T3-BSC-880

THE SOCIAL BASIS OF EUROPEAN FASCIST MOVEMENTS

THE SOCIAL BASIS OF EUROPEAN FASCIST MOVEMENTS

Edited by DETLEF MÜHLBERGER

CROOM HELM
London • New York • Sydney

Croom Helm Ltd, Provident House, Burrell Row,
Beckenham, Kent, BR3 1AT

Croom Helm Australia, 44-50 Waterloo Road,
North Ryde, 2113, New South Wales

Published in the USA by
Croom Helm
in association with Methuen, Inc.
29 West 35th Street
New York, NY 10001

British Library Cataloguing in Publication Data

The Social basis of European fascist
movements.
1. Fascism — Europe 2. Social classes —
Europe 3. Europe — Politics and
government — 1945-
I. Mühlberger, Detlef
320.5′33′094 JF2071

ISBN 0-7099-3585-4

Library of Congress Cataloging-in-Publication Data

ISBN 0-7099-3585-4

Printed and bound in Great Britain by Mackays of Chatham Ltd, Kent

CONTENTS

CONTRIBUTORS

Martin Blinkhorn is Senior Lecturer in History and Head of the Department of History at the University of Lancaster, England.

Gerhard Botz is Professor of Austrian History at the University of Salzburg, Austria.

Detlef Mühlberger is Lecturer in Modern European History at Oxford Polytechnic, England.

Henning Poulsen is Professor of Modern History at the University of Aarhus, Denmark.

Marco Revelli is Lecturer in Political Science at the University of Turin, Italy.

Robert J. Soucy is Professor of History at Oberlin College, Ohio, United States of America.

Raphael Vago is Lecturer in Modern East European History and Acting Director of the Russian and East European Research Center at the University of Tel-Aviv, Israel.

G. C. Webber is an Administrator at the University of Newcastle-upon-Tyne, England.

Herman van der Wusten is Professor of Political Geography at the University of Amsterdam, The Netherlands.

LIST OF TABLES

For Sue and Tania

PREFACE

It is over a decade ago, in June 1974 to be precise, that a group of historians and social scientists met at a conference at Bergen in Norway to deliberate on the question of the sociology of European fascist movements in the period 1919 to 1945, the proceedings of which were published in 1980. In the intervening years considerable further effort has been devoted to establishing the social types attracted to fascism, based on relatively extensive empirical data which has either not previously been subjected to detailed evaluation or has only been discovered in recent years. The present volume summarises these findings and provides an up-to-date review of the current research in the field.

As editor I obviously owe grateful thanks to the efforts of the contributors, who have made the idea behind this volume a reality. My thanks are also due to my colleague Roger Griffin, who undertook the translation of the essay on Italy at very short notice. To Gill Brooks I am much indebted for her sterling efforts in word-processing the manuscript. Also much appreciated was the advice and assistance given to me by Julia McKendry of the Oxford Polytechnic Computer Department. Finally, I would like to acknowledge the support and encouragement I have received from Richard Stoneman of Croom Helm, and thank him above all for his patience in the various delays to the manuscript.

Oxford — Detlef Mühlberger

Chapter One

ITALY

Marco Revelli

Translated by Roger Griffin

There is now a wide consensus among political sociologists that fascism is in some way or other connected with a pathological interaction between modernity and backwardness. That in other words it is one of the possible permutations of modernisation.

There is however less unanimity on the chief characteristics of such modernisation. To what category of 'perverse modernity' does it belong? Then again, *what level* of backwardness should be taken as the yardstick for measuring the degree of underdevelopment, and, in the same context, *what type* of backwardness are we to take as our model? Gino Germani, in the essay which has since become a classic, *Fascismo e classe sociale*, seems in a way to be referring to a predominantly *political* type of backwardness when he ascribes the gravity of the crisis of the early 1920s to the inadequacy of 'channels of integration' offered by the Italian political system which might have contained the radical mobilisation of the masses which followed the First World War.[1] Simultaneously, however, he refers to a relatively *advanced* stage of economic and social development when he considers fascism primarily as the product of a secondary mobilisation accomplished, that is, by members of the 'middle classes' whose secure position of social pre-eminence was already being undermined by the growing strength of the working-class movement. In the interpretation by A.F.K. Organski, on the other hand, the overriding impression given is one of *economic* backwardness. In fact, in his *The Stages of Political Development*, political phenomena are presented as strictly related to the stages of economic development defined by Rostow's model, and hence to the various phases in the process of industrialisation, in terms of which fascism is identified with a low category of development.[2] In contrast to Nazism, which he associates with the advanced stage of the 'welfare state', fascism is seen in fact as one of the political forms typical of the second stage, that of 'forced accumulation'. What is more, it is according to him one of the least modernised examples of these forms in that, as a compromise between residual agrarian elites and emerging industrial elites it clearly qualifies as the product of 'retarded industrialisation'. To take another example, the analysis of Barrington Moore Jr. focuses on the various permutations in the process by which the city becomes divorced from rural life and forms an elite endowed with a mercantile and entrepreneurial mentality, giving rise to a concept of backwardness which is more specifically *social*.[3] According to this approach fascism is seen as the outcome of two aspects of society being drastically out of phase: on the one hand the *advanced* stage reached by the rapid development of a mass-society in some countries which had started industrialising late but were subjected to violent social pressures in the 'take-off' period, and on the other hand the *backward* nature of the elites (and hence of the political institutions) called upon to govern in such a dynamic situation. A parallel diversity of points of view is to be found in the controversy over the quality and type of social representation peculiar to the fascist movement. This topic forms, as it were, the 'subjective dimension' of the debate on backwardness, once the social groups which formed the mass-base and exerted hegemony within it are – in terms of their response to the forces of innovation within the social structure – treated merely as the embodiment of demands and attitudes which are broadly speaking 'modernising', and in some respects the product of relatively advanced levels of social development. Was fascism, as Lasswell and Lipset maintain, the political expression of the psychological characteristic of the early stage of industrialisation, and thrown into panic when confronted by processes of concentration and organisation symptomatic of advanced capitalism?[4] Was it, therefore, to use the definition offered by Parsons and Bendix, a radical form of resistance to rationalisation?[5] Or, on the contrary, did it not constitute a specifically modern form of mobilisation carried out by the new technical and technocratic caste which emerged at the heart of advanced industrial and social structures, as Burnham seems to argue?[6] Or was it on the other hand, to quote the famous definition formulated by Dimitrov at the 18th plenary session of the Third International, the manifestation of the extreme stage in the development and crisis of capitalism, embodying the most destructive and corrupt section of the bourgeoisie, 'the most reactionary, chauvinist and imperialist elements of finance capital'?[7]

Unfortunately, in the face of such a lively theoretical debate and such a wide spectrum of conflicting points of view, the data and the methodologies which might allow an empirical verification of the different interpretations when applied to Italian Fascism are far from adequate. The statistical records compiled by public bodies on Italy's demographic and economic structures, indispensable to locate the genesis of fascism within the socio-economic *continuum* of her industrialisation process, are patchy. The *Inchieste*, or official inquiries, carried out by government agencies into the country's social conditions (dealing with family incomes, salary structures, consumer spending, social mobility, etc.) are practically non-existent. Research to produce documentary evidence concerning the ruling class and its forms of political organisation and association, whose traditions were nevertheless well established in the period leading up to the First World War, has been totally neglected.[8] Even in the spheres of science and political culture Fascism, in fact, marked a profound break with the past which contributed to the dissolution, or at least the dilution, of the positivistic and scientistic climate in the social matters which had brought about a significant apparatus for carrying out statistical surveys in the first two decades of the century. Having come into being in the 'Giolittian era' as a direct product of the growing concern with the 'social question', the Italian statistical bureaux had become a source of annoyance and embarassment at a time when everything was meant to be subordinated to the 'national question'. Moreover, reliability and objectivity of data was hardly to be expected in a political situation in which heavy-handed government interference in the operations of the bureaucratic and administrative apparatus was the order of the day. What is more, the take-over and monopoly of the state agencies by a single party with a charismatic leader inevitably marked the end of the practice of official parliamentary inquiries which had provided such precious material to politicians and academics of the liberal era, and simultaneously sealed the fate of all documentary or statistical work sponsored by other political organisations (whether parties or trade unions).[9] Once the Fascist Party was in power it controlled, true to its totalitarian principles, the information channels on all aspects of the country's political life, issuing its own abundant ideological and propagandistic bulletins, but keeping confidential data relating to its own organisational structure and membership. The modern Behemoth shows its head but keeps its body well-hidden. What strikes the reader of the *Annuari del Partito Nazionale Fascista* (Statistical Year Books of the National Fascist Party) is precisely the total lack of any statistical information when contrasted with the detailed documentation on every single activity and every public appearance of the party leadership. This perfectly reflects the image of a movement which claimed to epitomise, in a way which is both classless and anti-class, the unity and totality of a nation by means of the creative force of a heightened spirituality and radical nationalism. A movement which thus tended, in the presentation of its own social make-up, to lay special emphasis on the all-embracing 'totalitarian' power of its own ideology.

The studies on Fascism which have appeared since the Second World War have been dominated, at least until recent years, by a historiographical approach rather than by applying methodologies based on sociology or political science.[10] It is thus easy to understand the difficulties involved in trying to arrive at a definitive socio-economic classification of Fascism and hence the largely theoretical nature of the debate over the most appropriate interpretation.

I

As things stand, if we discount the data provided by the ten-yearly government *Censimenti* (censuses) of Italy's population and economy,[11] the only source we have to go on for a socio-economic analysis of Fascism are two systematic and scientifically carried out reworkings of data which give us, in complete chronological sequence, an overall picture of its demographic and economic dynamics. These are the *Documentazione statistica di base* compiled by P. Ercolani for the period 1861-1972,[12] and the *Appendice statistica* published by R. Romeo as an appendix to his *Breve storia della grande industria in Italia (1861-1961)*.[13] As for the analysis of social classes in Italy, the only documentation providing systematic quantitative data is still the *Saggio sulle classi sociali* by P. Sylos Labini.[14]

What emerges from these is a picture of a country both agrarian and industrial. On the one hand it clearly possessed a solid manufacturing base in an advanced stage of development, which in its leading sectors had already reached an 'oligopolistic' stage with a few companies dominating the market. At the same time the economic and social hegemony of the rural world still remained intact and continued to influence in various ways the majority of the population and make the most significant contribution to private incomes and to the national product. In short, a hybrid country in which over 60 per cent of the population still lived in rural areas and where nevertheless the iron and steel industry was producing more than a million and a half tonnes of steel a year. At the beginning of the 1920s, when Fascism came to power, 54.8 per cent of the active work-force was still employed in agriculture, as against 25.1 per cent in industry, 15 per cent in the tertiary sector and 5.1 per cent in public administration.[15] Moreover, in 1922, 34.2 per cent of the gross national product (in terms of output by value) was contributed by agriculture, as against 25.2 per cent by industry, 32 per cent by the tertiary sector and 18.6 per cent by public administration.[16] If we consider only the gross product of the private sector (leaving aside the rather remarkable figures attributed to the State's productive activities), the hegemonic role played by agriculture is even more in evidence: it accounted for as much as 41.3 per cent, as opposed to 30.5 per cent from industry and 28.2 per cent from the tertiary sector.[17] The overall situation is thus one of relative backwardness (but not of underdevelopment, given the presence of a substantial industrial base already well established), which seems to situate the origins of Fascism within the delicate phase of development in which take-off had already had its characteristic *technical* repercussions, but where, nonetheless, the *social* consequences of the great transformation had not yet affected a configuration of social classes and groups which has remained essentially similar to that of traditional societies. This is amply demonstrated by the pathological hypertrophy of autonomous middle-class groups, both rural and urban, which was a feature of Italian society in the inter-war years, and which in many respects formed an exception, or at the very least an anomoly, when compared with the profile of industrialised countries in general. In fact in Germany and Great Britain the social polarisation brought about by the second industrial revolution had reduced the traditional middle-class groups (both urban and rural small independent producers, artisans, tradesmen, etc.) to being a relatively minor percentage, partly replacing them with a new class of white-collar workers integrated into the technological structure of modern companies. Thomas Geiger has calculated, for example, that in the Weimar Republic the 'traditional middle class' did not exceed 34 per cent of the total population and that another 34 per cent was made up of employees with average to high-level qualifications.[18] By contrast there are some extraordinarily high figures for the most 'obsolete' elements of the Italian middle class, which was already overrepresented (53.3 per cent of the total population according to the estimate by P. Sylos Labini): in fact 37 per cent of the population would seem to be classifiable as rural 'independent petty bourgeois' and another 10.3 per cent as urban 'independent petty bourgeois', while only 3.2 per cent are included under the heading 'white-collar petty bourgeois' (see Table 1.1). If to this we add the fact that the bulk of the proletariat was made up of wage-earning *agricultural* workers (21.8 per cent as compared with 19.6 per cent of wage-earning industrial workers), we gain some idea of the enormous pockets of social immobility and resistance to change which existed in Italy, an expression of economic practices and life-styles which were in many respects anatagonistic to the basic demands for rationalisation exerted by the new industrial processes and bound to react radically to the threats being posed to the social *status quo*. This was the class whose composition was therefore in many ways *backward*, but undoubtedly was not *inert*. Even less was it 'normalised'. It was already being affected by the tensions which in the course of the next fifteen years would, in the economic sphere, bring about a reversal of the relationship between agriculture and industry (in the 1930s the latter made the major contribution to the GNP), as well as the transfer of about one million men from

Table 1.1: The major social groupings in Italy, 1921-36 (by %)

	1921	1936
Haute bourgeoisie (upper class)	1.7	1.6
Subtotal	1.7	1.6
White-collar petty bourgeoisie	3.2	5.0
Independent rural petty bourgeoisie	37.0	35.6
Independent urban petty bourgeoisie	10.3	11.5
Other petty-bourgeois elements	2.8	2.7
Subtotal	53.3	54.8
Wage-earning agricultural workers	21.8	16.2
Wage-earning industrial workers	19.6	21.4
Others	3.6	6.0
Subtotal	45.0	43.6
TOTAL (%)	100	100

Source: P. Sylos Labini, *Saggio sulle classi sociali* (Bari, 1974), p. 156.

agricultural to industrial work. It is precisely against the background of tensions, of growing insecurity throughout wide strata of society and of the frenetic processes of political mobilisation triggered off by them, that the institutional crisis took place which, on the eve of the advent of Fascism, was to paralyse the Italian political system.

II

In the two years between September 1920 (the 'Occupation of the Factories', the high-water mark of social agitation in the aftermath of the First World War) and October 1922 (the 'March on Rome' by about 50,000 Fascist *squadristi* and the appointment of Mussolini as head of government), there was a succession of as many as four different experiments in forming a government (Giolitti, Bonomi, Facta I and Facta II), all very feeble and ineffectual. It amounted to an extremely serious power vacuum - not to mention an actual dissolution of the political system - which had come about in the midst of an explosively tense social crisis coupled with an extreme polarisation of civil society into antagonistic factions.

The causes of such a crisis in the stability and efficiency of a liberal political system are complex. First of all they are to be sought in the erosion of the 'liberal middle ground' which had served as the basis of the national state ever since the unification of Italy. This erosion came about as a result of the rise of mass politics which occured in the period immediately before and after the First World War. The Italian political system had in fact emerged profoundly transformed from the twin electoral reforms of 1913 (the introduction of universal suffrage) and of 1919 (the adoption of proportional representation on the model of the Weimar Republic). These reforms had been introduced as an attempt to accommodate and integrate into the political system the increasingly broad and radical pressures exerted by the lower classes, but had the effect of depriving the already fragile political system of its centre, signalling the decline and fragmentation of the old 'parties of notables' and the appearance on the scene of modern 'mass parties'. The *Partito Socialista* (Socialist Party) - in many respects conforming to the model of 'parties for the integration of the masses' outlined by Kirchheimer[19] - which as early as 1913 had obtained 57 seats in parliament, won as many as 156 in 1919.[20] The *Partito Popolare* (Popular Party), on the other hand - a party based on religious convictions with no class boundaries - did not exist until 1919 when it obtained 100 seats straight away, taking from the Liberals a substantial percentage of their voters, especially in rural areas. At the same time the 'Giolittian centre', which had traditionally ensured the equilibrium of the political system, disintegrated, the 200 seats it had obtained in 1913 being reduced to 91 in 1919, without the formation of any other block which was capable of providing a rallying point to serve as a stable political force.

The instability was aggravated by a second factor which highlighted the profound historical watershed brought about by the war and the corresponding transformation of the socio-political situation, namely the emergence of unprecedented splits within the same political factions, and in particular the division between 'neutralists' and 'interventionists'.[21] Adding an extra dimension to the traditional division between right and left, this new element had the effect of further fragmenting parliamentary allegiances, creating a 'horizontal' schism across the whole political spectrum. When this fragmentation was perpetuated even after the end of the war, it led to a further restriction of the already narrow room to manoeuvre and limited opportunities for the formation of effective coalition alliances, thus creating new barriers. Liberals on the right (Salandra, Sonnino, Orlando) as well as the moderate left (Nitti), both interventionists, refused to support the neutralists under Giolitti. Nor could this centre block restore equilibrium to the system by taking advantage of the parliamentary strength of the *Partito Socialista* (neutralist), which was undergoing a severe crisis in its relations with its own social base and was incapable of making any definitive pledge to collaborate with the government. On the other hand, given the moderate and sectarian character of the Popular Party, any alliance between it and the Socialist Party was out of the question.

As a result, while the 'parties of the notables' were inexorably losing control of parliament, the new forces which were making their presence felt, the new 'mass-parties', were not succeeding in establishing the stable hegemony which on paper the parliamentary arithmetic made possible. This was the beginning of a period of vertical crisis in the institutional system which was to culminate in the Government of Mussolini, a period which Italian political science, in particularly P. Farneti[22] - ingeniously adapting the model proposed by Bracher for Germany in the early 1930s[23] - has subdivided into three successive phases. A first phase, whose central feature was the 'progressive loss of autonomy of the political society'[24] - i.e. the 'loss of power' by the traditional political establishment and the inability of political institutions to mediate in the struggles within civil society. This corresponded to the final period of Giolitti's time as head of government (October 1920 to June 1921). In these tumultuous months the now aged Liberal leader made exhaustive efforts to win political allies via a series of concessions to the most varied and contradictory social and political interest groups, which only succeeded in dissatisfying all of them and definitively losing their support. The growing hostility of the right was compounded by the weakening of the domination of the reformist left and the growing strength of the ultra-radicals. The second phase, that of the 'exhaustion of legitimate political alternatives', leading to the spate of extra-parliamentary agitation carried out on the '*piazza*' or from the 'barracks', opened with the Bonomi administration (July 1921 to February 1922) and closed with the two successive governments presided over by the Right Hon. Facta. In the course of this phase any residual good-will necessary to bring about a government majority by co-opting the interventionist factions within the Popular Party and Socialist Party was exhausted. The power vacuum created by the failure of such hybrid alliances, by the total impotence of the institutional decision-making machinery, and by the progressive fragmentation of Parliament, in which there were now as many as twelve main factions, was filled by the increasingly widespread and ruthless use of extra-parliamentary violence. Tasca has calculated that in less than ten months of activities during 1921 the *squadristi* destroyed in Italy 700 premises used by working-class organisations, killed 166 workers, and wounded a further 500.[25] Salvemini refers to over 1,500 workers and peasants being killed by Fascists and by the police by October 1921.[26] Thus, in this intermediary phase which witnessed the decline, and the ebbing of the tide of working-class agitation unleashed in the years immediately following the war, as well as the dramatic paralysis of the forces of law and order, the Fascist movement, still in its infancy, launched its own campaign of violence, thus forcing the pace of developments towards the third phase: that of the 'seizure of power'. On 16 November 1922, Mussolini, leader of a faction whose deputies in Parliament numbered a mere 35, obtained in the *Camera* the vote of confidence to become head of government with 306 votes for, 116 against and 7 abstentions. In the *Senato* the votes against were only 19. Achieving hegemony over the entire right and winning the consensus support of the representatives of the moderate mass-vote (the Popular Party), Fascism thus succeeded in monopolising the 'political society' of the day, and brought about a genuine 'change of regime'.

III

But 'Who were the Fascists?'. And what was their numerical strength? In the beginning their numbers were small - very small in fact. In his report to the First Congress of the *Fasci di combattimento* held in Florence on 9 October 1919, the secretary of the new movement, Umberto Pasella, spoke of 137 *fasci* formed so far with 40,385 registered members. But less than three months later, after the disastrous electoral failure of 16 November when the Fascists who stood at Milan obtained as little as 2 per cent of the votes (4,657 out of 270,000 votes cast), the figure had dropped to only 31 *fasci* and 870 members.

In this phase Fascism - Fascism *statu nascenti*, one might say - was still a volatile and fluid amalgam of frustrated minorities drawn from the most varied political and cultural backgrounds (nationalism, individualist anarchism, revolutionary syndicalism, socialism, futurism, etc.). Their common denominator was a radical rejection of the political realities of the day and, characterised above all by the *combattentismo*, the war-veteran's cult of the fighting spirit. It was first and foremost an *urban* phenomenon, a phenomenon of the big cities in fact, almost exclusively confined to the North, and found especially in Milan, the only large-scale concentration of industry and commerce in Italy. Of the 112 'founders' of the Fascist movement present at the meeting of 23 March 1919 in Piazza San Sepolcro, as many as 60 were Milanese and another 14 came from the immediate surroundings (such as Monza and Sesto San Giovanni). Of the remainder, ten came from Lombardy, eight from Liguria, seven (including the *squadrista* Farinacci) from Emilia, five from the Veneto region, three from Piedmont, and one from Sardinia. Only one came from Rome and two from the South.[27] Among these 112 there were nine lawyers, five army or navy officers, five professors, five doctors, three accountants, two parliamentary deputies and one senator. All the rest appear to have had no particular professional or academic qualifications. Over a year later, in May 1920 when, on the occasion of the Second Congress of the movement, a new census of its organisational strength was carried out, of the 118 *fasci* referred to in the report by the secretary Pasella (representing a total of 24,430 registered members), as many as 82, amounting to 70 per cent of the total, turn out to be centred in Milan. The fact that the most important executive body elected at the congress, the *Commissione Esecutiva Integrata* (Integrated Executive Commission) made up of regional representatives, had the same social composition noted earlier, testifies to the persistence of the prevalently urban and petty-bourgeois character of the movement. It included, in fact, six lawyers, two freelance professionals, two teachers, three journalists, three clerical workers, two railway workers, one tradesman, one artisan and one manual worker:[28] a blend, in many ways novel, between, on the one hand, 'classic' middle-class groups, mainly with an education in the humanities, self-employed and embodying the professional structures typical of what, in the last analysis, is a superseded and obsolete phase of urbanisation, and, on the other, newly emerging groups whose social and cultural profile was still not established, partly 'produced by' and partly 'displaced by' the war. All of them, however, had certainly become politically active as a result of being caught up in the 'total mobilisation' that continued well beyond the end of the war itself.

It is precisely the hybrid, contradictory and novel character of the social base of Fascism in its initial stage which makes it difficult to classify using traditional political categories, starting with the antithesis 'left/right' and the closely related 'progressive/conservative' dichotomy. However, this phase was of short duration.

From the middle of 1920, in fact, processes were already at work which in a very short space of time were to bring about both an extremely rapid numerical growth in the support of Fascism and a profound change of its political identity and its social composition, a change in a conservative direction. The month of October added to the endemic institutional crisis of the parliamentary system the catastrophic failure of the 'Occupation of the Factories', heralding the final collapse of the revolutionary expectancy of the lower classes and the profound crisis which was to convulse the entire working-class and trade union movement in Italy. On the 21 November of the same year the Palazzo d'Accursio massacre in Bologna had been the first and bloody episode of a protracted 'civil war' which was to drag on for the next two years, and marked the 'quantitative leap' in the use of extra-parliamentary violence. From that moment on the ranks of the Fascist movement swelled unabated: from 88 *fasci* and 80,476 members in December 1920, to 317 *fasci* and 80,476 members in March 1921, to 1,333 *fasci* and 218,453 members in December 1921, to reach their highest point in May 1922 with 2,124 *fasci* and 322,310 members (see Table 1.2). The increase in the

Table 1.2: The strength of the Fascist Movement between March 1921 and May 1922

	Number of *fasci* (branches)	Total Membership	Average number of members per *fascio*
March 1921	317	80,476	253
April 1921	471	98,399	208
May 1921	1,001	187,098	186
June 1921	1,192	204,506	171
July 1921	1,234	209,385	169
Aug 1921	1,253	221,919	177
Sept 1921	1,268	213,621	168
Oct 1921	1,311	217,072	165
Nov 1921	1,318	217,256	164
Dec 1921	1,333	218,453	163
April 1922	1,381	219,792	159
May 1922	2,124	322,310	151

Source: R. de Felice, *Mussolini il fascista* (2 vols., Turin, 1966), vol. 1, pp. 8-11.

period March 1921 to May 1922 amounted to over 300 per cent, and had all the signs of extensive dynamics (typical of rapid and superficial territorial expansion 'through contagion'), rather than of the intensive dynamics necessary for a movement to put down deep roots. The figures for branches (*fasci*) formed grew much more rapidly than those for new members, and to such an extent that the average number of new memberships per *fascio* fell steadily throughout the period, from its maximum of 253 in March 1921 to a record low of 151 in May 1922. This means that the territorial gains by new party organisations, their spread into new areas of recruitment, was not matched by a corresponding growth in the size of the individual organisations themselves, which in fact seem to be reduced to a state of relative stabilisation, not to say stagnation. As will occur so often in the course of the two decades in power, Fascism responded to the sudden change in its social and political identity without due qualms about coherence or continuity, trying to ride out events as best it could and turn them to its own advantage (this is a decidedly modern trait).

The geographical distribution of the movement

Table 1.3: The regional distribution of the Fascist membership, March 1921 to May 1922

	March 1921 Membership		December 1921 Membership		May 1922 Membership	
	No.	%	No.	%	No.	%
Piedmont	2,411	3.0	9,618	4.4	14,526	4.5
Lombardy	13,968	17.4	37,939	17.3	79,329	24.5
Liguria	2,749	3.4	7,405	3.4	8,841	2.7
Veneto	23,549	29.3	44,740	20.4	46,978	14.3
Northern Italy	42,677	53.1	99,702	45.5	148,774	46.0
Emilia	17,652	21.9	35,647	16.3	51,637	16.0
Tuscany	2,600	3.3	17,768	8.1	51,372	15.9
Umbria	485	0.6	4,000	1.8	5,410	1.8
Marches	814	1.0	2,072	0.9	2,311	0.8
Latium	1,488	1.8	4,163	1.9	9,747	3.0
Abruzzi	1,626	2.0	6,166	2.8	4,763	1.5
Central Italy	24,657	30.6	69,816	31.8	125,240	39.0
Campania	3,550	4.4	13,423	6.1	13,944	4.4
Apulia & Lucania	4,211	5.2	19,619	9.0	20,683	6.4
Calabria	712	0.9	2,406	1.1	2,066	0.6
Sicily	3,569	4.4	10,110	4.6	9,546	3.0
Sardinia	1,100	1.4	3,372	1.5	2,057	0.6
Southern Italy	13,142	16.3	48,930	22.3	48,296	15.0
Totals	80,476	100	218,448	100	322,310	100

Source: De Felice, *Mussolini il fascista*, vol. 1, pp. 8-11.

emerged considerably altered from this development. The original concentration in northern Italy was to give way to a more balanced - or, rather, a less unbalanced distribution (see Table 1.3 above). It could be said that in this way Fascism 'nationalised' itself, tranforming itself from an almost exclusively *local* phenomenon into a *national* movement, with a presence in every province of the Peninsula, the form and extent of which admittedly varied widely. Between March and December 1921, in fact, the percentage of members registered in the North fell from 53.1 per cent to 45.5 per cent, while that for the South rose proportionately from 16.3 per cent to 22.3 per cent. The figures for the Centre remained constant (rising only from 30.6 per cent to 31.8 per cent), but were to grow instead over the first five months of 1922, eventually reaching 39 per cent. What changed above all was the relationship between metropolitan and peripheral areas, between recruitment in the big cities and recruitment in the country, symptomatic of a cultural and social transformation in the nature of Fascism. From being a strictly urban phenomenon it became an ambiguous phenomenon with a dual identity, both urban and rural, dynamic and regressive. If at the beginning of 1921 membership in the big cities (Turin, Milan, Trieste, Bologna, Florence, Rome, Naples, Palermo) accounted for 39.4 per cent of the total number of militant Fascists (see Table 1.4), at the end of the year they were to plunge to 28.9 per cent to level out by May 1922 at 25.2 per cent (a completely unexceptional percentage, and, if anything, a low one in some ways, in view of the city's traditional role as a centre of intense politicisation, much more conducive to activism and political commitment than the provinces). If we take into account only the major cities of the North (which are precisely the ones where the movement was born), the transformation is even more obvious: the percentage of members actually fell from 26.5 per cent at the beginning of 1921 to 14.2 per cent in December of the same year, to sink to a mere 8.5 per cent by May of 1922. While at the start of the period under consideration more than a quarter of the Fascist movement proves to have been concentrated in the metropolitan zones of the North, on the eve of the 'seizure of power', after a period of frenetic growth and 'turn-over' of support, this percentage turns out to have dwindled to less than a tenth. Fascism, apart from becoming 'nationalised' had, so to speak, also become 'provincialised'. Milan, which in March 1921 represented 42.9 per cent of Fascists in Lombardy, could by May 1922 only lay claim to 17.6 per cent of the membership. Trieste, which accounted for 62.7 per cent of the total number of Fascists from the Veneto, declined to having

Table 1.4: Fascist membership in the big cities in relation to the total size of the membership of the movement, 1921-1922

	March 1921 Membership		December 1921 Membership		May 1922 Membership	
	No.	%	No.	%	No.	%
Turin	581		4,312		2,922	
Milan	6,000		10,000		13,697	
Trieste	14,756		16,697		10,522	
Northern Cities	21,337	26.5	30,991	14.2	27,411	8.5
Bologna	5,130		11,845		11,773	
Florence	500		6,353		20,880	
Rome	1,480		4,163		9,747	
Central Cities	7,110	8.8	22,361	10.2	42,400	13.2
Naples	2,850		9,545		10,395	
Palermo	380		380		1,030	
Southern Cities	3,230	4.0	9,925	4.5	11,425	3.5
Total Big Cities	31,677	39.4	63,177	28.9	81,236	25.2
Total Membership	80,476	100	218,448	100	322,310	100

Source: Calculations based on data provided by De Felice, *Mussolini il fascista*, vol. 1, pp. 8-11.

only 22.8 per cent. Turin suffered the same fate if only on a smaller scale (but Piedmont is generally regarded as peripheral to the epicentres of the Fascist movement): a fall from 24 per cent to 20.1 per cent. The wave of new recruits shifted from the great centres of population to the periphery, from the city to the countryside.

All this seems to confirm the thesis put

forward by some historians which maintains that the delicate transitional phase between 1920 and 1922 was a watershed for Fascism, marking a significant change in its dynamics as a movement, suddenly abandoning positions which were 'subversive', and to some extent 'revolutionary' - at any rate representing a radical break with the prevailing social and political order - to take up conservative and reactionary ones.[29] The reasons for this they see in the grafting onto the original body of Fascism of a new component destined, at least in the ensuing period, to gain hegemony: so-called 'agrarian fascism', openly siding with the landed interests, rural and violent in nature. A component which was thus the expression of 'backward' socio-economic interests, defined in terms of political objectives by the urge to wipe out the organisations which had grown up in defence of the new wage-earning working masses, and in terms of methods by the systematic use of *squadrista* violence.

The social make-up of the Fascist movement - statistically 'photographed', as it were, on the occasion of the Congress of Rome in November 1921 - reflects the nature of the transformation and the emerging dichotomy between 'urban fascism' and 'rural fascism' (see Table 1.5). A survey of 151,644 members of the *fasci* represented at the congress - equivalent to about half of the total membership - shows that the urban petty-bourgeois component, divided as we have seen into traditional independent middle-class groups (15.8 per cent) and salaried middle-class groups (14.1 per cent), had ceased to be the sole major constituent of the movement. Tradesmen, artisans, freelance professionals on the one hand, along with public and private officials and teachers on the other hand, amounted to no more than 29.9 per cent of all the members involved. Even when we add the figures for students (13 per cent) this percentage only rises to 44.9 per cent. Alongside these there was now in evidence a substantial block of more than 36 per cent formed by members from rural districts, a fair number of whom (12 per cent) was made up of large, medium and small land-owners. These provided - on this historians are unanimous - the backbone of the Fascist movement in the countryside, acting as catalysts of agrarian *squadrismo* and forming its hierarchy of command. In addition to these there is a figure of 15.4 per cent for workers, whose level of qualifications and provenance is however not specified (industry, transport, the construction

Table 1.5: The social composition of the Fascist Movement in November 1921 (the data relates to half of the total membership)

	Number	% of sample
Industrialists	4,269	2.8
Agrarians (large, medium and small landowners)	18,094	12.0
Free professions	9,981	6.0
Tradesmen and artisans	13,979	9.2
Private employees	14,989	9.8
Public employees	7,209	4.8
Teachers	1,668	1.1
Students	19,783	13.0
Workers	23,410	15.4
Agricultural workers	36,847	24.3
Totals	151,644	100

Source: PNF, *Il Partito Nazionale Fascista* (Rome, 1935), p. 26.

industry?), and a further 2.8 per cent made up of industrialists. The only common denominator capable of uniting to some extent people from such diverse social backgrounds is the fact that the bulk of them (57 per cent or 87,182) were ex-servicemen, which underlines the decisive role played by the war in determining the preconditions for the existence of Fascism.

The breakdown of the membership into social categories presented to the Third Congress captures and epitomises the image presented by Fascism at this significant cross-roads in its history. It was precisely at the Congress of Rome, in fact, in November 1921, that the Fascist movement was in the process of completing its own internal conversion to a right-wing position, incorporating the nationalist faction (traditionally monarchist, conservative and rabidly anti-socialist), turning itself into a party. The *Partito Nazionale Fascista* (PNF - National Fascist Party) originated as an amalgam of politically heterogeneous forces, but with an increasingly clear steer towards a reactionary, authoritarian and anti-proletarian position. It came into being as a 'politico-military machine', its goals the seizure of state power and the totalitarian representation of the nation within the framework of a political programme of 'order' and restoration. In many respects its internal composition reflected its new political identity. In fact, if the data concerning the social make-up of the party membership are compared with those for the stratification of Italian society (given in Table 1.1), it can be observed how the social structure of the party was a fairly faithful reflection of the general distribution of classes and occupational groups (achieving in a sense the ambition of representing organically and faithfully the whole nation), except for some significant cases of over- and under-representation in certain categories. Industrialists, for example, accounted for 2.8 per cent of members (while, according to the figures given by P. Sylos Labini, the entire *haute bourgeoisie* numbered at the time only 1.7 per cent). The figures tally almost perfectly for the middle classes (56.5 per cent in the party compared with 53.3 per cent in society), but there was a conspicuous imbalance in favour of the petty bourgeoisie formed by white-collar workers in the public and private sectors (15.7 per cent in the party as against 3.2 per cent in society). On the other hand workers were underrepresented (a mere 3.2 per cent discrepancy). Thus the social structure of the PNF in this phase appears to be partly determined by the presence of two poles, *economic power* on one side and *social renewal* on the other, with the industrial class forming the decisive element in assuring the internal equilibrium of the dominant class, while middle-class professional groups constitute the rising social group within a more general trend towards the rationalisation of the mode of production ('scientific organisation of work') and bureaucratisation (the growth of the state apparatus as a function of the increasing role of the state in controlling economic and social developments). These are features which would explain the extraordinary *dynamism* of Fascism at the level of political movement, and its ability to occupy the social and political void created by the crisis of the liberal system and by the defeat of the working-class movement, maximising its own advantages and achieving hegemony in an extremely disjointed and ambiguous political situation. They both coexist in a state of contradiction with the other basic component of Fascism in its phase leading up to the seizure of power, namely 'agrarian fascism', undoubtedly less dynamic and involving radically 'anti-modernising' pressures, but no less 'innovative' for all that. It is the presence of 'agrarian fascism' which accounts for the massive influx of a *squadristi* element and the systematisation of the use of violence: a 'political innovation' through and through (marking a drastic break with the parliamentary and institutional tactics applied by the other political forces), which put the political faction resorting to it first in a position to 'capitalise' on the crisis (suggesting an analogy with the 'innovative entrepreneur' in Schumpeter's theory). This dramatically new factor may also explain the remarkable spread of Fascism 'by contagion' in these two years. The interaction of these two elements (the urban and the agrarian, the dynamic and the regressive) will give rise to the 'political oxymoron' which Fascism has been held to represent as a phenomenon simultaneously *revolutionary* (in its methods) and *conservative* (in its ends), which was to manifest itself in all the decisive moments of its chequered history.

Table 1.6: The membership of the PNF, 1922-33

1922	299,876
1923	782,979
1924	642,246
1925	599,988
1926	940,000
1927	1,262,824
1930	1,723,400
1931	2,411,133
1932	2,418,123

Source: PNF, *Il Gran Consiglio nei primi dieci anni dell'era fascista* (Rome, 1932), pp. 31-411; PNF, *Il Partito Nazionale Fascista*, pp. 9-40; De Felice, *Mussolini il fascista*, vol. 1, p. 57.

The beginning of the third phase in the evolution of Fascism can be dated from 28 October 1922. The three years following the appointment of Mussolini as head of government saw the progressive 'fascistisation' of the state. In other words the transformation of institutions to embody an authoritarian and anti-liberal spirit via a process of creeping reform (the assumption of full powers, the promulgation of new legislation using governmental decrees, the Acerbo electoral law, etc.) culminated, after the Matteotti assassination, in the so-called *coup d'etat* of January 1925 (emergency laws, dissolution of political organisations, the gagging of the press). The formation of the PNF heralded the conversion of Fascism into a mass-movement. At the end of 1923 it claimed to have 782,979 members and in 1926, after a drop in recruitment due to the crisis which resulted from the killing of Giacomo Matteotti, this was to exceed 900,000 (see Table 1.6). Even the territorial distribution, already altered, as we have seen, in the two previous years, would progressively even out. In July 1923 some 36.7 per cent of members turned out to live in the North, 40.3 per cent in the Centre and 23 per cent in the South and the Islands (see Table 1.7). Admittedly the 'original' heartlands of the movement, Lombardy, Emilia and Tuscany - where 'agrarian fascism' had always had its strongholds - continued to present anomalies (they accounted for 40.2 per cent of the national total by themselves). But in general the distribution from now on appears more even, though central Italy turns out to be surprisingly overrepresented when compared to the North and the South, which have percentages of membership lower than the average territorial distribution of the population (North 48.2 per cent; Centre 16.3 per cent; South 35.2 per cent). The same make-up of the executive bodies of the party, on the other hand, suggests extreme concern to ensure uniform representation throughout the nation: in the *Comitato Centrale* (in the first phase when this body still existed) and in the *Direzione politica* the members prove to be distributed relatively equally according to region.

But the numerical expansion of these years also coincided, paradoxically, with the beginning of a twin process of 'autonomisation' - the Fascist state became independent from the party on the one hand, and the party from its *squadrista* component on the other - which was to bring about a relative weakening of the PNF within the Fascist system of power and a certain blurring of its identity.

As far as the first aspect of this process of 'autonomisation' is concerned - the emancipation of Fascism *qua* state from Fascism *qua* party - the turning-point came with the elections of 7 April 1924, which marked the electoral triumph of Fascism. The so-called *listone* (the list of candidates which included all the factions in the government bloc with an overwhelming majority of Fascists) obtained

1.7: The regional distribution of the membership of the PNF, July 1923

	Number of members	% of total membership
Piedmont	46,655	7.5
Liguria	19,675	3.1
Lombardy	100,230	16.0
Venezia Giulia	13,050	2.1
Venezia Tridentina	4,000	0.6
Veneto	46,503	7.4
Northern Italy	(230,113)	(36.7)
Emilia	68,848	11.0
Tuscany	82,526	13.2
Umbria	14,567	2.3
Lazio	36,060	5.8
Marches	12,274	1.9
Abruzzi	37,446	6.1
Central Italy	(251,721)	(40.3)
Campania	45,325	7.3
Basilicata	10,913	1.8
Puglia	35,100	5.6
Calabria	19,135	3.0
Sicily	25,031	4.0
Sardinia	8,052	1.3
Southern Italy	(143,556)	(23.0)
Italy (totals)	625,290	100

Source: PNF, *Il Gran Consiglio*, pp. 67-8.

66.3 per cent of the votes and, in compliance with the Acerbo electoral law, 75 per cent of the seats, 374 out of a total of 535: a virtual monopoly of parliament.[30] But these elections also demonstrated that the distribution and composition of the electoral consensus behind Fascism was different and, in many ways, independent from what they were for the PNF. As a result Mussolini's conception and control of the state became divorced from the action of the party, which was thereby partially relieved of its *political* responsibilities (policy-making now became mainly the responsibility of the state) and relegated to subsidiary functions within the movement (mediating between the various pressure groups and factions inside the movement, propaganda, support for government initiatives, recruitment of youth, etc.). The *listone* secured the greatest amount of support precisely in the South (81.5 per cent of the votes for the government, 18.5 per cent for the opposition) where, as has been noted, the PNF was organisationally at its weakest. However in the North, where the Fascist movement was born and the party had retained a solid structure and wide support, the *listone* actually failed to secure a majority vote (48.8 per cent of the votes cast). Only Central Italy registered a relative equilibrium between the 'electoral weight' of Fascism and the 'organisational weight' of the party: the government coalition prevailed over the opposition with 76 per cent of the votes. Particularly in regions where 'agrarian fascism' had been at its strongest and best organised - and where the destruction of opposing organisations, whether socialist or communist, had been the most ruthless - its electoral success was spectacular.

The dynamics of consensus and the dynamics of the organisational strength thus reveal themselves to be in many respects independent of each other. All of which only tended to reinforce, on a statistical and quantitative level as it were, a process which has been highlighted by historical research into the actions taken by the government and the choices made by Mussolini in the period after the March on Rome: namely the tendency of the *duce* to make his party (which, it should be said, he had always treated with a remarkable lack of scruples and a relative detachment) increasingly peripheral to the running of the government and to rely instead on his own capacity for political manoeuvring and on his control of state institutions to consolidate his own power and to widen the consensus behind him.

The *squadrista* element, with its activist wing and organisational backbone, proved to be a hindrance to this move by Mussolini, or at least to pose problems for him. It was the most 'intransigent' component of Fascism, partly 'subversive' and revolutionary, partly 'agrarian' and ultra-reactionary, and either way it was committed to defend its own role as the 'soul of Fascism' as well as its own organisational territory, independent from the *raison d'état* and its demands for action to be formally mediated via official institutions. The years of the 'fascistisation' of the state were also the years of the 'normalisation of Fascism', of the reduction of the movement to the role of a suitable *instrumentum regni* via a concerted effort to cut down to size, contain and control the *squadrista* component, concentrated in a hard political campaign designed to thwart the power of the so-called *ras*, the most popular leaders of the *squadre* (authentic 'natural leaders' who, like feudal lords, wielded undisputed authority over local areas of command). The constitution of the *Milizia volontaria per la sicurezza nazionale* (MVSN - Voluntary Militia for National Security) - an intermediary body between the party's armed force and the state institutional apparatus - was an important step in such a process of normalisation. Set up officially on 1 February 1923 as the 'armed guard of the revolution', this organisation absorbed practically the whole *squadrista* structure (20,460 men in August 1923), the original nucleus of Fascism, imposing on it rigid military discipline and putting it under the command of the head of government. In this way it was turned into an apparatus subservient to the state, performing duties either for the public (maintaining law and order in place of the earlier *guardie regie*, being employed in the event of a natural disaster, etc.) or for the party. Significantly Mussolini was later to assert:

> It is the party which says: 'I take a proportion of my supporters and instead of imposing on them the easy-going discipline that is involved with being a card-holding member, I impose instead a rigorous discipline as is found in the army.' However this is yet another remarkable symptom of how our people is again learning a sense of discipline.[31]

By this tactic he was able to wrest the party from highhanded and frenetic domination by the most openly revolutionary element, containing them within a purpose-built, 'specialised' structure and, above all, one which was hierarchically and rigidly controlled. The very social composition and age profile of the *Milizia* (see Tables 1.8 and 1.9), corresponding so closely to those of the membership of Fascism in its first phase, is a clear indication of the process by which the *squadrista* element became isolated and incorporated into a corps separate from the party itself.[32]

Table 1.8: The composition of the MVSN by occupational groups, 1923-33 (by %)

Occupational category	
Professionals	0.9
Landowners	2.8
Traders	0.9
Artisans	16.0
Peasants	11.3
Public employees	10.3
Private employees	5.7
Students	12.4
Servicemen	18.9
Workers	17.9
Unemployed	2.8
Total (%)	100
Frequency (*N*)	374

Source: Ufficio storico della MVSN, *I morti della milizia* (Rome, 1933), pp. 16-215.

Once the PNF had become freed from the constraints of the intransigent *squadrista* component, and was relieved of the responsibility of formulating policy, something which was now largely carried out at government level (i.e. 'depoliticised'), it was in a position to be rapidly converted into a pure instrument (with totalitarian tendencies) for the regimentation of the masses. Into an entity, that is, designed for the manipulation of consensus, the planning of communal leisure pursuits, and the integration of the masses into the Fascist state model, in many respects assuming the role of 'conveyor belt' between the government and 'civil society'. The party organisations henceforth fitted in with and infiltrated the daily life of the masses, both in the work-place (obligatory membership of the Fascist Corporations) and in the cultural sphere (taking over responsibility for recreational and educational activities, etc.). Entire sectors of 'society' (the young, professional groups, etc.) were co-opted into the PNF, which from 1927 to 1932 expanded its membership to

Table 1.9: The age-structure of the MVSN in 1922

Age group	% of membership
Under 13	2.0
13 to 17	19.2
18 to 22	34.2
23 to 27	21.9
28 to 32	8.9
33 to 37	7.6
38 to 47	5.4
over 47	0.7
Total (%)	100
Frequency (*N*)	374

Source: Ufficio storico della MVSN, *I morti della milizia*, pp. 16-215.

reach a record total of 2,418,123 (see Table 1.6). Of these 1,007,231 comprised members of male *fasci*, 147,210 members of female *fasci*, and the rest were members of associate mass organisations which had been incorporated into the party such as *l'Associazione fascista della scuola* (108,127), *l'Associazione del Pubblico Impiego* (191,269), *l'Associazione dello Stato* (68,854), *l'Associazione fascista ferrovieri* (122,096), *l'Associazione fascista postelegrafici* (69,357), the *Gruppi Universitari Fascisti* (57,996), the *Fasci giovanili* (608,669), and the *Giovani fasciste* (39,314).[33] It is significant that almost 25 per cent of members (leaving aside the 30 per cent represented by the youth organisations) was made up of public employees. Their massive presence was therefore to continue to be a distinctive feature of the PNF after the consolidation of the party's position was completed, and it is a clear indication of its nature: an organisation of mass control and regimentation, based on petty- and middling-bourgeois rank-and-file membership and *haut-bourgeois* hegemony (industrialists and landowners).

If these figures are compared with the results of a survey conducted in 1927 of a large number of PNF branch organisations throughout Italy, a survey which was certainly 'random' but which nevertheless produced statistics which are undeniably interesting, not just to political scientists but also to sociologists, what emerges relatively clearly is the transformation of the social make-up of Fascism in this phase to one prevalently white-collar middle class (see Table 1.10). In fact in the cities where a breakdown of the figures by social categories is possible, the percentage of the white-collar middle class ranges from 80 per cent in Reggio Calabria to 48 per cent in Rome, to 44 to 45 per cent in Trento and Verona. In addition there was a conspicuous presence of upper-class occupations (landowners, industrialists, landlords, higher civil servants). As for the political and social background of workers who are shown to be members of the PNF, the survey situates it in the 'category of "reformist socialism" - typographers, glaziers, dockers, members of cooperatives, who had better work-contracts than the other workers and convinced themselves that they would be able to preserve the differential which they had won by abandoning the rest of the working class to the forces of reaction and by submitting to Fascism'.[34] In his overview of the data as a whole Silone concluded that generally 'in none of the Fascist federations is there more than a minute and negligible number of industrial and agricultural labourers'.[35] What this highlighted was, in the author's words, 'the intimate connection which exists between the forces of Fascism and the structure of Italian capitalism', at every level.[36] According to this point of view Fascism therefore reflected, sector by sector, context by context, the existing mode of production relations, the degree of development of the productive forces, the overall maturity of the social relations. Firmly in the hands of the industrial *haute bourgeoisie* in areas where capitalism was mature, where industry had achieved hegemony as a manufacturing process, the Fascist Party functioned at times as if it was simply the extension into public life of decisions taken at company level. Elsewhere, in areas in a transitional stage and still predominantly rural, where the modernisation of the productive forces came up against the resistance of landed interests and the desire for the conservation of the social structure, the party was the expression of agrarian classes and the political demands of the landowners. Meanwhile in the loosely-knit network of urban social relations it was generally an organisation for the protection of the growing class of middle-ranking bureaucrats (as distinct from the technically skilled 'productive middle classes' linked to industry), who were by their very nature predisposed

Table 1.10: The social composition of the PNF branches in Verona, Trento, Reggio Calabria and Rome in 1927

	No. of members	% of membership
Verona:		
Free professionals	60	6.3
Dependent (salaried) professionals	90	9.4
Landowners	56	5.9
Tradesmen	80	8.4
Industrialists	50	5.2
Private employees	110	11.5
Public employees	325	34.0
Pensioners	160	16.7
Military Officers	25	2.6
Totals	956	100
Trento:		
Professionals and students	700	8.7
Landowners and industrialists	2,500	31.3
Public and private employees	3,500	43.7
Workers and peasants	1,300	16.3
Totals	8,000	100
Reggio Calabria:		
Professionals	-	10.0
Tradesmen	-	3.0
Employees	-	80.0
Students	-	5.0
Workers	-	2.0
Total (%)		100
Rome:		
Free professionals	-	15.1
Tradesmen	-	8.3
Industrialists	-	3.1
Private employees	-	14.0

Table 1.10 (cont'd)

Rome (cont'd)	No. of members	% of membership
Public employees	-	34.1
Students	-	5.5
Workers	-	18.7
Peasants	-	9.6
Total (%)		108.4[a]

Note: a. Silone's data is not an example of statistical accuracy (the inaccuracy relating to the percentage for Rome is probably due to Silone's use of different statistical sources). Problematical also is the use of different occupational groupings in the data presented by Silone, which makes comparisons between the branches on which there is data difficult. Nevertheless, despite these defects, Silone's material is too interesting to omit, given the lack of information on the social and occupational structure of individual PNF branches.

Source: I. Silone, 'La società italiana e il fascismo. Una vecchia inchiesta sul PNF', *Tempo presente*, no. 12 (December 1962), pp. 857-65.

to foster political *clientelismo* and were willing to submit to authority. This therefore suggests a political and structural model which is in many respects dualistic, consisting of a petty-bourgeois *form* and '*haut-bourgeois*' *politics* symptomatic of a country caught up in a delicate phase of economic and social transition to the stage of advanced capitalism, as was already heralded by a significant industrial sector and, simultaneously, by the more professional 'interventionist' role of the state as the determinant of social and economic life.

IV

In practice the definition of Fascism as a dualistic phenomenon, which Silone's survey suggests, does appear to be the one which most adequately accounts for the contradictory and heterogeneous social and economic characteristics of the Fascist regime, characteristics which in the past, precisely because of their complexity, have given rise to a plethora of interpretations, often in marked contrast to each other.

In the 1920s, the unprecedented nature of Fascism in both political and social terms had given considerable credence to the theory that the war experience was its main, if not only, cause, and as a result it was widely dismissed as an ephemeral phenomenon doomed rapidly to play itself out. The Liberal Missiroli wrote:

> It was inevitable that the war was to be followed by an extremely difficult period during which an outlet and a safety-valve would be found for the passions which had been stirred up in the course of the war, the anxieties generated by military actions, diplomatic disappointments, betrayed hopes, broken promises; a safety-valve, too, for the prolonged tensions that minds have been exposed to, the disruption of classes and social groups, the crisis in the economy, the anomalies of high finance, the contradictions of the spirit.[37]

With these words he was expressing the point of view of a large section of the liberal intelligentsia and liberal politicians, from Nitti to Croce, who saw in Fascism nothing more than a 'parenthesis', a transitional political phenomenon devoid of social and ideological significance. Others, especially the Communists, emphasised instead the close connection which existed between Fascist violence and the failure of the working-class revolution, reading into the activity of the new movement all the signs of it being a counterrevolutionary reaction launched by the bourgeoisie and thus attributing to Fascism a substantial degree of continuity with the previous ruling power blocks. Giulio Aquila, writing under the pseudonym of D. Sas, took the view that:

> Fascism is neither a terrorist militia of agrarian landowners... nor a revolt by the ranks of the *déclassés*, nor a revolutionary movement of the petty bourgeoisie, but rather it is an attack by the bourgeoisie, and one which can therefore only be repelled through a conscious struggle against the bourgeoisie itself.[38]

This line of interpretation was intended to react against and counter the position of those within the working-class movement who insisted on the 'agrarian' nature of Fascism so as to foster, from a reformist position, a *rapprochement* with the more 'democratic' elements of the industrial bourgeoisie and bring about alliances (such as the 'Aventian' pact) with the Liberal left.

There were also those, such as the socialist Zibordi, who stressed instead the composite nature of the 'Fascist revolution', made up of a 'counter-revolution of the bourgeoisie in the true sense of the word directed against a "red" revolution which did not exist except as a threat', 'an outburst of middle-class unrest and discontent', and finally 'a military coup'.[39] However nearly all observers drew attention to the heterogeneous make-up of Fascism's social base, and the difficulties involved in classifying it within the traditional criteria of political and class analysis. 'A miscellaneous agglomeration of old feudal landlords and *nouveaux riches*, of landowners and shopkeepers, of rich fools and discontented and rebellious working-class intellectuals, of traditional reactionaries and democrats', was Zibordi's description of it.[40] While in a famous article Gramsci spoke of *the two Fascisms*, one comprising

> the movement's urban nuclei, petty bourgeois, predominantly parliamentary and collaborationist, [the other] its rural nuclei, formed by large and medium-sized landowners and their farmworkers, with a vested interest in the struggle against the poor peasants and their organisations, resolutely anti-union, reactionary, and more prepared to put their trust in armed violence than in the authority of the state.[41]

These two components, he went on to say, were bound to develop an implacable enmity with each other, announcing the imminent end of the Fascist movement.

Moreover, almost all tried to address the problem posed by the role of the middle classes in the definition of Fascism's identity, for even if it was a difficult one to resolve they were aware of its crucial importance. The revolutionary Liberal, Piero Gobetti, attributed the numerical preponderance and political influence of the parasitic middle classes within the movement to the backwardness of Italian capitalism, its failure in the past to produce a genuine 'bourgeois revolution', which caused the perpetuation of a social situation conditioned by the presence of obsolete social groups, and inert both productively and culturally. 'It is only the provincial weaknesses of Italian capitalism', he wrote, 'that gave birth to the illusion of being able to make use of Fascism'.[42] This intuition was to be spelled out with great lucidity by Luigi Salvatorelli in Gobetti's periodical *Rivoluzione liberale*. Salvatorelli did not deny that 'Fascism has functioned as an anti-proletarian reaction to the advantage of the *haute bourgeoisie*',[43] but maintained that its essence was nevertheless not defined by this role since it was bound to be rapidly transcended giving way to a new movement with a substantial degree of political and social autonomy, the authentic expression of the turmoils of 'that section of society which, while not belonging to capitalism, and not even forming an element within the productive forces, will remain equally aloof from the proletariat'.[44] Seen in these terms the real social base of Fascism is thus the petty bourgeoisie steeped in a classical education, largely concentrated in the South, and surviving parasitically on the periphery of capitalism as an unproductive caste, which accounts for its autonomy *vis-à-vis* the political representation of the two fundamental social forces: bourgeois liberalism and proletarian socialism.

Another commentator who was to insist on the crucial role of the middle classes was Giovanni Ansaldo, who also worked on the *Rivoluzione liberale*. However in contrast to Salvatorelli he saw the social base of Fascism in a technical caste, already integrated into the processes of the rationalisation of industry's methods of production and the growth of a mass society.[45] It is worth recalling that the first theory will give rise to many of the interpretations of Fascism later elaborated by social scientists, ranging from the 'classic' ones of Bendix and Lipset - who defined it as a form of 'extremism of the Centre', of radicalisation of the middle classes (traditionally the natural habitat of parliamentarism) faced by the twin threat posed by capitalist accumulation and working-class militancy[46] - to historical approaches (in particular the one applied by Renzo de Felice),[47] all the way to psycho-sociological analyses (e.g. Lasswell).[48] The second theory is the interpretation which concentrates on the role and distinctive features of technocracy (Burnham).[49]

These early interpretations were to be challenged from the mid-1920s onwards by the Marxist school of political thought (from Togliatti to Trotzky, from Guerin to Dimitrov), which stressed instead the structural lack of autonomy of the middle classes, and the need to look for the 'organising principle', the necessary condition, of Fascism within the ruling classes themselves.[50] While not denying that the middle-class elements outnumbered the other groups in the Fascist organisations for the manufacture of consensus, the Marxists saw as the decisive factor the different political strategies which emerged out of the conflict between the historically distinct classes.

In point of fact if we superimpose onto the debate over the appropriate interpretative framework (a necessarily theoretical issue) the data at our disposal, however limited, and attempt an *empirical analysis*, we can show how in many respects the various interpretations prove to be complementary (at least in part). Politically and structurally the Italian Fascist system is shown to consist of a number of heterogeneous social strata but at the same time functionally (and hierarchically) these are interconnnected: a mass party base, increasingly dominated, as we have seen, by the presence of the white-collar middle classes - i.e. 'dependent', but in this case not necessarily 'productive' given the ubiquitous presence of the public civil servant - onto which was superimposed, in the event, an executive structure, a *'cadre'* of command preponderantly in the hands of upper-class elements (landowners, industrialists, high-ranking military personnel, notables). In 1928, the 93 federal secretaries of the Fascist Party included two marquises, two barons, one count, one duke, seven engineers, twenty lawyers, seven lecturers, eleven freelance professionals, and eight consuls of the *Milizia*. In the new *Camera*, elected by the plebiscite of 24 March 1929, 16.8 per cent of the deputies comprised landowners, industrialists, bankers and senior public or private officials, 9.5 per cent were university lecturers, 19.3 per cent were lawyers, and 3.6 per cent high-ranking soldiers. Among the 400 new members there were 27 nobles. A further 35 per cent consisted of professional politicians, 19.5 per cent of whom belonged to the upper class and 67.4 per cent to the middle class (see Table 1.11).

These data are particularly significant in as far as the *Camera* of 1929 was elected on the basis of a list of 400 names to be accepted or rejected *en bloc*, half of them proposed by the regime at Mussolini's discretion and the other half selected by various Fascist associations and corporations. Its composition thus reflects exactly the image and conception that Fascism had of its own leadership. In this sense it mirrors faithfully the Fascist power structure: a core formed by the traditional political and social elite complemented by a certain number of party officials drawn largely from the middle ranks of the bourgeoisie (the only novel feature, serving as a bridge between the ruling bloc and the mass social base). This epitomises the political model which can be pictured as combining a relatively high degree of economic modernisation but forced to coexist with a considerable resistance to the dynamics of social and political change. In this arrangement the social strata exposed to the most intense pressures exerted by the process of organisational and political innovation (the rising

Table 1.11: The composition of the Fascist Chamber according to occupations and age groups in 1929 (by %)

Occupational category	
University lecturers	9.5
Landowners	4.4
Industrialists and financiers	7.8
Higher civil servants	4.6
Lawyers	19.3
Professionals	0.3
Engineers	1.4
Journalists	3.6
Public employees	1.8
Technicians	1.8
Workers	0.3
Servicemen	3.6
Artists	0.8
Artisans	0.3
Professional politicians (from the PNF)	22.9
Professional politicians (from the syndicates)	12.7
Others	4.9
Total (%)	100

Table 1.11 (cont'd)

Age group:	
Born:	
before 1870	2.6
between 1870 and 1874	7.3
between 1875 and 1879	10.6
between 1880 and 1884	19.0
between 1885 and 1889	19.3
between 1890 and 1894	23.6
between 1895 and 1899	14.2
between 1900 and 1904	3.4
Total (%)	100

Source: *La nuova camera fascista* (Rome, 1929), pp. 91-483.

middle class on the one hand and the declining ones on the other), once integrated into the mass-organisation formed by the Fascist Party, are subject to the hierarchical domination of the traditional ruling caste, still 'enfeoffed' at the institutional summit of the state.

Notes

1. G. Germani, 'Fascismo e classe sociale', *La critica sociologica*, vol. 1 (1976). Cf. his work *Autoritarismo, fascismo e classi sociali* (Bologna, 1975).
2. A. F. K. Organski, *The Stages of Political Development* (New York, 1975).
3. B. Moore Jr., *Social Origins of Dictatorship and Democracy. Lord and Peasant in the Making of the Modern World* (Boston, 1966).
4. H. D. Lasswell, *Psychopathology and Politics* (New York, 1930); S. M. Lipset, *Political Man. The Social Bases of Politics* (Baltimore, 1959).
5. T. Parsons, 'Some Sociological Aspects of the Fascist Movement' in T. Parsons (ed.), *Essays in Sociological Theory* (New York, 1954), pp. 124-41; R. Bendix, 'Social Stratification and Political Power' in R. Bendix and S. M. Lipset (eds.), *Class, Status and Power* (Glencor, 1953).
6. J. Burnham, *La rivoluzione dei tecnici* (Milan, 1946).

7. J. Dimitrov, *La Terza Internazionale* (Rome, 1946), p.3.
8. It should not be forgotten that at this time Italy had found in Gaetano Mosca and Vilfredo Pareto two outstanding thinkers in the field of 'ruling class theory', and that the work of Robert Michels was enjoying considerable success in Italy.
9. Examples are Jacini's *Inchiesta agraria* of 1885 or the extremely important *Inchiesta industriale* of 1872-4.
10. Only recently has there been any real interest shown by political scientists in the Fascist Party and the Fascist movement. For an overview of the situation see P. Farneti, 'Social Conflict, Parliamentary Fragmentation, Institutional Shift and the Rise of Fascism: Italy' in J. Linz and A. Stepan (eds.), *The Breakdown of Democratic Regimes* (London-Baltimore, 1978). Of particular interest are some local studies on the social base of Fascism by P. Corner, 'La base di massa del fascismo: il caso di Ferrara', *Italia contemporanea*, vol. 26 (1974), pp. 5-31 (this is especially useful to document the agrarian movement); M. Zangarini, 'La composizione sociale della classe dirigente nel regime fascista: il caso di Verona', *Italia contemporanea*, vol. 30 (1978), pp. 27-47. Again on agrarian Fascism in the Po Valley see M. Barnabei, 'La base di massa del fascismo agrario', *Storia contemporanea*, vol. 6 (1975), pp. 123-53. An approach based on the national perspective is provided by J. Petersen, 'Elettorato e base sociale del fascismo negli anni venti', *Studi storici*, vol. 16, no. 3 (1975). Useful material is also to be found in the various contributions on Italian Fascism in S. U. Larsen a. o. (eds.), *Who were the Fascists? Social Roots of European Fascism* (Bergen-Oslo-Tromsø, 1980).
11. Cf. in this context the publications of the *Istituto Centrale di Statistica* (ISTAT).
12. P. Ercolani, 'Documentazione statistica di base' in G. Fua (ed.), *Lo sviluppo economico in Italia* (Milan, 1975).
13. R. Romeo, *Breve storia della grande industria in Italia (1861-1961)* (Bologna, 1961).
14. P. Sylos Labini, *Saggio sulle classi sociali* (Paris, 1974).
15. Ercolani in Fua, *Lo sviluppo economico*, p. 414.

The data relates to 1921.
16. Ibid.
17. Romeo, *Breve storia della grande industria*, p. 422.
18. T. Geiger, *Die Klassengesellschaft im Schmelztiegel* (Cologne, 1949).
19. O. Kirchheimer, 'The transformation of the Western European Party Systems' in J. La Palombara and M. Weiner, *Political Parties and Political development* (Princeton, 1966).
20. For this and the following data see P. Farneti, *La crisi della democrazia italiana e l'avvento del fascismo* (Bologna, 1975), p. 57.
21. Ibid.
22. Farneti in Linz and Stepan, *Breakdown of Democratic Regimes*, pp. 6-7.
23. K. D. Bracher, *Die Deutsche Diktatur. Entstehung, Struktur, Folgen des Nationalsozialismus* (Cologne-Berlin, 1969). The author distinguishes three phases in the events immediately preceding the Hitlerian regime: 'loss of power', 'power vacuum', and the 'seizure of power' by the Nazi Party.
24. Farneti in Linz and Stepan, *Breakdown of Democratic Regimes*, p. 6.
25. A. Tasca, *Nascita e avvento del fascismo* (Florence, 1950).
26. G. Salvemini, *The Fascist Dictatorship in Italy* (London, 1925), pp. 102-107.
27. R. Lazzero, *Il partito nazionale fascista* (Milan, 1985), pp. 24-6.
28. Ibid.
29. The historian R. de Felice writes that 'The *Fasci di combattimento* originated as a peculiarly urban phenomenon and the bulk of their members were at first ex-servicemen who had belonged to the revolutionary parties and movements of the pre-war period. In 1920 their ranks were swelled by students, petty-bourgeois elements, ex-servicemen of a later generation... Thanks to agrarian fascism and the wave of "consensus" which this brought the Fascist movement, the situation changed radically in 1921. From being an urban phenomenon Fascism became also, even predominantly, a phenomenon of agricultural areas and spread through the whole country, though it continued to be most strongly represented in the Northern regions.' R. de Felici, *Mussolini il fascista* (2 vols., Turin, 1966), vol.1, p. 6.
30. On the result of the election of 7 April 1924

and for the figures relating to the geographic distribution of the *listone* vote see U. Giusti, *Dai plebisciti alla Costituente* (Rome, 1945), pp. 102-103.

31. Lazzero, *Partito nazionale fascista*, p. 46.
32. These data are the result of an interesting piece of research based on the register of members of the *Milizia* who lost their lives and were contained in the *Albo d'onore*, or Roll of Honour, as published by the Historical Office of the MVSN in *I morti della Milizia* (Rome, 1939). While their documentary value is therefore not beyond doubt, they nevertheless provide some insight into the social composition of the *Milizia*.
33. I.e. The Fascist School Association; The Fascist Association of Public Employees; The Fascist Association of State Employees; The Fascist Association of Railway Employees; The Fascist Association of Post Office Employees; The Fascist University Association; The Boys' *Fasci*; the Girls' *Fasci*.
34. I. Silone, 'La società italiana e il fascismo. Una vecchia inchiesta sul PNF', *Tempo presente*, no. 12 (December 1962), pp. 857-70, here p. 867.
35. Ibid., pp. 865-6.
36. Ibid., p. 865.
37. M. Missiroli, *Il fascismo e la crisi italiana* (Bologna, 1921), p. 56.
38. See the material by D. Sas (G. Aquila) 'Der Faschismus in Italien' (first published in Hamburg in 1923) in R. De Felice (ed.), *Il fascismo e i partiti politici italiani. Testimonianze del 1921-1923* (Bologna, 1966), pp. 421-33.
39. G. Zibordi, *Critica socialista del fascismo* (Bologna, 1966), pp. 421-33.
40. Ibid.
41. A. Gramsci, *Sul fascismo* (Rome, 1973), pp. 133-5.
42. P. Gobetti, 'Capitalismo e liberta', *La rivoluzione liberale* (1923).
43. L. Salvatorelli, *Nazional-fascismo* (Turin, 1923), p. 11.
44. Ibid., p. 10.
45. G. Ansaldo, 'Il fascismo come odio piccolo borgese', *La rivoluzione liberale* (1922).
46. See in particular Lipset, *Political Man*.
47. R. De Felice (with M. Ledeen), *Intervista sul fascismo* (Bari, 1975).

48. Lasswell, 'Psychopathology and Politics'.
49. Burnham, *Rivoluzione dei tecnici*.
50. P. Togliatti, *Lezioni sul fascismo* (Rome, 1970), and *Opere (1917-1936)* (Rome, 1967); L. Trotzki, *Scritti 1929-1936* (Turin, 1962); D. Guerin, *Fascismo e gran capitale* (Verona, 1979); and Dimitrov, *La Terza Internationale*.

Chapter Two

Germany

Detlef Mühlberger

The phenomenon of Nazism has been subjected to the most intensive investigation since its appearance in the 1920s, and even before the brutality and barbarity of German behaviour during the Third Reich were fully exposed in 1945, numerous studies had attempted to get to grips with the complexity of this political movement. The revelation of the mass murder of European Jewry, and of the atrocities committed by Germans in occupied Europe - especially Eastern Europe - as well as the inhumanity of the Nazi regime towards sections of German society itself, generated a growing volume of literature on all aspects of the history and development of Nazism, the extent of which is now, one suspects, even beyond the control of the experts working in the field.[1] In the quest to find the causal factors behind Nazism diverse factors - socio-economic, historical, cultural and psychological - have been examined and re-examined constantly since the 1930s. Even before the Nazis secured power in 1933 the question as to the social composition of the membership, leadership and electoral constituency of the *Nationalsozialistische Deutsche Arbeiterpartei* (NSDAP - National Socialist German Workers' Party [Nazi Party]) was first raised in an effort to identify which social group - or groups - were carriers of the disease. From the late 1920s political scientists, historians and political commentators began tackling the question of the sociology of Nazism in a somewhat desultory fashion, providing impressionistic assertions not substantiated by any significant or meaningful empirical evidence. The usual route taken by most analysts attempting to reach conclusions as to the social make-up of the supporters of the NSDAP was one which concentrated on identifying its electorate.[2] On the basis of this approach a general consensus was reached in the early 1930s by Marxist and non-Marxist scholars alike, which deemed that Nazism was essentially a lower-middle-class movement. The 'middle-class image' of the NSDAP became strongly entrenched in the literature on Nazism long before the collapse of the Third Reich, and continued to dominate the debate on the nature of Nazism in the post-war period.[3] The counter-argument, which suggested that the NSDAP was a mass movement drawing support from all social groupings - a hypothesis which also rested primarily on observations relating to the electoral performance of the NSDAP in the endphase of the Weimar Republic - was very much a minority view in the debate on the social structure of Nazism until the 1970s.[4]

It is only in the last decade or so that the question of 'Who voted for the NSDAP?' has been subjected to renewed and systematic analysis by a number of historians and social scientists whose work - despite differences in the methodologies employed and conclusions reached - suggests that the electoral basis of Nazism was not simply confined to the lower middle class.[5] The allied, and more central, question as to the social make-up of the membership and leadership of the NSDAP, as well as the nature of its auxiliary organisations such as the *Sturmabteilung* (SA - Storm Section) and the *Hitlerjugend* (HJ - Hitler Youth), which allows one to identify the committed, hard-core elements of the movement, was largely neglected as far as empirical statistical analysis is concerned until the beginning of the 1960s.[6] The few studies available on the social basis of Nazism were generally limited in terms of their utility or restricted in their scope.[7] One source, which did readily allow an insight into the social structure of the Nazi Party, the *Partei-Statistik* produced by the Nazis themselves for internal party purposes in 1935, was understandably treated with great suspicion and generally ignored in the debate, although Schäfer did use it extensively in his study on the NSDAP which first appeared in the late 1950s.[8]

The statistical data on the social make-up of the NSDAP and on a number of its more important auxiliary organisations has increased by leaps and bounds since the 1960s. Unlike the problem of the paucity of information facing analysts of the social basis of fascist movements in most of the other European states, the quantitative data available on the social structure of the NSDAP is extensive, though much of the material has only begun to be utilised in recent years. It is surprising that the various membership lists contained in the NSDAP *Hauptarchiv*, which became available in microfilm form in the early 1960s, were not generally used until the 1970s, and then only patchily.[9] There is considerable material in the *Hauptarchiv*, especially on the membership attracted to the NSDAP in its formative stage of development, as well as data on the SA and the HJ. This data has either not been subjected to detailed analysis or has not been used at all.[10] It has to be noted, however, that the bulk of the material in the *Hauptarchiv*, barring a few exceptions, relates to Bavaria. To compensate for this bias, there are a number of membership lists relating to other regions of Germany which have been discovered in various archives in recent years and which allow an albeit limited insight into the nature of the NSDAP outside of Bavaria, and it is highly probable that more such material will ultimately be released - at least by West German archives. This hopefully will provide a more comprehensive insight into the undoubtedly often marked regional variations in the sociology of Nazi membership. Of critical importance also, of course, are the approximately 8.5 million membership cards contained in the Nazi Party Master File in the Berlin Document Center, the potential of which has only been tapped of late, primarily by Michael Kater.[11]

It was in the 1960s that new ground was broken in the quest to establish which social elements made up the Nazi membership. The first not very satisfactory attempts were made by Franz-Willing and by Maser in their studies of the history of the early NSDAP, in which they examined fragments of the general membership of the NSDAP before 1923, as well as analysing the composition of the membership of a number of Nazi branches situated in southern Germany.[12] Although these analyses have the merit of involving original calculations based on archival sources, the methodology employed in their evaluation is very primitive. Thus in the occupational classification adopted by Maser, for example, shopkeepers are placed into three different occupational categories, while no differentiation is made by him between skilled workers and artisans, or between dependent and independent artisans. Subsequent analysts working on the problem of the sociology of Nazism, such as Kater, have quite rightly made the point that Franz-Willing's and Maser's statistical material has little value.[13] It comes as a surprise therefore that Kater has used their material in his recent work on the subject.[14]

The first 'modern' studies on the social structure of the Nazi Party, which were based on sophisticated quantitative techniques involving the use of the computer, appeared in the 1970s.[15] The pioneering studies by Professor Kater, especially his work on the NSDAP's structure in 1923, has done much to stimulate research on the subject in the last decade or so. The social composition of the early NSDAP has been subjected to further analysis by both Douglas and Madden.[16] Studies on the NSDAP beyond its Bavarian context, and dealing with the later phases of the party's development, have also began to appear.[17] Still further insight into the sociology of Nazism has also been provided by a number of regional studies which touch upon the theme and hint at the often quite contrasting nature of the movement in different regions of Germany.[18] Of late attention has also began to be focused on the most significant of the Nazi Party's auxiliary organisations, the SA, on which there are now a number of studies dealing with the sociology of both its rank-and-file membership and of its leadership corps.[19]

The present study attempts to summarise the quite extensive empirical data now available on the social structure of the Nazi movement, and to provide additional new material to extend the data base. In the analysis the major focus falls on the pre-1933 period, in which three phases virtually suggest themselves: firstly, the formative stage of the development of the party from the time of its foundation in 1919 up to the abortive Munich putsch of November 1923; secondly, the period following the re-formation of the party in February 1925 up to 1929, when its fortunes were dramatically improved with the onset of the World Economic Depression, the impact of which on Germany was especially catastrophic; and finally the period from 1930 up to Hitler's elevation to the chancellorship in January 1933, a period during which the NSDAP became a dominant factor in the politics of the Weimar Republic. Little attention is given to the social make-up of the Nazi movement after 1933, although a brief summary of the trends discernible in the period 1933 to 1945 is made. The justification for the almost total neglect of the post-1933 period rests on the view that the millions of Germans who swelled the ranks of the NSDAP in and after 1933 were prompted by quite different motives in comparison with those who joined before 1933. Although opportunism may have played a part in determining the marked influx of members into the party after the *Reichstag* election of September 1930 - disparagingly called *Septemberlinge* by the 'old' Nazis - opportunism and indeed necessity undoubtedly conditioned the behaviour of many of the *Märzgefallenen* (a derogatory term used by the Nazis to describe those who joined the Nazi Party after its 'success' in the Reichstag election of 5 March) in 1933, as well as those involved in the stampede to join the party subsequently. Concentration therefore falls on those Germans who made the *choice* to support Nazism before 1933, since the operational environment, as it were, in which individuals made this choice was obviously vastly different in the pre- and post-1933 periods.

I

Before turning to the data available on the social make-up of the NSDAP it is prudent to look at the methodological and interpretational problems involved in evaluating the material. Problems and disagreements about the utility and reliability of the data, and the difficulty of finding agreed definitions of terms employed in interpreting the statistical evidence, are central to the theoretical and conceptual conflicts which surround the debate.[20] In the first place there is the problem - one with which social scientists have unsuccessfully wrestled with for decades - of what is meant by 'class'.[21] Because there are so many objective and subjective determinants which can be used in the construction of class models, and because political standpoints are involved in determining class boundaries, there is more than the usual amount of room for disagreement. For our purposes the type of approach used in defining class boundaries is critical, for depending on the method used, the same material can produce quite different results.[22] A second problem relates to the assignment of various occupational groups to specific classes. Although it is relatively unproblematical to put unskilled labourers or semi-skilled factory workers into the lower class, or to place salaried white-collar workers in the middle class, there are problems as regards the 'margins' of specific classes. Obviously the placement of, say, skilled craft workers or dependent artisans into either the lower class or lower middle class has a critical bearing on the debate surrounding the social structure of Nazism.

Even if it were possible to create a class model to which all scholars would subscribe (and this is highly unlikely), there remains the problem of the nature of the material on which analysis is based. The data on the occupations of individuals recorded in the Nazi membership lists and in the police files involves self-assigned job descriptions, some of which, such as 'worker' or 'businessman', are imprecise. Moreover, these self-assigned job descriptions are, at times, far removed from objective reality.[23] The fact that one has to establish the social structure of the NSDAP's membership on the basis of the occupational information provided by the members themselves results inevitably in a degree of uncertainty and imprecision. Another limitation is that except for information on the occupation of members (as well as on their sex, age and place of residence in most instances), there is generally no information on the family background, education or income levels of the individuals involved, all of which are held as important factors by contemporary social scientists in determining an individual's position in social space. Given these limitations, one must view the data provided in this study - as well as in all other studies published so far - as suggestive rather than as definitive of the sociology of Nazism.[24]

In view of all the problems outlined above, it is not surprising that the various studies dealing with the sociology of the Nazi movement which have appeared since the 1970s are based on diverse methodological and interpretational frameworks. This unfortunately restricts direct comparison of the results contained in them. I have suggested elsewhere that a possible way to overcome this problem is to establish a class model to which at least non-Marxist scholars could subscribe by working towards a compromise based on a judicious mix of contemporary views about social and occupational stratification with ideas current in the 1920s.[25] The basis for such a compromise is now available in Michael Kater's recently published work on the sociology of the Nazi Party.[26] The present study rests on his approach - admittedly with some modifications - as far as the class and occupational classification models which he employs are concerned (for an 'outline' of Kater's model see Table 2.1). In part the modifications proposed here, as far as

Table 2.1: The occupational and class structure of the gainfully employed German population, summer 1933 (by %)

Class	Occupational subgroup	Frequency	% of total
Lower	1. Unskilled workers	10,075,782	37.25
	2. Skilled (craft) workers	4,478,803	16.56
	3. Other skilled workers	203,737	0.75
Subtotal		14,758,322	54.56
Lower middle	4. Master craftsmen (independent)	2,585,551	9.56
	5. Nonacademic professionals	483,208	1.79
	6. Lower/intermediate (petty) employees	3,359,248	12.42
	7. Lower/intermediate civil servants	1,402,189	5.18
	8. Merchants (self-employed)	1,624,118	6.00
	9. Farmers (self-employed)	2,082,912	7.70
Subtotal		11,537,226	42.65
Elite	10. Managers	143,659	0.53
	11. Higher civil servants	128,794	0.48
	12. Students (upper school/university)	129,292	0.48
	13. Academic professionals	259,310	0.96
	14. Entrepreneurs	91,296	0.34
Subtotal		752,351	2.78
TOTAL		27,047,899	100.00

Source: M. Kater, *The Nazi Party. A Social Profile of Members and Leaders, 1919-1945* (Oxford, 1983), p. 241, Table 1 (reprinted by permission).

class labels are concerned (see Table 2.2), involve little more than changes in the terminology employed. The preference for describing those whom Kater collectively terms 'lower middle class' as 'lower- and middle-middle class', and the substitution of the term 'elite' with that of 'upper-middle class and upper class' reflects an attempt to spell out more clearly where in social space these elements are placed. More than semantic quibbling is involved here, since the use of the term 'lower- and middle-middle class' does take into consideration the space which exists in status terms between, say, white-collar workers in low or intermediary positions within subgroup 6, or between farmers with small- or medium-sized holdings within subgroup 9. There are nuances within classes in terms of status gradations which the preferred terms employed here try to accommodate. More important is the addition in the tables presented here of the 'status unclear' category, to which those individuals have been allocated whose class status is either not readily determinable or impossible to establish due to absence of data. Kater, in his book on the NSDAP, does not take into consideration those Nazi members with no job indication, the unemployed, pensioners, housewives and party officials. The omission of these categories of the membership obviously affects the percentage values arrived at, and to avoid distortions these categories have been taken into account in my own calculations.[27]

The method employed in calculating the data contained in Tables 2.2 to 2.12 - as far as these involve the processing of archival sources - was to assign, in the first instance, the occupations recorded in membership lists and police reports to 39 occupational categories. Several of these were in turn amalgamated to form one of the 18 to 19 subgroups generally used in the tables.[28] In the assignment of specific occupations to various subgroups I have generally followed the guidelines provided by the statisticians involved in the production of the 1925 census returns.[29] Admittedly this did involve placing occupations under one subgroup which fit uneasily together, such as the inclusion in subgroup 2 (skilled craft workers) of butchers and bakers along with plumbers and carpenters, as well as locksmiths, spinners and weavers.

It is impossible - for reasons of space - to list all of the hundreds of occupations encountered in the membership files under the specific occupational subgroups to which they are assigned. The following is designed to give some insight into the types of occupations which are 'typical' of specific subgroups:

Subgroup 1 (unskilled workers) - includes those in menial occupations which did not involve any significant skill or training, namely agricultural workers (e.g. farm workers, herdsmen, ploughmen); domestic and catering staff (e.g. cleaners, chambermaids, chauffeurs, waiters); unskilled and semi-skilled workers (e.g. all those described as 'workers', as well as those whose job description involved the use of the suffix 'worker' (e.g. factory workers, textile workers).

Subgroup 2 (skilled craft workers) - includes skilled blue-collar workers and apprentices in traditional artisanal crafts usually involving formal training (e.g. bakers, butchers, carpenters, plumbers, bricklayers, wheelwrights, printers, locksmiths).

Subgroup 3 (other skilled workers) - includes skilled workers in occupations not associated with artisanal ones traditionally embraced in the guild system (e.g. car-mechanics, electricians).

Subgroup 4 (master craftsmen) - includes independent craftsmen and tradesmen who had either acquired their 'master' (*Meister*) title, or who indicated their independent status in some other way (e.g. proprietors of bakeries).

Subgroup 5 (nonacademic professionals) - includes agricultural specialists (e.g. foresters, reeves); professionals who had gone through some form of higher (non-university) education (e.g. engineers, dentists); and artists and writers (e.g. sculptors, musicians, dancers).

Subgroup 6 (lower employees) - includes salaried white-collar employees (*Angestellte*) in lower and intermediary positions (e.g. clerks, bookkeepers, sales and office staff, technical staff), as well as supervisory staff (e.g. foremen).

Subgroup 7 (lower civil servants) - includes blue-collar salaried workers in the public sector (e.g. engine drivers, railway guards); and civil servants in lower and intermediary grades (e.g. school teachers, policemen, clerical administrative staff).

Subgroup 8 (merchants) - includes those listed as merchants (*Kaufmann*), shopkeepers, publicans, and café owners.

Subgroup 9 (farmers) - includes self-employed farmers, vintners, and fishermen of independent status.

Subgroup 10 (managers) - includes salaried white-collar employees in leading positions in the private sector (e.g. business executives, directors, and managers).

Subgroup 11 (higher civil servants) - includes those in the higher civil service grades (e.g. grammar school teachers, university lecturers and professors, leading administrators in government, judges).

Subgroup 12 (university students) - includes those who could be positively identified as studying at university (e.g. those described as *stud. phil.*, *stud. rer. pol.*, etc.).

Subgroup 13 (academic professionals) - includes self-employed, academically (university) trained professionals (e.g. lawyers, architects, engineers, physicians, consultants).

Subgroup 14 (entrepreneurs) - includes factory owners, estate owners.

Although the occupational classification model outlined above is based on that used by Kater, the present work does diverge from his approach in a number of ways.[30] Beyond the introduction of further subgroups in the 'status unclear' category noted earlier, there are some differences in the methods used here in the process of assigning various occupations to specific subgroups. In part the differences have only a marginal statistical consequence, such as my placement of foremen in mines (*Steiger*) into subgroup 6 (lower employees), as suggested in the 1925 census, rather than into subgroup 3 (other skilled workers) as Kater does.[31] More significant is that I have not followed Kater's decision to allocate 36.6 per cent of all skilled craft workers (subgroup 2) into the master craftsmen (subgroup 4) category. Kater's approach, based on the assumption that just over one-third of all skilled workers appearing in Nazi membership lists were in reality of independent status, is debatable.[32] The method employed here in differentiating between dependent and independent craftsmen rests upon the hierarchic issue of whether or not a craftsman had acquired his master title. Craftsmen without master status were deemed dependent and assigned to subgroup 2 (skilled craft workers), whereas those who described themselves as masters (or proprietors) are included in subgroup 4 (master craftsmen).[33] Similarly Kater's formula by which he assigns 2.2 per cent of all merchants, farmers, owners and leaseholders to subgroup 14 (entrepreneurs), on the assumption that these were in the highest income bracket and the suggestion that the small percentage of farmers involved in the transfer were in reality estate owners, has also been ignored. It is highly unlikely that estate owners would not have indicated their superior status, and as far as those who described themselves as 'merchants' are concerned, it is much more likely that many of these were little more than dependent commercial employees (*Handlungsgehilfen*).[34] In the classification used here only those merchants who described themselves as wholesale merchants (*Grosshändler*) are assigned to subgroup 14 (entrepreneurs). There is also the problem of the placement of blue-collar salaried staff in the public sector. Kater's description of this occupational category suggests that he has only included the 'white-collar' civil servants in this subgroup.[35] In this study, salaried blue-collar workers in the public sector, such as those employed in the postal and telephone services, workers employed in municipal enterprises, as well as railway workers, are combined with white-collar civil servants to form subgroup 7. By including salaried manual workers in the public sector in this subgroup I may well have erred on the side of caution, given the routine and often menial nature of the jobs many of them performed. However, various legislative acts passed during the Weimar era did elevate many public employees from wage-earners to salaried employee status, and they were generally regarded as of lower-middle-class status at the time.[36] Finally the problem of where one should place students on the social scale demands attention. Kater assigns university students and what he terms 'a handful of senior upper-school students... found in the party files' - the latter appear much more frequently in membership lists than he implies - to the social 'elite', arguing that they would secure prestigious and well-paid professional occupations following their graduation.[37] The latter assumption is questionable given the problem of unemployment among graduates even before the massive unemployment problem hit the Weimar state in the early 1930s. Nor was it inevitable that a grammar school pupil would necessarily go on to attend university. But more problematical appears to be Kater's placement of individuals into his 'upper school and university student' subgroup who fit uneasily into this category, leading to a distortion in the size of the 'elite' element in some Nazi branches which he has evaluated.[38] In this study university and non-university students have been separated. Those students who clearly indicated their 'university status' by describing themselves as *stud. phil.* or *cand. med.* have been assigned to subgroup 12 (university students), while those described as 'student' or as 'grammar school pupil' are placed in subgroup 15 (non-university students). This is a rough and ready method of differentiation, but guards against the error of crediting a high 'elite' component to Nazi branches if 'students' recorded in the membership lists are all automatically given 'university status'.[39]

Although the differences between Kater's approach and the one used here cumulatively mount up, the percentage values produced in my calculations are nevertheless *broadly* comparable with his data. This is not to ignore the consequences which result from the different methods used to establish the size of a number of subgroups, especially subgroups 2 (skilled craft workers) and subgroup 4 (master craftsmen), which have a bearing on the overall size of the three social 'blocks' into which the Nazi membership is divided.

II

In its formative phase of development the NSDAP was primarily a south German, predominantly a Bavarian phenomenon, a peripheral movement in the national politics of the Weimar Republic. Founded in Munich on 5 January 1919 by Drexler and Harrer, the *Deutsche Arbeiterpartei* (DAP - German Workers' Party) - renamed NSDAP in February 1920 - led, for much of 1919, a sectarian existence, forming part of the amorphous *völkisch* fringe active in Munich. When Hitler first came into contact with the DAP in September 1919, its membership most likely revolved around the two to three dozen mark. By the time the first membership census was made, probably in late November or early December, the number of members had risen to 168, which increased to 189 by the beginning of January 1920.[40]

It was in the course of 1920 to 1922 that the Nazi Party began to grow modestly, its membership rising to just over 2,000 by the end of 1920, to around 4,100 by the end of the following year, to reach a strength of 7,768 by September 1922.[41] In the spring of 1920 the party began to extend its activities outside of Munich, with the establishment of a series of branches in Bavaria, the first of which being formed in Rosenheim in April 1920. Also significant for the future development of the party was the appearance of isolated branches established outside of Bavaria, which were to develop as focal points for the growth of Nazism in other regions of Germany, such as the formation of a branch at Stuttgart in Württemberg in May 1920, the foundation of the first Nazi branch north of the river Main at Dortmund in Westphalia by May 1920, the emergence of a branch at Pforzheim in Baden in October 1920, and at Hannover in the spring of 1921.[42] The expansion of the party at the national level was seriously handicapped outside of southern Germany following its prohibition in most of the federal states (*Länder*) in November 1922. A number of branches did, however, continue to lead a shadowy existence north of the Main in late 1922 and in 1923. It was in the course of 1923 that the NSDAP first recorded a significant surge in its membership growth against a background of severe economic and political crises and the emotion-laden atmosphere occasioned by the occupation of the Ruhr by French and Belgian troops in January 1923. The passions aroused by the Ruhr invasion, combined with hyper-inflation, seriously tested a democratic system which had tried unsuccessfully to resolve a series of difficulties - such as the restructuring of the economy following the end of the First World War, the healing of the deep social and political divisions inherited from the Second Reich, the issues of Versailles and that of reparations, to name but a few - since its inception. The political instability combined with the economic malaise of the post-war years conditioned the growth of radicalism both on the left and right of the political spectrum and undermined the entrenchment of progressive, democratic forces. One of the beneficiaries of the deteriorating situation in 1923 was the NSDAP, which markedly increased its support in 1923. By the time of the abortive Munich putsch of November 1923, some 55,287 membership cards had been issued by the NSDAP. We do not know how many of these members were still in the party in November 1923. If the bulk of the total registered membership had not left the movement, it would suggest that it had experienced a possible seven-fold increase in membership in less than a year. What we do know is that some 10,000 membership cards alone were issued between September and November 1923. Details on 4,786 of these newly registered members have survived and their places of residence indicate that a large share of the rapid expansion of the Nazi movement was due to its growth in Bavaria, for 67.7 per cent of the new members were resident in that *Land*.[43] It does seem that the party was indeed a considerable force in Bavarian politics by 1923 and the data on its membership recruitment in Bavaria shows a movement which had penetrated into all parts of the *Land*, with branches numbering several thousand strong in Munich and Nuremberg, and sizeable branches in a number of towns, especially in the Protestant regions of Franconia, a major area of Nazi growth in 1923.[44]

The information available on the social and occupational structure of the Nazi Party's membership for the 1919 to 1923 period is relatively extensive, especially on the Munich branch (see Table 2.2). There are a number of lists relating to the DAP for late 1919 and early 1920, and a breakdown of 678 members registered in the Munich branch in May 1920, as well as a list of 2,548 members enrolled at Munich by August 1921 (which includes a small percentage of members resident in other parts of Bavaria, as well as a few entries from members resident in other parts of Germany and, in a few isolated cases, Nazis living abroad). In addition, for 1920 to 1923 there are also branch membership lists for six Bavarian towns (Reichenhall, Rosenheim, Passau, Landshut, Berchtesgaden and Ingolstadt), as well as lists which record the branch membership in Stuttgart, in Mannheim (in Baden), and in Hannover (in the Prussian province of the same name). Finally, there is also the data on 4,786 members mentioned earlier. It should be noted that whereas the data on the DAP and on the early NSDAP

Table 2.2: The social and occupational structure of the membership of the *Deutsche Arbeiterpartei* (DAP - German Workers' Party), and of the *Nationalsozialistische Deutsche Arbeiterpartei* (NSDAP - National Socialist German Workers' Party) in various towns, 1919-23

Class	Occupational subgroup	(A) DAP Munich[a] Dec. 1919	(B) DAP Munich[b] early Jan. 1920	(C) DAP Munich[a] late Jan. 1920	(D) NSDAP Munich[c] May 1920	(E) NSDAP Stuttgart[d] May 1920	(F) NSDAP Wielenbach[a] Aug. 1921
LOWER CLASS	1. Unskilled workers	5.4	4.7	4.8	3.9	8.3	31.6
	2. Skilled (craft) workers	13.7	15.9	11.8	11.8	16.7	15.8
	3. Other skilled workers	5.9	2.6	4.7	3.8	0	0
Subtotal		25.0	23.2	21.3	19.5	25.0	47.4
Lower- and middle-MIDDLE CLASS	4. Master craftsmen	5.4	5.8	6.1	2.8	0	5.3
	5. Non-acad. professionals	9.5	4.2	8.5	6.0	0	5.3
	6. Lower employees	7.2	9.4	6.9	10.6	0	0
	7. Lower civil servants	4.7	4.8	4.2	5.8	25.0	15.8
	8. Merchants	13.0	11.5	10.4	16.0	33.3	10.4
	9. Farmers	0	0	0	0.1	0	15.8
Subtotal		39.8	35.7	36.1	41.3	58.3	52.6
Upper-MIDDLE CLASS/ UPPER CLASS	10. Managers	2.4	2.1	1.9	1.3	0	0
	11. Higher civil servants	0	0.5	0	1.5	8.3	0
	12. University students	3.6	3.2	2.8	1.3	0	0
	13. Academic professionals	5.9	7.4	6.1	6.0	8.3	0
	14. Entrepreneurs	3.0	2.1	2.3	1.0	0	0
Subtotal		14.9	15.3	13.1	11.1	16.6	0
STATUS UNCLEAR	15. Non-univ. students	1.8	1.6	2.3	5.8	0	0
	16. Pensioners/Retired	0.6	0	0.9	0.9	0	0
	17. Wives/Widows	3.5	3.2	3.8	2.2	0	0
	18. Military personnel	8.9	11.6	11.8	4.1	0	0
	19. Illegible/no data	5.4	9.0	10.4	14.3	0	0
Subtotal		20.2	25.4	29.2	27.3	0	0
TOTAL (%)[1]		100	100	100	100	100	100
Frequency (*N*)		168	189	212	678	12	19

Table 2.2 (cont'd)

Class	Occupational subgroup	(G) NSDAP Kinding[a] Aug. 1921	(H) NSDAP Konstanz[a] Aug. 1921	(I) NSDAP Munich[a] Aug. 1921	(J) NSDAP Reichenhall[e] Oct. 1921	(K) NSDAP Hanover[f] Dec. 1921	(L) NSDAP Rosenheim[g] Aug. 1922
LOWER	1. Unskilled workers	40.0	15.3	8.5	0	8.0	5.3
CLASS	2. Skilled (craft) workers	20.0	7.7	12.6	18.2	12.0	7.5
	3. Other skilled workers	8.0	7.7	3.4	9.1	4.0	3.8
Subtotal		68.0	30.7	24.5	27.3	24.0	16.6
Lower-	4. Master craftsmen	4.0	0	3.8	0	8.0	11.2
and	5. Non-acad. professionals	0	0	6.4	27.2	4.0	2.5
Middle-	6. Lower employees	16.0	15.3	13.0	9.1	8.0	15.2
MIDDLE	7. Lower civil servants	0	7.7	6.4	9.1	12.0	17.1
CLASS	8. Merchants	4.0	7.7	14.3	9.1	20.0	14.6
	9. Farmers	4.0	0	0.9	0	0	0.6
Subtotal		28.0	30.7	44.8	54.5	52.0	61.2
Upper-	10. Managers	0	0	1.1	0	0	0.3
MIDDLE	11. Higher civil servants	0	0	0.6	0	0	1.2
CLASS/	12. University students	0	0	3.8	0	0	0
UPPER	13. Academic professionals	0	0	4.2	0	0	1.6
CLASS	14. Entrepreneurs	0	0	1.0	0	8.0	2.5
Subtotal		0	0	10.7	0	8.0	5.6
STATUS	15. Non-univ. students	0	23.0	4.9	0	0	2.8
UNCLEAR	16. Pensioners/Retired	0	0	1.7	0	0	1.2
	17. Wives/Widows	0	7.7	4.1	0	16.0	9.1
	18. Military personnel	0	0	2.3	0	0	0
	19. Illegible/no data	4.0	7.7	7.0	18.2	0	3.1
Subtotal		4.0	38.4	20.0	18.2	16.0	16.2
TOTAL (%)		100	100	100	100	100	100
Frequency (*N*)		25	13	2,548	11	25	320

Table 2.2 (cont'd)

Class	Occupational subgroup	(M) NSDAP Passau[h] Aug. 1922	(N) NSDAP Mannheim[i] Aug. 1922	(O) NSDAP Landshut[j] Sept. 1922	(P) NSDAP Berchtesgaden[k] Sept. 1923	(Q) NSDAP Ingolstadt[l] Oct. 1923
LOWER	1. Unskilled workers	4.8	7.8	5.3	9.0	8.3
CLASS	2. Skilled (craft) workers	3.6	14.0	14.9	16.8	18.7
	3. Other skilled workers	3.6	7.3	6.3	10.1	3.0
Subtotal		12.0	29.1	26.5	35.9	30.0
Lower-	4. Master craftsmen	4.8	1.1	10.3	2.2	4.2
and	5. Non-acad. professionals	1.2	3.9	3.1	3.3	3.9
middle-	6. Lower employees	12.0	15.1	8.0	6.7	18.0
MIDDLE	7. Lower civil servants	37.3	6.1	25.6	18.0	11.4
CLASS	8. Merchants	10.8	28.7	10.7	4.4	10.8
	9. Farmers	0	0.6	3.6	0	4.1
Subtotal		66.1	55.5	61.3	34.6	52.4
Upper-	10. Managers	0	0.6	0.4	1.1	0.9
MIDDLE	11. Higher civil servants	1.2	0	1.8	1.1	0.4
CLASS/	12. University students	0	3.4	0	0	0.2
UPPER	13. Academic professionals	1.2	0.6	1.3	5.6	2.2
CLASS	14. Entrepreneurs	1.2	0.6	1.7	0	1.1
Subtotal		3.6	5.2	5.2	7.8	4.8
STATUS	15. Non-Univ. students	0	1.7	0	0	2.6
UNCLEAR	16. Pensioners/Retired	1.2	0.6	0.9	0	0.7
	17. Wives/Widows	6.0	1.7	0.4	2.2	2.8
	18. Military personnel	0	0	0	0	0.7
	19. Illegible/no data	10.8	6.2	5.0	19.1	6.0
Subtotal		18.0	10.2	6.3	21.3	12.8
TOTAL (%)		100	100	100	100	100
Frequency (*N*)		83	178	222	89	535

Table 2.2 (cont'd)

Note:

1. The total percentage figure given in the columns of all of the tables are rounded up.

Sources:

a. Percentages calculated on the basis of data taken from a membership list entitled 'Adolf Hitlers Mitkämpfer 1919-1921'. The members of the DAP in 1919 and 1920 were resident in Munich and surroundings. The complete list for the NSDAP membership by the time the entries ended in August 1921 includes a small percentage of Nazis resident in various parts of Germany, though the bulk of the entries relate to Munich and a number of places scattered throughout Bavaria and southern Germany. Nazi Party members resident in Wielenbach (Upper Bavaria), Kinding (Middle Franconia) and Konstanz (Baden) are included in the list, which is in the Hoover Institution NSDAP *Hauptarchiv* Microfilm Collection (hereafter *HA*), Reel 2A/Folder 230.

b. Percentages calculated on the basis of data in 'Mitgliederverzeichnis (aufgestellt im Herbst 1919) der Deutschen Arbeiter-Partei, Ortsgruppe München', *HA* 8/171.

c. Percentages calculated on the basis of data in 'Mitglieder-Liste' (date of last entry 29 May 1920), *HA* 10/215.

d. Percentages calculated on the basis of data provided by Eugen Hang, 'Aufzeichnungen zur Vorgeschichte der Entstehung der NSDAP in Stuttgart', *HA*, 8/166.

e. Percentages calculated on the basis of data listed in a report on the 'Sprechabend zur Gründung einer Ortsgruppe der N.S.D.A.P.'. The report is dated 4 October 1921, and lists the branch committee and the membership, *HA*, 8/179.

f. Percentages calculated on the basis of data in 'Mitgliederliste der alten Ortsgruppe Hannover der N.S.D.A.P.', *HA*, 6/141.

g. Percentages calculated on the basis of data provided by the membership list 'Ortsgruppe Rosenheim' (date of last entry 2 August 1922), *HA*, 10/215.

h. Percentages calculated on the basis of data provided by the membership list 'Ortsgruppe Passau' (date of last entry 24 August 1922), *HA*, 10/215.

i. Percentages calculated on the basis of data provided by the membership list 'Ortsgruppe Mannheim', (date of last entry 28 August 1922), *HA*, 10/215.

j. Percentages calculated on the basis of data provided by the membership list 'Ortsgruppe Landshut' (date of last entry 20 September 1922), *HA*, 10/215.

k. Percentages calculated on the basis of data provided by the membership list 'Ortsgruppe Berchtesgaden' (date of entry 5 September 1922), *HA*, 8/175.

l. Percentages calculated on the basis of data provided by the 'Verzeichnis der NSDAP-Mitglieder aus den Jahren 1922/23' relating to Ingolstadt and surroundings (date of last entry 9 October 1923), *Staatsarchiv München*, NSDAP/469.

covers the bulk of the known membership and can thus be seen as an accurate guide to the social profile of the party in its infancy, the material from 1921 to 1923 is less comprehensive and although it does allow a useful insight into the social make-up of the membership in this period, it cannot be taken as representative for the party as a whole. The data is, however, extensive enough to reveal certain features of the sociology of the NSDAP which were to emerge in a more pronounced fashion in the post-1925 period: marked regional and local variations in the social types constituting the party.

It is not possible to establish the social structure of the DAP's membership before Hitler became a member of the party, at least not on the basis of data that is available to date. Madden's approach used to determine the structure of the pre-Hitler DAP, which is based on analysing the data relating to membership numbers 501 to 554 provided in the '*Adolf Hitlers Mitkämpfer*' list (the DAP membership started at number 501), rests on a basic error.[45] Although the number entered for Adolf Hittler (sic), described as a 'writer' (the first job designation 'painter' having been deleted) is indeed number 555, the number given to him was due not to his being the 55th person joining the party, but due to the fact that his name came alphabetically at that point in the first party census.[46] If one looks at the '*Mitkämpfer*' list carefully, it emerges that a number of consecutive membership numbers are usually listed under each letter of the alphabet before there is a jump in the sequence of the numbers recording those in the same alphabetic group who joined at a later stage. This allows one to calculate the strength of the movement and the rate of recruitment, especially once the 'date of entry' column is regularly filled in , as happenend from January 1920.[47]

The occupational data relating to the Munich DAP/NSDAP branch for the period spanning late 1919 to May 1920 suggests that the core of the party was made up of lower- and middle-middle-class types, with a not insignificant number of members drawn from the lower class, and a considerable degree of support also coming from the upper-middle class and upper class (see Table 2.2, columns A, B, C and D). Clearly the party was not, as its name would have it, a 'workers' party', but neither was it a predominantly lower-middle-class affair. The party's heterogeneous composition mirrored the social structure of Munich society, even if the lower class was somewhat underrepresented in its membership.[48] The social mix of the Munich Nazi branch was to remain broadly constant in subsequent years, but the fairly high percentage of 'military' elements within it declined by mid-1920.[49] The numeric strength of the Munich branch increased significantly in the course of 1920 and 1921, the enrolled membership standing at 2,548 by August 1921, a figure which includes just over 14 per cent of members not resident in Munich itself. The balance between the classes represented in the branch in comparison with that of late 1919 was hardly affected by the expansion, though there was a slight increase of 5 per cent in lower- and middle-middle-class support and a marginal decrease of 4.2 per cent in the membership drawn from the upper-middle class and upper class, while the percentage for the lower class hardly changed (see Table 2.2, column I). Included in the Munich branch membership list for August 1921 is data on members registered at the Munich branch, but resident elsewhere, on the basis of which one can establish the composition of small groups of Nazi supporters living in the villages of Wielenbach (Upper Bavaria) and Kinding (Middle Franconia), and the small town of Konstanz in *Land* Baden (see Table 2.2, columns F, G and H). It is true that the numbers involved are small, but the social make-up of Nazi support in these communities does highlight marked differences with that of the Munich NSDAP. Particularly striking is the high percentage figure for the lower-class component of the Kinding membership.

The ability of the NSDAP to transcend the class divide, to recruit from all social groups, is a feature of the pre-1923 period. The nucleus of the party was undeniably provided by the lower- and middle-middle class, which was overrepresented in the party, as was the upper-middle class and upper class. But support from the lower class - the largest social group in German society (see Table 2.1) - was not negligible, even if this social group responded less enthusiastically to the Nazi appeal and was underrepresented in the party. In terms of the new recruits entering the party in 1920, 1921, 1922 and 1923, the figures for the lower class share are quite high, at 35.3 per cent, 42.3 per cent, 28.1 per cent, and 38.4 per cent respectively.[50] In all but one of the Bavarian branches on which we have detailed evidence for 1922 and 1923 (Rosenheim, Passau, Landshut, Berchtesgaden and Ingolstadt), the lower- and middle-middle class made up the majority of the membership (see Table 2.2, columns L, M, O, P and Q). The exception, Berchtesgaden, may well be explained by reference to the high percentage of illegible entries contained in the membership list. The lower class was underrepresented in all of these branches, especially those in Passau and Rosenheim, though in Landshut and Ingolstadt and their immediate hinterland the party enjoyed a considerable degree of lower-class support, while in Berchtesgaden this social stratum appears to have been overrepresented in relation to the social structure of the working population in this part of Bavaria.[51]

That the NSDAP in its infancy had a relatively easy task in recruiting heavily from the lower- and middle-middle class, and great difficulty in making a serious impact on the lower class, is clearly demonstrated in the detailed data there is on one Nazi branch situated in the more industrialised city of Mannheim (see Table 2.2, column N). Given the size of Mannheim, the branch was still numerically weak some two years after its formation, suggesting that the Nazi movement lacked the popularity which it clearly had in many urban centres in Bavaria. Of the 31.8 per cent of the membership which can be identified as coming from the lower class (which accounted for 45.2 per cent of Mannheim's working population), only a handful of the unskilled and skilled workers could be deemed to have been 'industrial workers' on the basis of the type of occupational titles registered in the membership list.[52]

However, it should be borne in mind when one looks at the high profile of the lower- and middle-middle class in the NSDAP in southern Germany in the period 1919 to 1923, that this reflects to some degree the dominance of this class in a region which was not highly industrialised. There is limited evidence which suggests that the NSDAP was able to attract a greater degree of lower-class support in industrialised regions. In a number of Westphalian towns situated in the eastern half of the Ruhr, towns in which the lower class - especially the 'industrial working class' - was the dominant social group, workers played a more important role in the development of the NSDAP, limited though this was in the area until the mid-1920s. In Dortmund the lower-class membership was apparently strong enough by 1922 to oust the petty-bourgeois leadership which had dominated the branch since its formation in early 1920, while a police report on the Hagen branch (formed in the spring of 1922) speaks of it as having '304 members drawn from working-class and middle-class circles, with skilled workers and office employees predominating' by May 1922.[53] In two small branches established in the Dortmund area in 1922, at Mengede and Westerfilde, miners figured prominently in the membership, the Westerfilde branch being solely composed of around a dozen miners.[54]

The social and occupational groups involved in the surge towards the NSDAP in 1923 is captured in some detail in the most sizeable membership fragment which has survived from the pre-1923 period, which lists 4,786 members out of a probable 10,000 or so who joined the party between September and November 1923 (see Table 2.3). The data provides a useful insight into the party on the eve of its - unfortunately only temporary - disintegration, and the 'micro' analysis presented here throws up a number of interesting features which past 'macro' analysis of this data has failed to reveal.[55] Although only 32.3 per cent of the new membership came from outside of Bavaria, and indeed only a mere 24.2 per cent from outside of southern Germany - not surprising in view of the ban of the Nazi Party in most parts of central and northern Germany - the data does suggest that one is looking at a party which was in the process of establishing a toehold in virtually all regions of Germany by late 1923. It is true that the number of newly registered members involved in the case of central, northern and eastern Germany were very small in comparison with those who swelled the ranks of many of the branches in Bavaria, but a limited, usually clandestine, presence can be detected in the federal states of Hesse (especially in the Marburg, Bad Homburg and Bad Nauheim areas), Thuringia (centred on Eisenach and Gotha), Brunswick (particularly in the city of Brunswick), Anhalt (the Dessau region), and Saxony (primarily Chemnitz and its surroundings, where lower-class members were present in some force, as well as in Dresden and Plauen). In a number of Prussian provinces small clusters of Nazis were enrolling in the Rhine province (in the textile belt around Elberfeld-Barmen), in Westphalia (in the north-east of the province in the Bielefeld-Minden region, and in the county of Siegen in the south), and in Saxony (primarily around Halle a. d. Saale, Naumburg a. d. Saale, and in Döllnitz, where a few farmers joined as a group). Even in Silesia (in the areas around Breslau and Liegnitz) and East Prussia (in Königsberg, Wehlau and Insterburg) Nazism had

Table 2.3: The social and occupational status of persons joining the NSDAP in various *Länder* and provinces, in Germany as a whole, and in various towns and localities, September to November 1923 (by %)

Class	Occupational subgroup	(A) Baden	(B) Bavaria	(C) Bremen	(D) Brunswick [State]	(E) East Prussia	(F) Hanover	(G) Hessen	(H) Lippe-Detmold
LOWER	1. Unskilled workers	3.3	11.1	5.2	1.3	3.4	4.5	10.4	0
CLASS	2. Skilled (craft) workers	14.6	20.5	0	8.8	6.9	11.4	11.1	12.5
	3. Other skilled workers	11.2	4.7	5.2	3.8	3.4	2.3	6.0	4.2
Subtotal		29.1	36.3	10.4	13.9	13.7	18.2	27.5	16.7
Lower-	4. Master craftsmen	4.6	4.4	0	2.5	6.8	2.3	2.2	0
and	5. Non-acad. professionals	2.0	4.3	5.2	10.1	10.3	11.4	6.7	0
middle-	6. Lower employees	19.2	8.7	26.1	24.0	13.7	11.4	19.4	33.3
MIDDLE	7. Lower civil servants	5.3	8.0	15.8	1.3	20.7	2.3	8.9	8.4
CLASS	8. Merchants	21.9	11.9	26.3	25.3	13.7	22.7	18.6	12.5
	9. Farmers	0.7	11.0	0	1.3	3.4	9.1	2.2	0
Subtotal		53.7	48.3	73.4	64.5	68.6	59.2	58.0	54.2
Upper-	10. Managers	0.7	0.9	0	1.3	0	4.5	0.7	0
MIDDLE	11. Higher civil servants	0	0.1	0	0	0	0	0.7	0
CLASS/	12. University students	4.0	1.2	0	3.8	6.9	4.5	3.7	16.6
UPPER	13. Academic professionals	2.0	1.3	0	2.5	3.4	4.5	2.2	0
CLASS	14. Entrepreneurs	1.3	1.4	0	0	0	2.3	0	0
Subtotal		8.0	4.9	0	7.6	10.3	15.8	7.3	16.6
STATUS	15. Non-univ. students	7.2	1.6	0	5.1	0	2.3	1.5	12.5
UNCLEAR	16. Pensioners/Retired	1.3	0.8	0	0	0	0	2.2	0
	17. Wives/Widows	0.7	1.2	0	2.5	3.4	0	0.7	0
	18. Military personnel	0	0.1	5.2	2.5	0	0	0	0
	19. Illegible/no data	0	6.4	10.5	3.8	3.4	4.5	2.2	0
Subtotal		9.2	10.1	15.7	13.9	6.8	6.8	6.6	12.5
TOTAL (%)		100	100	100	100	100	100	100	100
Frequency (*N*)		151	3,241	19	79	29	44	134	24

Table 2.3 (cont'd)

Class	Occupational subgroup	(I) Saxony	(J) Saxony-Anhalt [*Wahlkreis*]	(K) Silesia	(L) Thuringia	(M) Westphalia	(N) Württemberg	(O) Germany
LOWER	1. Unskilled workers	8.6	9.6	11.8	5.0	7.1	4.7	9.7
CLASS	2. Skilled (craft) workers	16.1	16.3	23.5	18.7	20.2	12.3	18.4
	3. Other skilled workers	8.0	6.7	3.9	7.5	4.8	3.4	5.0
Subtotal		32.7	32.6	39.2	31.2	32.1	20.4	33.1
Lower-	4. Master craftsmen	2.3	2.9	9.8	5.0	1.2	6.7	4.3
and	5. Non-acad. professionals	5.7	6.7	5.9	2.5	9.5	5.1	4.5
middle-	6. Lower employees	18.4	10.6	9.8	16.2	17.8	12.3	11.5
MIDDLE	7. Lower civil servants	5.7	6.7	9.8	10.0	2.4	8.9	7.7
CLASS	8. Merchants	17.8	22.1	13.6	15.0	19.0	15.2	14.4
	9. Farmers	2.3	6.7	2.0	1.2	4.8	15.2	9.1
Subtotal		52.2	55.7	50.9	49.9	54.7	63.4	51.5
Upper-	10. Managers	1.7	1.0	0	1.2	1.2	0.4	0.8
MIDDLE	11. Higher civil servants	0	1.0	0	0	1.2	0	0.1
CLASS/	12. University students	0.6	1.0	0	2.5	1.2	0.8	1.5
UPPER	13. Academic professionals	2.3	2.9	2.0	5.0	2.4	2.1	1.7
CLASS	14. Entrepreneurs	1.1	0	0	0	0	0	1.1
Subtotal		5.7	5.9	2.0	8.7	6.0	3.3	5.2
STATUS	15. Non-univ. students	6.3	1.9	0	7.5	0	8.0	2.4
UNCLEAR	16. Pensioners/Retired	0.6	0	2.0	0	1.2	0	0.8
	17. Wives/Widows	0.6	1.0	0	0	1.2	0	1.0
	18. Military personnel	0	0	2.0	0	1.2	0	0.2
	19. Illegible/no data	1.7	2.9	3.9	2.5	3.6	4.7	5.5
Subtotal		9.2	5.8	7.9	10.0	7.2	12.7	9.9
TOTAL (%)		100	100	100	100	100	100	100
Frequency (*N*)		174	104	51	80	84	236	4,786

Table 2.3 (cont'd)

Class	Occupational subgroup	(P) Augsburg (Swabia)	(Q) Bamberg (Upper Franconia)	(R) Bielefeld (Westphalia)	(S) Brunswick [City] (Brunswick)	(T) Chemnitz (Saxony)	(U) Dresden (Saxony)	(V) Erlangen (Middle Franconia)
LOWER	1. Unskilled workers	20.2	17.0	0	1.7	5.4	0	9.0
CLASS	2. Skilled (craft) workers	30.2	18.5	26.6	6.8	25.4	16.6	13.0
	3. Other skilled workers	5.5	4.4	6.7	0	9.1	13.3	4.4
Subtotal		55.9	39.9	33.3	8.5	39.9	29.9	26.4
Lower-	4. Master craftsmen	2.7	1.4	6.7	3.4	1.8	0	0.5
and	5. Non-acad. professionals	4.6	5.9	20.0	11.8	7.3	3.3	3.5
middle-	6. Lower employees	9.1	6.6	6.7	20.3	18.1	26.7	3.0
MIDDLE	7. Lower civil servants	1.8	15.6	0	0	9.0	3.3	1.5
CLASS	8. Merchants	17.4	18.4	20.0	25.4	21.8	10.0	4.9
	9. Farmers	0	1.5	0	1.7	0	0	40.2
Subtotal		35.6	49.4	53.4	62.6	58.0	43.3	53.6
Upper-	10. Managers	0	0.7	0	1.7	0	0	0.5
MIDDLE	11. Higher civil servants	1.8	0	0	0	0	0	0
CLASS/	12. University students	0.9	1.5	0	5.1	0	0	4.0
UPPER	13. Academic professionals	0	0.7	0	3.4	0	3.3	2.9
CLASS	14. Entrepreneurs	0	0	0	0	0	0	0.5
Subtotal		2.7	2.9	0	10.2	0	3.3	7.9
STATUS	15. Non-univ. students	3.7	0	0	6.8	0	13.3	1.5
UNCLEAR	16. Pensioners/Retired	0.9	0.7	0	0	0	3.3	0.5
	17. Wives/Widows	0.9	1.5	0	3.4	0	0	0.5
	18. Military personnel	0	1.5	0	3.4	0	0	9.4
	19. Illegible/no data	0	3.7	13.3	5.1	1.8	6.7	0
Subtotal		5.5	7.4	13.3	18.7	1.8	23.3	11.9
TOTAL (%)		100	100	100	100	100	100	100
Frequency (*N*)		109	135	15	59	55	30	201

Table 2.3 (cont'd)

Class	Occupational subgroup	(W) Fürth (Middle Franconia)	(X) Gotha (Thuringia)	(Y) Günzburg (Swabia)	(Z) Hof (Upper Franconia)	(AA) Ingolstadt (Upper Bavaria)	(BB) Karlsruhe (Baden)	(CC) Kempten (Swabia)
LOWER	1. Unskilled workers	2.7	0	17.2	4.6	11.8	7.2	17.6
CLASS	2. Skilled (craft) workers	12.2	23.5	26.6	25.6	23.5	14.3	12.9
	3. Other skilled workers	9.4	5.9	0	11.6	5.9	3.6	9.7
Subtotal		24.3	29.4	43.8	41.8	41.2	25.1	40.2
Lower-	4. Master craftsmen	2.7	5.9	9.4	11.6	0	3.6	1.6
and	5. Non-acad. professionals	6.7	0	1.5	2.3	15.7	3.6	4.8
middle-	6. Lower employees	24.3	23.5	6.2	7.0	3.9	21.3	6.4
MIDDLE	7. Lower civil servants	10.8	5.9	9.4	4.6	9.8	3.6	14.5
CLASS	8. Merchants	21.6	23.5	4.7	7.0	5.9	32.1	24.1
	9. Farmers	0	0	10.9	9.3	11.8	0	4.8
Subtotal		66.1	58.8	42.1	41.8	47.1	64.2	56.2
Upper-	10. Managers	0	0	1.5	0	0	0	0
MIDDLE	11. Higher civil servants	0	0	0	0	0	0	0
CLASS/	12. University students	1.3	5.9	0	0	0	0	0
UPPER	13. Academic professionals	0	0	0	0	0	0	0
CLASS	14. Entrepreneurs	2.7	0	1.5	7.0	0	0	1.6
Subtotal		4.0	5.9	3.0	7.0	0	0	1.6
STATUS	15. Non-univ. students	2.7	5.9	1.5	2.3	0	10.7	0
UNCLEAR	16. Pensioners/Retired	0	0	0	0	0	0	0
	17. Wives/Widows	0	0	1.5	0	1.9	0	0
	18. Military personnel	0	0	0	0	1.9	0	0
	19. Illegible/no data	2.7	0	7.8	7.0	7.8	0	1.6
Subtotal		5.4	5.9	10.8	9.3	11.6	10.7	1.6
TOTAL (%)		100	100	100	100	100	100	100
Frequency (*N*)		74	17	64	43	51	28	62

Table 2.3 (cont'd)

Class	Occupational subgroup	(DD) Kirchenlaibach (Upper Franconia)	(EE) Kronach (Upper Franconia)	(FF) Kulmbach (Upper Franconia)	(GG) Langquaid (Lower Bavaria)	(HH) Memmingen (Swabia)	(II) Münchaurich (Middle Franconia)
LOWER	1. Unskilled workers	9.6	7.5	16.5	5.4	20.5	6.7
CLASS	2. Skilled (craft) workers	25.0	28.0	20.0	14.8	30.8	8.9
	3. Other skilled workers	1.9	4.1	5.2	7.4	0	0
Subtotal		36.5	39.6	41.7	27.6	51.3	15.6
Lower-	4. Master craftsmen	9.6	2.6	5.1	5.5	7.7	0
and	5. Non-acad.professionals	3.8	3.4	1.6	0	2.5	0
middle-	6. Lower employees	1.9	4.4	11.3	11.1	0	0
MIDDLE	7. Lower civil servants	44.2	4.8	0.8	12.9	2.5	2.2
CLASS	8. Merchants	0	13.7	16.4	9.2	2.5	0
	9. Farmers	0	20.9	0.8	5.5	23.1	82.2
Subtotal		59.5	49.8	36.0	44.2	38.3	84.4
Upper-	10. Managers	0	0.7	0	3.7	0	0
MIDDLE	11. Higher civil servants	0	0	0	0	0	0
CLASS/	12. University students	1.9	0.4	0	0	0	0
UPPER	13. Academic professionals	0	0	0.8	7.4	2.5	0
CLASS	14. Entrepreneurs	0	1.9	1.6	11.0	0	0
Subtotal		1.9	3.0	2.4	22.1	2.5	0
STATUS	15. Non-univ. students	0	1.1	0	0	0	0
UNCLEAR	16. Pensioners/Retired	0	0.4	0.8	0	0	0
	17. Wives/Widows	0	0	0.8	3.7	0	0
	18. Military personnel	0	5.9	0	0	0	0
	19. Illegible/no data	1.9	0	17.4	1.8	7.7	0
Subtotal		1.9	7.4	19.0	5.5	7.7	0
TOTAL (%)		100	100	100	100	100	100
Frequency (*N*)		52	268	115	54	39	45

Table 2.3 (cont'd)

Class	Occupational subgroup	(JJ) Munich (Upper Bavaria)	(KK) Neustadt a.d.Aisch (Middle Franconia)	(LL) Nuremberg (Middle Franconia)	(MM) Pappenheim (Middle Franconia)	(NN) Pirmasens (Palatinate)
LOWER	1. Unskilled workers	7.5	8.2	18.9	31.1	5.6
CLASS	2. Skilled (craft) workers	11.5	13.0	21.0	21.3	9.8
	3. Other skilled workers	5.9	2.3	4.7	1.6	8.4
		24.9	23.5	44.6	54.0	23.8
Lower-	4. Master craftsmen	2.4	2.3	6.4	4.9	4.2
and	5. Non-acad. professionals	9.6	1.2	1.6	1.6	0
middle-	6. Lower employees	14.5	2.3	13.7	1.6	14.0
MIDDLE	7. Lower civil servants	7.1	5.9	2.5	0	14.0
CLASS	8. Merchants	14.9	7.0	15.0	3.3	40.8
	9. Farmers	0.6	38.8	0.8	27.9	0
Subtotal		49.1	57.5	40.0	39.3	73.0
Upper-	10. Managers	1.2	0	0.4	1.6	0
MIDDLE	11. Higher civil servants	0.6	0	0	0	0
CLASS/	12. University students	3.3	0	0.4	0	0
UPPER	13. Academic profesionals	2.5	2.3	0.4	1.6	2.8
CLASS	14. Entrepreneurs	1.2	2.3	0.8	0	0
Subtotal		8.8	4.6	2.0	3.2	2.8
STATUS	15. Non-univ. students	3.7	0	0.4	0	0
UNCLEAR	16. Pensioners/Retired	2.2	0	0.8	1.6	0
	17. Wives/Widows	4.3	0	0.4	0	0
	18. Military personnel	0.4	0	0	0	0
	19. Illegible/no data	5.9	14.1	10.8	1.6	0
Subtotal		16.5	14.1	12.4	3.2	0
TOTAL (%)		100	100	100	100	100
Frequency (*N*)		487	85	232	61	71

Table 2.3 (cont'd)

Class	Occupational subgroup	(OO) Starnberg (Upper Bavaria)	(PP) Stuttgart (Württemberg)	(QQ) Treuchtlingen (Middle Franconia)	(RR) Vilsbiburg (Lower (Bavaria)	(SS) Wunsiedel (Upper Franconia)	(TT) Zwiesel (Lower Bavaria)
LOWER CLASS	1. Unskilled workers	8.3	3.4	17.4	4.5	11.9	4.1
	2. Skilled (craft) workers	45.8	14.5	4.3	50.0	11.9	24.9
	3. Other skilled workers	4.2	1.7	0	4.5	7.1	0
Subtotal		58.3	19.6	21.7	59.0	30.9	29.0
Lower- and middle-MIDDLE CLASS	4. Master craftsmen	0	7.6	13.0	9.1	14.3	0
	5. Non-acad. professionals	12.5	2.5	4.3	0	0	0
	6. Lower employees	4.2	6.7	17.4	4.5	7.1	12.5
	7. Lower civil servants	0	8.5	30.4	13.6	11.9	29.1
	8. Merchants	12.5	19.6	0	9.1	26.2	0
	9. Farmers	0	11.1	4.3	4.5	2.4	0
Subtotal		29.2	56.0	69.4	40.8	61.9	41.6
Upper-MIDDLE CLASS/ UPPER CLASS	10. Managers	4.2	0	8.7	0	7.1	0
	11. Higher civil servants	0	0	0	0	0	0
	12. University students	0	0.8	0	0	0	0
	13. Academic professionals	0	1.7	0	0	0	12.5
	14. Entrepreneurs	4.2	0	0	0	0	0
Subtotal		8.4	2.5	8.7	0	7.1	12.5
STATUS UNCLEAR	15. Non-univ. students	0	15.8	0	0	0	4.1
	16. Pensioners/Retired	0	0	0	0	0	0
	17. Wives/Widows	0	0	0	0	0	0
	18. Military personnel	0	0	0	0	0	0
	19. Illegible/no data	4.2	5.1	0	0	0	12.5
Subtotal		4.2	20.9	0	0	0	16.6
TOTAL (%)		100	100	100	100	100	100
Frequency (*N*)		24	120	23	22	42	24

Source: Percentages calculated on the basis of data provided by a list recording new members (*N*:4,786) joining the NSDAP between 25 September and 9 November 1923, *HA*, 10/215.

established a very limited presence. It was in the western and northern parts of Germany, in the federal state of Oldenburg and in the Prussian provinces of Hannover (except around Goslar and Osterode), and Schleswig-Holstein that the trickle towards the NSDAP is hardly measurable, while in Pommerania, Brandenburg and the two Mecklenburgs membership recruitment (as far as it is indicated in the 1923 list) was virtually absent, though a few groups of predominantly middle-class types - such as the small group at Cottbus in Brandenburg (seven merchants, five professionals of various kinds, along with one pastry-cook) - generated enough enthusiasm to enrol at Munich.

North of the Main the party was indeed a very marginal affair, in stark contrast to its position in Bavaria. The list for 1923 records seven cities and towns in which 100 or more individuals entered the party between September and November, as well as thirty-four towns and villages in which over 20 new recruits were attracted to it, and numerous localities scattered the length and breadth of Bavaria with 10 or more newly registered members. Beyond the 'star' performance of the branch at Munich, it was in Middle and Upper Franconia that high enrolments occurred (especially in the Kronach, Bamberg, Nuremberg, Fürth, Erlangen and Kulmbach areas), though Swabia (primarily in and around Augsburg, Günzburg and Kempten) and Lower and Upper Bavaria (particularly in Ingolstadt and Langquaid and their surroundings) were also involved in the surge. Only Lower Franconia (which shows only limited recruitment in the Würzburg and Schweinfurt regions) and the (Rhenish) Palatinate (where it seems that the party was hardly visible beyond the town of Pirmasens, which accounted for 95 per cent of new recruits recorded for the region) do not figure prominently in the data on Bavaria.

What sort of social groups were involved in the move towards the NSDAP in late 1923, and how representative were they in terms of the social make-up of members in established branches? The latter part of the question can only be answered tentatively, given the limited specific information that there is on established branches. However, such evidence as there is suggests that in Munich (compare Table 2.3, column JJ with Table 2.2, column I), Ingolstadt (compare Table 2.3, columm AA with Table 2.2, column Q), and Stuttgart (compare Table 2.3, column PP with Table 2.2, column E) the social mix involved in the expansion of the party in these towns in 1923 was broadly in line with the social make-up of members recruited in previous years, though in the case of Ingolstadt an increase in support from the lower class is indicated by late 1923.[56] It would seem that the social structures of the few established branches on which there is evidence over time do not seem to have been radically altered by the influx of the recruits, which were not drawn primarily or exclusively from any one class, except in the case of Bad Reichenhall (see Table 2.2, column J), where the new members joining in late 1923 were predominantly lower- and middle-middle class in status.[57]

The data relating to the new members joining the NSDAP on the eve of its attempt to stage a coup in November 1923 demonstrates that although the NSDAP recruited disproportionately from the lower- and middle-middle class and from the upper-middle class and upper class at the national and regional level (compare Table 2.1 and Table 2.3, columns A to O), it was able to mobilise lower class support, giving the party a heterogeneous social base. The material on the NSDAP's social profile to 1923 beyond its Bavarian power-base is limited, but does indicate a feature which was to become more clearly visible after 1925, namely the regional variations in the type of social elements which constituted the party. The extensive data on the members joining the party in Bavaria in late 1923 demonstrates another characteristic which marked the party as it developed: the often striking differences in its social structure *within* a particular *Land* or province (see Table 2.3, columns P to TT), which was influenced - though not inevitably - by the particular socio-economic and religious context in which regional or local Nazi groups evolved. Thus one can explain to some extent the high lower-class intake recorded for the Augsburg and Nuremberg branches (see Table 2.3, columns P and LL) by reference to the degree of industrialisation of these cities, in which even industrial workers (judging from the job descriptions recorded in the 1923 list) formed part of the Nazi recruits.[58] But other factors must have played an influential role also, such as the type of propaganda pushed out by the party and the targets chosen by local Nazi leaders, as well as the receptivity of the population to specific planks of the eclectic Nazi programme. The significance of local factors conditioning Nazi recruitment will only be revealed through numerous 'micro' studies.

The more one looks at the detailed picture provided by the 1923 data, the more difficult it is to make any generalisations about the social base of the NSDAP. In Bavaria one can point to a number of branches situated in both predominantly Protestant small towns, such as Hof and Kulmbach (see Table 2.3, columns Z and FF), and predominantly Catholic small towns, such as Günzburg, Kempten and Memmingen (see Table 2.3, columns Y, CC and HH) with a relatively high lower-class interest in Nazism.[59] In some very small towns and villages such as Pappenheim, Starnberg and Vilsbiburg (see Table 2.3, columns MM, OO and RR) and Sulzbach in Upper Franconia (where 13 of the 15 new recruits to the party followed working-class occupations), the influx of lower-class elements is very striking, while in other communities on which we have data, such as Münchaurich near Erlangen (see Table 2.3, column II), it is negligible.

Striking also is the degree of support given to the NSDAP by the farming community in some areas of Bavaria. The data for late 1923 suggests that farmers, and to a lesser degree agricultural workers, were moving towards the Nazi movement in some numbers.[60] This was especially true in Protestant parts of Middle and Upper Franconia, where in numerous villages farmers and farm workers constituted the bulk, if not the total, of newly registered members. Thus in Kleinsteinach (near Neustadt a. d. Aisch) the ten new members resident in the village were all farmers. In the nearby Emskirchen area the Nazi recruits in a number of villages were farmers and farm workers, while in the Münchaurich branch 37 of the 45 new members were farmers, two of the remainder being agricultural labourers. Interesting also, in that it shows the variability of the recruitment pattern *within* one branch, is the data on Erlangen (see Table 2.3, column V), which covered both the town and the surrounding countryside. Whereas the new members attracted by the party in the town were predominantly lower class, the members joining the branch in a number of nearby villages were overwhelmingly made up of farmers (e.g. in Grossdechsendorf 16 out of 21 recruits were farmers; in Möhrendorf and Uttenreuth around 90 per cent of the new members were farmers). Even in predominantly Catholic areas farmers were moving to join the party, though not to the same extent as in Protestant parts, with the partial exception of the Memmingen area, where they made up almost a quarter of the new membership.

One can detect a *Gemeinschaft* factor at work when one looks at the recruitment pattern in some of the villages noted above, a feature also discernable in other branches. Was it chance that a group of six policemen joined *en bloc* on the same day at Straubing, or that both blue- and white-collar railway employees formed the largest group among those joining the party at Kirchenlaibach (these account for the strong lower civil servants presence in the branch: see Table 2.3, column DD) near Bayreuth, or that groups of basket makers joined the party in large numbers in the Kronach area, especially in the villages of Oberlangenstadt and Küps, where they formed 40 and 50 per cent of the new recruits respectively? The precarious existence of the basket makers in north-eastern Bavaria (where they formed a prominent element in the lower class of the region), a perennial concern for the local authorities in the 1920s and 1930s, may well have conditioned their political behaviour.[61]

It is the infinite variety in the mix of social and occupational groups recorded in the 1923 list in various branches and localities throughout Bavaria which makes it difficult to categorise the NSDAP specifically as a *Mittelstandspartei* (middle-class party) or *Klassenpartei* (class party). The social profile of the branches varied quite enormously, even within the same region. It would seem that the rag-bag of ideas purveyed by the party attracted a socially-mixed following even in its early years, ranging from landowners and factory directors at the top of the social scale to day labourers and casual workers at the bottom. Though the generalisation holds that the core of the bulk of the party's branches and the mainstay of the party's membership was from the lower- and middle-middle class, support from the lower class made up a sizeable proportion of its early membership, while the upper-middle class and upper class was also (in relation to its size in society) strongly represented: the NSDAP had a pronounced heterogeneous social base in its early years.

III

That the NSDAP disintegrated into various factions following the shambles of the Munich putsch, contributing further to the divisions within the *völkisch* movement in 1924, is well-known. The imposition of a national ban on the party forced its erstwhile supporters, as far as they did not abandon active politics altogether, to find new political homes. Until the re-founding of the NSDAP in late February 1925 former Nazi supporters and sympathisers found refuge in a number of movements - some of only regional significance - both in Bavaria and in other parts of Germany. On the social make-up of the Nazi-*völkisch* successor organisations of the NSDAP which had more than just a regional significance, such as the *Grossdeutsche Volksgemeinschaft* (GDVG - Greater German People's Community) and, from mid-1924, the *Nationalsozialistische Freiheitsbewegung* (NSFB - National Socialist Freedom's Movement), there is virtually no information. The limited data there is on a number of branches of the NSFB in Upper Bavaria (see Table 2.4, columns A to D), suggests a movement in which, at least in this part of Bavaria, the lower- and middle-middle class was by far the largest element, and one in which the upper-middle class and upper class (see Table 2.4, columns E and F) secured a disproportionately high percentage of the leadership positions, both in Upper Bavaria as well as in the Bavarian NSFB as a whole. The lower class is conspicuous by its very limited presence in the membership. These lists, which provide limited data on the NSFB even for Upper Bavaria cannot, of course, be taken as representative of the NSFB's social composition as a whole, but there is evidence which suggests that lower-class interest and participation in *völkisch*-Nazi movements waned in 1924.[62]

Following Hitler's release from prison in late December 1924, the NSDAP was refounded by him in February 1925 after the ban on the party had been lifted, first in Bavaria, and then in other *Länder*. After an initial phase of comparatively rapid growth in 1925 and 1926, the subsequent period to late 1929 was a lean one for the party.[63] Despite the virtual stagnation of the movement in 1927 and 1928, and slow growth for much of 1928 and 1929, the period 1925 to late 1929 was a crucial one in the development of the NSDAP. It is in the late 1920s that the Nazi movement acquired the truly national presence which had eluded it before 1923, developed a rudimentary, increasingly centralised and bureaucratised organisational framework at the national, regional and local level, and began the creation of a more efficient propaganda arm. Although essentially an irritant and nuisance in Weimar politics, a peripheral factor of little significance until 1930, the party did make slow progress in terms of

Table 2.4: The social and occupational structure of the membership of the *Völkischer Block* (VB - *Völkisch* Bloc) and of the *Nationalsozialistische Freiheitsbewegung* (NSFB - National Socialist Freedom Movement) in various branches in Upper Bavaria, and of NSFB functionaries in Bavaria, 1924-25 (by %)

Class	Occupational subgroup	(A) VB Freilassing[a] Dec. 1924	(B) NSFB Traunstein[b] (Jan. 1925)	(C) NSFB Berchtesgaden[c] Jan. 1925	(D) NSFB Brannenburg[d] (Jan. 1925)	(E) VB/NSFB Upper Bavaria[e] (Branch leaders) (Jan. 1925)	(F) VB/NSFB Bavaria[f] (District/ branch leaders) (Jan. 1925)
LOWER	1. Unskilled workers	2.1	3.6	6.6	0	0	0
CLASS	2. Skilled (craft) workers	14.9	9.1	15.0	4.0	0	0
	3. Other skilled workers	2.1	1.8	3.3	4.0	0	0
Subtotal		19.1	14.5	24.9	8.0	0	0
Lower-	4. Master craftsmen	8.5	18.2	10.0	0	0	5.2
and	5. Non-acad. professionals	6.4	5.4	6.6	8.0	0	3.4
middle-	6. Lower employees	6.3	5.4	0	20.0	6.6	6.8
MIDDLE	7. Lower civil servants	27.6	5.4	36.6	8.0	13.3	31.0
CLASS	8. Merchants	6.4	21.8	11.6	32.0	19.9	6.8
	9. Farmers	2.1	0	0	4.0	6.6	3.4
Subtotal		57.3	56.2	64.8	72.0	46.4	56.6
Upper-	10. Managers	2.1	3.6	0	4.0	6.6	3.4
MIDDLE	11. Higher civil servants	0	3.6	1.7	0	0	5.2
CLASS/	12. University students	0	0	0	0	0	0
UPPER	13. Academic professionals	2.1	1.8	6.6	4.0	26.7	20.7
CLASS	14. Entrepreneurs	2.1	0	0	0	6.6	6.9
Subtotal		6.3	9.0	8.3	8.0	39.9	36.2
STATUS	15. Non-univ. students	0	0	0	4.0	0	0
UNCLEAR	16. Pensioners/Retired	0	1.8	0	0	6.6	3.4
	17. Wives/Widows	10.6	11.0	0	0	0	0
	18. Military personnel	0	0	0	0	0	3.4
	19. Illegible/no data	6.4	7.3	1.7	8.0	6.6	0
Subtotal		17.0	20.1	1.7	12.0	13.2	6.8
TOTAL (%)		100	100	100	100	100	100
Frequency (*N*)		47	55	60	25	15	58

Table 2.4 (cont'd)

Sources:

a. Percentages calculated on the basis of data in 'Mitgliederverzeichnis nach dem Stand vom 16. Dezember 1924, Völkischer Block, Ortsgruppe Freilassing', *HA*, 4/88.
b. Percentages calculated on the basis of data in 'Mitgliederverzeichnis des völk. Block der nat. soz. Freiheitsbewegung Ortsgruppe Traunstein', (n.d., probably January 1925), *HA*, 4/88.
c. Percentages calculated on the basis of data in membership list 'Nationalsozialistische Freiheitsbewegung Grossdeutschlands, Ortsgruppe Berchtesgaden', dated 10 January 1925, *HA*, 4/88.
d. Percentages calculated on the basis of data in membership list of the 'Brannenburg/Oberbayern' branch of the NSFB, (n.d., probably January 1925), *HA*, 4/88.
e. Percentages calculated on the basis of data provided in a list of branch leaders of 'Der Völkische Block. Nat. Soz. Freiheitsbewegung Grossdeutschlands. Kreisverband Oberbayern-Nord', (n.d., probably January 1925), *HA*, 4/88.
f. Percentages calculated from data relating to Upper Bavaria (source e) and a list of 119 district and branch leaders headed 'Nationalsozialistische Freiheitsbewegung Grossdeutschlands - Landesverband Bayern' (n.d., probably early 1925). The occupational status of 58 district and branch leaders could be established. Copy of list in *HA*, 4/88.

the growth of its membership. Madden estimates the strength of the party at approximately 27,000 by the end of 1925, which rose to 42,000 at the beginning of 1927, to 79,000 by the beginning of 1929, to reach a total of 125,000 by January 1930.[64] If one looks at the number of membership cards issued consecutively in these years, which reached the 170,000 mark by the end of 1929, it is clear that the NSDAP suffered from a considerable turn-over in its membership.[65] The 'take-off' phase of the party in 1930 is reflected in the tremendous jump in the issue of membership cards, which reached the 357,000 mark by the end of the year. According to Schulz the NSDAP had a strength of around 300,000 members by the time of its electoral breakthrough at the national level in September 1930, of which only 129,563 were still in the party at the beginning of the Third Reich.[66]

There is quite extensive data on the social and occupational status of the membership attracted by the NSDAP between 1925 and 1930. At the 'macro' level there are Kater's calculations based on Studentkowski's statistical material drawn up in the early 1930s (see Table 2.5, columns A to C), as well as material produced by Madden based on systematic sampling of party recruits between 1925 and 1929.[67] The second source is the ***Partei-Statistik***, produced by the Nazis for internal party purposes in 1935, which gives data not only for the party at the national level, but also provides a breakdown of its membership in each of the 32 *Gaue* into which the party was divided by the early 1930s.[68] Finally, there are two lists for established members in the southern half of the province of Westphalia and in the province of Thuringia for the period 1925 to 1928 (see Table 2.6, columns J and K), as well as a number of membership lists for various towns, which record the structure of Nazi branches at particular moments in time (see Table 2.6, columns A to I, and L to R).[69]

One has to be cautious in utilising data of such varied provenance, especially in view of the high turn-over rate of the Nazi membership in the period, but it does allow one to make a number of observations on the sociology of the party in this period. Studentkowski's material, which relates to the occupational background of new members joining the party in the period under review, suggests that after 1925 the Nazi movement secured once more a heterogeneous following, in which members drawn from the lower- and middle-middle class (on average 50 to

Table 2.5: The social and occupational status of persons joining the NSDAP in Germany, 1925-44 (by %)

Class	Occupational subgroup	(A) 1925	(B) 1927	(C) 1929	(D) 1930-32	(E) 1933	(F) 1937	(G) 1939	(H) 1942-44
Lower	1. Unskilled workers	12.7	19.1	18.7	15.4	12.6	15.7	15.9	18.3
	2. Skilled (craft) workers	19.5	23.5	20.0	18.1	15.4	15.1	20.1	18.6
	3. Other skilled workers	-	-	-	2.4	2.7	3.8	3.9	5.7
Subtotal		32.2	42.6	38.7	35.9	30.7	34.6	39.9	42.6
Lower middle	4. Master craftsmen	11.3	13.5	11.6	10.5	8.9	8.7	11.6	10.7
	5. Non-acad. professionals	-	-	-	4.2	4.2	3.4	3.0	2.9
	6. Lower employees	21.4	19.1	14.6	11.1	10.6	16.8	15.3	25.3
	7. Lower civil servants	11.4	5.0	5.5	4.6	11.7	16.3	7.6	3.3
	8. Merchants	11.3	8.3	11.1	11.9	12.8	5.5	6.7	3.3
	9. Farmers	3.6	5.2	12.0	12.6	8.9	6.7	9.7	9.1
Subtotal		59.0	51.1	54.8	54.9	57.1	57.4	53.9	54.6
Elite	10. Managers	-	-	-	0.9	2.3	1.6	2.0	1.0
	11. Higher civil servants	1.7	0.4	0.7	1.2	2.8	1.9	0.5	0.3
	12. Academic professionals	4.7	3.1	2.1	2.5	3.0	2.3	1.6	0.5
	13. Students	2.0	2.4	2.5	3.2	1.7	1.1	1.0	0.5
	14. Entrepreneurs	0.4	0.4	1.2	1.4	2.4	1.1	1.2	0.4
Subtotal		8.8	6.3	6.5	9.2	12.2	8.0	6.3	2.7
TOTAL (%)		100	100	100	100	100	100	100	100
Frequency (*N*)		22,795	15,900	61,785	1,954	3,316	3,977	1,001	1,492

Source: Kater, *The Nazi Party*, pp. 244-5, Table 3, columns A, E and I; p. 250, Table 6, column A; and pp. 252-3, Table 7, columns A, C, E and F (reprinted by permission). The data relating to new Nazi members provided by Michael Kater for 1925 to 1929 is based on statistical material produced by Werner Studentkowski around 1930 for the Nazi Party's internal purposes. Percentage figures for skilled workers (subgroup 3) and for non-academic professionals (subgroup 5) could not be established and are hidden in those for other subgroups. The figures for managers (subgroup 10) are included in those for lower employees (subgroup 6). The data for the period 1930 to 1944 is based on samples drawn systematically by Professor Kater from the NSDAP Master File in the Berlin Document Center.

Table 2.6: The social and occupational structure of the membership of the NSDAP in various regions and towns, 1925-29 (by %)

Class	Occupational subgroup	(A) Bad Nauheim[a] (March 1925)	(B) Hamburg[b] March 1925	(C) Barmen-Langerfeld[c] (Spring 1925)	(D) Munich[d] 1925-26	(E) Brunswick[b] [City] 1925-26	(F) Starnberg[e] May 1925
LOWER CLASS	1. Unskilled workers	5.9	17.9	33.3	7.6	13.3	0
	2. Skilled (craft) workers	0	13.8	25.6	7.6	13.9	7.7
	3. Other skilled workers	0	1.9	2.6	0.7	2.3	15.4
Subtotal		5.9	33.6	61.5	15.4	29.5	23.1
Lower- and middle-MIDDLE CLASS	4. Master craftsmen	0	7.9	0	5.6	8.0	15.4
	5. Non-acad. professionals	5.9	0	0	4.9	2.3	7.7
	6. Lower employees	0	14.2	0	11.1	19.5	0
	7. Lower civil servants	17.6	8.5	10.3	3.5	11.7	23.0
	8. Merchants	23.5	30.2	15.4	21.4	15.6	15.4
	9. Farmers	5.9	0	0	0	7.8	0
Subtotal		52.9	60.8	25.7	46.5	64.9	61.5
Upper-MIDDLE CLASS/ UPPER CLASS	10. Managers	0	0.9	0	4.1	1.6	0
	11. Higher civil servants	0	0.9	0	1.4	0	7.7
	12. University students	29.4	0	0	0.7	0.8	0
	13. Academic professionals	5.9	3.8	5.1	4.1	2.3	7.7
	14. Entrepreneurs	0	0	0	0	0.8	0
Subtotal		35.3	5.6	5.1	10.3	5.5	15.4
STATUS UNCLEAR	15. Non-univ. students	0	–	0	0	–	0
	16. Pensioners/Retired	0	–	0	3.5	–	0
	17. Wives/Widows	0	–	0	14.5	–	0
	18. Illegible/no data	5.9	–	7.7	9.0	–	0
Subtotal		5.9	–	7.7	27.0	–	0
TOTAL (%)		100	100	100	100	100	100
Frequency (*N*)		17	106	39	144	128	13

Table 2.6 (cont'd)

Class	Occupational subgroup	(G) Essen[f] July 1925	(H) Langerfeld[g] Aug. 1925	(I) Mülheim a.d.Ruhr[h] Nov. 1925	(J) Westphalia[i] 1925–28	(K) Thuringia[i] 1925–28	(L) Mettmann[j] Feb. 1926
LOWER	1. Unskilled workers	10.5	34.9	15.2	17.4	10.9	17.9
CLASS	2. Skilled (craft) workers	24.5	32.5	39.1	17.7	18.8	17.8
	3. Other skilled workers	8.8	4.6	0	5.8	2.5	10.7
Subtotal		43.8	72.0	54.3	40.9	32.2	46.4
Lower-	4. Master craftsmen	3.5	0	0	10.1	10.9	3.6
and	5. Non-acad. professionals	5.3	2.3	2.2	4.3	2.5	0
middle-	6. Lower employees	19.3	2.3	26.1	15.5	14.6	32.1
MIDDLE	7. Lower civil servants	8.8	4.6	2.2	7.3	10.0	7.2
CLASS	8. Merchants	12.3	13.9	10.8	15.2	14.3	0
	9. Farmers	0	0	0	1.3	7.3	3.6
Subtotal		49.2	23.1	41.3	53.7	59.7	46.5
Upper-	10. Managers	0	0	0	0.7	1.4	0
MIDDLE	11. Higher civil servants	0	0	0	0.5	0.9	0
CLASS/	12. University students	0	0	0	1.3	1.2	0
UPPER	13. Academic professionals	1.7	2.3	2.2	2.4	3.1	0
CLASS	14. Entrepreneurs	0	0	0	0.5	1.4	0
Subtotal		1.7	2.3	2.2	5.4	8.1	0
STATUS	15. Non-univ. students	3.5	0	0	–	–	7.1
UNCLEAR	16. Pensioners/Retired	1.7	0	0	–	–	0
	17. Wives/Widows	0	0	2.2	–	–	0
	18. Illegible/no data	0	2.3	0	–	–	0
Subtotal		5.2	2.3	2.2	–	–	7.1
TOTAL (%)		100	100	100	100	100	100
Frequency (*N*)		57	43	46	672	642	28

Table 2.6 (cont'd)

Class	Occupational subgroup	(M) Barmen[k] (early 1926)	(N) Starnberg[b] July 1927	(O) Rheinhausen[l] Dec. 1927	(P) Landsberg[m] (early 1928)	(Q) Königsberg[b] June 1929	(R) Schwabing[n] (Munich) 1929
LOWER	1. Unskilled workers	9.6	14.8	27.3	19.1	2.5	6.9
CLASS	2. Skilled (craft) workers	29.4	21.1	13.6	28.5	21.4	7.4
	3. Other skilled workers	5.8	11.1	27.3	9.5	3.8	2.8
Subtotal		44.8	47.0	68.2	57.1	27.7	17.1
Lower-	4. Master craftsmen	0	12.2	0	0	12.4	4.7
and	5. Non-acad. professionals	3.2	0	0	0	1.7	5.2
middle-	6. Lower employees	15.9	7.4	0	9.6	20.0	12.1
MIDDLE	7. Lower civil servants	0.6	11.1	0	4.8	6.7	3.7
CLASS	8. Merchants	11.5	0	22.7	4.8	18.3	13.0
	9. Farmers	0.6	0	0	0	0.8	0.2
Subtotal		31.8	30.7	22.7	19.2	59.9	38.9
Upper-	10. Managers	0.6	0	0	4.8	0.4	0.6
MIDDLE	11. Higher civil servants	0	14.8	0	0	0.8	1.2
CLASS/	12. University students	0.6	0	0	0	7.9	6.5
UPPER	13. Academic professionals	0	3.7	0	0	2.1	4.9
CLASS	14. Entrepreneurs	0	3.7	0	0	1.3	1.2
Subtotal		1.2	22.2	0	4.8	12.5	14.4
STATUS	15. Non-univ. students	0	–	0	0	–	5.0
UNCLEAR	16. Pensioners/Retired	0	–	0	0	–	3.3
	17. Wives/Widows	4.5	–	0	0	–	15.2
	18. Illegible/no data	17.3	–	9.1	18.9	–	5.9
Subtotal		21.8	–	9.1	18.9	–	29.4
TOTAL (%)		100	100	100	100	100	100
Frequency (*N*)		156	27	22	21	240	836

Table 2.6 (cont'd)

Sources:

a. Percentages calculated on the basis of data provided by a membership list for Bad Nauheim (Hesse-Darmstadt) attached to a letter by the branch leader Ernstberger to Hitler, dated 5 March 1925, *HA*, 6/142.
b. From Kater, *The Nazi Party*, p. 246, Table 4, columns A, E, G and I (reprinted by permission). Kater does not differentiate between university and non-university students, and does not provide details for subgroups 15 to 18.
c. Percentages calculated on the basis of data provided by the 'Mitglieder-Liste der N.S.D.A.P. Ogr. Barmen-Langerfeld' (n.d., probably early 1925), *Nordrhein-Westfälisches Hauptstaatsarchiv* [Düsseldorf] (hereafter *NWHStA*), RW23/Nr.85.
d. Percentages calculated on the basis of data provided by fragments of (incomplete) membership lists relating to 'Sektion Schwabing' and 'Sektion Innen-Stadt' (Munich) for 1925-6, *HA*, 2A/232, 8/177 and 8/182.
e. Percentages calculated on the basis of data provided by a membership list dated 9 May 1925 in F. Büchner, *Kamerad! Halt aus! Aus der Geschichte des Kreises Starnberg der NSDAP* (Munich, 1942), pp. 35-6.
f. Percentages calculated on the basis of data provided by 'Mitgliederliste der Ortsgruppe Essen - Monat Juli' (1925), *NWHStA*, RW23/Nr.38.
g. Percentages calculated on the basis of data provided by 'Mitgliederliste Langerfeld. 31 Aug. 1925', *NWHStA*, RW23/Nr. 85.
h. Percentages calculated on the basis of data provided by '1. Mitgliederliste der Ortsgruppe Mülheim-Ruhr der NSDAP' (date of last entry 16 November 1925), *NWHStA*, RW23/Nr.50-1.
i. From Kater, *The Nazi Party*, p. 248, Table 4, columns A and E (reprinted by permission). Kater does not differentiate between university and non-university students, and does not provide details for subgroups 15 to 18.
j. Percentages calculated on the basis of data provided by 'Mitgliederliste der NSDAP Ortsgruppe Mettmann, 28.2.1926', *NWHStA*, RW23/Nr.55.
k. Percentages calculated on the basis of data provided by 'Mitgliederliste NSDAP Barmen' (n.d., probably early 1926), *NWHStA*, RW23/Nr.49.
l. Percentages calculated on the basis of data provided by a membership list (date of last entry 1 December 1927) sent by the branch leader of Rheinhausen to the Ruhr *Gauleitung*, dated 27 January 1928. The covering letter suggests that only about 15 per cent of the total membership of the branch is recorded in this list, *NWHStA*, RW23/Nr.63.
m. Percentages calculated on the basis of data provided by a membership list 'Landsberg a. Lech' (n.d., probably early 1928 - the list is included in material dealing with the 1928 Reichstag election campaign), *HA*, 3/81-2.
n. Percentages calculated on the basis of data provided by a membership list for 'Sektion Schwabing/Nachtrag Ortsgruppe Schwabing 1929'; the list relates to the total strength of *Sektion* Schwabing (Munich) at the end of 1929, *HA*, 8/182.

60 per cent of the annual intake) were, as in the formative years of its development, overrepresented in comparison with the size of this class in German society (see Table 2.1). Studentkowski's figures for lower-class recruits, however, do indicate a growing success in the party's ability to mobilise support from this quarter, especially in the years immediately after the reconstruction of the party (as reflected in the figure of 42.6 per cent for 1927). This data, given its origins, could be dismissed as wishful thinking on the part of a party intent on demonstrating its self-proclaimed image as a *Volkspartei* (people's party) , were it not for independent calculations made by both Kater and Madden (based on random or systematic sampling of the NSDAP Membership Master File) for these years, which are in broad agreement with Studentkowski's values.[70] One can agree with Kater's comment that these percentages 'were still not very high', but they were certainly quite high.[71]

In the *Partei-Statistik*, published by the *Reichsorganisationsleiter* in 1935, the Nazis only claimed that 39,944 (23.4 per cent) out of a total of 121,151 members who had joined the movement before 14 September 1930 (and had not left it by the time the party census was taken - probably in late 1934) were 'workers'.[72] This would indicate, given the material provided by Studentkowski, Kater and Madden, that the turn-over for lower-class members was significantly greater than that of the total membership, though there is no way of verifying this hypothesis. The significance of the relatively low 'worker' percentage is, on another level, that it seems to show that the Nazis were giving an accurate picture of the social structure of the party and not merely engaged in falsifying the evidence and distorting reality, an accusation made by a number of historians who dismiss the *Partei-Statistik* too readily as representing little more than Nazi propaganda.[73] There are undeniable limitations in using this source, such as the vague occupational categories employed in it, and the fact that it does not allow one to establish the precise social structure of the party at any particular point in time before 1 January 1935 because the collated data is based only on the 'stable' membership (i.e. those who joined after 1925 and had not left the party by 1935). Given the high turn-over in membership before 1930 (and between 1930 and 1933 also), the *Partei-Statistik* can only provide at best a partial insight into the sociology of the NSDAP in the pre-1933 period, but cannot give us any indication as to the social background of the 40 to 50 per cent of the membership which joined the party temporarily in these years. Despite its limitations, the *Partei-Statistik* can be used as a general guide to the social structure of the Nazi movement at the national and regional level *because* in broad terms the data it contains is generally confirmed not only by the statistics produced by Kater and Madden at the national level, but also at the *Gau* level by a number of regional studies which have appeared in the last twenty years or so.[74]

At the *Gau* level the data in the *Partei-Statistik* indicates that the social make-up of the NSDAP was differently constituted from region to region, making it in the Ruhr, for example, a quite different animal from that in, for example, Schleswig-Holstein.[75] Although 'class' was a factor in determining recruitment, the socio-economic structure of the regions (as one would expect) and the religious composition of the population (as is well-known) were critical in determining the social mix at the *Gau* level. Thus in a number of *Gaue* the lower class made up around one-third of the membership recorded in the *Partei-Statistik*.[76] It was a prominent element in the rank and file in the heavily industrialised Ruhr region, accounting for 35.3 per cent of the members in Westphalia-South, 33.1 per cent in Essen and 32.4 per cent in Westphalia-North. The lower class also figures prominently, however, in the less heavily industrialised areas covered by *Gaue* Halle-Merseburg (34 per cent) and Koblenz-Trier (33.5 per cent). Although white-collar workers (*Angestellte*) were generally well-represented in the membership in all *Gaue*, they accounted for a striking 41.6 per cent in *Gau* Greater Berlin and 38.8 per cent in *Gau* Hamburg, but only 12.3 per cent in *Gau* Schleswig-Holstein. Civil servants were comparatively strongly in evidence in the membership of both Catholic and Protestant regions of Bavaria (as well as in Baden, Württemberg, and Thuringia), accounting for between 9.4 per cent to 16.3 per cent, an overrepresentation of 200 to 300 per cent in comparison with the percentage figure of this occupational group in Germany as a whole (see Table 2.1). In some regions, on the other hand, civil servants were hardly visible in the membership of the NSDAP, such as in Schleswig-Holstein (3.1 per cent) and *Gau* Hannover-East (4.1 per cent). The response rate of the farmers to the party was also highly variable before 1930. In some predominantly Protestant areas they constituted a major part of the rank-and-file membership in a number of *Gaue*, especially those of Schleswig-Holstein (a striking 37.2 per cent), Hannover-East (30.6 per cent), and Weser-Ems (27.3 per cent), whereas in the largely Protestant rural region of Franconia (5.7 per cent) farmers were less in evidence. In the agrarian parts of the industrialised Protestant *Land* Saxony the Nazis made hardly any impression on the farming community at all (farmers accounted for a mere 3.1 per cent of the Nazi membership in the region). While Protestant farmers were generally particularly susceptible to joining the NSDAP in the latter half of the 1920s, their Catholic counterparts (who had been quite visible among the party's membership in Bavaria by 1923) were conspicuous by their virtual absence, especially in Bavaria and in the Rhineland.

The data in the *Partei-Statistik* does imply that the NSDAP had a variable social structure at the regional level. This feature is confirmed by the admittedly more limited 'independent' data which we have on the party for 1925 to 1930 at the regional and local level (see Table 2.6), which also allows one, in the cases of Westphalia and of Thuringia, to make rough comparisons between the material in the *Partei-Statistik* at the *Gau* level with that derived from non-*Partei-Statistik* sources. The figure for the lower class among the 'established' members in Thuringia for 1925 to 1928 is given by Kater as 32.2 per cent, fairly close to the *Partei-Statistik* value of 29.4 per cent for the longer timespan 1925 to 1930. In the case of *Gau* Westphalia-South, Kater's analysis of those members who were recipients of the '*Goldene Parteiabzeichen*' (Golden Party Badge), that is members in the party who joined after 1925 and were still in the NSDAP at the outset of the Third Reich, shows that some 40.9 per cent of these were from the lower class, again fairly close to the *Partei-Statistik* figure of 35.9 per cent. Both for the national and - as far as there is material - regional situation the *Partei-Statistik* appears to be in line with, rather than contradicting, other evidence.

That it was not impossible for the Nazis to recruit often quite heavily from the lower class in industrialised areas of Germany is borne out in the social structure of the NSDAP in a number of branches situated in the Ruhr area, especially in the textile towns of Barmen and Langerfeld, and such centres of heavy industry as Rheinhausen and

Mülheim (see Table 2.6, columns C, G, H, I, L, M and O for details on branches situated in the Ruhr).[77] Data on some 780 members who joined the Nazi movement in the western Ruhr (that part which fell within the boundaries of *Regierungsbezirk* Düsseldorf) during 1925 to 1926 shows that about 50 per cent were from the lower class (which made up 60 per cent of the working population in the region).[78] The relative success of the NSDAP in attracting workers to its cause relates in part to the socio-economic structure of the area. Important however in the mid-1920s, when the Ruhr was a major centre of Nazi growth in Germany, were the consequences of the Ruhr occupation, which heightened the nationalist feelings of all classes in the region. The lower class was not immune to this form of irrationalism and even the German Communist Party (KPD) appealed to the nationalist sentiments of the working class in its propaganda in the Ruhr. Needless to say, the Nazis exploited the nationalist tendencies of the population in the Ruhr to the full, and secured support from 'nationalist-minded' Germans irrespective of their class background. Exploited by the party also were the problems of structural unemployment in the area connected with the rationalisation process which was in full swing in the mid-1920s, which combined with the effects of the economic recession of 1925 to 1926 to produce a bleak social environment. Important also in conditioning the right-wing political response of a section of the lower class, was the fact that even by the 1920s, the 'proletariat' of the region had still not acquired a strong working-class consciousness.[79] Critical also in explaining why the Nazis were able to penetrate the lower class in the Ruhr was the strong anti-capitalist (as well as racist) rhetoric which dominated the NSDAP's propaganda in the region throughout the 1920s and early 1930s.[80] Judging from the entries recorded in the Ruhr branch membership lists which have survived for the mid-1920s period, it appears that even sections of the industrial proletariat - such as miners, metalworkers, factory and textile workers - responded to the Nazi overtures.

Extensive material on the structure of individual NSDAP branches beyond those in the Ruhr towns is still lacking. Not surprisingly, the little data there is on a few branches situated in other parts of Germany presents a quite different pattern to that prevalent in the Ruhr. Although the lower class formed the bulk of the membership in small branches situated at Starnberg and Landsberg (both in Upper Bavaria) in 1927 and 1928 respectively (see Table 2.6, columns N and P), in branches situated in the large cities of Hamburg, Munich and Königsberg (see Table 2.6, columns B, D, Q and R) it was the lower- and middle-middle class, as well as the upper-middle class and upper class, which provided the great majority of the membership.[81] If it were not for the data on the Ruhr towns, one would be tempted to generalise along the lines that the smaller the town, the more probable that the lower class made up a significant proportion of the Nazi membership, and the larger the town, the less likely the chance that the lower class would be strongly represented in the Nazi ranks.

Collectively the data for the period 1925 to 1930 suggests that the Nazis recruited from all classes, though disproportionately. These were years when the NSDAP was able to mobilise the lower class in much greater numbers than in the pre-putsch period, especially in the Ruhr, where even industrial workers formed a not negligible part of its support. Clear also is that the party's social composition was very variable from region to region. It is the chameleon quality of the party which is so striking and which makes the party so difficult to pigeon-hole in class terms.

IV

The rapid rise in the NSDAP's membership recorded in 1930, which coincided with a marked deepening of the agrarian and industrial crisis which had set in in 1928 to 1929, plunged Weimar Germany into a sustained political crisis from the spring of 1930. The democratic process from mid-1930 onwards was basically 'frozen', with a succession of 'presidential governments' culminating in the final destruction of the Republic's pluralist parliamentary democracy with the establishment and consolidation of the so-called 'National Government' under the chancellorship of Hitler in the spring and summer of 1933. As unemployment rose to astronomic levels after 1930 (just short of 30 per cent of the working population by 1932), radicals of the left and right latched onto and exploited the deprivation and anxiety of large sections of German society. That the Nazis benefitted from the crisis more than any other party opposed to Weimar democracy is well-known. The ominous surge towards the NSDAP in 1930 was sustained in 1931 and 1932. After the electoral breakthrough at the national level - the Nazi vote rose from 2.6 per cent in the *Reichstag* election of May 1928 to 18.3 per cent in the *Reichstag* election of September 1930 - a veritable stampede towards the party took place as large numbers of '*Septemberlinge*', as established Nazi members dubbed the newcomers, joined the party. By January 1931 the 400,000th membership card had been issued (the 200,000th card had been issued as recently as February 1930), and in 1931 and 1932 a further 100,000 cards were issued on average at three-monthly intervals. By the time Hitler became chancellor in January 1933, a total of 1,435,530 membership cards had been handed out.[82] These figures allow one to measure the accelerating and sustained growth pattern of the NSDAP as it emerged from its relative obscurity in the late 1920s to become a major political force, securing a staggering 37.3 per cent of the votes by the time of the *Reichstag* election of July 1932.

In this period of massive expansion the membership of the NSDAP continued to exhibit the by now familiar features noticeable since the mid-1920s. Most striking is the continued volatility of the membership: of the 1,435,530 members who had joined the party at some stage before January 1933, only 849,009 remained by the time the party census was taken in late 1934. Since it is unlikely that many of the party members left the movement after its successful acquisition of power in 1933, it would seem that the party lost around 40 per cent of those who joined it between September 1930 and January 1933. The second characteristic of the membership is that in social terms it continued, as it had done since the early 1920s, to demonstrate the ability of the NSDAP to recruit from all classes. The marked heterogeneity of the NSDAP, even if it was unable to attract all classes in proportion to their size in German society, is demonstrated by the data which we have on its occupational and social structure. For the party as a whole, the random sampling undertaken by Kater again shows the familiar pattern: the members drawn from the lower- and middle-middle class and from the upper-middle class and upper class were over-represented in the party, and the lower class continued to be underrepresented, though the latter accounted for just over one-third of the membership influx recorded in these years (see Table 2.5, column D). In terms of the percentages for individual occupational groups which joined the party in the early 1930s, the pattern for 1929 (see Table 2.5, column C) continued, with very minor variations, up to 1933. Of significance is the fact that Kater's sample data for new entrants joining in the period 1930 to 1932 conforms quite closely with the values given in the *Partei-Statistik* for members who were in the party between September 1930 and January 1933. Thus while Kater's sample gives the figures of 35.9 per cent and 54.9 per cent for the lower class and the lower- and middle-middle class respectively, the *Partei-Statistik*'s comparable figures are 31.5 per cent and 57.9 per cent.[83] Even at the level of individual occupational groups where direct comparison can be made (the two sets of data measure, of course, different 'dimensions' of the membership, i.e. new and established members), there is remarkable congruence in the case of farmers (Kater's 12.6 per cent against the *Partei-Statistik*'s 12.5 per cent) and civil servants (Kater's 5.8 per cent against the *Partei-Statistik*'s 6.7 per cent).

The feature strongly in evidence in the *Partei-Statistik*'s breakdown of the social composition of the party at the *Gau* level - the marked variability from region to region - is again in evidence for the 1930 to 1933 period. Thus in the predominantly Protestant, agrarian regions, especially in *Gaue* Schleswig-Holstein, Hannover-East and Weser-Ems, the party continued to recruit heavily from the farming community. The percentage share of farmers in the party in these regions did, however, decline by between 5 to 10 per cent in comparison with the even higher values recorded in the years before 1930, as recruitment from other occupational groups, especially those from the lower class, increased.[84] In predominantly Catholic agrarian regions farmers continued to resist Nazi overtures, as they had done since the mid-1920s.[85] A partial exception is provided, however, by *Gau* Koblenz-Trier, where 12.4 per cent of the membership were farmers.[86] Civil servants also continued to be prominent in the party in Bavarian *Gaue*, as well as in Thuringia, Baden and Württemberg, though again the percentage values of this group shows a slight decline in comparison with pre-1930.

Although the NSDAP continued to mobilise the majority of its support from the lower- and middle-middle class (the percentage mix of the broad occupational categories used in the *Partei-Statistik* which cover this class - white-collar workers, self-employed, civil servants and farmers - was very variable in the 32 *Gaue*), the party was able to recruit much more successfully from the lower class following the onset of the economic crisis. According to the *Partei-Statistik* 'workers' increased their share of the membership in all of the *Gaue*, though the increase was markedly variable across the country, ranging from a mere 1.2 per cent in *Gau* Halle-Merseburg and 2 per cent in *Gau* Greater Berlin to 12.7 in *Gau* Main-Franconia and 13.5 per cent in *Gau* Westphalia-South. In the centre of Germany's heavy industry, the Ruhr, the party did particularly well in its efforts to attract lower-class support, which accounted for 43.8 per cent of the members in *Gau* Westphalia-South, 39.8 per cent in *Gau* Essen, and 37.6 per cent in *Gau* Westphalia-North. These relatively high percentages are rejected in Böhnke's study of the NSDAP in the Ruhr, who argues that a report by the *Regierungspräsident* for *Regierungsbezirk* Düsseldorf in 1930, in which the figure for industrial workers in the Nazi membership is a low 14 per cent and for agricultural workers a mere 5 per cent, is a more accurate reflection of the extent of lower-class participation in the NSDAP in the region.[87] Böhnke, in his somewhat one-sided interpretation of the social structure of the party in the Ruhr - he is reluctant to accept the idea that the working class could be involved with the NSDAP, which he characterises as a 'bourgeois party' even in the Ruhr - ignores the limitations of the statistics produced by the *Regierungspräsident*. For these figures relate to the whole of the *Regierungsbezirk* Düsseldorf, which includes predominantly agrarian areas, such as the counties of Cleve, Seldern and Rees, areas in which the percentage share of the lower class was probably much lower than in the Essen-Wuppertal-Duisburg triangle. A further problem is that the report fails to differentiate between dependent and independent artisans and craft workers, who account for 34 per cent of the total. If the bulk of these were dependent, and this is highly probable, even this source can be interpreted as showing a 40 to 50 per cent lower-class content for the party in the entire region.[88] An admittedly not perfect source which throws light on the Westphalian part of the Ruhr suggests that the lower-class participation in the NSDAP membership was even higher than that indicated in the *Partei-Statistik*. According to a 'secret report' sent by the Westphalian *Gauleiter* to the Munich party headquarters in November 1930, which covers the social make-up of the Nazi membership in the 'inner industrial area of Westphalia', the figure for 'workers' is given as 57.7 per cent (divided into 26.2 per cent for miners and 31.5 per cent for 'workers').[89] The ability of the party to make significant inroads into the lower class in the Ruhr is also indicated by the one detailed study available on the Duisburg region.[90] It is very likely that the *Partei-Statistik*'s data for the Ruhr *Gaue* actually understates the size of the lower-class element recruited by the party in the Ruhr in the early 1930s if, and this is likely, the lower-class membership registered a higher degree of turnover than that of others classes attracted to Nazism.[91] If the *Partei-Statistik* represents just an attempt by the *Reichsleitung* to statistically vindicate the Nazi claim that the party drew support from all strata, it is difficult to understand why in some of the areas with a highly concentrated, sizeable lower-class population, the *Partei-Statistik*'s values are so very low, as in the case of *Gau* Hamburg (only 24.4 per cent), and of *Gau* Greater Berlin (24 per cent).

Looking beyond the Ruhr region, the NSDAP also secured not inconsiderable support from the lower class in areas in which industry and crafts (light- and medium-scale industry in general) were the major employer, namely Thuringia (35.7 per cent), the Palatinate (35.2 per cent) and Saxony (35 per cent), as well as in a number of mixed agrarian-industrial areas, such as *Gaue* Koblenz-Trier (39.2 per cent) and Franconia (37.5 per cent). Even in predominantly agrarian Swabia the Nazis claimed that some 38 per cent of their support came from 'workers'.

There is, unfortunately, little additional information to check the veracity of the *Partei-Statistik*'s data on the extent of the lower-class support in the various *Gaue* noted above. Pridham, in his work on Bavaria, and Hambrecht, in his study of the development of the NSDAP in Middle and Upper Franconia, essentially base their relatively limited analysis of the sociology of the Bavarian NSDAP on the *Partei-Statistik*.[92] Only a few individual branch membership lists of the Bavarian NSDAP relating to the early 1930s have surfaced to date. The data on Pahres and Eltersdorf in Middle Franconia does show a high lower-class presence in the branches situated in these villages (see Table 2.7, columns L and M), the percentages being well above the values claimed in the *Partei-Statistik* for

Table 2.7: The social and occupational structure of NSDAP branches in various towns and localities, 1930-32 (by %)

Class	Occupational subgroup	(A) Züllichau[a] Jan. 1930	(B) Gassen[b] March 1930	(C) Laim[c] (Munich) June 1930	(D) Schloppe[a] Jan. 1931	(E) Märkisch-Friedland[a] March 1931	(F) Flötenstein[a] May 1931	(G) Deutsch-Krone[a] May 1931
LOWER	1. Unskilled workers	8.7	23.7	9.7	10.0	6.4	14.3	20.6
CLASS	2. Skilled (craft) workers	2.2	14.3	8.1	40.0	16.1	32.1	18.8
	3. Other skilled workers	2.2	0	3.2	5.0	12.9	3.6	4.1
Subtotal		13.1	38.0	21.0	55.0	35.4	50.0	43.5
Lower-	4. Master craftsmen	6.5	0	6.5	15.0	16.1	0	5.9
and	5. Non-acad. professionals	8.7	14.3	3.2	0	0	0	3.5
middle-	6. Lower employees	10.9	9.4	13.7	5.0	3.2	21.4	11.2
MIDDLE	7. Lower civil servants	6.5	0	10.5	5.0	0	0	3.5
CLASS	8. Merchants	15.2	0	11.3	10.0	12.9	3.6	2.9
	9. Farmers	19.6	28.6	0	5.0	12.9	14.3	7.0
Subtotal		67.4	52.3	45.2	40.0	45.1	39.3	34.0
Upper-	10. Managers	6.5	0	0.8	5.0	0	0	0.6
MIDDLE	11. Higher civil servants	0	0	2.4	0	0	0	1.8
CLASS/	12. University students	0	0	2.4	0	0	0	0
UPPER	13. Academic professionals	0	4.7	4.9	0	0	0	0.6
CLASS	14. Entrepreneurs	2.2	0	1.6	0	3.2	7.1	1.2
Subtotal		8.7	4.7	12.1	5.0	3.2	7.1	4.2
STATUS	15. Non-univ. students	6.5	0	0.8	0	0	0	10.0
UNCLEAR	16. Pensioners/Retired	4.3	0	4.1	0	0	0	0
	17. Wives/Widows	0	0	11.4	0	6.5	0	1.2
	18. Illegible/no data	0	4.7	4.9	0	9.7	3.6	7.0
Subtotal		10.8	4.7	21.2	0	16.2	3.6	18.2
TOTAL (%)		100	100	100	100	100	100	100
Frequency (*N*)		46	21	123	20	31	28	170

Table 2.7 (cont'd)

Class	Occupational subgroup	(H) Schneidemühl[a] (May 1931)	(I) Schlochau[d] May 1931	(J) Kraiburg[e] Feb. 1932	(K) Eutin[f] May 1932	(L) Pahres[g] May 1932	(M) Eltersdorf[h] June 1932	(N) Penzberg[i] Dec. 1932
LOWER	1. Unskilled workers	13.6	22.7	25.7	11.9	19.4	13.4	18.2
CLASS	2. Skilled (craft) workers	10.2	15.9	11.4	18.8	33.3	26.7	9.1
	3. Other skilled workers	1.1	0	2.8	5.7	2.8	6.7	3.0
Subtotal		24.9	38.6	39.9	36.4	55.5	46.8	30.3
Lower-	4. Master craftsmen	6.8	9.1	5.7	12.8	0	3.3	12.1
and	5. Non-acad. professionals	1.1	2.3	19.9	2.5	0	6.6	0
middle-	6. Lower employees	14.6	11.4	0	19.4	0	10.0	33.3
MIDDLE	7. Lower civil servants	4.5	6.8	0	3.0	2.8	0	3.0
CLASS	8. Merchants	12.4	2.3	17.1	10.9	5.6	10.0	0
	9. Farmers	13.6	9.0	5.7	1.3	27.7	20.0	0
Subtotal		53.0	40.9	48.4	49.9	36.1	49.9	48.4
Upper-	10. Managers	2.3	4.5	0	0.6	0	0	0
MIDDLE	11. Higher civil servants	2.3	2.3	0	0	0	0	0
CLASS/	12. University students	0	0	0	–	0	0	0
UPPER	13. Academic professionals	1.1	0	0	1.5	0	0	3.0
CLASS	14. Entrepreneurs	1.1	4.6	0	0.4	0	0	3.0
Subtotal		6.8	11.4	0	2.5	0	0	6.0
STATUS	15. Non-univ. students	4.5	0	0	1.9	2.8	3.3	0
UNCLEAR	16. Pensioners/Retired	0	2.3	2.8	0.4	0	0	0
	17. Wives/Widows	7.9	2.3	8.6	8.7	2.8	0	6.1
	18. Illegible/no data	2.3	4.5	0	0	2.8	0	9.1
Subtotal		14.7	9.1	11.4	11.0	8.4	3.3	15.2
TOTAL (%)		100	100	100	100	100	100	100
Frequency (*N*)		88	44	35	469	34	30	33

Table 2.7 (cont'd)

Sources:

a. Percentages calculated on the basis of data in D. Mühlberger, 'The Occupational and Social Structure of the NSDAP in the Border Province Posen-West Prussia in the early 1930s', *European History Quarterly*, vol. 15 (1985), pp. 292-3, Table 4.
b. Percentages calculated on the basis of data provided by the membership list 'Ortsgruppe Gassen' (Lower Silesia), dated 8 March 1930, *HA*, 10/212.
c. Percentages calculated on the basis of data provided by the membership list 'Ortsgruppe Laim. 25. Bezirk. Nach dem Stand v. 26.6.30', *HA*, 90/1869.
d. Percentages calculated on the basis of data provided by 'Mitgliederliste nach dem Stand vom 1. Mai 1931' for the NSDAP branch at Schlochau (Border Province Posen-West Prussia), *HA*, 10/207. The percentages revise those provided for Schlochau in Mühlberger, 'NSDAP in the Border Province Posen-West Prussia', pp. 292-3, Table 4.
e. Percentages calculated on the basis of data provided by 'Mitgliederstand am 1. Februar 1932. Ortsgruppe Kraiburg a. Inn' (Upper Bavaria), *HA*, 8/176.
f. Percentages calculated on the basis of data on the NSDAP branch at Eutin (Schleswig-Holstein) in L. D. Stokes, 'The Social Composition of the Nazi Party in Eutin, 1925-32', *International Review of Social History*, vol. 23 (1978), p. 6, Table 1, and pp. 8-13. Subgroup 15 (non-university students) includes both school children and students; if any of the latter were university students is unclear.
g. Percentages calculated on the basis of data in a membership list for 1 May 1932 of the NSDAP branch at Pahres (Middle Franconia) sent to the *Kreisleitung* Neustadt a. d. Aisch by the Pahres branch leader Elbinger on 20 June 1942, *Staatsarchiv* Nürnberg (hereafter *SAN*), NSDAP Mischbestand/Nr.96.
h. Percentages calculated on the basis of data provided by a membership list for June 1932 of the NSDAP branch at Eltersdorf (Middle Franconia) attached to a memorandum of the branch leader, dated 19 June 1942, *SAN*, NSDAP Mischbestand/Nr.96.
i. Percentages calculated on the basis of data on the NSDAP branch at Penzberg (Upper Bavaria) in K. Tenfelde, 'Proletarische Provinz. Radikalisierung und Widerstand in Penzberg/Oberbayern 1900 bis 1945' in M. Broszat a. o. (eds.), *Bayern in der NS-Zeit* (6 vols., Munich-Vienna, 1977-1983), vol. 4, p. 199, Table 37.

'workers' in *Gau* Franconia, especially in the case of Pahres, where the lower class formed the absolute majority of the branch membership. How representative these two branches are of the sociology of the party in the region as a whole is impossible to determine. The same limitation applies to the data on the social structure of the NSDAP in county Memmingen in *Gau* Swabia, which does however have the advantage of being based on the original source material submitted to the *Reichsleitung* for the purpose of calculating the structure of *Gau* Swabia's membership recorded in the *Partei-Statistik*.[93] In this predominantly Catholic agrarian region some 44.6 per cent of the 456 established members (*Altparteigenossen*) who had joined the party before 1933 were 'workers' (13.4 per cent agricultural workers; 8.3 per cent unskilled workers; and 23.2 per cent skilled workers). In comparison with the social structure of county Memmingen, the workers in the Nazi membership were markedly overrepresented in the area. Fröhlich and Broszat suggest that the NSDAP projected itself as a 'proletarian' party in county Memmingen, an 'image projection' which may well account for the relatively high 38 per cent of 'workers' recorded in the *Partei-Statistik* for *Gau* Swabia as a whole. Beyond the material on the two branches in Franconia and that on county Memmingen, there are three further branch lists for Bavaria, which show different recruitment patterns. There is information on two branches situated in the small towns of Kraiburg and Penzberg in Upper Bavaria (see Table 2.7, columns J and N) for 1932. Although in Kraiburg the lower class constituted almost 40 per cent of the membership at the beginning of 1932 (the branch temporarily folded-up in late 1932 due to lack of support), in the mining community of Penzberg the figure is only 30 per cent.[94] The variable response of the lower class to Nazism is further indicated by the Laim branch in Munich (see Table 2.7, column C), in which 'workers' made up only 21 per cent of the membership in June 1930 in a branch situated in a predominantly working-class district of the city.[95]

The often quite different social configuration of branch membership in *one* region - in which such factors as economic structure, level of urbanisation, religious conviction and the social structure of the population are almost constant - is shown by the data we have on the Border Province of Posen-West Prussia, a largely agrarian, predominantly Protestant region.[96] The social composition of Nazi branches situated in Züllichau, Schloppe, Märkisch-Friedland, Flötenstein, Deutsch-Krone, Schneidemühl and Schlochau (see Table 2.7, columns A, D to I), show quite distinct patterns. Particularly striking is the dominance of the lower- and middle-middle class in the Züllichau (67.4 per cent) and Schneidemühl (53.0 per cent) branches, the strong presence of the upper-middle class and upper class among the membership of the Schlochau branch (11.4 per cent), and the strength of the lower class in the Schloppe (55 per cent) and Flötenstein (50 per cent) branch memberships. One very unexpected feature which emerges when one looks more closely at the specific occupational groups represented in the party in the Border Province is that in an area dominated by agriculture (according to the 1925 census 62.6 per cent of the working population depended on agriculture for its living), the party was unable to attract agricultural workers, for only 2.4 per cent of Nazi members were from this occupational group, which accounted for 20.4 per cent of the working population. In the case of farmers, the percentages in the party and in the working population were almost identical (10.6 per cent and 12.8 per cent respectively).[97]

In reports made in the early 1930s by the *Regierungspräsident* of Koblenz on the NSDAP active in the predominantly Catholic Koblenz region, the often stark differences in the social structure of the party in one area also emerges.[98] Whereas in the Koblenz branch (780 members) artisans and craftsmen made up 40 per cent of the membership, with a further 20 per cent drawn from industrial workers and 23.5 per cent from commercial employees, in Daaden, Weitefeld, Flammersfeld, Kirchen and Gebhardshain (there were about 30 members in each of these Nazi branches) in county Altenkirchen, industrial workers were the largest occupational group (40 per cent), followed by farmers (20 per cent), artisans and craftsmen (15 per cent) and commercial employees (15 per cent). In a number of relatively small branches in county Simmern, on the other hand, 80 per cent of the membership came from farmers, 10 per cent from 'workers', and 10 per cent from craftsmen and artisans. In county Meisenheim (no specific percentages for individual occupational groups are given) the majority of the members were also engaged in agriculture, while in the rural parts of county Neuwied 60 per cent were farmers, as against the predominance of craftsmen and artisans (50 per cent) in the branches situated in the small towns of Neuwied and Linz. In county Ahrweiler, artisans and craftsmen (around 60 per cent) and commercial employees (around 20 per cent) formed the bulk of the membership in the three small branches situated in the area. While the upper-middle class and upper class is conspicuous by its absence in the majority of the counties subjected to analysis in the report, academic professionals made up 10 per cent of the membership in Koblenz, and some 15 per cent of the membership in the county of Ahrweiler. The social structure of the party in the Koblenz area underlines once again the remarkable capacity of the NSDAP to 'blend in' with the social and economic environment in which it operated.

On the eve of the Nazi seizure of power, following two years of very rapid and sustained membership growth, the NSDAP represented in many ways a microcosm of German society. Within its ranks were people from all walks of life, from casual labourers to aristocrats. The party had penetrated into all corners of Germany and mobilised support from all 'Christian' persuasions. This is not to deny that the NSDAP reflected the social and religious structure of German society imperfectly, for both the lower class and the Catholic population were underrepresented within its ranks. But although the lower- and middle-middle class was overrepresented in the party in comparison with its size in German society, the overrepresentation was not so overwhelming as to allow one to characterise the movement as a 'predominantly lower-middle-class affair'. It was the remarkably heterogeneous structure of the party, the infinite variability in terms of the social components which constituted the movement's rank and file, which is so striking.

V

In sharp contrast to the diversity of social types which formed the membership of the NSDAP, its party cadre was overwhelmingly made up by members of the lower- and middle-middle class and by the upper-middle class and upper class. The fact that it was the social background of party functionaries which was the initial focal point of analysis of the party's social structure in the 1940s and 1950s probably contributed strongly to the entrenchment of the 'lower-middle-class thesis' of Nazism in the post-war era, with the transfer of the social structure of the party cadre to that of the rank-and-file membership. The detailed evidence available on the party's functionary corps (see Table 2.8) does show a fairly consistent pattern throughout the period 1923 to 1945. At the lower and intermediary level of the party's organisational hierarchy, lower- and middle-middle class types occupied the majority of the posts, while at the *Gau* level and above, the functionary corps shows a massive overrepresentation of the upper-middle class and upper class and a virtual absence of the lower class. It is obvious that the party's functionary corps did not reflect the social make-up of the rank and file of the party.

The acquisition of power within the party hierarchy by the middle and upper classes is strongly in evidence by 1928. The first group of leaders who 'emerged' or were (more generally) elected by the branch members by 1923 were almost exclusively from the lower- and middle-middle class, even in areas such as Middle and Upper Franconia, where the lower class, as we have seen, was quite strongly in evidence in a number of branches.[99] From the time of the re-formation of the party in 1925 up to the collapse of the movement in 1945, the functionaries at the branch and district level continued to be heavily recruited from middle-class elements in most of the regions on which there is detailed evidence. Even in *Gau* Greater Berlin in the latter half of the 1920s, a period in which *Gauleiter* Goebbels made efforts to mobilise working-class support for the movement, the functionary corps at the branch level was nevertheless overwhelmingly based on the lower- and middle-middle class (see Table 2.8, column F).[100] The exception to this general pattern is provided by the Ruhr region, where the strong presence of the lower class within the rank and file of the party does appear to have had an influence on the social composition of the local leadership corps (see Table 2.8, columns B and G). The attitude of the *Gauleiter* in the region was probably also instrumental in the advancement of 'workers' within the movement to a position of authority, at least at the branch level. The Westphalian *Gauleiter* Wagner certainly took the class factor into consideration when appointing branch leaders, ensuring that these were drawn from the lower class in the industrial areas of his *Gau*.[101] However, when it came to appointments at the *Gau* level itself, Wagner (and Terboven in the adjacent *Gau* Essen) depended - and this is true of *Gauleitungen* in general - on the administrative skills

Table 2.8: The social and occupational status of Nazi Party functionaries at the national, regional and local level, 1923-41 (by %)

Class	Occupational subgroup	(A) Branch Leaders Middle/Upper Franconia[a] May 1923	(B) Branch Functionaries Western Ruhr[b] 1925-26	(C) *Gauleiter* Germany[c] 1925-28	(D) Branch Leaders Baden[d] 1927	(E) District Leaders Baden[e] 1928	(F) Branch Leaders Greater Berlin[f] Oct. 1929
LOWER	1. Unskilled workers	13.3	10.0	3.7	0	5.0	7.7
CLASS	2. Skilled (craft) workers	6.6	20.0	0	3.0	0	11.5
	3. Other skilled workers	0	15.0	1.9	3.0	0	0
Subtotal		19.9	45.0	5.6	6.0	5.0	19.2
Lower-	4. Master craftsmen	0	0	0	12.1	25.0	0
and	5. Non-acad. professionals	0	5.0	3.7	0	0	3.8
middle-	6. Lower employees	0	25.0	7.4	12.1	10.0	23.1
MIDDLE	7. Lower civil servants	40.0	10.0	27.8	0	10.0	26.9
CLASS	8. Merchants	20.0	15.0	9.3	36.4	25.0	19.2
	9. Farmers	13.3	15.0	0	21.2	15.0	0
Subtotal		73.3	55.0	48.2	81.8	85.0	73.0
Upper-	10. Managers	0	0	11.1	0	0	0
MIDDLE	11. Higher civil servants	0	0	13.0	0	0	0
CLASS/	12. University students	0	0	3.7	0	0	0
UPPER	13. Academic professionals	0	0	14.8	12.1	10.0	0
CLASS	14. Entrepreneurs	6.6	0	3.7	0	0	3.8
Subtotal		6.6	0	46.3	12.1	10.0	3.8
STATUS	15. Non-univ. students	0	0	–	0	0	3.8
UNCLEAR	16. Pensioners/Retired	0	0	–	0	0	0
	17. Miscellaneous	0	0	–	0	0	0
Subtotal		0	0	–	0	0	3.8
TOTAL (%)		100	100	100	100	100	100
Frequency (*N*)		15	20	54	33	20	26

Table 2.8 (cont'd)

Class	Occupational subgroup	(G) Branch Functionaries *Bezirk* Essen[f] Oct.1929	(H) Branch Leaders *Untergau* Swabia[f] Oct. 1929	(I) *Gauleiter* Germany[c] 1930	(J) Branch Leaders Northern Hesse[g] July 1930	(K) Leaders Middle/Upper Franconia[h] 1930-33
LOWER	1. Unskilled workers	27.3	0	5.3	10.8	0
CLASS	2. Skilled (craft) workers	22.7	14.3	0	0	5.9
	3. Other skilled workers	0	0	2.6	0	0
Subtotal		50.0	14.3	7.9	10.8	5.9
Lower-	4. Master craftsmen	0	7.1	0	19.3	5.9
and	5. Non-acad. professionals	9.1	7.1	0	0	0
middle-	6. Lower employees	9.1	21.4	10.5	12.0	11.7
MIDDLE	7. Lower civil servants	9.1	21.4	36.8	3.6	41.2
CLASS	8. Merchants	9.1	7.1	5.3	12.0	11.7
	9. Farmers	0	14.3	0	26.5	11.7
Subtotal		36.4	78.4	52.6	73.4	82.2
Upper-	10. Managers	0	7.1	10.5	0	0
MIDDLE	11. Higher civil servants	0	0	15.8	0	0
CLASS/	12. University students	0	0	0	0	0
UPPER	13. Academic professionals	9.1	0	7.9	8.4	11.7
CLASS	14. Entrepreneurs	0	0	5.3	3.6	0
Subtotal		9.1	7.1	39.5	12.0	11.7
STATUS	15. Non-univ. students	0	0	–	1.2	0
UNCLEAR	16. Pensioners/Retired	4.5	0	–	2.4	0
	17. Miscellaneous	0	0	–	0	0
Subtotal		4.5	0	–	3.6	0
TOTAL (%)		100	100	100	100	100
Frequency (*N*)		22	14	38	83	17

Table 2.8 (cont'd)

Class	Occupational subgroup	(L) Branch Leaders North-eastern Hanover[l] April 1931	(M) District Leaders Gau Munich-Upper Bavaria[j] June 1931	(N) *Gauleiter* Germany[c] 1933	(O) District Leaders Germany[c] 1941	(P) *Gauleiter* Germany[c] 1941	(Q) Agency Heads Germany[c] 1941
LOWER	1. Unskilled workers	12.5	0	11.4	2.0	7.0	0
CLASS	2. Skilled (craft) workers	12.5	0	0	7.3	7.0	3.1
	3. Other skilled workers	1.4	0	2.9	2.0	2.3	0.6
Subtotal		26.4	0	14.3	11.3	16.3	3.7
Lower-	4. Master craftsmen	5.5	7.7	0	4.0	0	1.2
and	5. Non-acad. professionals	1.4	7.7	0	6.3	2.3	5.5
middle-	6. Lower employees	1.4	0	14.3	16.3	14.0	17.8
MIDDLE	7. Lower civil servants	1.4	30.8	28.6	17.9	25.6	6.7
CLASS	8. Merchants	16.7	23.0	2.9	16.6	7.0	11.7
	9. Farmers	40.3	0	0	9.3	2.3	3.7
Subtotal		66.7	69.2	45.7	70.4	51.2	46.6
Upper-	10. Managers	0	0	11.4	2.7	4.7	6.7
MIDDLE	11. Higher civil servants	0	0	14.3	4.7	7.0	13.5
CLASS/	12. University students	0	0	0	3.0	0	0
UPPER	13. Academic professionals	0	30.8	11.4	5.6	16.3	26.4
CLASS	14. Entrepreneurs	1.4	0	2.9	2.3	4.7	3.1
Subtotal		1.4	30.8	40.0	18.3	32.6	49.7
STATUS	15. Non-univ. students	0	0	–	–	–	–
UNCLEAR	16. Pensioners/Retired	0	0	–	–	–	–
	17. Miscellaneous	5.5	0	–	–	–	–
Subtotal		5.5	0	–	–	–	–
TOTAL (%)		100	100	100	100	100	100
Frequency (*N*)		72	13	35	301	43	163

Table 2.8 (cont'd)

Sources:

a. Percentages calculated on the basis of data in R. Hambrecht, *Der Aufstieg der NSDAP in Mittel- und Oberfranken (1925-1933)* (Nuremberg, 1976), p. 36.
b. Percentages calculated on the basis of data on the occupational status of branch leaders, party treasurers and secretaries in membership lists for Nazi branches at Mülheim/Ruhr, Essen, Hamborn, Barmen-Langerfeld and Hammerthal, *RWHStA*, RW23.
c. From Kater, *The Nazi Party*, pp. 256-7, Table 10 (reprinted by permission). Kater does not provide details for subgroups 15 to 17.
d. Percentages calculated on the basis of data in J.H. Grill, *The Nazi Movement in Baden 1920-1945* (Chapel Hill, 1983) p. 159.
e. Ibid., p. 574, note.
f. Percentages calculated on the basis of data provided by a police report, Berlin, 'Gliederungen der NSDAP in Gaue, Untergaue, Bezirke, Kreise und Ortsgruppen innerhalb des deutschen Reichsgebietes ... nach dem Stande vom. 1. Oktober 1929', *HA*, 70/1510.
g. Percentages calculated on the basis of data in E. Schön, *Die Entstehung des Nationalsozialismus in Hessen* (Meisenheim a. Glan, 1972), p. 99. The data relates to Nazi branch leaders in *Regierungsbezirk* Kassel.
h. Percentages calculated on the basis of data in Hambrecht, *NSDAP in Mittel- und Oberfranken*, p. 307.
i. Percentages calculated on the basis of data in C-D. Krohn and D. Stegmann, 'Kleingewerbe und Nationalsozialismus in einer agrarisch-mittelständischen Region. Das Beispiel Lüneburg 1930-1939', *Archiv für Sozialgeschichte*, vol. 17 (1977), pp. 92-4. The data relates to Nazi branch leaders in Gau Hanover-East (the Lüneburg region). Listed under subgroup 17 (miscellaneous) are those who described themselves as 'Haussohn' (probably sons of farmers).
j. Percentages calculated on the basis of data in G. Pridham, *Hitler's Rise to Power. The Nazi Movement in Bavaria 1923-1933* (London, 1973), p. 190, note 11.

and expertise drawn primarily from the lower- and middle-middle class.[102]

The representation of the lower- and middle-middle class within the *Gauleiter* corps - the 'middle management' of the movement, as it were - is less in evidence, being severely reduced by a massive overrepresentation of the upper-middle class and upper class, a feature also strikingly in evidence at the Reich level of the party (see Table 2.8, columns C, I, N, P and Q).[103] From 1925 onwards, following the re-establishment of the party, only a handful of 'workers', such as the agricultural labourer Hildebrandt, who became *Gauleiter* of Mecklenburg, were able to carve out a power base at the *Gau* level. In the scramble for power within the party at the *Gau* level and above, elements drawn from the upper-middle class and upper class were much more successful in acquiring leadership positions than any other social group. The marked difference between the social structure of the leadership cadre and of the rank and file of the NSDAP should not surprise one. In the Weimar era even largely lower-class organisations such as the *Reichsbanner* had a leadership corps based on middle-class types for functional reasons.[104] One can but agree with Kater's observation that the Nazi functionary corps

> was closely related to the complex system of administrative tasks to be performed by the party hierarchy: the higher the degree of skill required, the more qualified and sophisticated were the administrative personnel. The NSDAP thus appears to have been ruled by the same laws of rationality that governed other institutions, corporations, and even other political parties in the Weimar Republic.[105]

It comes as no surprise that the dominance of the middle and upper classes in the party cadre is also reflected in the share out of the spoils accruing from the growth in the electoral support of the Nazi movement in the early 1930s, since the leading party functionaries figure strongly in the list of candidates in *Landtag* and *Reichstag* elections (see Tables 2.9 and 2.10).[106] It was only at the local town and district council level that the lower-class members of the party could hope to be sufficiently highly placed on the party slate to have a reasonable chance of being elected (see Table

2.9, column G). In the more prestigious *Landtag* elections, lower-class candidates were squeezed out by the middle- and upper-class elements, who dominated the list of candidates in virtually all of the *Länder*. The headline in the *Völkischer Beobachter* announcing the results of the elections to the Hamburg Senate in October 1931, 'Our 43 in Hamburg's Parliament. A true *Volksgemeinschaft* (people's community) and *Volksvertretung* (people's representation)', and the commentary which emphasised the 'picture of our *Volksgemeinschaft* ... unifying all occupations and classes', was hardly feasible in, say, Bavaria, where the lower class was almost totally absent even at the candidate level (see Table 2.9, colums A and B).[107] This is not to say that in the propaganda pumped out in the *Völkischer Beobachter* in its commentaries on regional elections, the assertion that the party advanced and represented the interests of all occupations and classes was a constant feature, even in regions such as Thuringia, where the lower class was patently underrepresented in the group of Nazi deputies elected to the Thuringian *Landtag* (see Table 2.9, column F).[108]

Similar disingenuous attempts were made by the party hierarchy to hide the dominance of the middle and upper classes in the growing corps of deputies elected on the Nazi ticket to the *Reichstag*.[109] The very limited participation of lower-class Nazis in the acquisition of the advantages and privileges accruing to MPs - for all the anti-parliamentarian rhetoric of Nazi propaganda, there was keen competition among Nazis to be nominated as a *Reichstag* candidate - is a feature throughout the 1928 to 1933 period, and even more so in the Third Reich (see Table 2.10). In the *Pöstchenjägerei* (scramble for posts) which unfolded in the party in earnest from the late 1920s, the upper-middle class and upper class did extremely well, as is reflected in the strong overrepresentation of this social group in the Nazi faction in parliament in comparison with its size in the Nazi membership. In the distribution of this form of patronage, Hitler and the Munich party headquarters generally had the last word in accepting or rejecting names on the lists of candidates submitted by the *Gauleiter*. The latters attempts - primarily for propaganda purposes one suspects - to take into consideration the social make-up of the population in their *Gaue* by advancing, for example, a lower-class candidate, were more often than not frustrated by the decisions

Table 2.9: The social and occupational status of regional and local Nazi parliamentary candidates and deputies, 1931-33 (by %)

Class	Occupational subgroup	(A) Hamburg[a] Senate Deputies Oct. 1931	(B) Bavaria[b] *Landtag* Deputies April 1932	(C) Prussia[c] *Landtag* Candidates April 1932	(D) Württemberg[d] *Landtag* Candidates April 1932	(E) Mecklenburg-Schwerin[e] *Landtag* Deputies June 1932	(F) Thuringia[f] *Landtag* Deputies Aug. 1932	(G) Germany[g] Local Deputies 1933
LOWER	1. Unskilled workers	13.9	0	5.0	1.8	13.3	3.8	8.7
CLASS	2. Skilled (craft) workers	4.6	2.3	8.2	5.5	6.7	3.8	13.0
	3. Other skilled workers	7.0	0	2.5	5.5	0	0	3.1
Subtotal		25.5	2.3	15.7	12.8	20.0	7.6	24.8
Lower-	4. Master craftsmen	0	4.5	3.2	9.3	10.0	7.6	7.5
and	5. Non-acad. professionals	0	0	5.6	7.4	3.3	3.8	4.9
middle-	6. Lower employees	16.2	6.8	12.1	7.2	3.3	3.8	10.1
MIDDLE	7. Lower civil servants	11.6	31.8	7.0	14.8	20.0	23.1	12.0
CLASS	8. Merchants	13.9	9.1	7.0	7.4	6.7	7.6	14.7
	9. Farmers	2.3	20.4	19.1	18.5	23.3	27.0	9.9
Subtotal		44.0	72.6	54.0	64.6	66.6	72.9	59.1
Upper-	10. Managers	4.6	2.3	0.6	0	0	0	3.4
MIDDLE	11. Higher civil servants	2.3	4.5	2.5	5.5	3.3	15.4	3.2
CLASS/	12. University students	0	0	0	0	0	0	0
UPPER	13. Academic professionals	11.6	11.4	7.6	11.1	3.3	3.8	6.4
CLASS	14. Entrepreneurs	6.9	2.3	4.4	5.5	6.6	0	3.1
Subtotal		25.4	20.5	15.1	22.1	13.2	19.2	16.1
STATUS	15. Party officials[1]	0	4.5	4.4	0	0	0	-
UNCLEAR	16. Miscellaneous[2]	4.6	0	10.2	0	0	0	-
Subtotal		4.6	4.5	14.6	0	0	0	-
TOTAL (%)		100	100	100	100	100	100	100
Frequency (*N*)		43	44	157	54	30	26	4,404

Table 2.9 (cont'd)

Notes:

1. Includes those party officials whose occupational status could not be established.
2. Includes those listed as 'retired' and those who did not provide details of their occupations.

Sources:

a. Percentages calculated on the basis of data provided by list 'Unsere 43 im Hamburger Parlament', *Völkischer Beobachter* (hereafter *VB*), 7 October 1931.
b. Percentages calculated on the basis of data provided by list 'Die gewählten bayerischen Abgeordneten der NSDAP', *VB*, 26 April 1932.
c. Percentages calculated on the basis of data provided by list 'Die nationalsozialistischen Landtagskandidaten in den preussischen Wahlkreisen', *VB*, 27 March 1932.
d. Percentages calculated on the basis of data provided by list 'Die Kandidaten der N.S.D.A.P. für die württemb. Landtagswahl', *VB*, 23 April 1932.
e. Percentages calculated on the basis of data in *Der Mecklenburgische-Schwerinsche siebente ordentliche Landtag gewählt am 5. Juni 1932* (Herausgegeben vom Büro des Mecklenburg-Schwerinsche Landtages, n.d.), p. 10.
f. Percentages calculated on the basis of data provided by list 'Die nationalsozialistischen Abgeordneten im neuen Thüringer Landtag', *VB*, 6 August 1932.
g. From Kater, *The Nazi Party*, p. 257, Table 10 (reprinted by permission).

Table 2.10: The social and occupational status of Nazi *Reichstag* candidates and deputies, 1928-36 (by %)

Class	Occupational subgroup	(A) Candidates[a] May 1928	(B) Deputies[a] May 1928	(C) Candidates[b] Sept. 1930	(D) Deputies[b] Sept. 1930	(E) Candidates[c] July 1932	(F) Deputies[c] July 1932
LOWER	1. Unskilled workers	7.4	0	7.7	6.5	6.4	6.1
CLASS	2. Skilled (craft) workers	4.5	8.3	4.9	5.6	6.7	5.6
	3. Other skilled workers	3.0	0	4.4	1.9	0.8	1.7
Subtotal		14.9	8.3	17.0	14.0	13.6	13.4
Lower-	4. Master craftsmen	2.2	0	4.8	2.8	5.1	3.5
and	5. Non-acad. professionals	0.7	0	3.6	2.8	4.2	6.1
middle-	6. Lower employees	5.9	8.3	12.2	8.3	11.0	8.7
MIDDLE	7. Lower civil servants	27.6	8.3	12.4	14.0	16.0	7.8
CLASS	8. Merchants	5.2	0	8.3	9.3	7.9	8.3
	9. Farmers	20.1	8.3	14.1	8.4	13.7	13.9
Subtotal		61.7	24.9	55.4	45.6	57.9	48.3
Upper-	10. Managers	2.2	0	1.5	2.8	1.7	1.3
MIDDLE	11. Higher civil servants	1.5	0	5.1	7.5	4.9	7.8
CLASS/	12. University students	0	0	0	0	0	0
UPPER	13. Academic professionals	12.0	41.7	9.5	13.1	10.6	13.5
CLASS	14. Entrepreneurs	1.4	0	3.9	2.8	4.2	6.1
Subtotal		17.1	41.7	20.0	26.2	21.2	28.7
STATUS	15. Party officials[1]	0	0	4.4	4.7	2.1	4.8
UNCLEAR	16. Miscellaneous[2]	6.0	25.0	2.9	9.3	4.6	4.8
Subtotal		6.0	25.0	7.3	14.0	6.7	9.6
TOTAL (%)		100	100	100	100	100	100
Frequency (*N*)		134	12	410	107	838	230

Table 2.10 (cont'd)

Class	Occupational subgroup	(G) Deputies[d] Nov. 1932	(H) Deputies[e] March 1933	(I) Candidates[f] Nov. 1933	(J) Deputies[f] Nov. 1933	(K) Deputies[g] March 1936
LOWER	1. Unskilled workers	5.6	5.5	3.2	3.4	1.7
CLASS	2. Skilled (craft) workers	5.1	4.9	5.7	5.6	2.4
	3. Other skilled workers	2.0	1.7	1.2	1.4	0.5
Subtotal		12.7	12.1	10.1	10.4	4.6
Lower-	4. Master craftsmen	4.6	3.1	4.7	4.6	3.0
and	5. Non-acad. professionals	6.1	7.6	6.6	6.1	5.3
middle-	6. Lower employees	8.2	7.3	8.2	7.9	4.7
MIDDLE	7. Lower civil servants	8.2	7.6	9.7	5.6	5.4
CLASS	8. Merchants	8.2	9.4	6.9	7.3	6.9
	9. Farmers	12.2	13.2	10.9	11.7	10.6
Subtotal		47.5	48.2	47.0	43.2	35.9
Upper-	10. Managers	1.0	1.0	2.4	2.4	1.3
MIDDLE	11. Higher civil servants	8.7	6.2	12.3	12.2	18.4
CLASS/	12. University students	0	0	0	0	0
UPPER	13. Academic professionals	14.3	12.5	6.8	6.9	5.1
CLASS	14. Entrepreneurs	6.6	6.2	2.6	3.1	0.6
Subtotal		30.3	25.9	24.1	24.6	25.4
STATUS	15. Party officials[1]	4.6	6.2	14.9	17.9	32.4
UNCLEAR	16. Miscellaneous[2]	4.6	7.3	3.6	3.8	1.3
Subtotal		9.2	13.5	18.5	21.7	33.7
TOTAL (%)		100	100	100	100	100
Frequency (*N*)		196	288	995	699	1,030

Table 2.10 (cont'd)

Notes:

1. Includes those party officials whose occupational status could not be established.
2. Includes those listed as 'retired' and those who did not provide details of their occupations.

Sources:

a. Percentages calculated on the basis of data in *Statistik des Deutschen Reichs* (hereafter *StDR*) vol. 372, I (Berlin, 1930), pp. 110-58; M. Schwarz, *MdR. Biographisches Handbuch der Reichstage* (Hanover, 1965), pp. 555-63.
b. Percentages calculated on the basis of data in *StDR*, vol. 382, I (Berlin, 1932), pp. 121-83; 'Wir vertreten das Volk. Die nationalsozialistischen Abgeordneten und ihre Berufe', *VB*, 6 November 1930; Schwarz, *MdR*, pp. 571-80.
c. Percentages calculated on the basis of data provided by a list of candidates submitted by Frick to Hitler, 1 July 1932, copy in *HA*, 29/552; 'Die nationalsozialistischen Reichstagsabgeordneten', *VB*, 6 and 9 August 1932; Schwarz, *MdR*, pp. 580-89.
d. Percentages calculated on the basis of data provided by Schwarz, *MdR*, pp. 589-97.
e. Ibid., pp. 597-606.
f. Percentages calculated on the basis of data in *StDR*, vol. 449 (Berlin, 1935), pp. 10-20.
g. Percentages calculated on the basis of data in *StDR*, vol. 497 (Berlin, 1937), pp. 8-26; 'Die Mitglieder des Reichstages nach dem Stand vom 6. April 1936', *Deutscher Reichsanzeiger und Preussischer Staatsanzeiger*, 7 April 1936.

reached at Munich.[110] A 'good name', which would give 'respectability' to the party, was obviously very useful for getting onto the Nazi list.[111] A post of some status within the party or its numerous auxiliary organisations was also a decisive criteria for those aspiring to be Nazi *Reichstag* deputies. All the 12 successful Nazi candidates in the 1928 election were party functionaries, and *Gauleiter* and their cronies, as well as the Reich leadership (as one would expect), were prominent among the Nazi MPs elected in the early 1930s. By the time of the *Reichstag* 'election' of 1936, 77.2 per cent of the MPs selected from the 'unity list' held posts in the movement. The social background of the great majority of the Nazi MPs did not bear much resemblance to the social structure of the party's rank and file even before the Third Reich was established.

VI

Beyond the data now available on the NSDAP's rank-and-file membership and on its leadership cadre, there is also material relating to the social structure of the rank and file and leadership of a number of its auxiliary organisations, primarily the HJ and the SA, which throws further light on the sociology of the Nazi movement.

The revelation in Stachura's work on the HJ that this admittedly small organisation of the Nazi Party - it had a total membership of only about 55,000 by 1933 - drew the bulk of its membership from the lower class before 1933, passed largely unnoticed when the book was published in 1975.[112] Stachura did not analyse any raw material on the social structure of the HJ's membership as such, but relied instead on, and generally accepted, the broad summaries relating to the social background of the HJ membership contained in various Nazi reports on *Gaue* Munich-Upper Bavaria, Hamburg, South Bavaria and the Rhineland. These reports led him to the conclusion that the ordinary membership of the HJ was 'predominantly working class', with the representation of working-class members averaging out at 65 to 70 per cent during the pre-1933 period.[113]

Stachura's assessment of the social profile of the HJ is confirmed in the case of my breakdown (it is the only detailed breakdown that we have at present) of the HJ in the Palatinate (see Table

Table 2.11: The social and occupational structure of the *Hitlerjugend* (HJ - Hitler Youth) in the Palatinate, 1928-April 1932 (by %)

Class	Occupational subgroup	(A) Palatinate Members joining in 1928	(B) Palatinate Members joining in 1929	(C) Palatinate Members joining in 1930	(D) Palatinate Members joining in 1931	(E) Palatinate Members joining in 1932	(F) Palatinate Members joining in 1928-32	(G) Palatinate HJ Leaders 1932
LOWER	1. Unskilled workers	25.9	19.7	15.6	15.8	15.5	16.8	7.9
CLASS	2. Skilled (craft) workers[1]	34.5	40.3	45.1	28.5	34.7	36.3	21.0
	3. Other skilled workers[1]	10.3	4.1	5.5	3.9	3.1	4.3	2.6
Subtotal		70.7	64.1	66.2	48.2	53.3	57.4	31.5
Lower-	4. Master craftsmen	0	0	0	0	0	0	0
and	5. Non-acad. professionals[1]	1.7	0.7	0.6	0.5	0.4	0.6	2.6
middle-	6. Lower employees[2]	6.9	10.5	10.6	6.4	6.6	8.3	28.9
MIDDLE	7. Lower civil servants	0	0	0	0.3	0.2	0.1	0
CLASS	8. Merchants[3]	1.7	0.2	0.4	0	0	0.2	7.9
	9. Farmers[4]	5.2	7.1	6.6	13.2	16.6	10.9	10.5
Subtotal		15.5	18.5	18.2	20.4	23.8	20.1	49.9
Upper-	10. Managers	0	0	0	0	0	0	0
MIDDLE	11. Higher civil servants	0	0	0	0	0	0	0
CLASS/	12. University students	0	0	0.2	0.1	0.4	0.2	7.9
UPPER	13. Academic professionals	0	0	0.2	0.1	0	0.1	2.6
CLASS	14. Entrepreneurs	0	0	0	0	0	0	0
Subtotal		0	0	0.4	0.2	0.4	0.3	10.5
STATUS	15. Non-university students	0	0.2	0.4	0.5	0	0.3	2.6
UNCLEAR	16. School children	1.7	6.4	9.8	10.0	13.0	9.6	5.3
	17. No data	12.1	10.7	4.7	20.5	9.3	12.1	0
Subtotal		13.8	17.3	14.9	31.0	22.3	22.0	7.9
TOTAL (%)		100	100	100	100	100	100	100
Frequency (*N*)		58	437	468	638	452	2,053	38

Table 2.11 (cont'd)

Class	Occupational subgroup	(H) Annweiler 1928-32	(I) Bergzabern 1930-32	(J) Frankenthal 1929-32	(K) Grünstadt 1929-32	(L) Kaiserslautern 1928-32	(M) Kusel 1930-32	(N) Landau 1929-32
LOWER	1. Unskilled workers	29.7	6.4	9.8	22.0	9.9	12.1	6.2
CLASS	2. Skilled (craft) workers[1]	32.8	40.3	49.0	58.0	39.1	42.4	43.7
	3. Other skilled workers[1]	7.8	6.4	3.9	8.0	15.2	3.0	6.2
Subtotal		70.3	53.1	62.7	88.0	64.2	57.5	56.1
Lower-	4. Master craftsmen	0	0	0	0	0	0	0
and	5. Non-acad. professionals[1]	0	0	0	0	1.3	0	0
middle-	6. Lower employees[2]	10.9	8.0	9.8	4.0	18.5	21.2	0
MIDDLE	7. Lower civil servants	0	1.6	0	0	0.6	0	0
CLASS	8. Merchants[3]	0	0	0	0	0	0	0
	9. Farmers[4]	1.6	11.3	0	8.0	0	12.1	0
Subtotal		12.5	20.9	9.8	12.0	20.4	33.3	0
Upper-	10. Managers	0	0	0	0	0	0	0
MIDDLE	11. Higher civil servants	0	0	0	0	0	0	0
CLASS/	12. University students	0	0	0	0	0	0	2.1
UPPER	13. Academic professionals	0	0	0	0	0	0	0
CLASS	14. Entrepreneurs	0	0	0	0	0	0	0
Subtotal		0	0	0	0	0	0	2.1
STATUS	15. Non-university students	0	0	0	0	0	3.0	18.7
UNCLEAR	16. School children	1.6	3.2	23.5	0	7.9	0	0
	17. No data	15.6	22.6	3.9	0	7.3	6.1	22.9
Subtotal		17.2	25.8	27.4	0	15.2	9.1	41.6
TOTAL (%)		100	100	100	100	100	100	100
Frequency (*N*)		64	62	51	50	151	33	48

Table 2.11 (cont'd)

Class	Occupational subgroup	(O) Landstuhl 1929-32	(P) Ludwigshafen 1928-32	(Q) Miesau 1929-32	(R) Neustadt 1928-32	(S) Pirmasens 1928-32	(T) Waldfischbach 1929-32	(U) Zweibrücken 1928-32
LOWER	1. Unskilled workers	12.5	8.5	6.2	17.8	41.2	26.2	9.1
CLASS	2. Skilled (craft) workers[1]	60.0	40.3	59.4	37.0	37.9	23.8	50.6
	3. Other skilled workers[1]	10.0	3.9	3.1	5.5	2.6	0	2.6
Subtotal		82.5	52.7	68.7	60.3	81.7	50.0	62.3
Lower-	4. Master craftsmen	0	0	0	0	0	0	0
and	5. Non-acad. professionals[1]	0	5.4	0	1.4	0	0	0
middle-	6. Lower employees[2]	7.5	10.1	15.6	13.6	1.3	7.1	9.1
MIDDLE	7. Lower civil servants	0	0.8	0	0	0	0	0
CLASS	8. Merchants[3]	0	0	0	0	0	0	0
	9. Farmers[4]	0	0	12.5	2.7	0	4.8	0
Subtotal		7.5	16.3	28.1	17.7	1.3	11.9	9.1
Upper-	10. Managers	0	0	0	0	0	0	0
MIDDLE	11. Higher civil servants	0	0	0	0	0	0	0
CLASS/	12. University students	0	0	0	0	0	0	2.6
UPPER	13. Academic professionals	0	0	0	0	0	0	0
CLASS	14. Entrepreneurs	0	0	0	0	0	0	0
Subtotal		0	0	0	0	0	0	2.6
STATUS	15. Non-university students	0	0	0	0	0	0	0
UNCLEAR	16. School children	5.0	20.1	3.1	9.6	6.5	7.1	24.6
	17. No data	5.0	10.8	0	12.3	10.4	30.9	1.3
Subtotal		10.0	30.9	3.1	21.9	16.9	38.0	25.9
TOTAL (%)		100	100	100	100	100	100	100
Frequency (*N*)		40	129	32	73	153	42	77

Notes:
1. Relates primarily to apprentices and trainees.
2. Includes all non-adults who listed their occupations as 'Kaufmann'.
3. Relates only to adults listed as 'Kaufmann'.
4. Includes sons of farmers who listed their occupations as 'Landwirt', 'Winzer' or 'Bauer'.

Sources: Percentages calculated on the basis of data on the membership and on the leadership of the HJ in the (Rhenish) Palatinate in various lists in *HA*, 75/1555 and 86/1776.

2.11). At the time of the (temporary) ban on the uniformed auxiliary organisations of the NSDAP in April 1932, which affected the HJ, SA and the *Schutzstaffel* (SS - Protection Squad), the complete membership index of the HJ in the Palatinate, listing members in 100 towns and villages throughout the Palatinate, and covering the period 1928 to 1932, fell into the hands of the police. The data highlights a very strong recruitment from the lower class, especially in the formative stage of the development of the HJ in the area (see Table 2.11, columns A to C), and a strikingly high lower-class component in a number of relatively large branches, especially those at Annweiler, Grünstadt and Pirmasens (see Table 2.11, columns H, K and O). The lower-class dominance in the period 1928 to 1930 was reduced to some extent as the HJ took root in numerous towns and villages after 1930, when lower- and middle-middle-class individuals were attracted to the movement in many of the rural backwaters of the province. Thus farmers' sons made up the majority of the HJ membership in branches of between 10 and 35 members at Zeiskam (51.5 per cent), Wachenheim (53.3 per cent), Morschheim (55.5 per cent), St. Julian (57 per cent) and Geiselberg (64.7 per cent).

The social structures of the HJ branches in the Palatinate show the type of variation from place to place encountered in the analysis of the NSDAP itself. Thus factory workers were in the majority in the small branches at Miesenbach (50 per cent) and Bottenbach (63.6 per cent), while agricultural labourers represented the largest occupational group (accounting for 36.4 per cent of the membership) in the branch at Göllheim. Some branches had a very homogeneous social structure. Members drawn from the lower class made up the entire membership at Langmeil, and 92.8 per cent of the members at Limburgerhof, while in a number of other small branches, such as those at Breitenbach, Nussdorf and Obersülzen, the lower- and middle-middle class dominated the rank and file.

Despite the overall dominance of the lower class in the HJ in the Palatinate, however, the branch leadership was primarily in the hands of middle-class individuals, while the handful of upper-middle-class and upper-class members in the HJ in the region provided the *Gau* leadership (see Table 2.11, column G).

The politicisation of youth by the HJ mobilised for the NSDAP youngsters drawn primarily from a class, the lower class, in which the older age groups were relatively immune to Nazism. It was an important source for the recruitment above all of the SA and SS, and this function was noted and emphasised by the contemporary authorities monitoring and assessing the HJ movement.[114] Although we have no details as to how many HJ members actually joined the party or the SA or the SS on reaching the age of eighteeen, it would seem from the data on the Palatinate that all but a handful of the 1,101 members recorded in the membership list who reached that age went on to become 'adult' members of the movement.[115] The constant influx of predominently lower-class recruits into the SA and the SS obviously conditioned, to some extent, the social structures of these militant, activist sections of the Nazi movement.

The empirical data available on the rank and file of the SA does suggest that this very important Nazi auxiliary organisation was indeed primarily lower class in its composition, and quite different from that of the NSDAP, although unanimity on this point among historians has not, as yet, been reached. Detailed, empirically-based analysis of the pre-1923 SA is still lacking. The data analysed here, calculations based on fragments of the pre-1923 Munich SA and material on the SA in Nuremberg, is limited and inconclusive, and cannot be taken as representative for the structure of the SA as a whole since it involves only a small percentage of the pre-1923 SA (see Table 2.12, columns A to D). It is on the later stages of the development of the SA, for the period 1929 to 1933, when it became a mass movement (it reached a strength of approximately 300,000 by January 1933), that there is relatively extensive statistical material - and considerable disagreement among historians as to how to interpret it.

The argument that lower-class members dominated the rank and file of the SA in the post-1929 period has recently been most forcefully advanced by Conan Fischer.[116] Using various records listing 1,184 SA members, Fischer came to the conclusion that in the period 1929 to January 1933, 63.4 per cent of the SA was working class (a number of his sources are included in Table 2.12, columns F, H and BB).[117] The idea that the SA - at least in some regions of Germany - did indeed contain a higher percentage of lower-class members than did the NSDAP itself, is not new.[118] But Fischer's assertion that his 'sample' is representative for the SA as a whole has been seriously questioned on methodological grounds by Richard Bessel and Mathilde Jamin.[119] There are undoubtedly problems surrounding Fischer's 'sample': it is essentially urban-based and does rely heavily on data relating to the Munich SA.[120] The 'urban' nature of Fischer's material has been particularly questioned by Bessel, who has found material on the SA membership in the largely rural, less urbanised regions of Eastern Germany which suggests that both in Silesia and especially East Prussia - areas on which there is some data - the working-class presence in the SA was not particularly high or significant.[121]

My own investigation of the structure of the Bavarian SA at the time of its (temporary) prohibition in April 1932, based on 1,539 members, does not involve a sample, random or otherwise. It rests on material put together by the Bavarian police authorities following house-searches of SA members resident in literally hundreds of small towns and rural communities scattered throughout Bavaria, material which has not been evaluated before (see Table 2.12, columns S to AA). Despite the 'accidental' nature of the material, its utility as a guide to the Bavarian SA in its rural setting is enhanced by the fact that the job descriptions involved in classifying the membership were not self-assigned in the way that they were in the NSDAP's own membership records. It is probable that the occupational data is relatively accurate, since it is less likely that SA members subjected to police investigation lied about their real jobs, especially since the bulk of the data relates to members living in villages and small towns in which the local police compiling the data probable knew many of the individuals concerned. This is attested by the details attached to many of the reports which cover - beyond name, age, place of birth, occupation - such matters as marital status, religion, family background (occupation of parents in some cases), and even, in a minority of instances, the financial situation of the individual concerned.

In all probability the material represents a broad cross-section of the rural, small-town Bavarian SA membership. It shows a consistent pattern in all the regions of the *Land*: the lower class makes up more than half of the membership in all but the Palatinate, though even here it only marginally fails to reach the 50 per cent mark. Striking also - in contrast with the structure of

Table 2.12: The social and occupational structure of the leadership and membership of the *Sturmabteilung* (SA - Storm Section) and of the *Schutzstaffel* (SS - Protections Squad) in various regions and towns, 1921-32 (by %)

Class	Occupational subgroup	(A) SA Members Munich[a] Dec. 1921	(B) SA Members Nuremberg[b] 1922-23	(C) SA Members Munich[c] (late 1923)	(D) SA Members Munich[d] (Nov. 1923)	(E) SA Leaders Germany[e] 1925-29	(F) SA Members Nuremberg[b] 1925-29	(G) SA Members Eutin[f] Mid-1929
LOWER	1. Unskilled workers	14.1	7.8	6.5	4.5	4.9	2.8	20.0
CLASS	2. Skilled (craft) workers	18.9	35.2	9.5	6.8	6.2	42.9	36.4
	3. Other skilled workers	9.4	-	5.7	6.8	-	-	-
Subtotal		42.4	43.0	21.7	16.1	11.1	45.7	56.4
Lower-	4. Master craftsmen	2.7	2.0	2.8	0	2.3	0	0
and	5. Non-acad. professionals	5.4	-	6.7	2.3	-	-	-
middle-	6. Lower employees	15.4	35.3	15.2	6.9	33.4	24.2	23.5
MIDDLE	7. Lower civil servants	4.7	11.8	6.6	13.6	10.4	20.0	5.5
CLASS	8. Merchants	14.9	2.0	25.6	40.9	10.1	1.4	7.3
	9. Farmers	0.7	0	0	0	6.4	0	7.3
Subtotal		43.8	49.0	56.9	63.7	62.6	45.6	43.6
Upper-	10. Managers	0	0	0	2.3	2.4	0	0
MIDDLE	11. Higher civil servants	0	-	0	0	2.7	-	0
CLASS/	12. University students	8.1	-	5.7	6.8	0	-	0
UPPER	13. Academic professionals	2.0	7.8	5.7	2.3	1.4	2.8	0
CLASS	14. Entrepreneurs	0	0	0	0	2.4	1.4	0
Subtotal		10.1	7.8	11.4	11.4	9.4	4.2	0
STATUS	15. Non-university students	2.0	-	5.7	2.3	0	2.8	0
UNCLEAR	16. Military[1]	0.7	-	3.8	4.5	2.1	-	0
	17. Miscellaneous[2]	0.7	0	0	0	14.8	1.4	0
Subtotal		3.4	0	9.5	6.8	16.9	4.2	0
TOTAL (%)		100	100	100	100	100	100	100
Frequency (*N*)		148	51	105	44	1,006	70	55

Table 2.12 (cont'd)

Class	Occupational subgroup	(H) SA Members Hessen-Nassau[f] 1929	(I) SA Members Schwabing[g] (Munich) 1929	(J) SS Members Schwabing[g] (Munich) 1929	(K) SA Members Nuremberg[b] 1930-32	(L) SA Leaders Germany[e] 1930-33	(M) SS Members Munich[h] Oct. 1930
LOWER	1. Unskilled workers	37.7	13.2	28.0	5.3	6.6	18.6
CLASS	2. Skilled (craft) workers	23.0	16.0	12.5	35.9	5.5	16.7
	3. Other skilled workers	-	16.0	6.2	-	-	8.3
Subtotal		60.7	45.2	46.7	41.2	12.1	43.6
Lower-	4. Master craftsmen	0	0	3.1	0.8	2.6	2.1
and	5. Non-acad. professionals	-	0	0	-	-	4.2
middle-	6. Lower employees	6.6	14.6	9.3	35.8	36.3	25.0
MIDDLE	7. Lower civil servants	8.2	1.3	0	6.9	10.6	2.1
CLASS	8. Merchants	13.1	13.3	3.1	2.3	9.7	14.6
	9. Farmers	6.6	1.3	0	0.8	7.0	0
Subtotal		34.5	30.5	15.5	46.6	66.2	48.0
Upper-	10. Managers	0	0	0	2.3	3.6	0
MIDDLE	11. Higher civil servants	0	0	0	-	3.3	0
CLASS/	12. University students	1.6	12.0	15.6	-	0	2.1
UPPER	13. Academic professionals	3.3	2.6	3.1	5.3	1.8	0
CLASS	14. Entrepreneurs	0	0	0	0	2.0	0
Subtotal		4.9	14.6	18.7	7.6	10.7	2.1
STATUS	15. Non-university students	0	8.0	12.5	1.5	0	0
UNCLEAR	16. Military[1]	0	0	0	-	0.2	0
	17. Miscellaneous[2]	0	1.3	6.2	3.1	10.7	6.2
Subtotal		0	9.3	18.7	4.6	10.9	6.2
TOTAL (%)		100	100	100	100	100	100
Frequency (*N*)		61	75	32	131	879	48

Table 2.12 (cont'd)

Class	Occupational subgroup	(N) SA Members Weilheim[i] Dec. 1930	(O) SA Leaders Upper Bavaria[j] (1930)	(P) SS Members Munich[k] Nov. 1931	(Q) SA Leaders North-east Hanover[l] Dec. 1931	(R) SS Members Ludwigshafen[m] April 1932	(S) SA Members Palatinate[m] April 1932
LOWER	1. Unskilled workers	36.7	33.2	0	20.6	2.8	23.5
CLASS	2. Skilled (craft) workers	15.7	11.1	10.5	12.7	25.7	22.0
	3. Other skilled workers	10.5	0	5.3	4.8	5.7	3.7
Subtotal		62.9	44.3	15.8	38.1	34.1	49.2
Lower-	4. Master craftsmen	5.3	5.5	0	0	8.6	2.2
and	5. Non-acad. professionals	0	11.1	5.3	1.6	31.4	2.2
middle-	6. Lower employees	10.6	16.5	42.1	11.1	5.7	2.9
MIDDLE	7. Lower civil servants	10.6	5.5	0	0	8.6	5.1
CLASS	8. Merchants	0	11.1	10.5	7.9	11.4	13.2
	9. Farmers	0	5.5	0	27.0	0	19.8
Subtotal		26.5	55.2	57.9	47.6	65.7	45.4
Upper-	10. Managers	5.3	0	0	0	0	0
MIDDLE	11. Higher civil servants	0	0	0	0	0	0.7
CLASS/	12. University students	0	0	5.3	0	0	0
UPPER	13. Academic professionals	0	0	5.3	1.6	0	1.5
CLASS	14. Entrepreneurs	0	0	0	0	0	0.7
Subtotal		5.3	0	10.6	1.6	0	2.9
STATUS	15. Non-university students	5.3	0	15.8	0	0	0.7
UNCLEAR	16. Military[1]	0	0	0	0	0	0
	17. Miscellaneous[2]	0	0	0	12.7	0	1.5
Subtotal		5.3	0	15.8	12.7	0	2.2
TOTAL (%)		100	100	100	100	100	100
Frequency (*N*)		19	18	19	63	35	136

Table 2.12 (cont'd)

Class	Occupational subgroup	(T) SA Members Lower Franconia[m] April 1932	(U) SA Members Upper Franconia[m] April 1932	(V) SA Members Middle Franconia[m] April 1932	(W) SA Members Upper Palatinate[m] April 1932	(X) SA Members Swabia[m] April 1932	(Y) SA Members Lower Bavaria[m] April 1932
LOWER	1. Unskilled workers	22.9	16.7	27.4	21.8	29.3	36.0
CLASS	2. Skilled (craft) workers	26.1	43.1	34.1	36.3	28.7	22.1
	3. Other skilled workers	6.4	4.8	4.4	1.6	4.0	2.9
Subtotal		55.4	64.6	65.9	59.7	62.0	61.0
Lower-	4. Master craftsmen	0.6	2.4	1.1	4.8	5.7	5.2
and	5. Non-acad. professionals	8.3	3.6	1.1	5.6	2.3	4.1
middle-	6. Lower employees	7.0	4.8	1.1	4.8	4.0	5.8
MIDDLE	7. Lower civil servants	3.8	5.6	6.6	7.2	6.9	9.3
CLASS	8. Merchants	12.1	10.4	9.9	5.6	10.9	9.3
	9. Farmers	10.2	6.0	13.2	5.6	5.2	2.3
Subtotal		42.0	32.8	33.0	33.6	35.0	36.0
Upper-	10. Managers	0	0.5	0	3.2	0	0
MIDDLE	11. Higher civil servants	0	0.7	0	0.8	0	0
CLASS/	12. University students	0	0	0	0	0.6	0
UPPER	13. Academic professionals	0.6	0	1.1	0.8	0.6	0.6
CLASS	14. Entrepreneurs	0	1.0	0	0.8	1.1	0.6
Subtotal		0.6	2.2	1.1	5.6	2.3	1.2
STATUS	15. Non-university students	1.9	0.2	0	0	0	0.6
UNCLEAR	16. Military[1]	0	0	0	0	0	0
	17. Miscellaneous[2]	0	0	0	0.8	0.6	1.2
Subtotal		1.9	0.2	0	0.8	0.6	1.8
TOTAL (%)		100	100	100	100	100	100
Frequency (*N*)		157	413	91	124	174	172

Table 2.12 (cont'd)

Class	Occupational subgroup	(Z) SA Members Upper Bavaria[m] April 1932	(AA) SA Members Bavaria[m] April 1932	(BB) SA Members Munich[f] Summer 1932	(CC) SS Members Munich[n] Sept. 1932	(DD) SA Leaders Munich[o] Nov. 1932	(EE) SS Leaders Munich[p] Dec. 1932
LOWER	1. Unskilled workers	35.7	25.9	7.0	32.0	2.2	16.7
CLASS	2. Skilled (craft) workers	24.3	31.1	45.1	7.1	10.9	8.3
	3. Other skilled workers	6.6	4.6	-	7.1	8.6	4.2
Subtotal		66.6	61.6	52.1	46.2	21.7	29.2
Lower-	4. Master craftsmen	5.1	3.5	0.5	7.1	2.2	4.2
and	5. Non-acad. professionals	2.6	3.7	-	17.8	8.6	8.3
middle-	6. Lower employees	3.7	4.5	19.1	3.6	19.5	33.3
MIDDLE	7. Lower civil servants	5.1	6.0	8.1	3.6	4.4	0
CLASS	8. Merchants	4.8	9.3	1.6	14.3	26.1	4.2
	9. Farmers	4.4	7.3	0.4	0	0	4.2
Subtotal		25.7	34.3	29.7	46.4	60.8	54.2
Upper-	10. Managers	0	0.4	0	0	0	0
MIDDLE	11. Higher civil servants	0.4	0.4	0	0	0	0
CLASS/	12. University students	0	0.1	12.0	0	2.2	0
UPPER	13. Academic professionals	0.7	0.6	4.3	0	15.2	8.3
CLASS	14. Entrepreneurs	1.4	0.8	0	7.1	0	0
Subtotal		2.5	2.3	16.3	7.1	17.4	8.3
STATUS	15. Non-university students	1.4	0.6	0	0	0	0
UNCLEAR	16. Military[1]	1.1	0.2	0	0	0	0
	17. Miscellaneous[2]	2.6	0.8	1.8	0	0	8.3
Subtotal		5.1	1.6	1.8	0	0	8.3
TOTAL (%)		100	100	100	100	100	100
Frequency (*N*)		272	1,539	773	28	46	24

Table 2.12 (cont'd)

Notes:

1. Lists those SA or SS members who were still in the Armed Services.
2. Includes ex-servicemen whose civilian occupations are unknown, as well as those who described themselves as 'unemployed' or 'retired'.

Sources:

a. Percentages calculated on the basis of data provided by 'Abschrift aus der Sturm-Abteilung der national-soz. Arbeiter-Partei (Maurice)', dated 2 December 1921, *HA*, 65/1483.
b. Percentages calculated on the basis of data provided by E. C. Reiche, *The Development of the SA in Nürnberg, 1922-1934* (Cambridge, 1986), p. 30, Table 2.4; p. 68, Table 3.3; p. 108, Table 4.5.
c. Percentages calculated on the basis of data provided by 'Stammrollen des SA Regiments München 1923', *HA*, 2A/234 and 4/102.
d. Percentages calculated on the basis of data provided by 'Namenverzeichnis der Angehörigen des Stosstrupps Hitler', police report, Munich (n.d., probably late 1923), *HA*, 68/1494.
e. Based on data in M. Jamin, *Zwischen den Klassen. Zur Sozialstruktur der SA-Führerschaft* (Wuppertal, 1984), pp. 166-9, Tables IV-1-3 and IV-1-4. Percentage figures for other skilled workers (subgroup 3) and for non-academic professionals (subgroup 5) could not be established and are hidden in those for other subgroups.
f. Based on data in C. Fischer, *Stormtroopers. A Social, Economic and Ideological Analysis 1929-35* (London, 1983), p. 26, Table 3.1. Percentage figures for other skilled workers (subgroup 3) and for non-academic professionals (subgroup 5) could not be established and are hidden in those for other subgroups.
g. Percentages calculated on the basis of data provided by 'Mitgliedergrundbuch Ortsgruppe Schwabing' [München] (for 1929). Nazi Party members who were also members of the SA or of the SS were also noted, *HA*, 8/182.
h. Percentages calculated on the basis of data provided by 'Mitglieder der SS-München', dated 14 October 1930, *HA*, 72/2546.
i. Percentages relating to the SA in Weilheim (Upper Bavaria) are calculated on the basis of data provided by 'Trupp Weilheim. Stärkebericht für den Monat Dezember 1930', dated 12 January 1931, *HA*, 90/1870.
j. Percentages calculated on the basis of data provided by 'Sturm 55-Führerverzeichnis', (Upper Bavaria, n.d., probably late 1930), *HA*, 90/1870.
k. Percentages calculated on the basis of data provided by 'Verzeichnis - Mitglieder der SS Sturm 1 Sturmnbann I' (Munich), 17 November 1931, *HA*, 72/1546.
l. Percentages relating to the SA leaders in the Lüneburg region (north-eastern part of the province of Hanover) calculated on the basis of data in Krohn and Stegmann, 'Kleingewerbe und Nationalsozialismus', pp. 95-8, Appendix 2. Included under miscellaneous (subgroup 17) are those who described themselves as 'Haussohn' (probably sons of farmers).
m. Percentages relating to the SS in Ludwigshafen (in the Rhenish Palatinate) and on the SA in various regions of Bavaria are based on data contained in numerous police reports compiled at the time of the ban of these organisations on 13 April 1932, *HA*, 75/1556 and 1557, and 87/1816.
n. Percentages calculated on the basis of data provided by a police report on 'SS-Motorsturm 2/II/1' (Munich), dated 1 September 1932, *HA*, 72/1546.
o. Percentages calculated on the basis of data provided by 'Verzeichnis der Führer der SA Münchens [Leibstandarte] nach dem Stand vom 1 November 1932', *HA*, 90/1870.
p. Percentages calculated on the basis of data provided by 'Verzeichnis der Führer der SS - Standarte München nach dem Stand vom 1 Dezember 1932', *HA*, 72/1546.

the SA in Munich (see Table 2.12, columns I and BB), is the virtual absence of the upper-middle class and upper class in all but the Upper Palatinate membership, where it did provide 5.6 per cent of the SA's rank and file. The mix of occupational subgroups at the regional level shows some significant variations. In Lower and Upper Bavaria unskilled workers (primarily agricultural labourers) are quite strongly in evidence, whereas in Upper Franconia and Upper Palatinate skilled (craft) workers are strongly represented. Master craftsmen do not generally figure to any extent (the youth of the SA membership is a factor here, of course) in any region, while merchants are conspicuous only in the Palatinate, and in Lower and Upper Franconia. The proportion of farmers in the regional membership ranges from the marginal 2.3 per cent in Lower Bavaria to the high figure of 19.8 per cent in the Palatinate.

Taken overall, the data on the predominantly rural Bavarian SA membership is in line with the values given in Fischer's work, rather than with Bessel's evaluation of the sociology of the SA in Eastern Germany. It may be that the latter region is the exception, given that the limited data on other regions of Germany generally supports, rather than contradicts, Fischer's views and further regional analysis may confirm his argument.[122]

There is little room for disputing the conclusions reached in Jamin's meticulous quantitative analysis of the leadership of the SA over time.[123] This shows, in sharp contrast with the evidence on the rank and file of the SA, that the lower class was markedly underrepresented in the higher echelons (i.e. *Standartenführer* - SA colonel - and above), which was dominated by lower- and middle-middle-class elements (see Table 2.12, columns E and L). In the ranks below that of *Standartenführer* the dominance of this class is less marked, and the lower class correspondingly more in evidence (see Table 2.12, columns O, Q and DD).[124] Overall the same applies to the leadership corps of the SA as to that of the NSDAP: it was quite different in social terms from the rank-and-file membership.

We do not have, as yet, any overall analysis of the SS.[125] The limited information advanced in Table 2.12 (columns J, M, P, R, CC and EE) relates, with the exception of the data on Ludwigshafen, exclusively to sections of the Munich SS between 1929 and 1932, and while it shows similarities with the pattern of the SA, is too restricted in scope to be taken as representative even of the Bavarian SS. Given that the SS did recruit its rank and file to a considerable degree from the SA in the pre-1933 period, the strong lower-class presence in the Munich SS is perhaps to be expected.

What we know about the social structure of the HJ and the SA does project a 'class image' markedly different from that discernible in the NSDAP itself. Whereas the lower class was clearly overshadowed by the lower- and middle-middle class within the NSDAP, in the two auxiliary organisations on which we have a considerable amount of evidence, the situation is clearly the reverse. Given the size of the SA by 1933 - and perhaps 50 per cent of its membership (according to Fischer) was also simultaneously in the party itself - the implications of its social structure for the Nazi movement as a whole provides food for thought.

VII

At the time of the establishment of Hitler's so-called 'National Government' at the end of January 1933, the Nazi movement probably had about one million organised followers, of which around 850,000 were in the NSDAP, while its largest auxiliary organisation, the 300,000-strong SA probably included 150,000 members who were not party members as such. As the 'National Government' set about strangling the German democratic forces, liquidating the political pluralism which the Republic had represented in the process, hundreds of thousands of Germans flooded into the party, the membership of which catapulted to the two-and-a-half million mark by 1935, to reach just short of the five million mark by 1939, and to over eight million by 1945.

The movement which acquired power in the spring of 1933 had secured a large, though volatile, following in the comparatively brief timespan of four years, a following which was markedly heterogeneous. Despite the imbalance between the classes represented in the party, the NSDAP had support from all occupational groups and all segments of German society, from the lower class to the upper class. It was a national party, entrenched in both rural and urban areas, supported by both Protestants and Catholics. In only one very important respect did the party fail to represent the totality of German society - although its chauvinist leadership would not have considered this crucial omission as significant - it had few women members.

The Nazi hierachy was very much aware of the social imbalances within the NSDAP and the fact that the party membership mirrored the structure of German society imperfectly. This conditioned the recruitment policy laid down in the *Partei-Statistik*, which aimed at restricting a further influx of occupational groups such as civil servants and the self-employed, which were overrepresented in the movement, whereas workers and farmers were to be encouraged to join in greater numbers.[126] In part these objectives were to be realised during the Third Reich, for the lower class did begin to figure more significantly in the party, especially during the war years (see Table 2.5, columns F to H). It was the lower-class influx which reduced the share of the lower- and middle-middle class within the new membership in the late 1930s and early 1940s (it declined from around the 57 per cent mark in 1933 to 1937 to 53 to 54 per cent during the Second World War). More marked was the progressive disenchantment of the upper-middle class and upper class with Nazism: the share of this class among new recruits dropped very steeply, falling from 12.2 per cent in 1933 to 2.7 per cent between 1942 and 1944 (see Table 2.5, columns E to H). One of the ironies of the development of the party after 1933 is that the increasingly aged male leadership ruled over a membership which, during the war years, acquired a larger and larger degree of support from women. Thus by the 1940s the share of males in the party had fallen from 94 to 95 per cent registered in the period 1933 to 1936, to 65.3 per cent by the period 1942 to 1944.[127]

During the Third Reich the social structure of the NSDAP did not dramatically alter. It continued to exhibit the characteristic which had marked it from the beginning, one which also explains its remarkable success: it was a polymorphic movement in social terms, a party which effectively transcended the class divide. It was this feature which brought it success in the late 1920s, and gave it its electoral strength in the early 1930s. It was the popularity of the party with Germans from all occupations and from all class backgrounds which also provided the base for the relatively easy entrenchment of the regime which unfolded after 1933, which was sustained until the last critical stages of the Second World War. It is a sad reflection that the sordid system which dominated Germany for twelve years was there because of popular support, a regime which would probably not have been removed but for external, enforced intervention. All social classes, to a greater or lesser degree, were involved in creating and sustaining the Behemoth.

Notes

1. See the bibliographical guides provided by P. Hüttenberger, *Bibliographie zum Nationalsozialismus* (Göttingen, 1980); H. Kehr and J. Langmaid, *The Nazi Era 1919-1945. A Select Bibliography of Published works from the Early Roots to 1980* (London, 1982); P. Rees, *Fascism and Pre-Fascism in Europe, 1890-1945: A Bibliography of the Extreme Right* (Sussex, 1984), pp. 233-315.
2. For example W. Stephan, 'Zur Soziologie der Nationalsozialistischen Deutschen Arbeiterpartei', *Zeitschrift für Politik*, vol. 20 (1931), pp. 793-800; S. A. Pratt, 'The Social Basis of Nazism and Communism in Urban Germany: a correlation study of the July 31 1932 Reichstag elections in Germany', unpublished MA thesis, Michigan State University, 1948.
3. On the characterisation of the NSDAP as a middle-class movement see, for example, the works by T. Geiger, *Die soziale Schichtung des deutschen Volkes* (Stuttgart, reprint 1962), pp. 109-22; S. M. Lipset, *Political Man* (New York, 1960); H. A. Winkler, *Mittelstand, Demokratie und Nationalsozialismus* (Cologne, 1972) - but see his later essay 'Mittelstandsbewegung oder Volkspartei? Zur sozialen Basis der NSDAP' in W. Schieder (ed.), *Faschismus als soziale Bewegung* (Hamburg, 1976), pp. 97-118; and K. D. Bracher, *The German Dictatorship. The Origins, Structure and Consequences of National Socialism* (Harmondsworth, 1978).
4. See P. Sering, 'Der Faschismus', *Zeitschrift für Sozialismus*, nos. 24-25 (1936), pp. 765-92; W. Ehrenstein, *Dämon Masse* (Frankfurt/M., 1952); W. Zopf, *Wandlungen der deutschen Elite* (Munich, 1965).
5. J. W. Falter, 'Wer verhalf der NSDAP zum Sieg?', *Aus Politik und Zeitschrift*, B28-29 (1978), pp. 3-21; R. F. Hamilton, *Who voted for Hitler?* (Princeton, 1982); T. Childers, *The Nazi Voter. The Social Foundations of*

Fascism in Germany, 1919-1933 (Chapel Hill-London, 1983).

6. For a review of the literature see M. Jamin, *Zwischen den Klassen. Zur Sozialstruktur der SA-Führerschaft* (Wuppertal, 1984), pp. 11-45.
7. T. Abel, *The Nazi Movement. Why Hitler came to Power* (New York, 1938); H. Gerth, 'The Nazi Party: its Leadership and Composition', *The American Journal of Sociology*, vol. 45 (1940), pp. 517-41; E. M. Doblin and C. Pohly, 'The Social Composition of the Nazi Leadership', *The American Journal of Sociology*, vol. 51 (1945/46), pp. 42-9; D. Lerner, *The Nazi Elite* (Stanford, 1951).
8. *Partei-Statistik Stand 1.Januar 1935*. Herausgeber Der Reichsorganisationsleiter der NSDAP (3 vols., Munich, 1935). W. Schäfer, *NSDAP. Entwicklung und Struktur der Staatspartei des Dritten Reiches* (Hanover-Frankfurt/M., 1956).
9. G. Heinz and A. F. Peterson, *NSDAP Hauptarchiv. Guide to the Hoover Institution Microfilm Collection* (Stanford, 1964).
10. The extent of the data on the membership of the NSDAP available in the *Hauptarchiv* is reflected in the sources used in the tables in this essay. Beyond a number of branch memberships listed in Tables 2.2 to 2.4, 2.6 and 2.7, the data in Table 2.11 and much of that in Table 2.12 has not previously been evaluated.
11. Kater has published numerous articles since the early 1970s based on the membership data contained in the NSDAP Master File in the Berlin Document Center. The results of his investigations are summarised in his recent study: M. H. Kater, *The Nazi Party. A Social Profile of Members and Leaders, 1919-1945* (Oxford, 1983). Material from the Berlin Document Center has also been used extensively by J. P. Madden, 'The Social Composition of the Nazi Party, 1919-1930', unpublished PhD thesis, University of Oklahoma, 1976; Jamin has also made use of this source in her study of the leadership of the SA - Jamin, *Zwischen den Klassen*.
12. G. Franz-Willing, *Die Hitlerbewegung, der Ursprung, 1919-22* (Hamburg, 1962), pp. 129-30; W. Maser, *Die Frühgeschichte der NSDAP. Hitlers Weg bis 1924* (Frankfurt/M., 1965), pp. 254-5.
13. M. H. Kater, 'Zur Soziographie der frühen NSDAP', *Vierteljahrshefte für Zeitgeschichte*, vol. 19 (1971), pp. 124-59, here p. 126.

14. Kater, *Nazi Party*, pp. 242-3, columns C, D, H to K. The values given in this essay are based on the original *Hauptarchiv* material - see Table 2.2, columns C, D, L to O.
15. Kater, 'Soziographie'; M. H. Kater, 'Sozialer Wandel in der NSDAP im Zuge der nationalsozialistischen Machtergreifung' in Schieder, *Faschismus*, pp. 25-67; M. H. Kater, 'Quantifizierung und NS-Geschichte. Methodologische Überlegungen über Grenzen und Möglichkeiten einer EDV-Analyse der NSDAP-Sozialstruktur von 1925 bis 1945', *Geschichte und Gesellschaft*, vol. 3 (1977), pp. 453-84.
16. D. M. Douglas, 'The Parent Cell: Some Computer Notes on the Composition of the First Nazi Party Group in Munich, 1919-21', *Central European History*, vol. 10 (1977), pp. 55-72; P. Madden, 'Some Social Characteristics of Early Nazi Party Members, 1919-23', *Central European History*, vol. 15 (1982), pp. 34-56.
17. C-D. Krohn and D. Stegmann, 'Kleingewerbe und Nationalsozialismus in einer agrarisch-mittelständischen Region. Das Beispiel Lüneburg 1930-1939', *Archiv für Sozialgeschichte*, vol. 17 (1977), pp. 41-98; L. D. Stokes, 'The Social Composition of the Nazi Party in Eutin, 1925-32', *International Review of Social History*, vol. 23 (1978), pp. 1-32; D. Mühlberger, 'The Occupational and Social Structure of the NSDAP in the Border Province Posen-West Prussia in the early 1930s', *European History Quarterly*, vol. 15 (1985), pp. 281-311.
18. D. Mühlberger, 'The Sociology of the NSDAP: The Question of Working-Class Membership', *Journal of Contemporary History*, vol. 15 (1980), pp. 493-511. Cf. J. H. Grill, 'Local and Regional Studies on National Socialism: A Review', *Journal of Contemporary History*, vol. 21 (1986), pp. 253-294.
19. M. H. Kater, 'Ansätze zu einer Soziologie der SA bis zur Röhm-Krise' in U. Engelhardt a. o. (eds.), *Soziale Bewegungen und politische Verfassung* (Stuttgart, 1976), pp. 798-831; C. Fischer, *Stormtroopers. A Social, Economic and Ideological Analysis 1929-35* (London, 1983); Jamin, *Zwischen den Klassen*; R. Bessel, *Political Violence and the Rise of Nazism. The Storm Troopers in Eastern Germany 1925-1934* (New York, 1984); E. Reiche, *The Development of the SA in Nürnberg, 1922-1934* (Cambridge,1986).

20. For a brief review see Mühlberger, 'Sociology', pp. 494-5.
21. Cf. P. Hammerton, *Exercises in historical Sociology* (The Open University Press, 1974), p. 11.
22. This is illustrated most effectively by J. Genuneit, 'Methodische Probleme der quantitativen Analyse früher NSDAP-Mitglieder' in R. Mann (ed.), *Die Nationalsozialisten. Analysen faschistischer Bewegungen* (Stuttgart, 1980), pp. 34-66.
23. On this problem see C. Schmidt, 'Zu den Motiven "alter Kämpfer" in der NSDAP' in D. Peukert and J. Reulecke (eds.), *Die Reihen fast geschlossen. Beiträge zur Geschichte des Alltags unterm Hakenkreuz* (Wuppertal, 1981), pp. 21-43.
24. Jamin's carefully researched work on the SA leaders is exceptional in terms of the comprehensive data on which it is based - Jamin, *Zwischen den Klassen*.
25. Mühlberger, 'NSDAP in Posen-West Prussia', pp. 295 and 308, note 64.
26. Fortunately Kater has moved away from the narrow concept of the occupational groups which composed the German working class which characterised his earlier work on the sociology of Nazism. For his current approach see Kater, *Nazi Party*, pp. 5-7.
27. This is especially true at the 'micro' level of analysis. If one omits 25 members from a branch membership list of say 100, it can significantly inflate the percentage values given for the class groupings of those 75 members subjected to analysis. It can, for example, push up the figure for the lower-class section of the membership from 30 to 40 per cent.
28. Occupational subgroups 1 to 14 are used in all the tables. The subgroups in the 'status unclear' category listed in Tables 2.2 to 2.12 show some variations since it is obviously pointless to include, for example, pensioners in the HJ tables, or housewives in those relating to the SA.
29. The 1925 census returns are in *Statistik des Deutschen Reichs* (hereafter *StDR*) (Berlin, 1929-31), vols. 402-408. Thousands of occupational titles are listed alphabetically in *StDR* (Berlin, 1929), vol. 402, pp. 177-212; occupations to be found in 160 economic branches are also given, ibid., pp. 46-118.

30. In the case of data taken from Kater, his percentage values are used as they stand. Where I am dependent on material provided by other historians, I have adapted their data to fit my classification system.
31. Kater, *Nazi Party*, p. 6. In the 1925 census '*Steiger*' are assigned to the supervisory personnel category - see *StDR* (Berlin, 1929), vol. 402, p. 48.
32. On the method employed see Kater, *Nazi Party*, pp. 7-8.
33. Cf. Fischer, *Stormtroopers*, p. 19.
34. This is borne out by the use of the term '*Kaufmann*' by 15-year-old HJ members in the Palatinate to describe their occupational status (see Table 2.11, note 2). Cf. J. Kocka, 'Zur Problematik der deutschen Angestellten 1914-1933' in H. Mommsen a. o. (eds.), *Industrielles System und politische Entwicklung in der Weimarer Republik* (2 vols., Kronberg/Ts.-Düsseldorf, 1977), vol. 2, p. 800, note. That the word '*Kaufmann*' often lacks precision when used by Nazis to describe their occupation is also illustrated by J. H. Grill, *The Nazi Movement in Baden 1920-1945* (Chapel Hill, 1983), p. 84.
35. Kater, *Nazi Party*, p. 9.
36. Thus engine drivers and railway guards, for example, are assigned to the white-collar employees (*Angestellten*) category in the 1925 census - *StDR* (Berlin, 1929), vol. 402, p. 11. Cf. Fischer, *Stormtroopers*, p. 16.
37. Kater, *Nazi Party*, p. 12.
38. For example, in his breakdown of the membership of the Nazi branch at Mettmann in the Ruhr, Kater's figure for the 'elite' element within the membership is given as 3.6 per cent, based entirely on the 'students' subgroup - Kater, *Nazi Party*, p. 246, Table 4, column F. The only candidates in the membership list on which this percentage could be based is a schoolchild (*Schüler*) or a 'student' of photography (*Photoschüler*). Neither of these would merit inclusion in the 'elite'. Details on the Mettmann branch are given in 'Mitgliederliste der N.S.D.A.P. Ortsgruppe Mettmann, 28.2.1926', *Nordrhein-Westfälisches Hauptstaatsarchiv* (Düsseldorf),(hereafter *NWHStA*), RW23/Nr.55.
39. At the 'micro' level this would result in very high percentages for the upper-middle-class and upper-class component in some Nazi branches -

see, for example, the effect it would have on the branches at Konstanz (see Table 2.2, column H), or Dresden or Stuttgart (see Table 2.3, columns U and PP), or Deutsch-Krone (see Table 2.7, column G).

40. The figures are based on entries recorded in 'Mitgliederverzeichnis (aufgestellt im Herbst 1919) der Deutschen Arbeiter-Partei, Ortsgruppe München' in the Hoover Institution NSDAP *Hauptarchiv* Microfilm Collection (hereafter *HA*), reel 8, folder 171; cf. 'Adolf Hitler's Mitkämpfer 1919-1921', *HA*, 2A/230.
41. Madden, 'Social Composition', pp. 77, 86 and 93. Madden estimates the party's strength at around 8,100 by the end of 1922 - ibid., p. 93.
42. Grill, *Nazi Movement in Baden*, pp. 56-7; W. Böhnke, *Die NSDAP im Ruhrgebiet 1920-1933* (Bonn-Bad Godesberg, 1974), p. 41; J. Noakes, *The Nazi Party in Lower Saxony 1921-1933* (Oxford, 1971), p 14.
43. The percentages are calculated on the basis of data in a list of new members who joined the NSDAP between 25 September and 9 November 1923 - the list is in *HA*, 10/215.
44. Cf. R. Hambrecht, *Der Aufstieg der NSDAP in Mittel- und Oberfranken (1925-1933)* (Nuremberg, 1976), p. 35. In a number of towns in the predominantly Catholic regions of southern Bavaria the NSDAP also acquired considerable support, as in the Ingolstadt area, where the party had 535 members by 9 October 1923 (see Table 2.2, column Q).
45. Madden, 'Social Composition', p. 68. Kater's data for the pre-Hitler DAP is based on Madden's mistake - Kater, *Nazi Party*, p. 242, Table 2, column A.
46. In the 'Adolf Hitler's Mitkämpfer' list, the date of entry into the DAP of the early members is generally omitted, though number 550 is registered as entering the party on 27 August 1919 and number 669 joined on 1 October 1919. It is highly improbable that the names of the first 54 members in the DAP only started within the letter range A to H.
47. The first entries under the letter A cover the numbers 501 to 504; the first entries under the letter Z cover the numbers 666 to 668. The first entries under the letter B cover the numbers 505 to 516, before jumping to 669 for the next member.
48. Cf. F. L. Carsten, *The Rise of Fascism* (London,

1967), pp. 94-5; Madden, 'Social Composition', pp. 72-5. 'Workers' accounted for 41.1 per cent of Munich's working population in 1925 - percentage calculated from data in *StDR*, vol. 406 (Berlin, 1928), p. 612. The percentage of the membership in the Munich branch which can be positively identified as lower class in the period 1919 to 1920 fell from 31.3 per cent in December 1919 to 27.8 per cent by May 1920.

49. It is difficult to establish how many of those listing a military rank in early 1920 were actually still in the army. A small percentage did give their regiment in the 'address' column. It may well be that a fair number who listed their rank in lieu of their occupation had in reality left the army and had not obtained civilian employment. Cf. Madden, 'Social Characteristics', pp. 47-8.

50. Kater, *Nazi Party*, pp. 242-3, Table 2, columns E, G, L and M.

51. The lower class made up 41.3 per cent of the working population in Rosenheim, 38.8 per cent in Passau, 38.1 per cent in Landshut, 40.1 per cent in *Kreis* Berchtesgaden, and 45.8 per cent in Ingolstadt - percentages calculated from data in *StDR*, (Berlin, 1928), vol. 405, section 29, pp. 72-90. The values for the lower class which can be positively identified in the branch memberships of these towns is 21.4 per cent, 14.7 per cent, 28.2 per cent, 45.7 per cent and 34.5 per cent respectively.

52. Percentage figure for the lower class in the working population of Mannheim calculated from data in *StDR*, (Berlin, 1928), vol. 405, section 33, p. 90. On the social characteristics of the NSDAP's membership in Mannheim - and Baden generally - in the pre-1923 period, see Grill, *Nazi Movement in Baden*, pp. 81-6.

53. D. Mühlberger, 'The Rise of National Socialism in Westphalia 1920-1933', unpublished PhD thesis, University of London, 1975, p.140.

54. Ibid., p. 142.

55. The list has previously been analysed by Kater, 'Soziographie'.

56. In the case of new members enrolled in the Stuttgart branch, however, it has to be noted that a number of these were not resident in the city, but in various towns and villages in the region, such as Schwäbisch-Gmünd. The data for 1920 relates to members resident in the city,

who formed the membership at the time of the foundation of the branch.

57. Only one of the ten new members was from the lower class, the rest were all from the lower- and middle-middle class. Data on Reichenhall for members joining in 1923 in *HA*, 10/125.

58. That factory and textile workers formed part of the membership of the Nazi branch in Augsburg is noted by G. Hetzer, 'Die Industriestadt Augsburg. Eine Sozialgeschichte der Arbeiteropposition' in M. Broszat a. o. (eds.), *Bayern in der NS-Zeit* (6 vols., Munich-Vienna, 1977-1983), vol. 3, pp. 51-2.

59. For background on the NSDAP's development in the Günzburg area, see the study by Z. Zofka, 'Dorfeliten und NSDAP. Fallbeispiele der Gleichschaltung aus dem Kreis Günzburg', in Broszat, *Bayern in der NS-Zeit*, vol. 4, pp. 383-433. On the situation of the NSDAP in county Memmingen see E. Fröhlich and M. Broszat, 'Politische und soziale Macht auf dem Lande. Die Durchsetzung der NSDAP im Kreis Memmingen', *Vierteljahrshefte für Zeitgeschichte*, vol. 25 (1977), pp. 546-72.

60. Madden suggests that these occupational subgroups had a more limited presence in the pre-1923 NSDAP - Madden, 'Social Characteristics', p. 47.

61. On the economic position of the basket makers in northeastern Bavaria (and on the economic problems of the region in general) see the documents in 'Lage der Arbeiterschaft, Arbeiteropposition, Aktivität und Verfolgung der illegalen Arbeiterbewegung 1933-1945' in Broszat, *Bayern in der NS-Zeit*, vol. 1, pp. 193-325.

62. Cf. Grill, *Nazi Movement in Baden*, pp. 94-6; Hambrecht, *Aufstieg der NSDAP*, pp. 62-76.

63. On the general development of the NSDAP see D. Orlow, *The History of the Nazi Party* (2 vols., Newton Abbot, 1971-73), vol. 1 (1919-1933); W. Horn, *Führerideologie und Parteiorganisation in der NSDAP (1919-1933)*, (Düsseldorf, 1972).

64. Madden, 'Social Composition', pp. 137, 156, 203 and 218.

65. Calculated by Madden at 45 per cent for the period 1925 to 1928, Madden, 'Social Composition', p. 218.

66. G. Schulz, *Aufstieg des Nationalsozialismus* (Frankfurt/M.-Berlin-Vienna, 1975), p. 550.

67. Madden's data has been re-worked by Kater to

allow comparisons to be made with Studentkowski's material - see Kater, *Nazi Party*, pp. 244-5, Table 3.

68. *Partei-Statistik*, vol. 1, p. 146.

69. The Material on Westphalia and Thuringia relates to established members in *Gaue* Westphalia-South and Thuringia who are mentioned in Nazi 'histories' of the *Kampfzeit* ('the period of struggle') written in the 1930s. By checking the names of these members with the names of Nazi members recorded in the NSDAP Master File in the Berlin Document Center, Kater was able to discover the personal details relating to 672 out of 820 of the Westphalian Nazis and 642 out of the 941 Thuringian Nazis mentioned in the Nazi 'chronicles' - Kater, *Nazi Party*, p. 249.

70. Of Kater's sample of 2,339 new party entrants who joined the NSDAP between 1925 and 1932, 38.9 per cent came from the lower class - Kater, 'Quantifizierung und NS-Geschichte', p. 470. Kater's re-working of Madden's material (Madden places all artisans into the lower-middle class in the classification model he employs in his thesis) gives the following values for new members drawn from the lower class: 37.3 per cent in 1925; 45.9 per cent in 1927 and 36.6 per cent in 1929 - Kater, *Nazi Party*, pp. 244-5, Table 3.

71. Kater, *Nazi Party*, p. 35.

72. *Partei-Statistik*, vol. 1, p. 70.

73. Tyrell views the *Partei-Statistik* as representing an attempt by the Nazis to inflate the lower-class presence within the party membership - A. Tyrell, *Führer befiehl ... Selbstzeugnisse aus der Kampfzeit der NSDAP* (Düsseldorf, 1969), p. 379. Various doubts about the utility of the *Partei-Statistik* are also expressed by R. Kühnl, *Formen bürgerlicher Herrschaft. Liberalismus - Faschismus* (Hamburg, 1971), p. 82; and E. Hennig, *Bürgerliche Gesellschaft und Faschismus in Deutschland: Ein Forschungsbericht* (Frankfurt/M., 1977), pp. 164-5. There are problems surrounding the use of this source, but it can nevertheless be used (with care) to provide an insight into the sociology of Nazism - see Mühlberger, 'Sociology', p. 498; cf. the perceptive comments made by Jamin, *Zwischen den Klassen*, pp. 17-18 and 31-2.

74. For example, the relatively high lower-class

presence in the NSDAP in the Ruhr as indicated by the *Partei-Statistik* data is confirmed in my forthcoming article 'A "*Mittelstandspartei*"? The Social Structure of the NSDAP in the Ruhr'.

75. The variability of the social composition of the NSDAP from region to region is suggested by a number of regional studies which touch on the problem of the sociology of the NSDAP - see the studies by G. Pridham, *Hitler's Rise to Power. The Nazi Movement in Bavaria 1923-33* (London, 1973); Hambrecht, *Aufstieg der NSDAP*; Grill, *Nazi Movement in Baden*; Böhnke, *NSDAP im Ruhrgebiet* (who understates the extent of lower-class support for Nazism in the region); Noakes, *NSDAP in Lower Saxony*; K. Schaap, *Die Endphase der Weimarer Republik im Freistaat Oldenburg 1928-1933* (Düsseldorf, 1978); R. Heberle, *From Democracy to Nazism: a regional case study on political parties in Germany* (New York, reprint 1970); and R. Rietzler, "*Kampf in der Nordmark*" *- Das Aufkommen des Nationalsozialismus in Schleswig-Holstein 1919-1928* (Neumünster, 1982). Cf. R. Mann, 'Neue Untersuchungen zur Sozialgeschichte des Nationalsozialismus', *Kölner Zeitschrift für Soziologie und Sozialpsychologie*, vol. 21 (1979), pp. 155-64.

76. For the following percentages see *Partei-Statistik*, vol. 1, p. 146.

77. My provisional analysis of three further Nazi branch membership lists relating to the Ruhr show that in 1925 to 1926 the lower class constituted the majority of members in Hamborn (*N*:38 - 65.7 per cent), Essen (*N*:412 - 50 per cent), and Hammerthal (*N*:33 - 60.6 per cent). The calculations are based on membership lists in the *NWHStA*, RW 23.

78. The percentages are based on the membership of nine Nazi branches in the Ruhr.

79. On the mentality of the working class in the Ruhr see K. Rohe, 'Vom alten Revier zum heutigen Ruhrgebiet. Die Entwicklung einer regionalen politischen Gesellschaft im Spiegel der Wahlen' in K. Rohe and H. Kühr (eds.), *Politik und Gesellschaft im Ruhrgebiet* (Königstein/Ts., 1979), pp. 21-47, here p. 46.

80. Cf. D. Mühlberger, 'Central Control versus Regional Autonomy: A Case Study of Nazi Propaganda in Westphalia, 1925-1932' in T. Childers (ed.), *The Formation of the Nazi Constituency, 1918-1933* (London, 1986), pp. 64-103.

81. In the case of Munich this can be explained by reference to the fact that the 1925-6 and 1929 data relates to the Schwabing district of the city, which was predominantly bourgeois.
82. Tyrell, *Führer befiehl*, p. 352.
83. For these and the following percentages see *Partei-Statistik*, vol. 1, p. 148.
84. Cf. Noakes, *Nazi Party in Lower Saxony*, pp. 141 and 159.
85. See Pridham, *Nazi Movement in Bavaria*, p. 188.
86. Cf. F. J. Heyen, *Nationalsozialismus im Alltag. Quellen zur Geschichte des Nationalsozialismus vornehmlich im Raum Mainz-Koblenz-Trier* (Boppard, 1967), pp. 54-6.
87. Böhnke, *NSDAP im Ruhrgebiet*, p. 199.
88. Cf. Mühlberger, 'Sociology', pp. 500-501.
89. Mühlberger, 'National Socialism in Westphalia', p. 298.
90. I. Buchloh, *Die nationalsozialistische Machtergreifung in Duisburg: Eine Fallstudie* (Duisburg, 1980).
91. Madden, 'Social Composition', p. 265; see also Jamin, *Zwischen den Klassen*, p. 32.
92. Historians dealing with the regional development of the party do have access to various pieces of evidence - reports by the police and civil administration, information obtained from personality files of the party, fragments of regional or local membership lists, and material provided by the press - against which the *Partei-Statistik*'s data can be measured. These types of sources are used, for example, by Pridham to 'control' the *Partei-Statistik*'s values for the Bavarian *Gaue*. He suggests that in general the *Partei-Statistik*'s breakdown for Bavaria is confirmed by other evidence, though he questions the relatively high values given for 'workers' in the *Partei-Statistik* for Bavaria - see Pridham, *Nazi Movement in Bavaria*, pp. 186-7.
93. Fröhlich and Broszat, 'NSDAP im Kreis Memmingen', pp. 548-555.
94. On the Kraiburg branch see Pridham, *Nazi Movement in Bavaria*, p. 252, note. On Penzberg, see Tenfelde in Broszat, *Bayern in der NS-Zeit*, vol. 4, pp. 199-200.
95. In stark contrast to the social structure of the Laim branch of the NSDAP was that of the Laim SA, which was predominantly lower class (73.9 per cent of its members were working class) - Fischer, *Stormtroopers*, pp. 28, 68n.

96. Mühlberger, 'NSDAP in Posen-West Prussia', pp. 283-7.
97. Ibid., pp. 292-3, Table 4. The percentage of the working population dependent on agriculture is based on data in *StDR* (Berlin, 1928), vol. 403, section 6, pp. 2-3.
98. For the following see Heyen, *Nationalsozialismus im Alltag*, pp. 52-6.
99. Kater notes that some workers did hold leadership positions before 1923 in the Ruhr area and in Bremen - Kater, *Nazi Party*, p. 174.
100. On the efforts of the Nazis to secure working-class support in Berlin from the mid-1920s see M. Broszat, 'Die Anfänge der Berliner NSDAP, 1926/27', *Vierteljahrshefte für Zeitgeschichte*, vol. 8 (1960), pp. 85-118.
101. Wagner went so far as to remove branch leaders whom he considered to be too bourgeois (*bürgerlich*), as in the case of Theiler, branch leader in the industrial city of Hagen - see Wagner to RL Abteilung I, Bochum, 16 May 1931, *Bundesarchiv* Koblenz (hereafter *BAK*), NS 22/1076.
102. Böhnke, *NSDAP im Ruhrgebiet*, pp. 200-201.
103. Cf. R. Rogowski, 'The *Gauleiter* and the Social Origins of Fascism', *Comparative Studies in Society and History*, vol. 19 (1977), pp. 389-430.
104. This is shown by K. Rohe, *Das Reichsbanner Schwarz Rot Gold* (Stuttgart, 1965), p. 272.
105. Kater, *Nazi Party*, p. 177.
106. On the procedure involved in drawing-up the list of Nazi candidates see Orlow, *Nazi Party*, vol. 1, pp. 183, 252-3 and 266-8.
107. Report on the Hamburg election result in *VB*, 7 Oct. 1931.
108. In the commentary on the occupational background of the Nazi deputies elected to the Thuringian *Landtag*, the *VB* emphasised that 'the National Socialist faction represents a *Volksgemeinschaft* since it contains all occupational groups, (though) naturally the agrarian community is strongly represented' - *VB*, 6 Aug. 1932.
109. The occupations of the 107 Nazis elected to the *Reichstag* in September 1930 were given under the headline 'We represent the people' - *VB*, 1 Oct. 1930.
110. See, for example, the protest by *Gauleiter* Meyer of Westphalia-North at the arbitrary removal by the *Personalamt* in 1932 of a miner

from the list of parliamentary candidates in his *Gau*. Meyer was 'appalled' by the decision given that, as he stated in his letter of protest to Munich, 'the bulk of the party membership in my *Gau* is drawn from "workers of the fist" (*Arbeiter der Faust*) ... and the candidature of a worker is absolutely vital if this membership is not to be alienated' - Meyer to Loper, Personalamt, Gelsenkirchen, 20 Feb. 1932, *BAK*, NS 22/1075.

111. Hence the increasing frequency from the early 1930s onwards of 'royal' and 'aristocratic' elements in the Nazi *Reichstag* corps of deputies, headed by August Wilhelm, 'Prince' of Prussia, the 'Crown Prince' zu Waldeck und Pyrmont, a number of 'counts', such as von Bismarck-Schönhausen, von Helldorf, von Quadt zu Wykradt und Isny, von Wartenburg, and quite a few 'barons', such as von Stauffenberg, von Schorlemer, von Eltz-Rübenach and von Kanne.
112. P. D. Stachura, *Nazi Youth in the Weimar Republic* (Santa Barbara-Oxford, 1975). In a recent review of the social structure of the NSDAP Stachura, however, comes to the conclusion that 'the NSDAP was a predominantly lower-middle class affair' - P. D. Stachura, 'The Nazis, the Bourgeoisie and the Workers during the *Kampfzeit*' in idem (ed.), *The Nazi Machtergreifung* (London, 1983), pp. 15-32, here p. 28.
113. Stachura, *Nazi Youth*, pp. 58-62.
114. Cf. 'Bericht über die Auswertung der Akten der Hitler-Jugend, Gau Rheinpfalz beim Bezirksamt Neustadt a. d. Haardt', *HA*, 87/1776.
115. The strength of the HJ in the Palatinate was 952 at the time of the April 1932 ban: see 'Stand vom 2. April 1932', *HA*, 86/1776. The authorities assumed that only 1 to 2 per cent of those recorded as leaving the HJ did not go on to join the SA or the SS.
116. C. J. Fischer, 'The Occupational Background of the SA's Rank and File Membership during the Depression Years, 1929 to mid-1934' in P. D. Stachura (ed.), *The Shaping of the Nazi State* (London, 1978), pp. 131-59; see also his book - Fischer, *Stormtroopers*.
117. Fischer, *Stormtroopers*, p. 31, Table 3.3. Kater used the same material, but reached different conclusions (due to his exclusion of 'specialist workers' (*Facharbeiter*) and dependent artisans from the working class, arguing

that the SA was essentially petty-bourgeois in its composition - Kater in Engelhardt, *Soziale Bewegung*, p. 802.

118. E. G. Reiche reaches the conclusion that in the period 1925 to 1932, 43 per cent of the Nuremberg SA was working class - Reiche, *SA in Nürnberg*, pp. 140-1, Table 4.10. Stokes points to the 'proletarian nature' of the SA in Eutin - Stokes, 'Nazi Party in Eutin', p. 27.

119. R. Bessel and M. Jamin, 'Nazis, workers and the uses of quantitative evidence', *Social History*, vol. 4 (1979), pp. 111-16. See the rejoinder by C. Fischer and C. Hicks, 'Statistics and the historians: the occupational profile of the SA of the NSDAP', *Social History*, vol. 5 (1980), pp. 131-8; cf. the reply by R. Bessel and M. Jamin, 'Statistics and the historian: a rejoinder', ibid., pp. 139-40.

120. The Munich data (for late 1932) accounts for about two-thirds of Fischer's 'sample' - Fischer, *Stormtroopers*, p. 26, Table 3.1.

121. Bessel, *Stormtroopers in Eastern Germany*, pp. 36-9. Bessel's conclusions are based on a number of police reports which provide a rough breakdown of the membership of the SA for 1930 to 1931, primarily for East Prussia.

122. Cf. the breakdown of the membership of the SA in Berlin (*N*:1,824) for February 1931, in which unskilled and skilled workers account for 54 per cent - Bessel and Jamin, 'Nazis, workers', p. 113, Table 1.

123. Jamin, *Zwischen den Klassen*.

124. Ibid., p. 211, Table IV-I-17, column 2.

125. The SS leadership corps has been subjected to analysis by G. C. Boehnert, 'A Sociography of the SS Officer Corps, 1925-1939', unpublished PhD thesis, University of London, 1977. Cf. his essay 'The Third Reich and the Problem of "Social Revolution": German Officers and the SS' in V. R. Berghahn and M. Kitchen, (eds.) *Germany in the Age of Total War* (London, 1981), pp. 203-217., especially p. 205, Table 1. See also M. Kater, 'Zum gegenseitigen Verhältnis von SA und SS in der Sozialgeschichte des Nationalsozialismus von 1925-1939', *Vierteljahrshefte für Zeitgeschichte*, vol. 62 (1975), pp. 239-79.

126. *Partei-Statistik*, vol. 1, p. 56.

127. Women accounted for only 7.8 per cent of the members who joined the NSDAP between 1925 and 1932, and made up a mere 5.1 per cent of the

hundreds of thousands who rushed to join the movement in 1933 - Kater, *Nazi Party*, p. 254, Table 8. Cf. M. H. Kater, 'Frauen in der NS-Bewegung', *Vierteljahrshefte für Zeitgeschichte*, vol. 31 (1983), pp. 202-241. See also Madden, 'Social Composition', p. 254, Table 47.

Chapter Three

THE BRITISH ISLES

G. C. Webber

Sociological analyses of fascism in Britain have been hampered by lack of empirical evidence. The various movements of the 1920s were too small to be taken seriously even by the police; the Blueshirts in Ireland were often difficult to distinguish from traditional conservatives; and the records of the British Union of Fascists (BUF) were confiscated by the police in 1940, never to be seen again. In addition, because British fascism was never a serious electoral force it gives us little opportunity to study voting patterns, and because it was more of a nuisance than a threat to the status quo in the 1920s and 1930s it received less scholarly attention at the time than it has since. As a result, discussions of the social composition of fascist movements in Britain have tended to remain at the level of theoretical conjecture, and this has left us with a remarkably unclear picture of the kinds of people who were attracted to fascism, of their motivations, their number, and of the ways in which these fluctuated over time.

Theories current during and shortly after the inter-war years (most of which related specifically to the BUF) were confused and confusing. The Labour Party concluded in 1934 that the BUF chiefly attracted ex-officers, small-tradesmen, the middle classes and irresponsible youngsters, and having satisfied themselves that they were not losing support to the Communist Party in areas of fascist strength, ceased to worry about the movement thereafter.[1] The right-wing *Saturday Review* also thought that the BUF was composed largely of 'young Conservatives' at this time.[2] But by 1935 Harold Laski was talking of the movement as predominantly working class, and another left-winger, W. A. Rudlin, argued (with an eye to the future) that the fascist movement would attract a series of different groups each of which would eventually fall prey to the deepening crisis of capitalism: first 'blue-collar' workers, then 'black-coated' ones, and finally the 'real middle classes'.[3] Lionel Birch, writing in 1937, thought that fascism drew its support from psychological 'types' rather than particular social classes, but even he singled out public school and University 'hearties', ex-officers, and ex-Communist workers for special attention. And the journalist, Frederick Mullally, asserted retrospectively (in 1946) that the stereotypical Blackshirt was a lower-middle-class youngster from South London whose father was a Roman Catholic civil servant.[4]

More recently, academic studies have added to our knowledge, but have done so unevenly. In 1966, W. F. Mandle produced a study of the leadership of the BUF (based upon information from the fascist press), which confirmed that this group, at least, contained a disproportionate number of relatively-young, well-educated, widely-travelled, restless, middle-class ex-servicemen.[5] In 1980, Stuart Rawnsley published an essay based upon a regional study of membership in the North of England which concluded that although some groups - such as employed and unemployed cotton-workers, self-employed men, small-businessmen, shopkeepers and Catholics - were overrepresented, the BUF nevertheless attracted 'all sorts of people who joined for a variety of reasons'.[6] And in 1984, John Brewer published a study of the fascist movement in the Midlands which sought to achieve similar goals. However, this analysis must be treated with caution since it is based upon a sample of only 15 survivors - three farmers, two teachers, and a collection of diverse individuals divided about evenly between non-unionised working-class and lower-middle-class men.[7] On the other hand, our knowledge of the movement in other areas is even more sketchy. We still lack comparable studies of the South of England in general and of the East End of London in particular, and without them generalisations about fascism in Britain are likely to remain open to doubt (especially if they are merely extrapolations from small and possibly unrepresentative samples). Nevertheless, we are in a position to advance some tentative and necessarily impressionistic generalisations about the social bases of fascism in Britain by carefully weighing the existing evidence (of the 1920s as well as the

1930s, and of Irish as well as English fascism) and by making use of recently-released Home Office files relating to the BUF.[8]

I

The first English movement to call itself fascist was the British Fascisti (BF), better known as the British Fascists and referred to by wits as the B...F...s. Created early in 1923 by Rotha Lintorn-Orman, a 28-year-old woman with military ancestors and a fetish for uniforms, the movement represented little more than an over-reaction to militant trade unionism. It thought of itself as an apolitical organisation akin to the Scout movement (from which it drew much of its inspiration) and despite its paramilitary trappings it was far from being a threat to the status quo. Its stated aim was to defend the King in times of national crisis, and its policies were heavily influenced by fears of religious decline. The philosophy of the British Fascist movement was not unfairly regarded by Arnold Leese as nothing more than 'Conservatism with knobs on', and during elections the movement did, in fact, urge its supporters to vote for the Conservative Party.[9]

It seems likely that most of them already did. Although the movement was always small, its early membership was drawn heavily from the ranks of three different social groups: retired military men, obscure Peers, and class-conscious youngsters of the upper-middle classes. It attracted no more than a handful of the working-class 'toughs' which other fascist movements sought to recruit, and the only unusual feature of the movement was the existence of an all-women Patrol Group in London that roamed the streets in search of Communists and prostitutes. According to one writer, this represented a form of 'fascist feminism',[10] but the claim makes little sense, since most of the women who belonged to the fascist movement were not feminists, and most of the feminists who were politically to the right (such as Christabel Pankhurst and her anti-Bolshevik Women's Party, for instance) were not fascists.

The membership of the British Fascist movement was concentrated almost entirely in London. Elsewhere it was practically bereft of support, and as the years progressed the number and social status of its adherents declined along with its income (although its doctrine grew more interesting as it became more radical). Damaged by internal disputes in the mid-1920s and undermined by the creation of the BUF in the early 1930s, the movement was reduced to a pitiful rump of 300 by 1934 until, eventually, it died along with its founder member in 1935. If the British Fascists were of any significance it was only because the movement had at one time or another contained men such as Arnold Leese (a vet, who was later to establish the Imperial Fascist League), William Joyce (a part-time tutor in English literature at London University, later and better known as the Nazi broadcaster, Lord Haw-Haw), and Neil Francis-Hawkins (an over-weight surgical instrument salesman, and a leading member of the BUF in the 1930s). In other respects the movement was unimportant, and its rivals and offshoots more so. The National Fascisti, for example, a mixture of 'Ku Klux Klan and undergraduate rag',[11] which broke from the British Fascists in 1925, was simply smaller and nastier than the parent organisation. And it was by no means renowned for the quality of its members. Indeed, the Secretary to the President of the National Fascisti, Colonel Sir Leslie Barker, was arrested on firearms charges in 1929 and subsequently discovered to have been a transvestite woman who had successfully masqueraded as a man since 1922.[12]

Arnold Leese's Imperial Fascist League (the IFL, established in 1929) was similarly bizarre. Leese, a retired vet with an interest in currency reform and a hatred of Jews (he referred to Mosley as a 'Kosher Fascist'), was an early and unrepentant supporter of Nazi Germany. But even though the IFL resisted amalgamation with the BUF, the organisation itself remained small and unimportant. Membership was apparently restricted to those whose physiognomy accorded with their Aryan beliefs and even at the height of its success in 1939 it probably had no more than 1,000 members and possibly as few as 200. This makes it very difficult and possibly dangerous to generalise about its social composition. But insofar as the IFL had any discernible social profile it appeared to be that of a movement whose recruits were, like Leese himself, middle-class men in revolt against prevailing middle-class values, and as a result the IFL adopted a series of curious positions. The League was (even more than the British Fascists) noticeably lacking in young working-class 'shocktroops', but it retained an abstract admiration for the British working man; it was hostile to the existing aristocracy (which was thought to be permeated by Jews and which gave little if any support to the IFL), but it supported the concept of aristocracy as such; and it was particularly interested in eugenics as a means of raising the birth-rate of the middle classes, but it distrusted the (*nouveau-riche*) industrial and the (liberal) professional elements within it.[13]

In short, British fascist movements of the 1920s, though they included a few youngsters out for a thrill and a handful of adventurous women using their newly-found independence to press for a return to traditional social values, gained most of their support from amongst a small group of minor aristocrats and 'respectable' middle-class rebels concentrated in and around London. Socially, fascism attracted those who had been (or feared that they might become) 'marginalised' by the now-dominant cleavage of class. Politically, this was reflected in their fear that the Conservative Party might not be capable of resisting Socialist advances.

II

The pattern of support in the 1930s was more complicated.[14] The creation of the British Union of Fascists in October 1932 drew established fascists of all kinds (except Leese and the IFL) into one relatively large but shifting and unstable coalition, and although little is known about the first year of its existence, the best estimates suggest that by the end of 1933 the BUF could boast from 17,000 to 20,000 members and that this figure rose to 40,000 or 50,000 during the first six months of 1934 when Lord Rothermere's *Daily Mail* gave the fascists its support. At this time the membership was concentrated mainly in and around London (but in places such as Paddington, St. Pancras, and Ealing rather than in the East End), in Yorkshire (especially Leeds), in the South-East (particularly in the coastal towns), in Lancashire (especially Manchester and Liverpool), in East Anglia (amongst rural rather than urban communities), and in the Midlands (especially in Birmingham, Wolverhampton, and Stoke).[15]

Sociologically, the BUF of 1934 differed from the fascist movements of the 1920s in a number of ways. Support came from *all* social classes, but the balance between them varied in different parts of the country. In isolated branches such as those in Cardiff, Bristol, and (according to Home Office sources) Birmingham, most of the support came from small-traders despite efforts to attract other social groups. In rural areas such as East Anglia, Worcester and the West country (but also in some parts of South and South-East England and for a while in South-West Scotland), relatively-wealthy farmers were attracted to the movement. In other areas support came mainly from the unemployed, notably in Manchester, where the BUF published a regional journal entitled *The Voice of the Workless*, and in Liverpool, where the local headquarters resembled a 'doss house'.[16] But all of these areas were in some respects *unrepresentative* of the movement as a whole which was heavily middle class but nevertheless composed of two fairly distinct 'wings'. On the one hand, the BUF attracted working-class recruits who were almost invariably non-unionised, often unemployed, and very rarely of the 'steady workman' type. On the other hand, it attracted numerous members of the professional classes, a disproportionate number of ex-officers, and a fair collection of public schoolboys, sometimes recruited by BUF youth groups such as those at Beaumont College, Stowe School, Westminster College and Worksop College.[17]

However, after the violent Olympia meeting of June 1934, and the sudden withdrawal of Rothermere's support in July, the BUF entered a period of rapid contraction that lasted until late-1935. During this period the social base of the movement altered dramatically. Membership slumped from 50,000 to 5,000 and became concentrated primarily in the East End of London (especially Stepney and Shoreditch, where it had *not* previously taken root), in Manchester, Liverpool, Leeds, and Hull, with a handful of members (probably no more than 125) remaining faithful to the cause in Birmingham. As a result (and with the possible exception of Birmingham) the BUF came to rely heavily upon working-class support. In the North it found favour with employed and unemployed cotton workers, and in the East End it attracted an indeterminate collection of individuals about whom we know surprisingly little except that they probably did *not* come from the ranks of the 'ordinary' working-class Labour voters in the area - the non-Irish dockers, those who worked in the shipyards, and the transport workers.[18] But although the BUF had lost most of its active support in the middle-class areas of the South and the East during the latter part of 1934, the amount of *sympathetic* support received from the middle and upper-middle classes began to *increase* again during 1935.[19]

After 1935 the movement began to recover. From a base of 5,000 members in October 1935, the BUF had more than tripled its support by November 1936. However, this recovery is difficult to analyse in terms of social class. Indeed, we cannot even be sure how these new members were distributed across the country. The BUF obviously *hoped* to attract working-class support by concentrating upon 'industrial' issues via the Fascist Union of British Workers (the FUBW was an offshoot of the BUF run by an ex-communist, C. J. Bradford). But its success was limited. It seems that the movement did increase its support amongst working-class northerners in Yorkshire and Lancashire. Rawnsley, for instance, provides some evidence of an increase in support amongst cotton workers, railwaymen, chemical plant workers and the unemployed.[20] But these findings have to be set in context. For the BUF was also picking up support from northern taxi-drivers, shopkeepers and the like, and it appeared to recover *less rapidly* in these areas than it did in the country as a whole. Meanwhile, its support in the East End of London probably increased *more rapidly* than it did elsewhere, but this was a result of native anti-Semitism and the counter-productive agitation of the left (the so-called 'Battle of Cable Street') rather than a consequence of industrial dissatisfaction. Indeed, the BUF's 'Industrial' strategy was ill-organised and ineffective, and the unionised sections of the working class remained practically immune from the appeal of fascism.

Thus, although the evidence is far from conclusive, it seems possible that the BUF's recovery might be explained by a revival of 'respectable' *middle-class* fascism, especially in the South of England where the movement still intended to contest numerous seats in the General Election due in 1940. Moreover, the numerical strength of the BUF in this region may have been as high as 3,000 by late-1936 which, as a percentage of total national membership, would have been higher than it was in 1934. Such an explanation (though it must still be regarded as tentative) would also tally with what little we know about the movement in the years 1937 and 1938. For the introduction of the Public Order Act (which was expected to reduce the appeal of the BUF to hot-headed working-class youngsters) did *not* prevent the movement from increasing its membership to 16,500 by the end of 1938. And although we simply do not know how this support varied by region or by class we should certainly be wary of assuming that it was as heavily working class as it had been towards the end of 1935.

During 1939 the BUF underwent a series of changes. In the first place, its membership began to rise sharply once again, and was probably as high as 22,500 by the end of the year (a figure which was higher than at any time other than the first half of 1934). However, the turnover of members at this time seems to have been particularly rapid (even amongst the national leadership), and the movement of 1939 possessed a new social profile. Membership in London continued to increase numerically to a level of about 11,000 but this masked an underlying transformation. The anti-Semites of the East End, although they remained hostile to Jewish immigrants, became increasingly anti-German during 1938 and 1939, and consequently became distrustful of the BUF (which since 1936 had called itself the British Union of Fascists and National Socialists). In areas such as Bethnal Green, Limehouse, and East Ham support for the BUF fell away, but in areas to the West and North of London such as Chiswick, Dalston, and Stoke Newington, the BUF found new (or perhaps recovered old) supporters mainly from amongst the middle and upper classes, but especially from the ranks of 'disgruntled businessmen', independent taxi-drivers and small-shopkeepers whose support they had been *trying* to gain for some time.[21] Elsewhere in the country details are more difficult to determine, but it seems likely that the provincial pattern was very similar. There is some reason to believe that the BUF may still have attracted several thousand supporters in the middle-class areas of the South and the South-East, and even though the movement was still strong in the North (especially in Manchester, East Lancashire and Leeds) we cannot be sure that the support they received in these areas came from the working classes.

Reviewing the years from the formation of the BUF in 1932 to the outbreak of war in 1939, it is useful to regard the movement as having passed through three fairly distinct phases. The first period (October 1932 to mid-1934) was one in which the policy of the movement, originally defined by Mosley's *The Greater Britain* (1932), was increasingly blurred by its bid for respectability and during which the supporters of the movement were drawn from two very different social groups, the lower-working and upper-middle classes. During the second period (1935 to 1938) the policy of the BUF became more openly anti-Semitic and more deliberately geared towards sectional interests. Initially, the membership was concentrated in working-class areas of the North and in the East End of London but was later more varied and more difficult to characterise. During 1939 the BUF entered its third phase. Although the movement continued to stress local and regional problems it was really little more than a single-issue organisation associated with the middle-class peace movement and at this time it attracted many new members most of whom appeared to be middle class themselves.

In the light of such changes it is dangerous to make too many sweeping generalisations about the BUF because, as Rawnsley has quite rightly pointed out, the movement *did* attract 'all sorts of people', and they not only joined the movement for different reasons, but they did so at different times, and were concentrated in different areas. Consequently, it is a mistake to look for a fascist 'stereotype' and it may even be reckless to advance beyond the realms of well-established but negative assertions. Thus, leaving positive conclusions to one side for the moment, the most significant feature of the BUF was that it consistently *failed* to penetrate the most highly-unionised sections of the working class who were natural Labour voters and were overrepresented in the areas worst hit by the depression.

III

Although the Irish Blueshirt movement emerged more slowly and disappeared more rapidly than fascism in England, it too was a complicated phenomenon about which we know very little. In fact, it is difficult to know whether or not the Blueshirts should be classified as fascist. For the movement existed independently of traditional parliamentary parties only briefly, most of its leaders vigorously denied any association with continental fascism, and the emotions that the Blueshirts aroused did not really belong to Europe of the 1930s but to Ireland of 1922.[22]

The Blueshirts had their origins in the Army Comrades Association (ACA) which was established early in 1932. At this time the movement was composed almost exclusively of ex-National Army officers who had opposed De Valera and the Irish Republican Army (IRA) during the civil war of 1922 to 1923, and who were now worried that the (conservative) *Cumann na nGaedhael* party (from which the ACA drew most of its support) would not be capable of defending established interests in the face of a newly elected *Fianna Fail* government led by De Valera himself. Subsequently, however, the style and social composition of the movement altered. In March 1933, soon after De Valera had called a snap election which strengthened his parliamentary position, the ACA adopted blue shirts as a uniform; in July 1933 the leadership of the movement was offered to General Eion O'Duffy, the ex-chief of police recently dismissed by De Valera; at the same time it changed its name to the National Guard; and although we possess almost no reliable figures, membership of the movement appeared to rise rapidly.

However, the social composition of the National Guard was more complex than that of the ACA. Though the movement was led by a former police-chief and retained the support of many ex-officers, the vast majority of Blueshirts were now large cattle farmers and their families (especially in the cattle-intensive counties of Limerick, Cork, Waterford, and Kilkenny) who were concerned about the consequences of De Valera's so-called 'economic war' with Britain. In addition, the movement attracted some shopkeepers and professionals (but few businessmen), and a substantial number of shop-assistants (many of whom had farming backgrounds), labourers (most of whom were attracted to the movement by civil war loyalties), and the unemployed. At local levels, it was the ex-army men who tended to lead the movement and the sons of farmers who proved to be the most ardent activists.

Blueshirt followers were consequently less 'radical' than Blueshirt leaders and it by no means followed that support for the National Guard entailed opposition to democracy or admiration for dictatorship. Thus, after O'Duffy had abandoned a farcical attempt to organise a mass march in August 1933, he led the Blueshirts into an alliance with *Cumann na nGaedhael* and the National Centre Party to create *Fine Gael* in September. For a while O'Duffy led both the party and the Blueshirt contingent within it (which was re-constituted as the League of Youth and was more popular than ever). But his leadership was incompetent, and after another *Fianna Fail* victory in the local elections of June 1934 O'Duffy resigned (in September), the Blueshirts were gradually phased out, and Irish 'fascism' quietly withered away.

IV

British Fascism attracted a range of social groups who joined the movements for a variety of reasons. However, it is difficult to generalise about social characteristics other than class. We know, for example, that fascism was particularly attractive to the young, but we cannot be sure how youthful the movements were as a whole. Activists, especially the kind that got themselves arrested, were no doubt unrepresentative of most fascist sympathisers, and any sample of surviving members will inevitably be biased in favour of the young. Besides, fascism was only one 'youth movement' amongst many, and as such, age may not be a particularly significant variable. Likewise, although the fascists were overwhelmingly male, so was every other political organisation (particularly the British Labour Party), and few conventional parties had anything akin to the BF's all-women Patrol Group. We know also that Roman Catholics were overrepresented and that they too were attracted to fascism for various reasons. Some, especially in Ireland, saw fascism as a political counterpart to their religious beliefs. Others were swayed by the 1929 Concordat between Mussolini and the Pope. Others still were simply interested in extending the principle of hierarchy from the Church to the State. But we do not know how many fascists were Catholic, nor what proportion of Catholics were fascists.

Many of the early fascists (and at local levels, many of the subsequent leaders) were retired military men, but even they had no single reason for supporting the fascist movement. In England, fascism attracted ex-officers who felt at home with the para-militarism of the BUF and found it difficult to re-adapt to civilian life or hold down a regular job. But in Ireland, the ex-army Blueshirts tended to be in steady employment, were often men of substance, and were usually pulled towards a fascist-style organisation by traditional loyalties rather than being pushed into it by socio-economic pressures.

Farmers were another group attracted to fascism both in England and in Ireland. But in England rural enthusiasm for the BUF faded rapidly amongst ordinary farmers once the 'tithe wars' of the early thirties ceased to be an issue, and support became concentrated amongst minor aristocrats and wealthy 'gentlemen farmers' who disliked industrial development, disapproved of the growing power of business interests within the Conservative Party, and thought of fascism as a modern version of Tory Paternalism. In Ireland, too, it was the wealthier farmers who formed the backbone of the Blueshirt movement, but their fears were crudely economic and they were soon overcome.

Fascism also appealed to the working classes, but the pattern of support was very uneven. The movements always attracted a certain number of unemployed workers, but this varied according to the time and place, and in general we know little about this group *except* that they were out of work. It also attracted a degree of support from members of the working classes employed in sectors of the economy where Trade Unionism was weak or non-existent, but this too was subject to variation. In the North of England, the BUF found favour with cotton workers who wanted to protect their industry from foreign competition, but it soon *lost* support in areas with a strong tradition of working-class Conservatism such as Liverpool and West Lancashire. On the other hand, the BUF gained support in the East End of London by exploiting well-established sentiments of anti-alienism that had previously been the preserve of local Tories.

Elsewhere the fascists were supported by self-employed and independent professional men who felt that their status, and perhaps their livelihoods, were under threat from the interests of organised business above them and those of organised labour below. But fascism in Britain never conformed to the classic model of a petty bourgeois movement except in particular areas (Bristol, Cardiff and perhaps Birmingham) and at particular times, most notably in 1939, when the ranks of the BUF were swollen by independent taxi-drivers and small-shopkeepers. However, this was a period in which the BUF was least distinctively 'fascist' and increasingly difficult to distinguish from other right-wing groups who opposed the war.

Consequently, over-arching theories of fascism need to be handled with care. Static models that seek to construct fascist stereotypes are inadequate because fascism was a kaleidoscopic movement with a constantly shifting appeal. On the other hand, dynamic models that seek to relate support for fascism with economic crisis are weakened by the fact that where the 'crisis' was most severe the fascist movement was relatively weak, and that (with the exception of the early part of 1934) the BUF were most popular when the 'crisis' was least acute. As Brewer has pointed out, fascists might have emphasised the *idea* of a crisis as a means of *rationalising* their support for the BUF, but there simply wasn't one.[23] In fact, instead of constructing elaborate theories to explain why a few thousand people *did* support the fascist movement in Britain, it might be more profitable to ask why so many millions *didn't*. That, however, is a question that would take us well beyond the confines of the present chapter.

Notes

1. Labour Party, *Report on replies to fascist questionnaire*, 27 July 1934: LP/FAS/34/1, Labour Party Archives, London.
2. *Saturday Review*, 5 May 1934.
3. H. Laski, *Jewish Chronicle*, 14 March 1935. W. A. Rudlin, *The Growth of Fascism in Great Britain* (London, 1935).
4. L. Birch, *Why they join the Fascists* (London, 1937) and F. Mullally, *Fascism Inside England* (London, 1946).
5. W. F. Mandle, 'The Leadership of the British Union of Fascists', *Australian Journal of Politics and History*, vol. 12 (Dec. 1966), pp. 360-83.
6. S. Rawnsley, 'The membership of the British Union of Fascists', in K. Lunn and R. C. Thurlow (eds.), *British Fascism* (London, 1980), pp. 150-65.
7. J. D. Brewer, *Mosley's Men. The BUF in the West Midlands* (Aldershot, 1984). Brewer's 15 fascists include three farmers (aged 49, 35, and 28 - all ages given at the time of joining, but those dates unknown), two teachers (aged 27 and 20, the latter being the only female in the sample), a 29-year-old van driver, a 19-year-old unemployed steel worker, a 29-year-old commercial traveller, a 28-year-old shop

manager, a 20-year-old trainee chef, a 29-year-old clerk, a 41-year-old cinema owner, a 27-year-old brewery worker, a 14-year-old school-child, and a 19-year-old houseman in private service.

8. The Home Office files are mostly in the HO 144 series and consist mainly of Special Branch reports.
9. R. Benewick, *Political Violence and Public Order* (London, 1969).
10. B. L. Farr, 'The development and impact of Right-wing politics in Great Britain, 1903-1932', unpublished PhD thesis, University of Illinois, 1976, ch. 8.
11. C. Cross, *The Fascists in Britain* (London, 1961), p. 61.
12. J. Collier and I. Lang, *Just the Other Day* (London, 1932), pp. 222-5.
13. J. Morrell, 'The Life and Opinions of A. F. Leese', unpublished MA thesis, University of Sheffield, 1974. Refer also: *The Fascist* (1929-1939).
14. This section is based upon original research previously published as an article: G. Webber, 'Patterns of membership and support for the British Union of Fascists', *Journal of Contemporary History*, vol. 19 (1984), pp. 575-606. Detailed references can be found in the article.
15. Labour Party, *Report*; Home Office files; and Brewer, *Mosley's Men*.
16. HO 144/20144/167-171.
17. HO 144/20140/102-119.
18. R. Skidelsky, *Oswald Mosley* (London, 1981 edn.), ch. 16. W. F. Mandle, *Anti-Semitism and the British Union of Fascists* (London, 1968).
19. HO 144/20144/46-48.
20. Rawnsley, in Lunn and Thurlow, *British Fascism*, pp. 159-60.
21. Webber, 'Patterns of membership', pp. 593-4; Skidelsky, *Oswald Mosley*, ch. 16.
22. This section is based mainly upon M. Manning, *The Blueshirts* (Dublin and Toronto, 1971); M. Manning, 'The Irish Experience: The Blueshirts' in S. U. Larsen a. o. (eds.), *Who Were The Fascists? Social Roots of European Fascism* (Bergen-Oslo-Tromsø, 1980), pp. 557-67; and E. Rumpf and A. C. Hepburn, *Nationalists and Socialism in 20th Century Ireland* (Liverpool, 1977), pp. 128-34.

23. J. D. Brewer, 'The BUF: some tentative conclusions on its membership' in Larsen , *Who Were The Fascists*?, pp. 542-56; and idem, 'Looking Back at Fascism: a phenomenological analysis of BUF membership', *The Sociological Review* (Nov. 1984), pp. 753-4.

Readers should also consult the recently published work by R. Thurlow, *Fascism in Britain. A History, 1918-1985* (Oxford, 1987), especially pp. 122-30. The present chapter was completed before Thurlow's work was available.

Chapter Four

THE NORDIC STATES

Henning Poulsen

The history of the fascist parties in four of the five Nordic states is one of relative failure. The fascist movements which developed in Denmark, Norway, Sweden and Iceland were little more than pale imitations of the German Nazi Party. It was only in Finland, where the fascists developed a more independent ideological profile, that they fared a little better, as can be seen from Table 4.1, which records the electoral performance of the Nordic fascist movements in the various national elections of the 1930s and early 1940s.

Table 4.1: Votes cast for Nordic fascist parties in national elections, 1932-44 (by %)

	1932	1933	1934	1935	1936	1937	1939	1943	1944
Denmark				1.0			1.8	2.1	
Norway		(2.2)			1.8				
Sweden	0.6				0.7				0.1
Finland					8.3		6.6		
Iceland			0.7			0.2			

Source: S.U. Larsen a.o. (eds.), *Who were the Fascists? Social Roots of European Fascism* (Bergen-Oslo-Tromsø, 1980), pp. 597-9, 702, 715, and 748; G. Djupsund and L. Karvonen, *Fascismen i Finland. Högerextremismens förankring hos väljerkåren 1929-1939* (Åbo, 1984), pp. 71-2.

Analysis of these low electoral performances of Nordic fascist parties offers one way for historians and social scientists to tackle the questions 'Who were the fascist?' and 'Why did fascists secure support?'. But the 'electoral analysis' approach creates obvious difficulties since, in comparative terms, the returns secured by Nordic fascist parties were too small to have any real statistical significance, and when one asks the question as to why this or that group preferred fascism, the general answer is that it did not. Studies of fascism in the Nordic states involve the study of minorities, or more often than not of plain exceptions.

One way of overcoming the problem involved in evaluating the significance of the relatively poor electoral performance of fascist parties at the national level, is to break up the data and examine those areas of the Nordic states in which fascists fared comparatively better than elsewhere. Were such regions characterised by common economic, social or cultural features? If so, these features might provide clues for a general explanation as to why fascism secured support and allow one to identify specific groups which supported fascism, or formed at least a potential reservoir of fascist support.

Another approach can be used in the cases of Denmark and Norway. Information on the membership and leadership of the *Danmarks Nationalsocialistiske Arbejder Parti* (DNSAP - Denmark's National Socialist Workers' Party), and to a lesser extent on the *Nasjonal Samling* (NS - National Unity), has survived. An analysis of the material relating to the rank and file of these parties will allow one to identify their social base with greater precision than by looking at their leadership corps. The data on the DNSAP membership is virtually complete and is based on the membership application forms filled in by those who joined the movement during the 1930s and early 1940s. The material on the NS is not as comprehensive, being based on the trials of those members who were active in the NS during the Occupation and excludes, therefore, those who had left the party before 1940. Evaluation of this membership data, however, also creates problems since the social composition of the DNSAP and of the NS may not have been identical with the social profile of their electoral supporters. In addition, we are unable to compare the social structure of the membership of these parties with that of other parties active in these states at the time, since we do not have similar, relatively trustworthy, information on non-fascist parties for the 1930s and early 1940s.

A more problematical method, which has also been used to investigate the nature of fascist membership, is that which involves interviewing former fascists in order to determine as to why they joined fascist parties. If one uses this approach, the answers provided by individuals can be of value provided that the replies are corroborated by other evidence. However, the replies resulting from the 'oral history' approach generally only throw light on what was later regarded as being a socially acceptable reason for being a fascist. In Denmark the unreliability of this method was illustrated as early as the late 1940s, when around one hundred males, who had been sentenced for the crime of collaboration with the occupying power, were asked about their background. Only ten per cent admitted to having had fascist sympathies. But by using membership files, the investigator found that in reality some forty per cent had been members of the DNSAP.[1]

Given the generally unreliable nature of the 'oral history' approach, the analysis of the social base of fascism in the Nordic states will be confined to the use of the first two research methods outlined above. Before examining the nature of the fascist parties in the Nordic states, however, it is necessary to give a brief review of the development of the parties in question, and to examine the political and socio-economic context in which they operated in the pre-1945 period. Even if we collectively describe them as 'fascist', the parties operating in the Nordic states were not all alike. Some of them changed their image over time, and none of them can just simply be classified as 'fascist'.

I

In outlining the development of the fascist parties which were active in the Nordic states, the most straightforward situation to evaluate is that which prevailed in Denmark. Here the DNSAP established itself as the major fascist party, significant enough to participate in elections. Minor fascist groups did exist alongside the DNSAP, but these were generally shortlived and unable to attract any sizeable following. Nor is there any doubt about the fascist credentials of the DNSAP. As is indicated by its name, it was modelled on the German Nazi Party, and even if it claimed to be a national

Danish movement, it did not try to fool anyone about its strict adherence to the German example.

The DNSAP was founded in 1930 by a small circle of men who had got to know each other in earlier, but fruitless, attempts to form a fascist party along the lines of the Italian model.[2] None of these individuals, nor Frits Clausen, a country doctor from North Schleswig who was the leader of the DNSAP from 1933 to 1945, were politicians of prominence. Perhaps because the DNSAP started from scratch, it was the only Nordic fascist party which made, relatively speaking, steady progress. Its limited, but constantly increasing electoral support is recorded in Table 4.1. By the time of the national election of 1932 the DNSAP, despite the severe crisis into which the Danish economy had been plunged by the general European recession, was unable to collect the 10,000 signatures which would have allowed it to participate in the election. This defect was overcome in 1935, when the party acquired 16,000 votes, a figure which rose to 31,000 in the election of 1939. The system of proportional representation used in Denmark allowed the DNSAP to secure three seats in 1939, which it was able to retain in the election of 1943, when the party obtained its highest ever support, although this only involved a mere 42,000 votes.

The overall history of the DNSAP was a somewhat uneventful one. It was a small movement isolated from other parties and always on the fringe of Danish politics. The chief concern of the party's leadership related primarily to the problems posed by the organisation and propaganda activity of the movement. In the 1930s the DNSAP tried especially to appeal to the agrarian community, though it was always careful to project the claim that it was a national party embracing all classes and groups within society. When Denmark was occupied by Germany in 1940, Hitler recognised Clausen as the future leader of a nazified Denmark contained within the framework of a Greater German Reich. But despite the willingness of the DNSAP to co-operate with the Germans, and its effort to recruit several thousand volunteers for the *Waffen-SS*, it did not acquire any political power, since the Germans continued to allow the existing Danish constitutional government to function.

The history of fascism in Norway is only straightforward in the sense that here too only one party was able to attract a significant following and to participate in elections. The NS was founded in 1933 by Vidkun Quisling, a former army officer and well-known politician, who had only recently resigned from the post of Minister of Defence in the government led by the Agrarian Party.[3] The problem with the NS, however, is the ambiguous nature of the party. In the 1933 general election it presented its programme in vague nationalist terms, which might or might not have been regarded as 'fascist' by those few who voted for the party. Allied to the lack of a clear ideological profile is the problem of the actual size of the NS vote in 1933, since in a number of the constituencies in which the NS put up candidates it did so in joint lists with the *Bygdefolkets krisehjelp* (Farmers' Relief Association). In some areas these joint list secured around ten per cent of the votes. This makes it difficult to establish just how many of the 28,000 votes (2.2 per cent of the votes cast) acquired by the NS-*Bygdefolkets krisehjelp* electoral alliance can be regarded as votes for the NS.[4] Although the share of the national vote was low, it was not unimpressive, given that the NS was a new party and that it put up candidates in only some forty per cent of the constituencies. A rough estimate of the NS share of the poll would suggest that in its formative stage of development the NS was electorally stronger than its Danish counterpart, the DNSAP, ever became. However, even if one excludes the votes attracted by the *Bygdefolkets krisehjelp* for the joint ticket, were all the voters of the NS 'fascist' at this stage? There were basically three groups active within the NS in 1933: firstly, an ardent Nazi circle which was strongly anti-Semitic, and which left the party in the course of 1934 to 1935; secondly, a central fascist core around Quisling, which initially denounced, but from the middle of the 1930s gradually accepted, the Nazi racial outlook; and thirdly, a Christian group, which left the party in the late 1930s in protest against the emphasis on anti-Semitism, which dominated the ideology of the NS by that stage.

By the time of the national election of 1936, in which the NS put up its candidates all over the country, the party obtained a mere 26,000 votes (1.8 per cent of the total votes cast). The disillusionment resulting from this poor performance caused bitter strife within the party's inner circle, and the NS gradually ceased to function in most of the country. When Quisling announced, at the time of the German occupation of Norway on 9 April 1940, that he had formed an NS-government, it is debatable whether the NS was still in existence. Its last general meeting before the Occupation had attracted only eight people![5] Quisling's bid for power in April 1940 came to nought since the Germans established control over the civil administration under *Reichskommissar* Joseph Terboven. In the months following the invasion, the NS was reconstructed, and its fortunes were greatly enhanced by the German declaration of 25 September 1940 that it constituted the only legally permitted party in Norway.[6] Not surprisingly, the NS formed the nucleus of a German puppet government which began functioning on the same day and which was formally installed through the 'State Act' of 1 February 1942, under which Quisling became 'Minister-President' at the head of an NS government. These developments naturally benefitted the NS movement, which expanded its field of activity during the Occupation, aided by the prohibition of all other political parties. The German authorities gave Quisling and the NS their support in the NS objective to nazify Norwegian society, a task assisted by the rapidly rising NS membership after 1940. The NS quickly began to occupy key posts in the civil service, to head and infiltrate all forms of organisations, and to control the municipal councils. Countering this process of nazification became the primary goal of the Norwegian resistance movement throughout the 1940 to 1945 period.

Of all the parties in Scandinavia who described themselves as 'fascist', those in Sweden returned the poorest election results.[7] The low returns may well have been the consequence of the organisational divisions within Swedish fascism, for by the mid-1930s there was an intense rivalry between two fascist groups headed respectively by the veterinary surgeon Birger Furugård and the former artillery sergeant Sven-Olov Lindholm. Furugård had, as early as 1924, been involved in the formation of the *Svenska Nationalsocialistiska Frihetsbundet* (SNF - Swedish National Socialist Freedom League), which imitated the early German Nazi Party. Lindholm had participated in the foundation of the *Sveriges Fascistiska Folkparti* (SFF - Swedish Fascist People's Party) in 1926. Though the SFF reflected a pronounced racist slant, it was essentially a copy of the Italian fascist model. Both of these organisations underwent a number of name changes in the 1920s until Furugård and Lindholm united their small number of followers to form the *Sveriges Nationalsocialistiska Parti* (SNP - Swedish National

Socialist Party) in 1930. The SNP was modelled on the Nazi Party and was the only Scandinavian fascist movement to establish close links with the German Nazi hierarchy in the early 1930s.

In the national election of 1932 the SNP acquired a mere 15,000 votes (0.6 per cent of the total poll), and in the following year the fragile unity established in 1930 collapsed, with Furugård remaining as the leader of a rump SNP, while Lindholm formed the *Nationalsocialistiska Arbetar-partiet* (NSAP - National Socialist Worker's Party). By the time of the 1936 national election, these two parties attracted only 20,000 votes (0.7 per cent of the total poll), 17,000 of which falling to the NSAP. It was left to Lindholm to attempt the unification of the Swedish fascist fringe in 1938 in the shape of his *Svensk Socialistisk Samling* (SSS - Swedish Socialist Unity). Lindholm attempted to endow the SSS with a more independent image, partly through the name change and partly through the use of Swedish, instead of German, symbolism. The changes did not help Lindholm's efforts to give momentum to the fascist cause in Sweden, and the SSS, after failing to participate in the national election of 1940, secured a mere 4,000 votes (0.1 per cent of the votes) in the national election of 1944. The party collapsed shortly after the end of the Second World War.

In contrast with the other Nordic states, fascism acquired a relatively strong following in Finland.[8] The Finnish variant of fascism was mainly based upon the Lapua Movement, which emerged in 1929.[9] It was characterised by a pronounced anti-Communism, which expanded into a general attack on all left-wing movement, and even on centrist parties, in the early 1930s. The widespread terrorism employed by the Lapua Movement in its political struggle had a significant impact on Finnish politics between 1929 and 1932, and the threat posed by the movement apparently even made the leading political circles apprehensive for a brief spell. The Lapua Movement, although sometimes described as 'fascist', only reflected some features of fascist ideology, but lacked any traits of anti-capitalism and did not pretend to be the vehicle for a united people's movement, so that the term 'right-extremist' is perhaps more accurate to describe its nature. Essentially an expression of rural conservatism, the Lapua Movement rapidly acquired support from all over Finland. It also secured the backing of existing right-wing parties, and in alliance with the Conservative Party and the Agrarian Union, generated the popular pressure which led to the creation of a new conservative government in 1930. The right-wing forces, after an intense election campaign, succeeded in establishing a parliamentary majority, which enforced a ban on the Finnish Communist Party. In the following year the Lapua Movement led a campaign designed to extend the ban to the Social Democratic Party as well, but when the government rejected the demand, the Lapua Movement mobilised its forces and attempted a *coup d'état*, which ended in dismal failure, leading to the total collapse of the movement by 1932.

The hard-core of the Lapua Movement joined with other extreme right-wing elements to form a political party in June 1932, the *Isänmaallinen Kansanliike* (IKL - The People's Patriotic Movement), which became increasingly fascist.[10] Unlike the Lapua Movement, which had appealed for support from the Whites who had fought the Reds in the civil war of 1918, the IKL presented itself as a party of integration, determined to heal the White-Red division within Finnish society. The IKL received strong support from students organised in the Academic Karelia Society, who managed to persuade the party to adopt a Finnification programme aimed at the abolition of the use of Swedish, which was still the language of the older, bourgeois generation in the 1930s. The language issue rapidly ended the co-operation between the younger generation active within the IKL and elements drawn from the older generation active within the conservative right, and Swedish-speaking conservatives left the party. Although the IKL presented a joint list with the Conservatives in the national election of 1933, this electoral alliance split apart in 1934, and 14 IKL supporters formed their own parliamentary group. In 1936 the party secured the re-election of the same number of MPs when, standing as an independent party, it obtained 8.3 per cent of the votes. In 1939 the share of the IKL's vote was reduced to 6.6 per cent, and the number of its MPs dropped to eight.

The comparatively better electoral performance of the Finnish fascists can, in part, be explained by reference to their ability to avoid too open an identification with other European fascist movements. Although the IKL was influenced by Italian fascist ideas, reflected in its emphasis on a corporate constitution and the hierarchical leadership principle which determined its organisational structure, the IKL developed its own ideological framework, which was coloured by Christian values. It projected a specific Finnish stance on such issues as the language question and the problem of national reconciliation. By the late 1930s the strong anti-left sentiments and the revolutionary character of the IKL became less pronounced, and in 1941 the party was willing to join a government of national unity which included the Social Democrats. The party was banned under the requirements of the armistice with the Soviet Union.

Even in Iceland, which had a population of little more than 100,000, fascism made its appearance in the shape of the Icelandic Nationalist Movement founded in 1933 (it was renamed Nationalist Party in 1934).[11] It was formed and led at first by a group of middle-aged men, but was soon taken over by younger elements and transformed into a Nazi-type party. It imitated above all the racist, eugenic teachings of the German Nazi movement, and adopted the swastika as its organisational symbol. The Icelandic Nazis fared very badly at the polls, acquiring only 0.7 per cent of the votes in 1934, and a derisory 0.2 per cent in 1937. These poor results require some qualification in that the Nationalist Party contested only three constituencies in 1934, in which its candidates secured from between 1.4 to 4.4 per cent of the votes, while in 1937 all the votes given to it came from a single constituency, in which its candidate polled 4.9 per cent of the votes cast. The party never managed to organise itself outside of Reykjavik and the south-western part of the country.

II

Two aspects which conditioned the development of fascist parties in a number of Nordic states also require elaboration: their relationship with conservative movements and their association with Christian circles.

A number of fascist parties in the Nordic countries had close ties in their formative stage of development with conservative parties. When the Finnish IKL first participated in elections in 1933, it put forward a joint list with the Conservative Party, and its elected candidates initially belonged to the conservative group in parliament until the fascist-conservative alliance broke down in 1935.

In Iceland the founders of the Nationalist Party had close ties at first with the conservative Independent Party and initially regarded their party as the activist youth organisation of the Independent Party. In Denmark, Norway and Sweden the existing youth organisations of the right were also impressed by fascism in the years following Hitler's coming to power in 1933.[12] The pro-fascist tendency among right-wing youth movements was strongest in Sweden, where the independent *Sveriges Nationella Ungdomsförbund* (SNU - Swedish National Youth League) adopted a programme in 1934 which combined traditional right-wing ideas and aspects of fascist ideology. The leaders of the SNU went so far as to form a political party of their own, which reflected fascist characteristics. Although this party only marginally exceeded the size of the SNP, its very existence helps to explain not only the limited membership attracted by the latter, but also to account for its very poor electoral performance. The more radical character of Swedish conservatism, which embraced racist ideas, provided strong competition for Swedish fascism. Although conservative parties distanced themselves from fascism in the three Scandinavian countries under review, in the case of Sweden conservatism left less space for fascism because the conservatives covered more of the relevant ideological field.

It is clear that former conservatives made up a considerable proportion of the urban supporters of fascist parties in both Denmark and Norway. Thus in Copenhagen the application forms filled in by recruits to the DNSAP, which record previous party allegiances, show that more than half of the members had belonged to conservative or conservative youth organisations.[13] The detailed analysis which we have of the results of the municipal election of 1934 in Stavanger in Norway, in which the NS secured some twelve per cent of the votes, suggests that the Nazi vote was due primarily to the losses sustained by the Conservative Party, for the returns of the various electoral districts of the town show, in comparison with previous elections, a very close and consistent correlation between NS gains and conservative losses.[14] In the municipal election in Bergen in the same year the NS and the Conservative Party even put forward a common list of candidates, despite the fact that the Conservative Party headquarters in Oslo had deemed the NS to be an unacceptable movement.[15]

The relationship between a number of Nordic fascist movements and Christian circles provides an intriguing, if complex, backcloth to the development of Nordic fascism. Although neither the Swedish or Danish Nazis - only three clerics are to be found in the membership registrations of the DNSAP - attempted to project a pro-Christian outlook, Christian circles did play a role in the development of the NS and were prominent in the history of the IKL.

In its formative years the NS contained a group of supporters led by clergymen, who apparently viewed the party as an expression of the Christian way of life and as a force which showed respect for christian values.[16] A positive outlook *vis-à-vis* Christianity did indeed characterise NS propaganda in the election campaign conducted in the run-up to the Stavanger municipal election of 1934, which probably contributed to the exceptional twelve per cent share of the votes acquired by the NS in the town. The relationship between Christian circles and the NS was not permanent, however, and from 1935 clergymen in leading positions within the party left it in response to the increasing 'nazification' of the NS by Quisling and his acceptance of anti-Semitism as part of the ideological repertoire of Norwegian fascism. The withdrawal of Christian elements undoubtedly contributed to the decline of the NS in the latter half of the 1930s and was electorally damaging to its fortunes. In Stavanger, for example, the secession of Christian supporters from the NS contributed to its collapse in the town: only 3.5 per cent of the voters opted for the NS in the national election of 1936, as against the 12 per cent which the party had secured only two years previously. However, the NS did continue to retain some clergymen within its ranks, which encouraged Quisling to try to nazify the Protestant Church during the Occupation, an attempt which ended in failure.

It was in Finland that Christianity and fascism developed a close relationship in the shape of the IKL.[17] Christian values conditioned the ideology of the IKL and IKL-agitators used both the style and language of lay preachers in their propaganda efforts, persistently attacking marxism and, to some degree, capitalism as forces inimical to biblical teachings. It has been assumed, though not conclusively proven, that the gradual decline of the IKL in the 1930s was connected with the growing scepticism of the clergy towards fascism as a whole.

Certainly the number of clergy elected as IKL MPs declined from five to one by the time of the national election of 1939.

The detailed local study on the village of Ylistaro points to a special relationship between Finnish fascism and nonconformist Christian communities.[18] In Ylistaro nonconformists not only took the initiative in forming the local IKL organisation, but provided its leadership. It would appear that the revolutionary outlook of the IKL fitted in with the general mentality of nonconformists, to whom it was a duty to 'obey God rather than man'. Nonconformists did not show the respect for the authority of the state which characterised the outlook of the adherents of the dominant Lutheran Church in Finland. However, though the IKL did secure better electoral results in predominantly nonconformist areas of Finland, the extent of its support in these areas was not so startlingly different from that secured elsewhere. We do not have sufficient evidence to conclusively prove that there was an inevitably close relationship between the success of fascism and the strength of nonconformism. The major problem is that while nonconformism was widespread among Finnish smallholders, this social group generally rejected the overtures of the IKL.

III

Popular explanations for the failure of fascism to make much of an impression on the Nordic states are often very restricted in their approach. This or that fascist party is deemed to have failed because of poor leadership or because of internal rivalries or divisions. This type of explanation begs the question as to whether the failure was due to, rather than the consequence of, internal conflicts, for internal disputes often followed in the wake of a bad electoral performance, while inadequate leadership raises the question of why a party was unable to find a more effective leader. Another common approach used to explain the failure of Nordic fascism is simply to observe that it lacked support, an explanation which does not get one very far since one might just as well say that cold weather is due to low temperature.

Any meaningful explanation of the history of fascism must be related to the general societal context within which it operated. Fascism did not emerge from nowhere, but was based on individuals who had often been previously politicised by other parties, while in the case of the younger age groups one can assume that a considerable proportion of these would have been mobilised by existing political forces. Since political preference is based on choice between competing political parties, it has to be explained by considering all of them, for poor products might well be saleable in a market which contains only shoddy goods, while good products might well be rejected if even better ones are available.

In all but one of the Nordic countries fascism came face to face with well-established constitutional systems based on democratic values. Denmark had acquired its first progressive constitution, based on the principle of universal adult male suffrage for the election of the Second Chamber, in 1849. In 1915 this principle was extended to cover the election of the First Chamber, while the franchise was extended to women as well. Iceland, which was part of the Danish kingdom until 1918, mirrored this development pattern. The Norwegian constitution dated back to 1814, and full suffrage for men was introduced in 1899, and for women in 1913. In Sweden the somewhat conservative constitution of 1866 was liberalised step by step, and universal suffrage for men was granted in 1909, and for women in 1921. Finland provides the exception to the gradual democratisation process discernable in the Nordic states from the late nineteenth century. As part of the Russian tsarist autocracy, Finland only acquired a democratic constitution when it was granted its independence by the Soviet Union in 1918. Part of the explanation for the relatively greater strength acquired by fascism in Finland may well relate to the fact that it was operating within a newly formed democracy. In Finland fascism competed with democratic political forces which were also newcomers to the political arena, parties which lacked the weight of tradition to effectively withstand the fascist wave. The comparatively late emergence of democracy in Finland probably conditioned one other feature of political behaviour which differentiates Finland from other Nordic states: electoral participation was significantly lower than elsewhere in Scandinavia. In the inter-war period around 80 per cent of the Danish and Norwegian electorate exercised their right to vote, while in Sweden the number of voters participating in elections averaged out at around the 70 per cent mark. In Finland, however, only some 55 per cent of the electorate took part in the elections of the 1920s and 1930s.[19]

In the three Scandinavian kingdoms decenniums of constitutional struggle had left their mark on the political consciousness of the electorate. It was only after prolonged and bitter strife that the hallmark of parliamentarianism - the obligation of the Crown to form governments which enjoyed majority support in the Second Chamber - was victorious. This principle was established in 1884 in Norway, in 1901 in Denmark, and in 1906 in the case of Sweden. The fact that the struggle for parliamentarianism in these states was led by agrarian parties is of importance. The rural population, which was to be subjected to the severest pressure in the economic crisis of the 1930s, had demonstrated a strong commitment to democratic values for a considerable time. In the period following the First World War the acceptance of democracy was generally no longer the subject of dispute, and the parties of the right which had lost the struggle to halt democratisation, broadly accepted the new situation. This is not to ignore the marked difference in outlook between the Swedish Conservatives, who continued to adhere to their conservative attitudes, and their Danish counterparts who, in their eagerness to demonstrate their democratic nature, even joined the Social Democrats in 1939 in an attempt to have the First Chamber abolished.

It is tempting to accept the argument advanced by many historians that fascism failed in the Scandinavian kingdoms because their democratic structures enjoyed strong support. However, fascism was something new and not part of a traditional political order, and it can be argued that its very novelty gave it an advantage since opposition to democracy could not be channelled through alternative political ideologies. In this context the very poor performance of fascism in Sweden is perhaps illuminating. There is reason to believe that the relative failure of Swedish fascism was the consequence of the competition which it encountered in the shape of the established Swedish right, which had a number of ideological features in common with fascism, including a form of anti-Semitism.

A decisive factor working against the growth of fascism was the ability of the Nordic political systems not only to uphold the democratic order, but even to improve it during the crisis situation of the 1930s. The major political development in the

Nordic states after the First World War was the integration of workers' movements into society, and the progress made by socialist parties, primarily in the shape of the Social Democrats. It was only in Finland that the communists secured a sizeable following, whereas elsewhere, especially in Denmark and Norway, they were as marginal as the fascists.

The first governments led by Social Democrats took office for short periods in Sweden, Denmark and Norway during the 1920s. In 1929 a coalition government headed by Social Democrats took over in Denmark, which remained in power until the German occupation in 1940, when it was succeeded by a national coalition government in which Social Democrats still provided the leadership. From 1932 the Swedish Social Democrats led similar coalition governments until the war, when the government was expanded to include the major opposition parties as well. In 1938 the Swedish Social Democratic Party became the first socialist party in Europe to secure more than fifty per cent of the votes. In Norway the Social Democrats were also able to establish a stable government in 1935, while the relatively weaker Finnish Social Democratic Party joined a coalition for the first time in 1937.

These social-democratic governments did not, as prophesied and anticipated by the conservatives, effect a social revolution. On the contrary, the strengthening of the socialist movements furthered social compromise. When the depression set in in the late 1920s, the economic difficulties of the day were tackled by socialist-led governments in a pragmatic fashion. With the possible exception of the Swedish Social Democratic Party, no political movement of any importance advocated Keynesian measures to overcome the crisis, and government policies were generally restricted to social measures designed to help those who were most badly affected by the recession. In the first instance this meant giving assistance to farmers and to unemployed workers, and as a consequence most of the political compromises were made between the agrarian and social-democratic parties.

Of course, tensions between the right and the left still played a considerable role in political consciousness, but the compromises reached did allow the political systems to function throughout the depression era, a development which demonstrated the vitality of democracy. Thus the fascist thesis that dictatorship was necessary to overcome class antagonisms and to create national unity, was proven to be false in the Nordic states. The spirit of compromise and moderation extended beyond the political arena to the labour market. The number of working days lost by strikes or lock-outs in all of the Nordic countries went down in the 1930s to less than half the number recorded in the previous decade.[20]

IV

In broad terms the Nordic economies were not too badly affected by the depression which hit Europe in the late 1920s. The main reason for this was that the bulk of industry was geared to meet the demands of the home market and was favoured by protectionist policies. There were, however, some important exceptions provided by industries dependent on export markets, and both the Swedish iron industry and the Scandinavian ship-building industry in general, were adversely affected. Shipping also suffered due to the decline in international trade. But the major impact of the crisis fell on the primary sector, and especially those parts dependent on foreign markets. Agriculture in Denmark, forestry in Norway, Sweden and Finland, as well as the fishing industry in Iceland and Norway were all hit by the decline in export opportunities.

Although the economic crisis did not reach the acute form it took in comparatively highly industrialised states such as Germany, the difficulties experienced by the Nordic states nevertheless did create an adverse economic climate which could be exploited by fascist parties. Local studies available to us do suggest that there was a direct relationship between the severity of the depression and the growth of fascism. Of the Scandinavian towns, Stavanger in Norway and Gothenburg in Sweden stand apart as fascist strongholds. In the municipal election of 1934 in Stavanger, no less than 12 per cent of the votes were given to the NS, while in the national election of 1932 the Swedish Nazis obtained their best result, namely 5.7 per cent of the votes, in Gothenburg. Although these results might be explained by reference to particular local political circumstances, it is probably no coincidence that these two towns headed the national unemployment tables for Norway and Sweden respectively. Both towns were very badly hit by the depression since Stavanger was virtually dependent for its economic vitality on shipping, while shipping and ship-building were crucial for the Gothenburg economy.[21]

A similar correlation between the strength of fascism and the gravity of the economic crisis can be detected when one examines a number of rural fascist strongholds in Denmark, Norway and Sweden.[22] In Denmark the DNSAP did comparatively well in the rural districts of North Schleswig, an area which had been part of Germany until 1920. This was a region in which much money had been poured into the dairy industry in the 1920s, capital investment which became increasingly difficult to service when dairy prices declined in the early 1930s. As a consequence of increasing numbers of bankruptcies, the area recorded the highest number of forced sales of farms in Denmark. In Norway and Sweden two neighbouring districts on either side of the border, East Inland and Värmland, recorded the highest Nazi vote. These were areas in which forestry was the mainstay of the local economies, a sector of economic activity largely dependent on the export of timber and wood-pulp, which was hard-hit by the economic crisis. Although similar local studies are virtually totally lacking in the case of Finland, it may be significant that Ostrobothnia in western Finland, a stronghold of both the Lapua Movement and of the IKL, was also a forest district. However, the sole local study that we have, which deals with the village of Ylistaro in Ostrobothnia, broadly suggests that both the village and the region as a whole may not have been as badly affected by the economic crisis as many other parts of Finland.[23]

There are problems in demonstrating that a direct experience of economic difficulties was a major general factor behind the growth of fascism in the 1930s. The evidence available is contradictory and far from conclusive. In Norway, for example, the isolated Western Country district near Bergen, where the local economy produced primarily for the local market and was hardly touched by the economic crisis, recorded the lowest NS returns in the 1930s.[24] Yet in a number of quite prosperous towns also largely untouched by the recession, the NS was comparatively well-supported. In Denmark and Norway the geographical distribution of foreclosures in agriculture does broadly correspond with the strength of agrarian fascism, whereas in Finland we do not have any evidence as yet of a similar connection. It is significant, however, that an association of farmers formed to counter the forced sales of farms in Finland, opposed both the Lapua

Movement and the IKL. The expected positive correlation between people occupied in the primary sector and the fascist vote has been investigated for Denmark, Norway and Sweden, but the results are contradictory.[25] Whereas a positive correlation was found in Denmark only for the 1935 and 1939 elections, it turned out to be very small at .12, while a study of the 1936 election in Norway produced a negative correlation of -.23.

V

Detailed information on the social make-up of the rank-and-file membership of Nordic fascist parties is confined to the DNSAP and the NS, the files of which were confiscated following the end of the German occupation, to be used subsequently in the post-war trials of collaborators. The type of data these files provide - albeit that the data presents methodological and interpretational difficulties - is lacking as regards the various fascist movements active in Sweden, Finland and Iceland, and in the quest to identify the social groups drawn towards fascism in these states one is forced to draw inferences from the electoral performance of the fascist parties operating in these states. Obviously the use of such electoral data at best only allows one to identify the social profile of fascism in the broadest of terms, but in the absence of any more specific material, one is forced to resort to such an approach, which does not always get one very far, given the often very low electoral returns of the Nordic fascist parties. We know virtually nothing about the sociology of the Swedish and Finnish fascist movements and not even a qualified guess on their social composition is at hand as yet.

The confiscated files relating to the DNSAP contain the application forms filled in by some 39,000 members at the time of their entry into the party for the period 1930 to 1945. Of the registered party members a ten per cent sample of male members aged eighteen and over has been analysed (see Table 4.2.). For comparative purposes the result of the 1940 census - based on the male population aged eighteen and over - is also given. Since very few pensioners joined the DNSAP, the 1940 census breakdown without this group has been added in parenthesis.

The data in Table 4.2 provides only a tentative picture of the actual social composition of the

Table 4.2: Members joining the DNSAP according to period of recruitment and by occupational group, 1930-45 (by %)

Occupational subgroup	1930-35	1936-39	1940	1941	1942	1943	1944-45	Average 1930-45	Census 1940
Agricultural workers	27.5	26.4	10.0	13.0	10.1	7.6	-	15.9	12.3 (13.7)
Unskilled workers	6.1	10.6	16.6	24.9	29.5	37.4	36.0	18.6	19.0 (20.5)
Skilled workers	15.5	16.4	22.6	22.0	22.9	27.5	10.0	20.3	14.0 (15.5)
Self-employed	28.6	24.3	26.4	15.9	13.7	6.1	-	21.2	27.8 (30.8)
Civil servants	18.4	20.0	22.1	22.0	17.0	16.0	10.0	19.9	15.7 (17.4)
Pensioners	0.8	0.6	0.7	0.4	0.9	0.8	-	0.7	9.9
Others/no data	3.1	1.7	1.5	1.8	5.9	4.6	44.0	3.4	1.5 (1.7)
Total (%)	100	100	100	100	100	100	100	100	100
Frequency (*N*)	510	470	806	554	454	131	50	2,975	

Source: M. Djursaa, *DNSAP-danske nazister 1930-1945* (2 vols., Copenhagen, 1981), vol. 2, pp. 100-101.

DNSAP membership at any one time during the 1930 to 1945 period. One problem is that there are few reliable figures as to the actual number of members in the party at any specific stage of its development. We do know from the audit of party membership dues that the DNSAP had 2,740 registered members in April 1937, while the number of membership registrations by 1937 stood at around 8,500, figures which reflect a very high membership turn-over in the party's formative years of development, for only approximately one-third of known members were still in the party at the time the audit was made. By April 1939 the membership total was probably between 4,000 and 5,000, but it rose quite significantly by the time of the 1943 elections, when the DNSAP membership reached its peak at around the 21,000 mark.[26] Other evidence suggests that members drawn from higher occupational groups stayed in the party much longer than members drawn from lower status categories.[27] This suggests that the higher status groups made up a larger percentage of the actual membership than is indicated by their share of party entries given in Table 4.2.

Important also is the age-group distribution of the membership. The bulk of the DNSAP's members at the time of their entry into the party were very young. Of the 2,975 members analysed in Table 4.2, only thirty per cent were over thirty-five-years old.[28] The fact that the DNSAP attracted above all the younger generation may well be the reason for the underrepresentation of the self-employed category in the party when compared with the 1940 census returns (though the latter are based on the total male population aged eighteen-years and over), while the overrepresentation of agricultural workers - mostly farmhands - most probably is. There is, unfortunately, no way of testing these hypotheses, since the census of 1940 does not provide details on the age-profile of the various occupational groups.

An insight into the social structure of the rank-and-file membership of the NS is provided by the register of 55,000 persons who were NS members during the German occupation period, who were subsequently tried for collaboration after the war. Given that the NS party organisation - as noted earlier - had virtually disintegrated by the late 1930s, the information which we have on the pre-war membership is restricted to those who renewed their membership at some time following the reconstruction of the NS in 1940, that is a total of 2,700 individuals, who undoubtedly formed but a small fraction of the pre-1940 membership. These 2,700 re-registered members can be described as the hardcore of the pre-war NS, but the occupational status of these members may well be quite unrepresentative of the early NS membership. The occupational composition of the pre-1940 membership is given in Table 4.3, which is based on the male members aged twenty-three-years and over (for comparative purposes the 1930 census returns are also provided, though these relate to the male population aged twenty-one-years and over).[29]

Although the NS was able to attract a considerable number of young people into its ranks, it was not as pronounced a party of youth as was the DNSAP. Some 49 per cent of the NS members were aged thirty-five-years and over at the time of their recruitment.[30] A further contrast between the DNSAP and the NS was that the latter recruited more and more of its members from rural areas. Whereas only 39.8 per cent of the NS membership was resident in rural areas in the period 1933 to 1939, the figure increased to 53.5 per cent between 1941 and 1945.[31] In terms of the occupational background of the membership of the DNSAP and the NS, although there are some similarities, it is the differences which are more striking. Skilled workers are over-represented in the membership of both parties (in comparison with the respective occupational break-down of the working population of Norway and Denmark), unskilled workers are markedly under-represented in the NS membership, while workers as a whole are overrepresented in the DNSAP. More striking still is the obvious overrepresentation of civil servants within the NS.

The most surprising feature of the membership structure of the DNSAP is the overrepresentation of both unskilled and skilled workers during the Occupation period. There is a problem here concerning the skilled worker category: a person who described himself as a 'smith' or as a 'painter' is registered in the skilled workers subgroup, when in reality some of these may well have been self-employed. More detailed information (which is not at hand) might well have resulted in the reduction of the size of the skilled workers subgroup and a corresponding increase of the self-employed subgroup. The growing number of workers who joined the DNSAP during the Occupation can be seen as the consequence of the urbanisation of the party. Whereas only half of the members were resident in towns in the 1930s, the share rose to 80 per cent

Table 4.3: The composition of the membership of the NS according to occupational status, 1940-45 (by %)

Occupational subgroup	9 April 1940	1 Jan. 1941	1 Jan. 1945	Average 1940-45	Census 1930
Unskilled and agricultural workers	9.5	15.8	20.4	20.4	37.0
Skilled workers	10.2	10.1	11.4	11.6	8.0
Lower and intermediate employees	12.7	11.7	10.0	10.0	6.0
Engineers/technicians	5.2	2.8	2.4	2.5	0.5
Traders (self-employed)	5.8	4.4	3.8	3.9	3.5
Farmers (self-employed)	15.8	20.6	22.4	20.4	16.0
Lower and intermediate civil servants	7.8	12.5	10.5	11.8	5.0
Higher civil servants	14.1	8.3	6.7	6.9	0.5
Frequency (*N*)	1,352	15,101	20,231	25,224	

Source: M. Djursaa, *DNSAP-danske nazister 1930-1945* (2 vols., Copenhagen, 1981), vol. 1, pp. 174-5.

during the Occupations years.[32] The influx of a growing number of workers into the DNSAP, which significantly altered its social profile after 1940, is confirmed in a detailed analysis of its membership in Copenhagen, as well as by the electoral performance of the party in the capital in the 1943 national election, when it secured the bulk of its votes in the working-class districts rather than the more well-to-do areas of the city, a reversal of the pre-1940 situation.[33]

In comparison with the DNSAP, workers were underrepresented in the NS, though they did provide between a quarter to one-third of its membership during the Occupation, a period in which the proportion of workers in the party increased by more than thirty per cent in comparison with the pre-1940 period.[34] Workers did, however, dominate the membership in one of the strongholds of the party: the East Inland region, in which forestry dominated the economy, an area in which the NS achieved its best electoral results in 1936, obtaining 8.5 per cent and 7.6 per cent of the votes in the communes of Trysil and Elverum respectively.[35] In both places workers made up a high proportion of the known NS membership in the 1930s (in Trysil almost three out of four members were workers) and the local party organisations were both founded and led by workers.

In Trysil and Elverum, and in East Inland in general, the working-class support enjoyed by the NS came primarily from forestry workers organised in independent or 'yellow' trade unions. The latter were formed in 1927 - at a time of growing unemployment as the international crisis began to affect the forestry industry - and were backed by those forestry workers who were not prepared to support the strike action of those forestry workers who were members of socialist-led unions. The supporters of the yellow trade unions lost out when the forest owners decided to accept the socialist unions as contract partners in 1928. This development left the supporters of the yellow trade unions in a position of bitter antagonism towards both the employers and the socialist unions, in an ideal position therefore to be attracted by a party which was hostile to both capitalism and marxism. Significantly, at the national level, leaders of the yellow trade unions were to be among the founders of the NS in 1933.

The examples of Trysil and Elverum provide evidence for a possible explanation as to why workers were drawn towards the NS. The support can be seen as a reaction by workers against (socialist) trades unions directed by an often unknown hierarchy at the national level: inclusion in these was viewed by some forestry workers as a threat to their independence and an attack on their local autonomy. Moreover, a sense of proletarian consciousness among the forestry workers in the East Inland was hardly developed. They simply did not view themselves as workers oppressed by employers. As lumberjacks engaged in a high-risk occupation, they were pround and independent spirits, aware of their ability. Even if a large number of them did ultimately connect with the tendency of the mainstream of the working class to join national labour organisations, it is easy to understand why a not insignificant number of them decided to join a party which was in marked opposition to the growing labour movement.

It is difficult, however, to develop from the example of the behaviour of the forestry workers in the East Inland region a general theory which would explain the attraction of workers by the NS. The propensity of forestry workers in Trysil and Elverum to give their support to yellow trade unions and to the NS probably relates to local factors. Elsewhere in Norway workers shied away from giving any significant support to either of these movements. The highest number of workers claimed by the yellow trade unions before they were dissolved in 1936 was only 5,000. Significantly in Denmark this form of unionism was practically non-existent. Opposition to the socialist labour movement, of course, may have paved the way to fascism without the stepping-stone provided by yellow trade unions, but then it would be more reasonable to expect working-class support for fascism to have been more prominent in Norway than in Denmark since the Norwegian labour movement was more radical than its Danish equivalent. But the reverse was the case for, as noted earlier, workers were underrepresented in the NS and overrepresented in the DNSAP. The theory that pronounced anti-socialism was a significant factor in generating working-class support for fascism is difficult to sustain in the case of the DNSAP. Members joining the DNSAP were invariably asked if they had previously belonged to a political party and the bulk of the working-class members of the party usually described themselves as former social democrats or communists, while only approximately ten per cent indicated that they had previously given their support to liberal or conservative movements.[36] There are no reasons to believe that workers who were active in the DNSAP were in any way untypical of their social surroundings.

Explaining why Danish workers joined the DNSAP in relatively large numbers - a feature which is quite untypical of fascist movements as a whole - remains a problem. It has to be noted, however, that this was not a general phenomenon of the DNSAP throughout its entire history, but a special trend which marked the German occupation period. The economic situation in which the Danish workers were placed during the Occupation is probably the key to an understanding of the ability of the DNSAP to mobilise significant working-class support. For the Danish economy, the war and the Occupation resulted not only in the loss of imported raw materials essential for the smooth-running of the economy, but also led to the curtailment of investment in industry as a whole, particularly in the construction industry. This caused heavy unemployment in the urban centres, and tens of thousands of Danish workers were recruited to work in Germany, even though Denmark was exempted from the conscription of forced labour generally enforced by the Germans in other parts of occupied Europe. The DNSAP was given special facilities to agitate among the Danish workers in Germany, and was able to provide such inducements as offering free cinema tickets to party members. The party files contain indications that many new members joined the DNSAP while they were working in Germany. The advantages to be had through the DNSAP - rather than any real ideological conviction - probably persuaded workers to join the party. This would explain another feature of working-class membership: workers stayed in the party for a much shorter duration than members from other social groups, resulting in a high turn-over rate in working-class membership, with the result that the overrepresentation of workers among party entrants distorts the actual size of the working-class presence within the DNSAP in the early 1940s, which was lower than the figures available actually suggest.[37]

It would seem from the detailed analysis of the East Inland example that workers might join a fascist movement as a reaction to the growing strength of socialist-led organisations, while the DNSAP's ability to recruit workers can be explained primarily in terms of pure opportunism. Social or economic interests do not seem to explain the working-class recruitment to fascism in Norway and Denmark.

If the overrepresentation of workers is the striking feature of the DNSAP's membership, the most noticeable aspect of the membership of the NS is the overrepresentation of civil servants. The heavy overrepresentation of civil servants in the NS - a feature which is less marked in the case of the DNSAP's social profile - raises the question as to whether fascism generally had a special attraction for this occupational group, a question which must be tackled with caution. The strong presence of civil servants within the NS, and especially the high overrepresentation of higher civil servants during the Occupation, may essentially be put down to opportunism. The elevation of the NS to the position of being the sole legal political party in Norway in September 1940 was followed by serious attempts to nazify the administration, and even if this does not allow one to speak of an enforced enrolment of civil servants into the NS, 'persuasion' was undoubtedly accompanied by implied threats. It would seem that many civil servants thought it wise to become members of the NS in order to protect their jobs and to ensure the 'integrity' of their particular branch of the civil service. Here one can cite the example of the Oslo police force, half of which decided to join the NS in the autumn of 1940, including some individuals who were executed at a later date for resistance activity.[38] There is a problem, however, in explaining the overrepresentation of civil servants, and especially of higher civil servants, in the NS merely by reference to opportunism. It is undoubtedly a critical factor determining their behaviour following the occupation of Norway in April 1940, but it cannot explain the relatively large number of civil servants who had been party members before 1940. In the case of higher civil servants, membership of the NS seems to have been even greater before 1940 than during the Occupation period. The column headed '9 April 1940' in Table 4.3 includes all those who had been members of the NS at some time before that date and who renewed their membership at some time thereafter. The higher civil servants subgroup accounts for a staggering 14 per cent of this re-enrolled membership, whereas the subgroup made up but 0.5 per cent of the population. Even if one bears in mind the problem of the representative nature of the pre-1940 membership data, and if one works on the assumption that individuals belonging to occupational groups which were most prone to becoming NS members during the

Occupation probably renewed their membership more frequently than members drawn from subgroups which were less strongly represented, the conclusion is inescapable that the NS had a special attraction to civil servants, and to the higher grades in particular. Although the reasons for this strong attraction have not been analysed by historians as yet, it is probable that these relate to a general fascist tendency to be found among former conservatives who, as we have noted earlier, tended to lend their support to the NS in its formative stage of development. The similarly marked overrepresentation of engineers and of technicians in the NS is perhaps also due to their former conservative background, even if it is remarkable that directors and managers are only slightly overrepresented within this occupational group.[39]

The extent to which civil servants were attracted to fascism in Norway and Denmark does show a difference. Although civil servants were also prominent within the DNSAP membership, their slight overrepresentation would most likely disappear if the age distribution of civil servants active in the DNSAP is taken into account. In comparison with the age profile of the working population as a whole, civil servants who belonged to the DNSAP were, on average, much younger. The different rate of response to fascism by civil servants in the two countries may be due to the fact that they were a more marginal group in Norwegian society. Although civil servants represented a new and numerically expanding element in both societies, they were badly organised in Norway and less integrated into the established party system. On the whole civil servants did not consider themselves to be a special class within society. It is reasonable to argue that such a group - or to be more accurate a small section of it - was attracted to new movements, including fascism.

The factor which may account for the relative failure of the DNSAP - in contrast to the NS - to attract civil servants into its ranks in large numbers, is that in Denmark both the Social Democrats and the Conservatives paid special attention to the interests of the civil servants. Thus in 1938, for example, a law was passed which regulated the working conditions of the civil servants in a most favourable way. Another factor conditioning the different rate of response by civil servants in the two states may be the rural character of Danish fascism in its early years. As can be seen in the recruitment pattern of civil servants entering the DNSAP in Table 4.2, the percentage of civil servants grew as the party became more urbanised in the late 1930s and in the first two years of the Occupation. However, since we do not have any systematic studies on the relationship between civil servants and the DNSAP and the NS, the suggestions advanced above to explain the different recruitment patterns of civil servants remain hypothetical. What the data on the NS, and to a lesser extent on the DNSAP, does clearly show is the susceptibility of civil servants to fascism in certain circumstances.

As noted in section IV, the reaction of the agrarian population to fascism has to be measured against the background of the general economic crisis of the early 1930s. But the question of how, and to what extent, the crisis generated fascist support among the rural population is complicated since it also gave rise to other agrarian protest movements which were not fascist in nature.

Danish agriculture was hit severely by the crisis due to its heavy reliance on export markets. Farmers had been prosperous for decades and had acquired a strong belief in their own ability to overcome economic difficulties by accommodating themselves to the requirements of the world markets. Consequently the dominating political outlook among Danish farmers was a liberal one. This placed the agrarian parties and organisations in a difficult position when the crisis began to affect Danish agriculture in 1931. They could hardly ask the state - represented by the Social Democratic government - for subsidies since they had always claimed that these were harmful to the economy. The severity of the crisis, however, spawned a protest movement in the shape of the *Landbrugernes Sammenslutning* (LS - Union of Farmers), which may have had the support of about half of the farming community in the early 1930s. The LS was not a political party as such, but more of a pressure group of disgruntled farmers, and the DNSAP made a major effort to become its political mouthpiece.[40] But the fascist overtures were countered by the formation of a new agrarian party, the *Bondepartiet* (Agrarian Party) in 1934. A keen rivalry for the rural vote developed between the DNSAP and the Agrarian Party in subsequent elections. Although the DNSAP was able to increase its vote in rural areas in the national election held in the autumn of 1935 - in comparison with its performance in the local elections held in the spring of that year - it was unable to do so in the county of Lolland-Falster, where the Agrarian Party, which had not taken part in the local elections, now made clearly observable gains at the expense of the DNSAP. The competition between the parties did not, however, affect the situation in the rural areas of the province of North Schleswig, a stronghold of the DNSAP by the mid-1930s. In this area the Danish Nazis were firmly entrenched from the early 1930s and were successfully contesting elections from 1932. Based on an efficient organisation, the DNSAP was able to counter the agitation of the Agrarian Party in North Schleswig, the latter remaining weak as a consequence.

The DNSAP was primarily a rural movement in the 1930s and exploited the agrarian crisis to generate support, but it was never able to lead or dominate the agrarian population in its entirety, even if it was able to secure pockets of relatively strong support in some rural parts of Denmark. The party membership files indicate a slight overrepresentation of owners of large and medium-sized farming units within the DNSAP's membership - at least until the mid-1930s - while relatively few smallholders are to be found within its ranks.[41] The same pattern is assumed to pertain to the NS, though the imbalance in the recruitment pattern of farmers is less obvious since the information on membership only provides evidence on those farmers who joined the NS during the war.[42] In Sweden only the fascist stronghold of the forest district of Värmland shows evidence of significant agrarian support for the Swedish fascist movement, while in Finland the fascists were associated with the anti-communist Lapua Movement, but not with the agrarian protest organisations formed by indebted farmers.[43] In both countries agriculture essentially produced to meet the demands of the home market, which meant that existing parties and agrarian organisations traditionally acted as interest groups in relation to the state. Since they continued to fulfil this function during the crisis, the political space left open to new agrarian movements was restricted.

As far as the pattern of agrarian support for fascism in the Nordic states is concerned, the most unusual pattern developed in Norway, where agrarian support for the NS appears to have reached its peak during the war, at a time when the growing demand for food made Norwegian agriculture - and this applies to European agriculture generally -

increasingly prosperous. In Norway self-employed farmers increased their share of the membership of the NS (see Table 4.3) from around 16 per cent in April 1940 to some 22 per cent by the end of the Occupation. The Norwegian situation is in stark contrast to that prevalent in Denmark, where agrarian support for the DNSAP declined in the late 1930s when the agrarian crisis eased, to decline still further during the Occupation, when agriculture returned to prosperity. Thus while self-employed farmers made up some 16 per cent of the male membership of the DNSAP in January 1940 - fractionally more that their share of the male adult working population - by 1945 they accounted for only 10 per cent.[44]

VI

Historians dealing with Nordic fascism have generally devoted much of their energy to answering the question 'Why did fascism have so little success in the Nordic countries?'. Few have attempted to provide an answer to the opposite question 'Why did fascism have any followers at all?'. It has usually been considered as unsurprising that a movement which dominated Germany in the 1930s should also secure a share of the political spectra in small neighbouring states. And perhaps this may indeed suffice as a general explanation. However, such an approach ignores the question of the peculiar attraction of fascism. The tens of thousands of Scandinavians who joined fascist parties did not do so simply by circumstance or accident. They were not political novices who made their choice regardless of their former political convictions, or people who decided to join a fascist movement simply because they happened to attend a fascist meeting. Fascism must in some way have had an appeal to its followers, and fascist parties must, at some point, have projected a message which coincided with the essential features of a general view of society held by their supporters.

Scandinavian historians tend to emphasise the anti-modernist aspect of fascist ideology as the reason behind the general attraction of fascism. Norwegian historians in particular have placed a special emphasis on anti-modernism as the main factor which generated support for the Quisling movement.[45] Their arguments are based on the view that those supporting the NS regarded it as vehicle which would re-establish a traditional form of society. The theory is based on the observation that the NS fared best in those districts of Norway in which traditional ideals were still strongly entrenched in the inter-war era, areas in which the patriarchal family unit still dominated relationships and in which there was no organised form of modern class relationships. The theory is, moreover, further sustained by reference to the close relationship between conservatism and nascent fascism observable in all of the Nordic countries. It would seem that fascism was in accord with the main ideological value system prevalent in Nordic society.

In the relatively small Nordic states nationalism took on a special form. Imperialism was out of the question for obvious reasons and was generally replaced by romanticism. Nordic nationalism was exploited in the propaganda of fascist parties, which emphasised Nordic mythology, the cult of the heroic past, and the (presumed) need for a united people led by a single outstanding leader. Political issues as such played an astonishingly modest role in fascist agitation. The racial theories propagated by the Nordic fascists - which included forms of anti-Semitism - were most often presented as evidence of the special inherited values of the Nordic peoples. Even though the fascists claimed that they were committed to the formation of a new society by destroying the hated marxist and capitalist 'system', their vision of a new and truly national society was based essentially on past models.

There are some problems surrounding the utility of the theory of anti-modernism as the general, or at least as the dominant, factor behind the appeal of fascism. It is true that in Norway the strong presence of higher civil servants in the NS - in contrast to the more limited support given to it by industrialists - can be interpreted as a reaction to modernity by the old upper class. But how can one account for the strong support given to the NS by white-collar workers? And why should anti-modernism have had a special appeal to young people, who were generally prominent elements in the membership of fascist parties, especially in Denmark?

In explaining the attraction of fascism in the Nordic states one should emphasise not just its anti-modernism, which was dominant in the formative phase of its evolution when fascist parties were closely connected with existing movements of the right and even with Christian circles, but also its growing dependence on the model provided by Nazi Germany, which became noticeable in its later phase of development. The Nazi model did include some anti-modernist ideological features, but it also projected the image of a very modern, industrialised and efficient society of a new type. In the general political debates of the 1930s the meaning of the words 'Nazi' and 'fascist' was not formed by the programmes of the tiny Nordic fascist movements, but by the general image which Germany and Italy had at the time.

In Denmark the fascist leadership always took care to be in step with the actual developments unfolding in Germany. In the DNSAP the early emphasis on corporativism was soon superseded by the call for the creation of a dictatorship; the abolition of capitalist interests was soon forgotten when the capitalist system survived Hitler's seizure of power. In Norway Quisling began by denouncing anti-Semitism, but then quickly accepted it even at the price of losing the Christian wing of his movement. How can one account for this aping of National Socialist ideology? These changes were, after all, criticised even within party circles as signs of a lack of national independence.

The most plausible answer is that fascist leaders such as Quisling, Clausen and Lindholm knew that most of their followers were essentially followers of Hitler. They all tried hard to get some sort of official recognition of their positions from the German Nazi Party because they considered themselves to be leaders of national branches of the general Nazi Movement. This position left them with little room to cultivate their own ideas.

At the present stage of research into Nordic fascism the argument outlined above should be viewed as a hypothesis based on a general impression derived from my analysis of the party propaganda and the internal party discussions which took place in Nordic fascist parties, especially in the DNSAP. If it is difficult to perceive what the general public image of the German Nazis was in the Nordic states, it is even more difficult to ascertain that of the Scandinavian fascists. Having declared themselves to be fascists or Nazis, Scandinavians could no longer act in a truly independent fashion: they had to become Hitler's Scandinavian followers.

Notes

1. *K. O. Chrisiansen, Mandlige landssvigere i Danmark under Besaettelsen* (Copenhagen, 1950).
2. On the history of the DNSAP see H. Poulsen, *Besaettelsesmagten og de danske nazister* (Copenhagen, 1970) - it contains a summary in German.
3. A general history of the NS is still not available. On the foundation and first years of the party see H. O. Brevig, *NS - fra parti til sekt, 1933-37* (Oslo, 1970). Specific aspects of the party's development are contained in R. Danielson and S. U. Larsen (eds.), *Fra idé til dom. Noen trekk fra uitviklingen av Nasjonal Samling* (Bergen, 1976). On the Quisling regime during the German occupation see especially T. C. Wyller, *Nyordning og motstand: en framstilling og en analyse av organisasjonenes politiske funksjon under den Tyske okkupasjonen 25.9.1940-25.9.1942* (Oslo, 1958).
4. The electoral performance of the NS is evaluated by S. S. Nilson, 'Who voted for Quisling' and by H-D. Loock, 'Support for Nasjonal Samling in the Thirties' in S. U. Larsen a. o. (eds.), *Who were the Fascists? Social Roots of European Fascism* (Bergen-Oslo-Tromsø, 1980), pp. 657-66 and 667-76.
5. Loock in Larsen, *Who were the Fascists?*, p. 669.
6. Cf. S. U. Larsen, 'The social foundations of Norwegian Fascism 1933-1945' in idem, *Who were the Fascists?*, pp. 599-600.
7. On the history of fascism in Sweden see E. Wärenstam, *Fascismen och nazismen i Sverige* (Uppsala, 1972). See also B. Hagtvet, 'On the fringe: Swedish Fascism 1920-45' in Larsen, *Who were the Fascists?*, pp. 715-42.
8. For a brief review of the development of Finnish fascism see R. Alapuro, 'Mass support for fascism in Finland' in Larsen, *Who were the Fascists?*, pp. 678-86.
9. A detailed evaluation of the Lapua Movement is provided by R. Alapuro and E. Allardt, 'The Lapua Movement: the threat of rightist takeover in Finland, 1930-1932' in J. J. Linz and A. Stepan (eds.), *The Breakdown of Democratic regimes: Europe* (Baltimore, 1978), pp. 122-41.
10. For the following see R. E. Heinonen, 'From people's movement to minor party: the People's

Patriotic Movement (IKL) in Finland, 1932-1944' in Larsen, *Who were the Fascists?*, pp. 687-701.

11. The marginality of Icelandic fascism is reflected in the paucity of works on the subject. Beyond the old study by J. Adils, *Markmid Flokks thjódernissinna* (Reykjavik, 1939), there is a recent brief overview provided by A. Gudmundsson, 'Nazism in Iceland' in Larsen, *Who were the Fascists?*, pp. 743-50.
12. For the following see U. Lindström, *Fascism in Scandinavia 1920-1940* (Stockholm, 1985), pp. 144-54.
13. M. Djursaa, *DNSAP - Danske Nazister 1930-1945* (2 vols., Copenhagen, 1981), vol. 2, p. 140.
14. Nilson in Larsen, *Who were the Fascists?*, pp. 658-60.
15. Loock in Larsen, *Who were the Fascists?*, p. 670.
16. For the following see D. O. Bruknapp, 'Ideene splitter partiet' in Danielson and Larsen (eds.), *Fra idé til dom*, pp. 9-47; S. U. Larsen, 'Med korset mot hammeren' in I. Montgomery and S. U. Larsen (eds.), *Kirken, Krisen og Krigen* (Bergen-Oslo-Tromsø, 1982), pp. 279-92.
17. See Heinonen in Larsen, *Who were the Fascists?*, pp. 694-6.
18. K. Ihmanen (ed.), *Kansanliikkeitten Pohjanmaa* (1982). Cf. G. Djupsund and L. Karvonen, *Fascismen i Finland. Högerextremismens förankring hos väljerkåren 1929-1939* (Åbo, 1984), pp. 69-75.
19. Lindström, *Fascism in Scandinavia*, p. 115; Djupsund and Karvonen, *Fascismen i Finland*, pp. 56-7.
20. *Kriser och krispolitik i Norden under mellenkrigstiden*. Nordiska Historiskermötet i Uppsala 1974. Mötesrapport (Uppsala, 1974), p. 313, Table 1.15.
21. Lindström, *Fascism in Scandinavia*, pp. 125-9.
22. Ibid., pp. 117-25.
23. Djupsund and Karvonen, *Fascismen i Finland*, p. 24.
24. T. J. Thunshelle and H. Hendriksen, 'Den mislukka samlinga' in Danielson and Larsen, *Fra idé til dom*, pp. 104-27.
25. Lindström, *Fascism in Scandinavia*, p. 116.
26. Poulsen, *Besaettelsesmagten og de danske nazister*, p. 381.
27. Djursaa, *DNSAP*, vol. 1, p. 100; vol. 2, pp. 106, and 127-34.

28. Ibid., vol. 2, p. 172.
29. Beyond the data in Table 4.2 taken from Djursaa, *DNSAP*, vol. 2, pp. 174-5 (the work has a summary in English and English texts for all tables), see the detailed material in J. K. Myklebust, 'Hvam var de norske nazistene? Sammenheng mellom sosial, økonomisk og politisk bakgrunn og medlemskap i Nasjonal Samling', unpublished MA thesis, Bergen University, 1974; cf. Larsen in idem, *Who were the Fascists?*, pp. 595-620.
30. Larsen in idem, *Who were the Fascists?*, p. 606, table 3.
31. J. P. Myklebust and B. Hagtvet, 'Regional Contrasts in the Membership Base of the Nasjonal Samling' in Larsen, *Who were the Fascists?*, p. 606, table 3.
32. H. Poulsen and M. Djursaa, 'Social Basis of Nazism in Denmark: the DNSAP' in Larsen, *Who were the Fascists?*, p. 713, note 8.
33. Djursaa, *DNSAP*, vol. 2, pp. 101-03.
34. Larsen in idem, *Who were the Fascists?*, p. 607.
35. For the following see H. Hendriksen, 'Mennesker uten makt' in Danielson and Larsen, *Fra idé til dom*, pp. 68-103. Cf. H. Hendriksen, 'Agrarian Fascism in Eastern and Western Norway: a Comparison' in Larsen, *Who were the Fascists?*, pp. 651-6.
36. Djursaa, *DNSAP*, vol. 2, pp. 140-2.
37. Ibid., p. 107.
38. J. Andenes, *Det vanskelige oppgjoret* (Oslo, 1980), pp. 32-3.
39. Larsen in idem, *Who were the Fascists?*, p. 612.
40. Cf. Poulsen and Djursaa in Larsen, *Who were the Fascists?*, pp. 704-07.
41. Djursaa, *DNSAP*, vol. 2, p. 113.
42. On the relationship between the farming community and the NS see Hendriksen, as well as Myklebust and Hagtvet in Larsen, *Who were the Fascists?*, pp. 651-6, 621-50.
43. The situation in Sweden has been evaluated by Hagtvet in Larsen, *Who were the Fascists?*, p. 716. On Finland see Alapuro in ibid., pp. 679-81.
44. Djursaa, *DNSAP*, vol. 2, p. 113.
45. Myklebust and Hagtvet in Larsen, *Who were the Fascists?*, pp. 621-650.

Chapter Five

FRANCE

Robert J. Soucy

For historians of inter-war French fascism, there are essentially three kinds of sources that reveal its basic social dynamics: firstly, propaganda texts (including newspapers, pamphlets, books and speeches) that show what social groups fascists were trying to appeal to; secondly, autobiographical materials which help explain why some individuals became fascists; and thirdly, police reports at the *Archives Nationales*, the *Archives de la Préfecture de la Police* in Paris, and various regional archives which describe the financial backing of each fascist movement, the political and social backgrounds of their leaders, and, in a more general way, the social, economic and religious composition of their rank-and-file memberships. By combining these sources and keeping in mind the political and social context in which each movement prospered or declined, some important connections become apparent.[1]

Prior to the outbreak of the Second World War, fascism emerged in France in two major waves, each in response to new threats from the socialist left. In the minds of some social and economic conservatives, these threats could only be permanently repressed by overthrowing the Third Republic which allowed them to rise. The first wave of French fascism began in 1924 as a backlash to the election of the *Cartel des Gauches*, a coalition of Radicals and Socialists. The second wave developed during the Great Depression in reaction to an upsurge of the left that included the election of a new *Cartel des Gauches* in 1932, and the election of the Popular Front, a coalition of Radicals, Socialists, and Communists, in 1936. Each wave of fascism declined when conservative governments returned to power and demonstrated that they could defeat the 'red menace' within a framework of electoral democracy. Three 'moderate' premiers, Poincaré in 1926, Doumergue in 1934, and Daladier in 1938, made it unnecessary for the bulk of French social and economic conservatives ultimately to opt for fascism; parliamentary conservatism proved able to stem the socialist tide for them.

A minority of conservatives, however, were attracted to more authoritarian solutions, and some of the wealthiest were willing to finance various French fascist movements during periods of crisis. These movements, like fascism in Italy, were anti-parliamentarian, anti-liberal, anti-Marxist, supporters (despite their occasional talk of national 'socialism') of the upper- and lower-middle classes against the industrial working classes, intensely nationalistic, enamoured with military values and willing to employ paramilitary violence to attain their political ends. While the major financial backers of these movements were upper bourgeois or landed gentry, they realised that they needed to enlist the petty bourgeoisie and the peasantry if they were to develop the mass base necessary for effective political action. The socio-economic programmes of their movements were therefore 'centrist' within the French political context of the times, attempts in effect at winning lower-middle-class support for upper-middle-class interests. These programmes defended private property, low taxes, class conciliation and upward social mobility ('careers open to talent') and condemned the nationalisation of production, increased government spending, class conflict and social and economic equality ('decadence').

The election of the *Cartel des Gauches* in 1924 led not only to a general right-wing backlash, but the formation of three fascist movements in France: the *Légion*, the *Jeunesses Patriotes*, and the *Faisceau*. It also gave a shot in the arm to one of their major precursors, the *Action Française*, which joined them in their virulent denunciations of the *Cartel* and the 'communist' danger it represented.

The royalist *Action Française*, founded in 1898 in response to the Dreyfus Affair, was socially and economically conservative, blaming lower-class discontent not on low wages, long hours, poor working conditions or upper-class selfishness but on the corrupting influence of Jews, Protestants, liberals and foreigners. Violently anti-Marxist as well as anti-Semitic, it had little success in recruiting industrial workers to its cause, despite certain efforts in that direction. Between 1906 and 1912, it sought the collaboration of non-Marxist syndicalists on a common platform of hostility to the Third Republic and capitalistic Jews, but with the exception of a handful of renegades (some of whom were enticed by the prospect of royalist subsidies for their newspapers and for themselves) it was rebuffed. When in 1909 Maurice Pujo of the *Action Française* claimed that the left's revolutionaries were 'on our side', the syndicalist leader Victor Méric replied contemptuously 'you must be joking' and pointed out that his followers opposed the Third Republic 'on different grounds and with opposite aims'.[2]

In the light of the social composition of the membership of the *Action Française*, Méric's conclusion is not surprising. As Eugen Weber has shown in his classic study of the *Action Française* (partly by reviewing the professions of those who subscribed to its newspaper), the bulk of the *Action Française*'s troops came from the lower middle classes and the white-collar professions (shopkeepers, clerks, office workers, doctors, lawyers, travelling salesmen, etc.) and were highly nationalistic, Catholic and socially conservative. These characteristics were also typical of the memberships of the *Légion*, the *Jeunesses Patriotes* and the *Faisceau*, although the *Action Française* had a greater number of aristocrats in leadership positions. In 1907, as Weber has noted, over half of its sections were headed by titled persons and fifteen to twenty per cent of its support came from people with titles.[3] The Duc d'Orléans, the pretender to the throne, was one of the major financial supporters of the *Action Française*.

I

The *Légion*, founded one month after the *Cartel des Gauches* came to power, was more 'republican' in its fascism: that is to say, it wanted France ruled by a dictator (preferably a military figure) not a king. One of the major financial backers of the *Légion* was General Noël de Castelnau, who also helped subsidise the establishment of the *Jeunesses Patriotes* six months later. In 1924 Castelnau was president of the *Féderation National Catholique*, the *Ligue de la Défense Catholique*, and the *Ligue des Patriotes*, as well as a frequent contributor to two conservative newspapers, *L'Echo de Paris* and *La France Catholique*. Elected to the Chamber of Deputies in 1919 as a member of the *Bloc National*, he had lost his seat in 1924 to a *Cartel des Gauches* candidate. A police report from Lyons in 1925 claimed that the *Légion*'s political and social doctrines owed much to Castelnau and that a *Légion* meeting at which he had spoken was attended by 'persons known for their nationalist, conservative and clerical opinions'.[4] The offical leader of the *Légion*, however, was Antoine Rédier, editor of a conservative journal. Rédier damned the *Cartel des Gauches* for its 'attacks on private property and the family', equated its proposals to raise taxes with 'communism', called for reduced government spending, denounced 'anti-religious sectarianism' and 'depopulation', demanded a crackdown on brothels, and advocated the formation of paramilitary units to fight leftist revolutionaries in the event of civil war. What happened in Russia in 1917, he warned, could happen in France in 1924.

The ideology of the *Légion* reflected the social and economic as well as the religious and military backgrounds of its members. Rédier's *légionnaires* were middle class, Catholic and often war veterans. The organisers of the Strasbourg section of the *Légion* included several ex-army officers (one was a brigadier-general, another a colonel), a university professor, an engineer, and a shopkeeper.[5] The secretary of the movement at Lyons was the director of the Lyons Gas Company, and the president, a former member of the *Action Française*, was an *employé* (a white-collar worker). According to the police, the 'principal members' of the Lyons *Légion* were two engineers, a hardware store owner, a silk goods manufacturer, a silk merchant, a cutler, a metal merchant, and an industrialist.[6] The rank and file of the movement included a number of Catholic university and high school students, and it was towards the Catholic right in general that the *Légion* pitched much of its propaganda. In Nantes the *Légion* distributed copies of its programme to members of the *Action Française* and the *Ligue des Chefs des Familles Catholiques*, and in Strasbourg to 2,000 'selected' persons, who were all members of the *Action Française*, the *Jeunesses Catholiques*, the Catholic UPRN or the local clergy. In 1926 the police estimated that the *Légion* had some 10,000 members and that its four-page Sunday newspaper, *Rassemblement*, had a circulation of 15,000 to 20,000.[7] Geographically, the *Légion*'s greatest strength was in the provinces, especially in the cities of the North, West and South-west. It made little headway in Paris, where the *Jeunesses Patriotes* had captured much of its potential clientele, almost as if General de Castelnau, backing both movements, had parcelled out the territory. Indeed, a police report of September 1925 described the *Légion* as a 'seedbed' for the *Jeunesses Patriotes*, which, in fact, it turned out to be.

II

In June 1925 the *Légion* was absorbed into the *Jeunesses Patriotes*, a much larger and better financed organisation. Its programme was essentially the same as the *Légion*'s, and, except for its rejection of royalism, close to that of the *Action Française* also. Its leader, Pierre Taittinger, had been a member of the *Ligue des Patriotes*, headed by Castelnau, and the *Jeunesses Patriotes* had begun as a youth auxiliary to the *Ligue*. By 1925, however, it had adopted the trappings of fascism, including the fascist salute, blue-shirted paramilitary units (the French equivalent to Mussolini's Blackshirts), and cries of 'Dictatorship! Dictatorship!' at its political rallies. Taittinger accused the *Cartel des Gauches* of playing into the hands of the communists and pointedly observed in the party's newspaper that it had been the weaknesses of the State in Italy that had led to fascism. 'Communism', he declared, 'calls forth fascism'.[8]

Taittinger, a much-decorated war veteran, had been elected to the Chamber of Deputies in 1919 as a member of the right-wing *Bloc National*, and although he was re-elected in subsequent elections, he did not believe that the Third Republic had made France safe for conservatism (as was demonstrated, he said, by the triumph of the *Cartel des Gauches* in 1924). Taittinger himself was quite wealthy, for he owned four newspapers and was the owner or manager of twenty commercial enterprises, including the *Forces Motrices de la Vienne*, the *Société Française du Chocolat Suchard*, the *Omnium de Concentration Financière et Industrielle du Luxembourg*, the *Société du Louvre et de l'Hotêl Lutétia*, and *Champagne Taittinger*.[9]

The *Jeunesses Patriotes* was launched partly with Taittinger's money and partly with funds provided by Castelnau's Catholic associations. By March 1926, Taittinger had acquired a number of additional backers. According to the police:

> *Les Jeunesses Patriotes* has a great deal of money at its disposal. Besides the *Banque de Paris et des Pays-Bas* which allots an annual subsidy of 60,000 francs, the *Crédit Lyonnais*, the *Société Générale*, and the *Banque Nationale de Crédit* have agreed to finance Monsieur Taittinger, but for a lesser sum: 10,000 francs each.
> Among the large subscribers to the *Jeunesses Patriotes* is Monsieur Emile Laffont, the well-known publicity agent.
> The provinces, notably the region of the East, furnish large subsidies to Monsieur Taittinger. At Nancy, Monsieur Lucien Bailly, a mining engineer with a large fortune, gives a large amount, as does Monsieur Ernest Marie, a stockbroker.[10]

By 1926 the *Jeunesses Patriotes* had grown to some 65,000 members, by 1929 to 102,075 members, including 25,750 in Paris and 76,325 in the provinces.[11] These police estimates do not represent a steady rise, since there were fluctuations downwards at times, as in May 1926 when some 4,000 members abandoned the *Jeunesses Patriotes* to join its new rival, the *Faisceau*. The *Faisceau*'s decline after 1927, on the other hand, led to an increase in *Jeunesses Patriotes* recruitment.

The leaders of the *Jeunesses Patriotes* generally had wealthy, aristocratic or military backgrounds. At party rallies, Taittinger had shared the speakers' platform at various times with General Dessoffy, Baron André de Neufville (the owner of several automobiles, a yacht, a chateau in the Rhone Valley, a villa near the Alps, and a mine in Spain), Prince Murat (of the Bonapartist nobility), Henri de Kerillis (a wartime pilot and peacetime factory executive), Roger de Saivre (son of Baron Maurice de Saivre, owner of several anthracite mines in Indo-China), Count François de Gouvion de Saint-Cyr, Louis Madelin (a historian), and Count Charles des Isnards. The number of aristocrats on this list led critics, as Taittinger himself later recounted, to label the *Jeunesses Patriotes* an 'association of papa's boys, a phalange of dandies in gaiters and monocles grouped together to defend their parents' dividends'.[12] Taittinger insisted that this was not the case, that the movement was composed of persons from all classes and professions (workers, bourgeois, engineers and students) who were fraternally united by a common nationalism. One historian of the movement, Jean Philippet, says that the subscription lists to the party's newspaper, *Le National*, show that supporters came from all classes, but he provides no statistics as to the percentages of each, other than saying that the names of small industrialists appeared 'rather frequently' along with those of large landowners, lawyers and *rentiers* (investors).[13]

If the top leadership of the *Jeunesses Patriotes* came largely from upper-middle-class or aristocratic backgrounds, the rank and file was more lower middle class. Indeed, according to a reporter from *Le Temps* who visited its party headquarters in 1935, the movement had a populist flavour. Speaking of the Blueshirts he found there, he wrote:

> ... they did not feel constrained to act like intellectuals. Vigorous, healthy complexions, their eyes looking directly at you under their Basque berets, they chatted, laughed and spoke candidly, their pipes between their teeth...
> Those who are curious about Parisian folklore can learn something from the perpetual comings and goings of these tough-looking fellows. Vulgarity did not seem to be in favour, but they displayed a certain roughness in their language, mixing with the vocabulary of the Latin Quarter some of the slang of working-class neighbourhoods, or rather some of the spirit of the common people. It seemed to us, moreover, that some of the recruitment took place among the ranks of the people, including among those of some disabused communists.14

Although the police found that the *Jeunesses Patriotes* recruited its members from 'rather different backgrounds', they said nothing about ex-communists being involved. In 1925 they reported that the rank and file of the movement tended to come mainly from conservative war veterans' organisations, Catholic groups and Alexandre Millerand's Protestant youth association:

> They are for the most part war veterans already enrolled in the *Union Nationale* [a right-centre veterans' association], the *Ligue des Chefs de Section* [League of

> Platoon Leaders], or the *Camarades de Combat*. Or they are students, notably from the *Jeunesse Chrétienne Protestante*... and are very passionate supporters of Monsieur Millerand... Or, finally, they are Catholics devoted to General de Castelnau.
> A few *camelots du roi* [street fighters of the *Action Française*] joined in the beginning. They received an imperious order from Maurras [the head of the *Action Française*] to resign or be struck from the rolls.[15]

A 1929 police report on three *Jeunesses Patriotes* squad leaders, two of whom had been *camelots du roi*, gives some indication of the type of people who led the movement's 'shock troops' into action against its left-wing opponents. Georges Simonin was described as a 'mediocre and nondescript' clerk for the Paris Gas Company before becoming the secretary of Edouard Soulier, a right-wing parliamentary deputy who supported the *Jeunesses Patriotes*. Henri Meaux was the son of a family of wealthy potato and sugar beet producers. Achille Joinard for several years had owned a small shop specialising in religious articles, had worked for a time as an accountant for the *Crédit Lyonnais* banking firm, and had been the secretary of '*La Rose Blanche*', a Catholic royalist organisation. As a *camelot du roi*, he had participated in a number of violent disruptions of left-wing rallies and had been arrested and fined several times for assaulting political opponents or battling with the police.[16]

According to Taittinger, *Jeunesses Patriotes* recruitment soared following a bloody encounter between his followers and a group of communists in April 1925, which left four of his Blueshirts dead and thirty wounded. The 'rue Damrémont massacre' spurred an inflow of new money and men into the *Jeunesses Patriotes*, a paramilitary movement whose announced aim was to 'bar the road to communism'. The *Jeunesses Patriotes* itself was organised along military lines, authority flowing from the top down. Paris was divided, like a battlefield, into six 'sectors', each sector assigned to various 'centuries' (shock troops named after the armies of ancient Rome). It was the duty of each 'century' to obey the orders of the central committee without question. The central committee was composed of six war veterans, including two majors, one colonel, one general and one admiral. A police report of January 1926 described General Dessoffy as the 'veritable head of the general staff' of the *Jeunesses Patriotes* and noted that it was Dessoffy who had organised its paramilitary units, pinpointed the military specialities of its members ('machine-gunners, cannon men, etc.') and appointed liaison teams in case the need arose to resist a left-wing revolution. Dessoffy, a former royalist, had previously served as a military attaché in Rome where he had witnessed fascism in power.[17]

III

Another major fascist organisation formed in response to the *Cartel des Gauches* was the *Faisceau*, led by Georges Valois. For a few months, Valois stole some of Taittinger's thunder and some of his troops, but the *Faisceau* fizzled out when the conservative Poincaré government returned to power in 1926 and Valois' financial support evaporated. Although Valois had been an anarcho-syndicalist as a young man, by 1903 he had gone over to the extreme right. First as a member of the *Action Française* and then as head of his own movement, his socio-economic ideology was highly conservative (quite similar in its fundamentals to that of Rédier and Taittinger) despite Valois' occasional, and quite misleading, rhetoric to the contrary. A number of scholars, taking this rhetoric at face value, have seen Valois as an example of 'left fascism' and have described his ideology as a genuine attempt to synthesize nationalism and socialism. Yet, as a fascist, Valois denounced socialism, communism, anarchism, democratic syndicalism, class struggle and labour's use of the strike as a bargaining weapon against management. He praised capitalism (especially in its 'dynamic' form), Henry Ford, bourgeois paternalism, class conciliation and 'careers open to talent'. His solution to the 'social problem' was not to give workers a greater ratio of the profits but to increase their wages by increasing production. The latter was to be accomplished not by nationalising industry or giving workers more control in the work-place but by modernising production techniques and by ceasing strikes which hurt production. Valois damned the *Cartel des Gauches* for opening the floodgates to communism (he said its leader, Herriot, was France's 'Kerensky') and portrayed his *légionnaires* (right-wing war veterans) as mobilising to prevent capitalist and Christian Europe from being overrun by the 'barbarian hordes' of Bolshevik and atheistic Russia.

Valois did, it is true, make an attempt in 1925 and 1926 to attract some disgruntled communists to his cause, but he had little success. Two celebrated exceptions were Henri Lauridan, the former secretary of the *Union des Syndicats Unitaires du Nord* (Federation of United Unions of the North) and Marcel Delagrange, the former communist mayor of Périgueux. According to the police, when Lauridan offered his services to Valois in June 1925, the latter hesitated to accept him because of his 'troubled' past and his reputation of being 'a man easy to buy'.[18] Delagrange was no longer mayor when he was recruited by Valois, having, according to the police, fallen under the influence of his mistress, the Comtesse de Chasteigner, president of the Périgueux section of the *Action Française* and well-known for her 'royalist, reactionary and clerical opinions'. When Delagrange displayed support for Valois in November 1925, he was dismissed from the Communist Party. Shortly afterwards, he joined the *Faisceau*. In return for his services, Valois agreed to pay him 2,000 francs a month, help buy him a house in the suburbs of Paris, and cover his moving expenses.[19]

Although Valois was pleased to acquire Delagrange as a 'leftist' showpiece, as a means of attracting working-class support, he was apprehensive about the impression Delagrange might make on the bulk of his supporters, who were much more middle class and socially conservative. According to an informer, Valois went to some pains to transform Delagrange's proletarian image into a more acceptable one when Delagrange was scheduled to speak for the first time at a *Faisceau* rally in Paris:

> It was necessary that Delagrange force himself to eliminate from his language that which remained from his communist past. Three people, particularly, worked to obtain this result: G. Valois, P. Dumas and the Comtesse de Chasteigner... [The Comtesse], who had a great influence on Delagrange, gave him a passionate little discourse underscoring how important it was that he said *adieu* to Lenin and Trotsky... She completed her little

> sermon by giving advice to the former communist mayor on how to look and dress in the future.
> He for his part agreed with good grace to the necessity of shedding his old self.[20]

Despite Delagrange's willingness to adapt, some of the *Faisceau*'s financial backers did not trust him always to remain an obedient servant. One of these, Eugène Mathon, head of a large textile industry in the North, broke with Valois over his use of Delagrange and took some of his wealthy friends with him. The socialist and communist press, however, had no such reservations. *Le Peuple* damned Delagrange as a 'renegade', and *L'Humanité* accused him of stealing 35,000 francs when he left the Communist Party and of making himself a pawn of its enemies.[21]

Nor did Delagrange's attempt to attract communist and socialist rank and file to fascism make much headway. According to the police, 'the exclusively working-class element remained sullenly opposed despite all the appeals directed at them by the *Faisceau*'.[22] Delagrange claimed that this was because the *Faisceau* leadership had not given him enough money to do the job, but a more likely explanation is that *Faisceau* ideology itself prevented a more positive response from workers, especially communist workers. To imply the opposite, as some scholars have, to see Delagrange's adoption of fascism as an extension of his former communism, rather than as a repudiation of it, is to ignore the content of his speeches. Delagrange not only criticized the French Communist Party for 'provoking' strikes and other 'social troubles', but he also declared that the *Faisceau* associated itself with 'intelligent bourgeois' who, aware of the 'Russian example', were unwilling to 'stick their necks under the guillotine'.[23] In 1926, at a *Faisceau* rally in Paris, he made it clear that he had left his former communism behind him: 'We want the working masses to come to us and not let themselves be led astray by a communist ideology which would lead them to worse acts of violence and which would conduct the country to ruin'.[24]

According to Allan Douglas, an American historian, few blue-collar workers, communist or otherwise, responded to the *Faisceau*'s rhetoric:

> The Faisceau was never able to attract any large number of workers. The total may have run over 10%... but certainly

> not over 20%. No significant numbers of factory workers or workers in heavy industry were enrolled... There were owners and directors of enterprises, managers, a large number of engineers and other technical personnel. The *Faisceau* attracted shopkeepers and artisans, especially in the provinces. On the lower end of the social scale there were more employees and white-collar workers than blue-collar workers. The occupational mix of the *Faisceau* leaned heavily to the technical professions, engineers, architects, etc. and the financial ones, bankers, insurance agents, accountants. These middle-class groups, to which fascist ideology has always appealed, also reflected the technical and financial biases in Valois' thought.[25]

Most of the leaders of the *Faisceau* were middle class and Catholic. Many had been previously affiliated with the *Action Française* or the *Jeunesses Patriotes*. Many were also war veterans. Ninety-three per cent of the money that launched the party's newspaper, *Le Nouveau Siècle*, was put up by four industrialists: Franz van den Broeck d'Obrenan, Eugène Mathon, Antoine Cazeneuve, and Serge André. Van den Broeck d'Obrenan had a large fortune derived from the colonial trade. According to the police, he was the owner of a chateau and a villa, his Paris residence was staffed with 'numerous servants' and he was a member of several fashionable clubs in Paris, including the Polo Club and the Artistic Union. Prior to joining Valois' movement, he had belonged to the *Action Française* and had been a member of the retinue of the Duc d'Orléans, the pretender to the throne. In 1924 he had run for parliament on a right-wing platform, had lost, and saw the *Cartel des Gauches* come to power. Eugène Mathon was president of the Association of Textile Manufacturers of Roubaix-Tourcoing and had also previously supported the *Action Française*. Antoine Cazeneuve owned a large machine-tool manufacturing firm and was the founder of an association of 'unions' run by employers. Serge André was the largest stockholder in a petroleum firm, 'Sidoléine', which in 1925 had some fifteen million francs in assets.

Once the *Faisceau* was successfully launched, it acquired other financial backers as well, two of the most important being the cognac millionaires Maurice James Hennessy and Paul Firino-Martel. Another major contributor was Victor Mayer, a Jewish shoe manufacturer, who along with an engineer named Salomon, may help explain why the *Faisceau* avoided pandering to anti-Semitism in its propaganda.[26] Other backers included several industrialists, engineers and landowners, a countess, a professor, a Paris municipal *counselor*, a senator, and a lawyer. In November 1926 the police concluded that Valois had received at least 525,000 francs in official subsidies and that these did not include 'the sums he has received directly from the big industrialists of the region of the North and from heavy industry'.[27] Several private railway companies sent money, using Marcel Peschaud, Secretary-General of the Paris-Orléans railway, as their go-between.[28] Valois' opposition to nationalising the railroads (which were nationalised after the Second World War), and his attempt to replace communist railway unions with fascist unions, may have inspired some of their support. According to the police, the *Faisceau* also received unofficial subsidies from the *Confédération Générale de la Production Française* and the *Redressement Français*, through an intermediary, Gustave Gautherot, editor of the *Revue Antibolcheviste*.[29] Both were big-business associations with large political slush funds.

IV

With the defeat of the *Cartel des Gauches* in 1926, financial support for French fascist movements declined, and in the case of the *Faisceau* so much so that Valois' movement ceased to exist after 1928. The *Jeunesses Patriotes* survived by abandoning its call for dictatorship and supporting the right-wing Poincaré and Tardieu governments. Neither the *Jeunesses Patriotes* nor the *Action Française* was very militant in the late 1920s, a period of general prosperity with the left firmly under control.

The onset of the Great Depression in France in the early 1930s led to a revival of the fortunes of the *Jeunesses Patriotes* and the *Action Française* and to the rise of three new fascist movements in France: the *Solidarité Française*, the *Croix de Feu* and the *Francistes*. Again, it was in response to a threat from the left that these movements developed, a threat which culminated in the election of a new *Cartel des Gauches* government in 1932. On 6 February

1934, fascist groups joined forces with a number of right-wing veterans' organisations to hold a massive street demonstration against the *Cartel*. When some 40,000 demonstrators tried to storm the Chamber of Deputies to 'throw the rascals out', serious fighting erupted between them and the police. When the smoke cleared, sixteen rioters and one policeman had died, and 655 rioters and 1,664 policemen had been injured. The following day the *Cartel* government resigned and was replaced by a more conservative cabinet. A democratically-elected left-wing majority, hesitant to resort to the military to defend itself, had caved in to the 'fascist threat'.

The demonstration of 6 February 1934 represented the high tide of French fascism during the inter-war period. At that time, according to the police, some 370,000 persons belonged to various fascist organisations in France, over 100,000 of these persons in Paris. The largest fascist organisation in 1934 was the *Solidarité Française*, with 180,000 members, some 80,000 in Paris. Led by Jean Renaud, an ex-colonial officer, its paramilitary troops (dressed in blue shirts and berets, gray trousers and army boots) stood ready to resist any communist uprising, especially its elite battalion of fifteen hundred shock troops. Ideologically, the *Solidarité Française* was anti-socialist, anti-parliamentary, anti-Masonic, anti-Semitic, and a staunch defender of the French Empire. Its socio-economic progamme was essentially the same as that of its fascist rivals. Francois Coty, the perfume and newspaper millionaire, who had previously helped finance the *Action Française*, the *Jeunesses Patriotes* and the *Faisceau*, was instrumental in launching the *Solidarité Française*. In the wake of the 6 February riots, the movement also received a subsidy of two million francs from Georges Vautier, a member of the *Redressement Français*. The latter was a business lobby officially committed to 'leading an energetic propaganda campaign against the extreme left'. Vautier was himself the director of some fifteen hydro-electric and gas companies.[30] The rank and file of the *Solidarité Française* was largely lower middle class, although Renaud was not above 'recruiting' one squad of his shock troops from unemployed North Africans in Paris.

Colonel de La Rocque's *Croix de Feu* had some 130,000 members in 1934, including some 25,000 in Paris. It, too, had paramilitary units ('*dispos*') who could be mobilised on short notice to combat a communist insurrection, although, as the French

Minister of the Interior observed following the riots of 6 February, not all members of the *Croix de Feu*, especially its older ones, were willing to 'descend into the street with helmets on their heads'. The membership of the *Croix de Feu* was more upper class than that of the *Solidarité Française*. This was evidenced in the support La Rocque received among students at the *École Polytechnique*, Saint-Cyr and the French Naval Academy, all prestigious schools which trained sons of the *haute bourgeoisie* for top positions in the civil service and the military. Some 350 of these students paraded in their school uniforms with *Croix de Feu* units up the Champs-Elysées to the Arc de Triomphe on Armistice Day 1933. The police called shrewd attention to the support which the *Croix de Feu* had in the military services. Although officers on active duty were discouraged from joining political movements, many sympathised with La Rocque's ideals and many reserve officers, as well as cadets being groomed for high positions in the army and navy, belonged to the *Croix de Feu*. Many *Croix de Feu* members were also Catholic, although the official ideology of the movement welcomed members from all religious backgrounds, even Jews. Only the non-religious were excluded.

Like other French fascist organisations, the *Croix de Feu* was largely subsidised by big business groups, especially by certain banks, utility companies and the steel trust, the *comité des forges*. La Rocque himself was on the board of directors of a major hydro-electric company, the *Compagnie Générale d'Electricité*, which, like other private French utility companies, feared the coming to power of a left-wing government which might lower electricity rates or even nationalise the industry (which eventually happened after the Second World War). The head of the *Compagnie Générale d'Electricité* was Ernest Mercier, who in 1934 was also head of the *Redressement Français*, the same right-wing business lobby whose political slush fund helped subsidise the *Solidarité Française* (and in 1926 had helped finance the *Faisceau*). François Coty had also chipped in when the *Croix de Feu* was founded in 1927. The *Banque de France* seems also to have been involved; the treasurer of the *Croix de Feu* was one of the bank's lawyers, the assistant treasurer one of its cashiers. In 1937 it was discovered that the *Croix de Feu* had benefited from government subsidies between 1930 and 1932 when the conservative André Tardieu had been a government minister. Tardieu later testified that on the recommendation of a high 'military personality' he had provided La Rocque with secret government funds to help him expand his anti-socialist movement. Tardieu said he had participated in the transaction because 'I thought that it would be interesting to help in organising the forces of order against the forces of disorder'.[31] According to the police, important sums of money were also given to the *Croix de Feu* by François Wendel (an industrialist and President of the *comité des forges*), Ernest Mallet and Pierre Miraband (both bankers), Schwof d'Hericourt (an industrialist), Jacques de Neuflize (a banker and railroad director), and Otto de la Havraise (a major electrical industry stockholder).[32] Subsidies were also provided by the *Banque de Paris et des Pays Bas* and the *Banque Mallet Frères*, the latter acting as a go-between for some of France's richest nobility, particularly the Guise and Luynes families and the Duchesse d'Uzès.[33]

The official programme of the *Croix de Feu* in 1933 no doubt had something to do with this support. It called for lower taxes and 'the elimination of government intervention in areas belonging to free enterprise' and the protection of family property and 'legitimate profits' from savings.[34] It berated communists and socialists for fomenting class conflict and described itself as a 'moral' force devoted to class conciliation. Its motto was 'Fatherland, Family, Work', the same motto which was later adopted by the Vichy regime.

Marcel Bucard's *Francistes* had only 1,500 members in 1934 and only 300 in Paris. Bucard, a former member of *Faisceau*, called for a totalitarian state that would put an end to Marxist class struggle and liberal party politics. Poorly subsidised, lower middle class to *Lumpenproletariat* in its membership, it was too blatantly modelled upon the German brand of fascism to win much popular support in France.

V

In 1936 the Popular Front, a left-wing coalition of Socialists, Communists and Radicals led by Léon Blum, came to power in France. This was followed by a series of sit-down strikes in French factories aimed at pressurising management to make immediate concessions to labour. These concessions were forthcoming in the Matignon Accords, which granted workers higher wages, the forty-hour week and vacations with pay. Many conservatives were outraged, and some, since the paramilitary fascist leagues were now outlawed, threw their support behind Jacques Doriot's newly-founded *Parti Populaire Français* (PPF), which soon became one of France's largest fascist movements with a quarter of a million members (its chief rival being the *Parti Social Français*, a non-paramilitary offshoot of the *Croix de Feu*).

Doriot had been a communist before 1935, and his original constituency had been among the workers of Saint-Denis (where he had regularly won election until he was defeated by a communist candidate in 1938). As a fascist, he warned against the Soviet 'menace', called for an *entente* with Nazi Germany and Fascist Italy, criticised the Popular Front for not checking inflation, and urged workers to forego resorting to strikes in its dealings with management.[35] In an unabashed effort to extend his political base beyond the proletarians of Saint-Denis, he asked the petty bourgeoisie and the peasantry ('guardians of precious traditions') to support his movement against big capitalism on the one hand, and potential communism on the other. Like other French fascists, he denounced the nationalisation of industry ('the bureaucratisation of production'), paid homage to property rights, declared that individual profit would remain 'the motor of production', and advocated class conciliation in place of class struggle. He lamented the 'ruin' of the middle classes, which he blamed on inflation and high taxes. Within a short time, he won a number of *Action Française*, *Jeunesses Patriotes*, and *Croix de Feu* militants to his cause, which resulted in their former leaders complaining bitterly about his 'stealing' of their troops.[36] The PPF was especially successful in Algeria where French settlers were attracted to its strongly pro-colonial policy.

Between 1936 and 1938, a good deal of money poured into PPF coffers. As one Popular Front deputy wrote to the Minister of the Interior in 1938, the PPF disposed of resources 'out of proportion to its number of members. Millions are spent to cover the deficits run up by its evening newspaper, its string of weekly newspapers and its payments for a considerable number of regional headquarters'.[37]

According to Fernand Légey, who for a time had served on the Federal Committee of the PPF as a delegate from Algeria, much of this money was donated by conservative businessmen and landowners who felt that Doriot had a better chance of attracting the masses to fascism than Colonel de La Rocque. They believed that La Rocque had 'neither the audacity nor the cleverness of a Hitler or a Mussolini', while Doriot knew how to talk to the proletariat and the petty bourgeoisie in their own language. With the arrival of the Popular Front to power and the series of sit-down strikes that followed, 'the upper bourgeoisie finally understood that they could no longer ignore the anger of the people'. They chose to support a man who would 'install a dictatorship in France by making use of the working masses and by making fools of them'.[38] They hoped, Légey said, that the PPF, by combining communist methods of mobilising the masses with shock troops composed of former *Croix de Feu* members, would undercut the Popular Front and pose a serious obstacle to the communists. Légey noted that the programme of the PPF was 'popular in name only' since it was 'in sum the exact programme of the monarchists of the *Action Française*... and [was based on the same] system of corporatism that is dear to Maurras'.[39] Thus in December 1936 an editorial in the *Action Française*'s newspaper had expressed 'sympathy' for the PPF.[40]

Légey recalled that the PPF never lacked money, that its headquarters and offices were furnished quite handsomely, that its leaders travelled first class wherever they went, and that there was no way that the membership subscriptions and the sale of party insignias could cover a budget that ran into millions of francs. The movement was subsidised, he said, by 'big industrialists, big businessmen, bankers, that is by capitalism and management'.[41] In Algeria, the propaganda budget of the PPF was paid for by 'the biggest industrialists, *colons* and businessmen'.[42]

Since, Légey added, members of the central committee of the PPF were not elected and meetings were not open to the rank and file, deals with the *patronat* were easily made. Légey reported having received a letter from Victor Arrighi of the PPF central committee, instructing him to give certain 'sympathetic' industrialists the names of PPF workers whom they could hire when vacancies occurred. These workers were to support the *Confédération Générale du Travail* (CGT) and their local unions on wage demands and other grievances, but to oppose any calls for strikes. 'In return', wrote Arrighi, 'the owners to whom you have rendered service will thank you with a financial contribution'.[43] Légey recalled, too, how some of these owners had the PPF's newspaper, *L'Emancipation Nationale*, sent free to their workers as part of their effort to undermine working class unity. He found it ironic that a party that was 'subsidised by industrialists, businessmen and managers' would 'pretend to struggle against the social conservatism of these people'. There were only two hypotheses, he said, that might apply: either the PPF was betraying its bourgeois financial backers on behalf of the working classes, or it was betraying the working classes on behalf of its bourgeois financial backers. Légey concluded that the second was the case.[44]

Paul Marion, one of the leaders of the PPF, had declared that the PPF would ally with the devil and his grandmother to defeat communism, but Légey said that for a large number of party activists, 'for example, ex-royalists', this was not necessary. The same was true for 'the great colonial bourgeoisie' who approved of Doriot's plan for an electoral system in Algeria that would give 700,000 Europeans more voting power than 6,000,000 Moslems. In this, Légey concluded, 'the big colonial bourgeoisie, sister to the continental, has pushed its egoism to the limit against the indigenous population'.[45]

Police reports of the period tend to reinforce Légey's account. At PPF rallies Doriot presented himself as the defender of the working class, adding that 'workers and bosses must co-operate without, however, having to resort to strikes'.[46] Another PPF speaker declared that the principal objective of the movement was to combat communism by all possible means, and praised Doriot for admitting that he had made a serious 'error' in joining the communists as a young man. He added:

> In 1936 Doriot totally abandoned the Communist Party and created the *Parti Populaire Français* with the aim of grouping around him the middle classes that are pressed by the large trusts on the one side and the communists, directed by Moscow, on the other. The politics of the Soviets cannot be applied in France where there is a large number of small merchants, small artisans, small investors, and [small] owners. The situation of the Russian worker has perhaps been ameliorated, but it is far from being as

> good as that of the French worker. Bosses there will always be, and they are indispensable...
> We want neither a dictatorship of the right nor a dictatorship of the left, but the middle-class Frenchman who represent two-thirds of the population must live.[47]

Or, as another PPF speaker declared:

> Between the two hundred families which represent capital and the two hundred families that represent Stalin, there are many people in France. We are ready to welcome [all those opposed to communism], whether they be *Croix de Feu* or Radical Socialists or even disillusioned Socialists...[48]

Thus it was quite possible to have well-known conservatives speak at PPF meetings alongside former communists. At an April 1937 private meeting of the PPF in the ninth district of Paris, for example, two of the speakers were Joseph Delest, an editor of the *Action Française*'s newspaper and a member of the *Action Française*'s veterans' organisation, and Georges Lebecqu, the head of France's leading conservative veterans' association, the *Union Nationale des Combattants*.[49]

Pierre Drieu La Rochelle, a novelist and poet who admired Doriot's 'virility' and 'realism', and who wrote a weekly column for *L'Emancipation Nationale*, later emphasized the overwhelming petty-bourgeois nature of the PPF. Indeed, one of the reasons he joined the movement in 1936 was because he felt that, while the *Croix de Feu* drew most of its supporters from the upper bourgeoisie, the bourgeois who supported the PPF were small businessmen and artisans, self-made men, and not *fils de papa*. In 1935 he praised the 6 February 1934 rioters for defending the French bourgeoisie against the danger of communism, describing them as 'petit bourgeois who are afraid of becoming proletarians and workers who want to become petit bourgeois'.[50] He distinguished the fascist from the socialist 'who shouts provocatively under the nose of the capitalist: "Watch out! We are the men who are going to cut your throats!"' The fascist, he said, was much closer to the petty-bourgeois radical-socialist than to the proletarian communist in his social and economic goals.[51] He went on:

> Fascism will be nothing other than a new Radicalism, a new movement of the petite bourgeoisie, disciplined and organized into a party which will insert itself between big capitalism, the peasantry, and the proletariat and which, through terror and authority, will impose on their diverse interests an old charter in a renovated form.[52]

In his book *Fascist Socialism* of 1934, Drieu called not for a revolution of the proletariat but for a revolution of the bourgeoisie.[53] This was consistent with the conclusion that he had come to a decade earlier: 'If one withdrew from the capitalist camp, in truth there would be no other support for one's ideas, no other social category to fall back on'.[54] For Drieu, however, the major goals of fascism were 'spiritual' not material (he even praised Nazi Germany in 1934 for having *lowered* the standard of living!). What he wanted for France was virile asceticism and military hardness not soft living and hedonistic 'decadence'. Looking back on the collapse of fascism in 1943, he deeply regretted that fascism had been diverted to merely defending the economic interests of fearful bourgeois. In 1944 he concluded that fascism had been 'the marvelously efficacious camouflage of a great social upsurge of the petite bourgeoisie'.[55]

In the case of inter-war French fascism, this upsurge came in two waves in response to threats from the political left and was largely financed by upper-middle-class conservatives who saw fascism as one means of defending their social and economic interests.

Notes

1. Parts of the following analysis are excerpts from my recent book, R. J. Soucy, *French Fascism: The First Wave, 1924-1933* (Yale University Press: New Haven-London, 1986).
2. P. Mazçaj, *The Action Française and Revolutionary Syndicalism* (Chapel Hill, N.C., 1979), p. 19, pp. 43-5.
3. E. Weber, *Action Française* (Stanford, 1962), p. 63.
4. *Archives Nationales* (hereafter *AN*), Paris, F^7 13208, 25 February 1925.
5. Ibid., 30 March 1925.
6. Ibid., 25 February 1925.

7. Ibid., 30 March 1925.
8. P. Taittinger, *La Liberté*, 20 December 1924, p. 1.
9. H. Coston, *Dictionnaire de la politique française* (Paris, 1967), p. 998.
10. *AN*, F^7 13232, 4 March 1926.
11. Ibid., May 1925 and 3 June 1929.
12. Taittinger, *La Liberté* ,1 January 1926, p. 1.
13. J. Philippet, *Les Jeunesses Patriotes et Pierre Taittinger* (Paris, 1957), pp. 137-8.
14. *Le Temps*, 9 February 1935, p. 2.
15. *AN*, F^7 13232, May 1925.
16. Ibid., 9 November 1925.
17. Ibid., 15 January 1926 and 2 June 1925.
18. *AN*, F^7 13208, 7 June 1926.
19. *AN*, F^7 13210, 8 April 1926.
20. Ibid., 25 March 1926.
21. *Le Peuple*, 14 May 1926, and *L'Humanité*, 7 March 1926.
22. *AN*, F^7 13210, 27 August 1926.
23. Ibid., 5 October 1926.
24. Ibid.
25. A. Douglas, *Georges Valois and the French Right* (Ann Arbor, Michigan, 1981), pp. 375-6.
26. Ibid., pp. 377-8.
27. *AN*, F^7 13208, 3 November 1925.
28. Ibid., 1 December 1925.
29. Ibid., Summary of police reports on *Le Nouveau Siècle*, 1926.
30. *AN*, F^7 13238, 12 April 1934.
31. Chambre des Deputés, *Rapport général au nom de la commission d'enquête* (Paris, 1934), no. 3385, pp.17, 28, 34, 35. See also *Le Jour*, 27 October 1937.
32. *AN*, F^7 13241, 29 June 1935.
33. Ibid., 6 July 1935. See also *AN*, F^7 12965, 30 March 1936.
34. Chambre des Deputés, *Rapport général au nom de la commission d'enquête*, p. 120.
35. *AN*, F^7 12966, 24 February 1937.
36. *AN*, F^7 12964, 12965, and 12966.
37. Letter from Fernand Grenier to the Minister of the Interior, 28 September 1938, *Archives de la Préfecture de la Police*, Paris.
38. F. Légey, *Le vrai but de Doriot* (Algiers, no date), pp. 3, 5.
39. Ibid., p. 8.
40. Ibid., p. 9.
41. Ibid.
42. Ibid., p. 10.
43. Ibid.

44. Ibid., p. 11.
45. Ibid., p. 14.
46. *AN*, F^7 12966, 24 February 1937.
47. Ibid.
48. Ibid., 20 February 1937.
49. Ibid., 24 February 1937.
50. P. Drieu La Rochelle quoted in R.J. Soucy, *Fascist Intellectual: Drieu La Rochelle* (Berkeley-Los Angeles-London, 1979), p. 160.
51. Ibid., p. 159.
52. Ibid., p. 160.
53. Ibid., p. 152.
54. Ibid.
55. Ibid., pp. 165-6.

Chapter Six

THE LOW COUNTRIES

Herman van der Wusten

Fascism is an elusive concept and although many efforts have been made to remove it, as a generic term, from the discourse of the social sciences, these have been in vain.[1] I shall be using Linz's definition, as elaborated by Payne, as a starting-point.[2] Fascism, when set against major nineteenth-century ideologies, has three basic characteristics: it represents a positive ideal, mainly in terms of being a voluntarist creed which aims at the development of a nationalist authoritarian state; it has its own aesthetic in organised public settings; and it exalts youth and the personal charisma of leadership figures. Using these elements as a yardstick, I will analyse the fascist movements which operated in the Netherlands and in Belgium, and assess their social profiles. I shall not give any attention to the Grand Duchy of Luxembourg since no significant fascist movement developed in this very small state during the period 1919 to 1945.

The history of fascist movements in the Netherlands and Belgium is one of a confusion of mergers and splits among 'groupuscules' and a few larger units. Most would-be fascist leaders in both states lacked any sizeable following. Their party papers also had but a small circulation, or were practically not sold at all, even though they were for some time quite heavily subsidised by rich individuals, such as Haighton and Deterding in the Netherlands, and Baron de Launoit in Belgium. In most cases the fascist newspapers did not have any continuity.

In the Netherlands no fascist movement, with the exception of the *Nationaal Socialistische Beweging* (NSB - National Socialist Movement), ever had more than a little over one thousand members in the entire inter-war period. The NSB, which was founded in 1931, had nearly 50,000 members at one stage in its pre-war history. Just after the Occupation in 1940, fascist movements did start to grow quite considerably for a short time, but in 1941 they were all forced to merge with the NSB. For the Netherlands an analysis of the NSB undoubtedly does allow one to cover an extremely large proportion of the population which was attracted to fascism. In the case of Belgium, however, the analysis of the social basis of fascism is more difficult since not one of the Belgian fascist movements ever outgrew the others to the same extent as in the case of the Dutch NSB. It seems certain that four movements became, at some stage in their history, larger than the pragmatic yardstick of 'just over one thousand members' applied in the case of the Netherlands. There were, in chronological order of their appearance: the *Légion Nationale* (formed in 1922), the *Verbond van Dietsche Nationaal Solidaristen* (Federation of Dutch National Solidarists) or *Verdinaso* (formed in 1931), the *Vlaamsch National Verbond* (VNV - Flemish National League, formed in 1933), and *Rex* (formed in 1935). It was not until the 1930s that fascism secured some significance in the Low Countries. There is, however, a debate as to whether or not all of these movements had a 'fascist nature'. Although they undoubtedly demonstrated, for the major part of their existence, most of the features which characterised fascism (bearing in mind Payne's definition introduced above), there is a problem with the multi-faceted nature of some of them, particularly the VNV, and their changing nature over time, which applies to all of them. I shall be returning to this problem in section II.

The debate on the social composition of fascist movements has primarily been conducted in terms of occupational class and status, and of former political allegiance, as well as in terms of age, sex and place of residence, but more rarely in other terms. However, the importance of region, linguistic category, and religious beliefs and practices are also generally accepted as highly relevant differentiating features in the study of social cleavages and political response. There is no reason to suppose that these factors should be of less importance when applied to fascist movements. It is my intention to demonstrate the essential role played by these factors when analysing the social profile of fascist movements in the Low Countries.

There are no detailed studies on the social composition of the membership of fascist movements in the Low Countries along the lines of Kater's recent monograph dealing with the NSDAP.[3] Such studies are, in fact, hardly feasible, since more or less complete membership registrations with information on individual members have not been preserved. However, extensive NSB archives have survived, which enable one to secure a relatively detailed insight into this Dutch fascist party. This is achieved primarily by listing individuals who turn up in the NSB files (because they register, complain, enquire, accept a position, resign, etc.), and then tracking down their particulars, as far as it is possible, from other sources. Some NSB membership lists for districts - at some particular moment in time - are also available, as well as, especially for later years, tables of the overall membership produced by the NSB headquarters, though these often involve the use of inappropriate occupational classifications. For other fascist movements in the Low Countries, the type of information available for the NSB is either completely lacking or very limited in scope, and we have to rely on circumstantial evidence, such as impressions by eye-witnesses and analysis of electoral data.

I

In some major respects the Netherlands and Belgium were remarkably similar in the inter-war period as regards their socio-economic structures. In 1930 the distribution of the employed population in terms

Table 6.1: Distribution of the employed population by economic sectors in 1930 (by %)

	Netherlands	Belgium
Agriculture/horticulture/ fisheries	20	18
Industry	39	46
Commerce/transport	23	23
Civil service/liberal professions	9	8
Domestic service/odd jobs	9	5
Total (%)	100	100

Note: From the censuses held in both countries in 1930, with adjustments for reasons of comparability.

of economic sectors clearly reflects a picture of two thoroughly developed countries.

The Netherlands, a more recently industrialised state, had a smaller proportion of its economically active population engaged in industry compared with Belgium. Women formed about a quarter of the employed population in the Low Countries. There is no comparable information on the occupational stratification of the Netherlands and Belgium in the inter-war years, though for the Netherlands there is a six-fold classification ranging from academic professionals, managers, and higher civil servants in class I, to unskilled labour in class VI. The data is based on calculations relating to the male employed population over the age of eighteen:

Table 6.2: The social stratification of the Netherlands in 1933 (by %)

Class I	2
Class II	7
Class III	18
Class IV	32
Class V	30
Class VI	9
Unknown	2
Total (%)	100

Source: J. J. M. van Tulder, *De beroepsmobiliteit in Nederland van 1919 tot 1954. Een sociaal-statistische studie* (Leiden, 1962), p. 278.

In view of the basic similarities between the sectoral distributions of the Netherlands and Belgium (see Table 6.1), one would not expect very large differences in the occupational stratifications of these countries, though the self-employed elements in classes II, III and IV were probably a little larger in the Netherlands (there were more farmers), while one would expect to find relatively more industrial labour within classes IV, V and VI in Belgium.

By European standards the Low Countries were, of course, of relatively small size, but both did possess significant colonial possessions. By 1930 both states had a population of around 8 millions. In each of them nearly a quarter of the population lived in the four largest cities, the largest of which (Brussels and Amsterdam) had a population approaching the million mark. Overall the Netherlands were the more urbanised, while Belgium had a more densely populated countryside.

The Netherlands did not have any significant linguistic divisions, whereas Belgium had been marked by social cleavages based on differences of language, long before 1930. In the Walloon (the southern) and Flanders (the northern) regions large majorities, of around 80 per cent of the inhabitants, spoke French and Flemish respectively, with the French-speakers in Flanders being especially prominent in the traditional regional elite. In the Brussels area, originally within the Flemish region, an uneasy co-existence of Flemish and Walloon peoples had developed by the 1930s, since people had migrated to this core area of Belgium from all parts of the country. Significant progress towards the full emancipation of Flanders was made during the inter-war period, a development which constituted the dominant political issue of these decades.[4] Finally, a very small, politically insignificant number of German-speakers were concentrated near the eastern border of Belgium.

With regard to religion, the Netherlands showed great diversity in comparison with Belgium. In Belgium, Catholicism had been firmly entrenched since the Counter-Reformation, though there was, of course, a significant variation in religious observance by the 1920s and 1930s, with Flanders being generally the more religious region. In the cities, and in the industrialised areas in general, a large section of the inhabitants had loosened their ties with the Church. In the Netherlands, despite an extraordinary proliferation of belief systems and religious sects within Protestantism, a three-fold classification is feasible. The southern provinces were predominantly Catholic, with significant Catholic enclaves scattered around the country as a whole. A ribbon of Protestant orthodoxy stretched from the south-west to the north-east, whereas latitudinarian Protestant views and secular perspectives were concentrated in the north-west and the north generally, a pattern which was basically instituted during the Reformation. A general process of secularisation was accelerated in the 1920s, though this had not, by any means, reached the levels discernible in the post-1960 period. In the inter-war years, Catholics made up just over one third of the Dutch population, orthodox Protestants accounted for around a quarter, while the rest of the population held more latitudinarian or secular views.

In constitutional and political terms, both the Netherlands and Belgium were parliamentary democracies, with a monarch as head of state in both countries. Since the end of the First World War, general elections were conducted on the basis of a system of proportional representation, with compulsory voting. In the Netherlands all adults had voting rights, whereas women were only enfranchised in Belgium after 1945. In both countries, no single party obtained an absolute majority, and governments were based on coalitions. In the Netherlands, six relatively large parties (two of which were Protestant, two Liberal, one Socialist, and one Catholic) had coalition potential. The Socialist Party was, in fact, excluded from cabinet responsibility until 1939. Most cabinets were formed on the basis of coalitions among the religious parties, occasionally supplemented by the Liberal parties. In Belgium, there were three large parties (which stood for Catholic, socialist and liberal interests respectively), while various Flemish parties were also a constant feature of the political landscape. The Catholic Party held power virtually uninterruptedly in the 1920s and 1930s, usually in combination with the Liberal Party, though the Socialist Party was also at times involved in coalitions. Although the stability of cabinets was significantly lower in Belgium than it was in the Netherlands, the longevity of individual ministers was often considerable in both countries.

Political allegiances were generally stable in both countries for most of the period under review. Religious parties, both Protestant and Catholic, as well as socialist parties, were political organisations closely connected with such institutions as the churches, trades unions, and leisure and mutual benefit associations, which more or less effectively segmented the bulk of the population into separate blocks. The overlap and inter-connections between party formations and institutional organisations, often under a co-ordinated leadership, has become known in the Netherlands as the system of '*verzuiling*' ('pillarisation').[5] Political leaders of these 'blocks' pondered over the reform of public institutions during the inter-war years in terms somewhat akin to the organisational principles which are characteristic of authoritarian regimes.[6] The intellectual climate, therefore, for fascist concepts and proposals, was not entirely absent.

Table 6.3 shows the support pattern of the major Dutch and Belgian parties during the inter-war period. In the Netherlands the support patterns were very stable, whereas in Belgium there was a steady decline in the support enjoyed by the three major parties. It is clear that the religious parties were more important in the Netherlands, although they obviously did have problems in keeping their support intact. The Socialists were more important in Belgium, reflecting the more industrialised character of the labour force.

Table 6.3: Mean proportion of votes in national inter-war elections for major parties (by %)

	Netherlands		Belgium
Catholic Party	29.1		34.9
Protestant Party	13.5		-
Protestant Party	9.1		-
Liberal Party	5.5	)	15.8
Liberal Party	7.2	)	
Socialist Party	21.9		35.2
Rest	13.7		14.1
Total (%)	100		100

Source: T. Mackie and R. Rose, *The international almanac of electoral history* (London, 1974), tables 3.16, 16.8.

Two final factors conditioning political developments in the 1920s and 1930s should also be noted: the respective experience of the two states during the First World War, and the course of the economic crisis at the end of the 1920s. The experience of the war, and the position of the states and their social rearrangements after the war, were all material to the formation and institutionalisation of the fascist creed. The impact of the economic crisis from 1929 rekindled post-war fears, tensions and expectations, and created situations in which new socio-political movements were given another chance of securing support. This could occur even after some considerable time-lag, as in the case of *Rex*. The Netherlands were least touched by the war, since the country remained neutral. The war had an impact, of course, if only indirectly, for it made foreign trade difficult and led to an influx of war refugees, especially from Belgium. Belgium felt the impact of the war directly from the outset, being invaded and occupied, with the exception of a small part of south-west Flanders, by the Germans. Flemish so-called 'activists' collaborated with the German occupation authorities, and secured concessions for their Flemish demands (such as parity of the Flemish language with the 'official language', French; greater regional autonomy, etc.) in return. At the same time, however, Flemish soldiers were also fighting in the Allied armies on behalf of the Belgian government, temporarily removed to Le Havre for the duration of the war. Both the Belgian war cabinet and the higher ranks of the Belgian Army were largely dominated by French-speakers, a fact resented by Flemish soldiers, who started a 'Front' movement in order to get Flemish demands accepted. After the war some of the leaders of the 'Front' movement went into politics and won seats in Flanders. Many 'activists', of course, were prosecuted for collaboration with the Germans. Gradually, however, the relations between 'activists' and 'fronters' were harmonised under the common banner of a set of Flemish demands, one of which became, in due course, a call for an amnesty for 'activists'. The Belgian economy was severely damaged by the ravages of war by 1918, but recovered remarkably quickly. During the economic crisis of the 1930s, both the Netherlands and Belgium were hard hit, with the impact of the recession being somewhat deeper, and lasting longer, in the Netherlands than in Belgium, although these features reflect only a very relative difference between the harsh economic situations which both countries experienced.[7]

II

Fascism was, in Linz's apt word, a 'latecomer'.[8] It only entered the arena of electoral politics as the party systems of European democracies were in the process of being 'frozen', at a time when the principal existing political movements had only just accommodated themselves to post-war conditions, which often involved enlarged franchises and new electoral laws introduced in the wake of the First World War. In the Low Countries the major existing parties did rather well in terms of holding on to their electoral support, and new political movements were peripheral and played only a marginal role.

Thus fascism never succeeded in becoming a major political force in the Low Countries, although fascists tried very hard to win support and a number of would-be contestants for the position of mentor and leader of fascism presented themselves in the 1920s and 1930s. Some of these aspiring fascist leaders may not have started out as fully-fledged fascists, and some of them probably did not attract only a purely fascist following. But the examples of fascist movements and regimes provided by Italy, and later by Germany, and the opportunities left in political space by existing political parties, drew potential leaders and their followers who exhibited authoritarian nationalist ideals, inexorably towards fascism.

As indicated earlier, the focus of attention will fall on one Dutch and four Belgian fascist movements, since these generally conform to the three common elements which characterised fascism according to Payne. A few additional points have to be made, however. The first relates to the third element of Payne's definition, that is, the specific style and organisation of the movements. The NSB was apparently hardly able to generate the high level of mobilisation and membership activism which the definition requires. My impression is that the same is probably also true of the VNV, which was never an extremely activist, highly mobilised organisation. It also had difficulty in keeping up a very stylised appearance at its public meetings, since the mixture of a traditional fair and the choreography of a homogeneous mass movement, which characterised its gatherings, did not easily go together.[9] It is primarily the low mobilisation aspect which could allow one to place the NSB and VNV at some stages of their development, or even during their entire existence, within the broad conservative right. However, this aspect was involuntary, for the leaders of these parties did set out to create highly mobilised mass movements, but were unable to realise their objective.

The social position and recruitment pattern of fascist leadership figures is another point which should initially be considered. Payne has stressed that one difference between fascism and the radical Right, within the context of authoritarian nationalism, was their respective connections with existing elites, the differentiating feature being that the radical right should be commanded by existing elites, such as the military, directly.[10] As far as the principal fascist leaders in the Low Countries are concerned, the record is somewhat variable. The leader of the NSB, Mussert, was the son of a primary school teacher, who had risen to become a well-connected, higher civil servant in an important government agency dealing with matters relating to roads and waterways. Forced by the government to make a choice between his political ambitions and his civil service career, Mussert renounced his civil service status in 1934. De Clercq, leader of the VNV, had initially been a primary school teacher, became an ambulance-man during the First World War, before starting a lengthy career as an MP representing the cause of Flemish nationalism. Van Severen and Degrelle, the leaders of *Verdinaso* and *Rex* respectively, came from families of small-town notables. Both attended university without taking their degrees. Van Severen served as a Belgian officer, was demoted, and became a 'frontist' MP after the war. He was not, however, re-elected in 1929. Degrelle, who was born in 1906 and was by far the youngest of the fascist leaders under review, was at first an organiser and propagandist for the Catholic Party. After a confrontation with its leadership, he broke with the party and started *Rex*. Hoornaert, the leader of the *Légion Nationale*, was a lawyer in Liège after serving as an officer in the Belgian Army. Although not one of these fascist leaders belonged to the national elite (and some, such as Mussert and Degrelle, apparently lost important connections by starting their own movements), all seem to have contemplated the use of their links with the elite at various times in order to further their aims. This is particularly true of Degrelle, as well as Van Severen, in the late 1930s. Both Degrelle and Mussert enjoyed some support from the elite throughout their party careers. An even more obvious fusion with existing elites, however, would have altered the nature of their movements.

Finally, in the case of the VNV, another factor needs to be stressed. The VNV was founded by De Clercq as a reaction to the creation of the *Verdinaso* movement by Van Severen. Van Severen had been active in the Flemish nationalist movement, and after the formation of *Verdinaso* attempted to capture the support of Flemish nationalists by using a fascist message. The VNV was a counter-movement to this development, and although some of its intellectual supporters, and a major part of its rank and file, initially viewed it merely as a continuation of organised Flemish nationalism, key national party figures preferred to regard it as a fascist movement (as defined in our terms), and steered it in that direction.[11] It was a mass movement, but it never became the sole representative of Flemish nationalism. Not only did the Flemish section of the Catholic Party cater for Flemish demands, but MPs explicitly chosen on the Flemish nationalist ticket in these years were not necessarily VNV supporters, though most of them were. It is therefore difficult to equate electoral support for Flemish nationalism with VNV sympathy in general, let alone see it as a sign of support for fascism. There are also other, somewhat peculiar, aspects in the relationship between the VNV and Flemish nationalism. Although De Clercq was the object of efforts to construct a true leadership cult, he was merely a member, but not the president, of the parliamentary party composed of Flemish nationalists, and was by no means the most extreme figure in this company. The VNV was to a great extent a continuation of Flemish nationalist associations, and too entangled with other organisations active in the field of Flemish nationalism to be able to develop its fascist character without strain.

When fascist movements failed to achieve a high degree of mobilisation, or when they became too closely associated with existing elites, or when they remained entangled with other movements and associations, then they could take on the appearance of being part of the conservative or of the radical right, or reflect characteristics of both of these 'directions' within the right. In the examples provided by the fascist movements of the Low Countries this is not merely a hypothetical question. However, these features of the Dutch and Belgian fascist movements can be considered as handicaps which hampered the full realisation of the fascist potential which they embodied. The NSB and the VNV wavered towards the conservative right, while *Verdinaso* and *Rex* were inclined towards the radical right. The *Légion Nationale* was, as far as we know, totally fascist, without ever growing into a true mass movement.[12]

With the exception of the *Légion Nationale*, the movements under discussion all started in the 1930s. The membership of the NSB peaked at around the 50,000 mark towards the end of 1935. *Rex* was by far the largest of the Belgian fascist parties in the mid-1930s, with a membership of perhaps 115,000 during its peak period of 1936 to 1937, which declined dramatically to around 12,500 by 1939. The membership estimates available have to be treated with caution, however, for they are made from a very narrow source base.[13] If we set aside all the difficulties involved in a comparison between the NSB and Belgian fascist movements (such as the lower membership fees levied by *Rex*, for example), the figures suggest a larger following for Belgian fascism during the mid-1930s. It is probable that by 1939 Belgian fascist parties still had a larger membership than that of the NSB in the Netherlands. Schepens estimates the total membership for all four Belgian movements at less than 35,000 in 1939, but his figure for the VNV, at 12,000 to 13,000 'active members', is probably too low.[14] If we take Willemsen's figures, the total would be around the 47,500 mark, of which roughly 25,000 were in the VNV.[15] By 1939 the NSB's membership had fallen to around 30,000.

The *Légion Nationale* and *Verdinaso* always shunned electoral politics. The NSB felt too weak to participate in the 1933 national elections, but did take part in 1937 and secured 4.2 per cent of the votes. It scored its biggest electoral triumph in April 1935, when it entered the electoral arena for the first time to contest the Provincial Estates election, and obtained 7.9 per cent. This election took place a few months before the NSB's membership peaked. By the time of the Provincial Estates election of 1939, support for the NSB had dwindled from the 1937 level, falling to 3.9 per cent. Flemish nationalists, bearing in mind the differences with the VNV, polled 5.9 per cent, 7.1 per cent, and 8.3 per cent in the Belgian national elections of 1932, 1936 and 1939 respectively. *Rex* obtained 11.5 per cent of the votes in 1936, but only 4.4 per cent in 1939. In electoral terms, therefore, both the NSB and *Rex* peaked in the middle of the 1930s and then declined, whereas the vote for the Flemish nationalists slowly increased over the whole period. The NSB and *Rex* both lost support as a consequence of their identification with increasingly threatening foreign examples of fascism. Flemish nationalism secured support for quite different reasons, of course, and the fascist nature of the VNV was not repellent enough to deter Flemish nationalists from continuing to support it.

After the German occupation of the Low Countries in May 1940, there was some influx of new members into the fascist parties of the Netherlands and Belgium, a development which was looked at with mixed feelings by the 'old guard'. In the Dutch movement the new recruits were somewhat contemptuously called 'May-beetles'. The NSB, VNV and *Rex* movements were all deeply involved in collaboration.[16] Degrelle fought for Nazi Germany on the Eastern Front. Members of the various fascist parties served in important positions in the civil administration. Fascists formed militias to assist in 'territorial defence activities', such as fighting the resistance movement, rounding up Jews, etc., as well as promoting recruitment for military service on the Eastern Front. Van Severen was arrested by the Belgians at the outset of the war and transported to the north of France, where he was shot by French soldiers. Some of his supporters collaborated with the Germans, while others joined the Belgian resistance movement. Hoornaert's *Légion Nationale* put up armed resistance against the German occupation. Hoornaert was seized and later died in a German concentration camp.

The social profiles of the various fascist movements are difficult to establish. On the *Légion Nationale* there is very little data available. It does not seem to have attracted any significant support outside its initial base of ex-servicemen. I will therefore focus my attention on the NSB, *Verdinaso*, VNV and *Rex* movements. For the NSB, VNV and *Rex*, use will be made of electoral results, which is the richest data source available. The fit of members and voters at the ecological level, although far from perfect, is present as far as the NSB is concerned.

The NSB increased its membership only very gradually after its formation in December 1931, and during its first year of existence a thousand members joined the movement. From the beginning of 1933 onwards, the NSB grew at a tremendous rate, a surge in support which continued, with some interruptions, until the summer of 1935. Its growth then levelled off at the 47,000 mark, and a decline set in, which continued until the occupation of the Netherlands in May 1940, by which time membership stood at 28,000. Following the Occupation, new entrants joined in relatively large numbers until the all-time peak was reached in the third quarter of 1941, when the NSB had 75,000 members. Thereafter it declined again until the end of the war, when the movement disintegrated in chaotic circumstances.[17] The net membership figures take into account the in- and outflow of members. In both 1936 and 1937 more than 10,000 people left the NSB, but these losses were compensated by an influx of roughly the same number of new members in 1936, whereas the number of new entrants was down by around 50 per cent in 1937.[18] The increase from May 1940 was due largely to an increased inflow, though the outflow of members also went down immediately, which suggests that the NSB at that stage no longer had any significant number of supporters committed to a fascist principle of national autonomy. The ebb and flow in support before the war may well be explicable by reference to international politics, Dutch political factors and movement dynamics. In explaining the membership fluctuations of the NSB, however, it is not easy to determine the contribution made by each of these factors.

We lack a clear picture of the occupational and social status of the NSB membership. In Table 6.4, two membership distributions are presented, which can only be considered as very rough approximations of the occupational and social structure of the (male) members of the NSB in the 1930s.

In Table 6.4 the first column is based on the aggregate of data provided by five regional studies dealing with the early membership of the NSB. Four of these case studies deal with NSB members situated in the western part of the Netherlands, involving the analyses of the two large cities of The Hague and Rotterdam, the small town of Alkmaar along with some of its neighbouring municipalities, and the wealthy commuter belt of het Gooi south-east of Amsterdam. The fifth study is based on the NSB membership in the rural region of Drente in the north-east of the country. With the exception of the study by Loogman on Drente, the data involves only party functionaries, most of whom were at the lowest echelons of the party hierarchy. This factor is important, for party position within the NSB and occupational status were closely correlated. A problem here is that by no means all functionaries and members were recovered, and the occupations of those who were identified could only be retraced in part. I have excluded the 'without occupation' category, in which quite a number of 'rentiers' were listed, a group in which individuals who had been repatriated from the Indies were prominent. There is obviously a considerable degree of uncontrolled bias in the first column. The second column is based on membership statistics produced by the NSB headquarters in 1936 and 1937, and covers a number of places in the western provinces of the Netherlands, as well as the mining areas of southern Limburg, in which a very large part of the working-class membership of the NSB was recruited. This may

Table 6.4: Two distributions of the occupations of male members of the NSB (by %)

	(A) Aggregates based on 5 regional studies 1933-35	(B) Partial list 1936-37
Liberal professions	19	15
Salaried employees	30	19
Independent middle class	33	23
Farmers	5	4
Working class	13	39
Total (%)	100	100
Frequency (*N*)	346	4,146

Sources: Column A is based on data in the unpublished theses submitted to the University of Amsterdam relating to The Hague by R. E. Smit, 'Kring 5 en kring 32, de Nationaal-Socialistische Beweging in Den Haag en omgeving (van December 1931 tot Juni 1935)' (Amsterdam, 1975); Rotterdam by M. O. van Ossenbruggen, 'De ontwikkeling van de Nationaal-Socialistische Beweging in Rotterdam van December 1931 tot April 1935' (Amsterdam, 1975); Alkmaar by D. J. Hagtingius, 'Groei en afval van de NSB in Alkmaar en het Geesterambacht 1933-1939' (Amsterdam, 1976); Drente by P. Loogman, 'De NSB in Drente. Een onderzoek naar de factoren die de spreiding van de NSB in de provincie Drente heben beïnvloed' (Amsterdam, 1976); and het Gooi by A. J. W. Veen, 'De NSB in het Gooi van haar oprichting in December 1931 tot Juni 1935' (Amsterdam, 1978). Column B is based on data provided by L. de Jong, *Het Koninkrijk der Nederlanden in de Tweede Wereldoorlog. Deel I. Voorspel* ('s-Gravenhage, 1969), p. 285.

also be a biased sample, given the strong possibility that the occupations of members were wrongly classified. The category 'rentiers and pensioners' has again been excluded.

A comparison of the two columns may suggest changes in the composition of the NSB over time, or merely illustrate the differences in the occupational status of functionaries and members reflected in these two samples. I think that the latter case may well apply, though the first possibility should not be excluded. There are some suggestions in the literature on the NSB that it did attract more lower-class people over time, and that these accounted for quite a large proportion of its membership during the war years.[19] A comparison between Tables 6.2 and 6.4 suggests that the higher middle class was overrepresented in the NSB, an overrepresentation which may have been more extreme if (and there is quite a strong possibility of this) it turned out that some salaried employees were in fact managers, and that some of those listed as 'independents' were in reality entrepreneurs. The middle class is definitely overrepresented within the NSB, bearing in mind that a considerable part of the working class is to be found in Table 6.2 in Class IV. Farmers were underrepresented within the middle-class membership section of the NSB, but it would be imprudent to make a statement on the relative over- or underrepresentation of the 'old' as against the 'new' middle classes in the NSB as a whole. What is clear is that the working class was underrepresented in the party.

In its early stage of development the NSB was very much a big city movement. In October 1932 all the support it had came from four large cities, apart from a few members resident in a small university town. By the summer of 1933, half of the growing NSB membership was still concentrated in these centres of initial support. Of the remaining half, some 20 per cent lived in the other parts of the three most urbanised western provinces of Utrecht, North and South Holland, and 30 per cent came from the rest of the country. NSB membership in the big cities was therefore heavily overrepresented, but somewhat underrepresented in the rest of the western provinces (except for the commuter areas, in which it was again overrepresented), and strongly underrepresented in the rest of the Netherlands. This distribution pattern was very stable up to 1940, with in- and outflows of membership determined nationally. The surge of membership support for the NSB after May 1940 was more evenly spread, but it still came predominantly from the western provinces.

There are a number of other features of significance in determining the membership profile of the NSB. One factor which influenced the recruitment pattern of the NSB was religion, and Kooy's monograph on the eastern border-town of Winterswijk shows an overrepresentation of latitudinarian

Protestants and of non-believers among NSB members.[20] This feature conforms with the geographic distribution of members at the national level. The NSB members who joined during the war years also reflect an overrepresentation of adherents of the Dutch Reformed Church (which contained a large number of latitudinarians and marginal Christians), but not of non-believers.[21] Females played a largely supplementary role in the NSB, accounting for 28 per cent of the membership in the lists produced by the NSB in 1936 and 1937, and 32 per cent of the entire membership in 1942.[22] In its age composition, the NSB was by no means a 'youth movement'. It seems that within the NSB there was less emphasis on the exaltation of youth than was customary in other fascist movements. Kooy's analysis of Winterswijk demonstrates that people of all age groups entered the NSB in numbers, though one of his tables suggests some overrepresentation of the age group 30 to 40.[23] Data published by Vos, based on the NSB's national membership in 1942, also shows a significant overrepresentation of the age group 35 to 45.[24] Among the NSB members, males of around 40 years of age, from the higher income brackets and living in and around cities, with only a slight attachment to Protestantism or atheism, were over-represented.

As to the allied question as to who voted for the NSB, the geographic distribution of NSB voters in the election of 1935 suggests that the main centres of electoral support were primarily concentrated in the western parts of the Netherlands, as well as in a few areas of very strong support in the extreme east of the country, where proximity to the German border may be the causal explanation for the relatively strong NSB vote. There are some indications in Kooy's work that personal links with Germany may have had a positive influence on the turn-out for the NSB, but it is difficult to prove that proximity to the German border can be isolated as a significant general factor in the voting pattern of the eastern parts of the Netherlands.[25] An analysis of the Dutch municipalities as electoral units (the mean vote for the NSB of 6.2 per cent is much lower than the national figure of 7.9 per cent, which suggests a concentration of NSB votes in larger municipalities) demonstrates that the following factors were important in determining the electoral strength of the NSB.[26] Wealthy municipalities (described as such on the basis of income tax returns) consistently show a larger degree of NSB support than less wealthy ones. We know from other studies that NSB voters in the cities were concentrated in high status neighbourhoods.[27] It is extremely likely that this relationship also holds true at the level of the individual, with wealthier people being more prone to supporting the NSB. There is also a relationship between the NSB turnout and the rural-urban factor, as well as the degree of support given to the principal political blocks represented in the system of 'pillarisation'. In general the support for the NSB was lowest in rural municipalities in which the population was tightly organised in one or more compartments of 'pillarised' society. The rural-urban and 'pillarisation' factors, however, were not as consistent in determining the NSB electoral support pattern than the wealth factor.

Since the NSB secured support which originated primarily from outside the block-like segments represented in 'pillarisation', such support as it acquired must have come from any of the following two sources: from Liberal parties; or from small, special interest and protest parties. If one compares the 1933 and 1935 election results, it appears that the NSB picked up votes from all of these sources, with the special interest and protest parties suffering the sharpest decline of support.[28] In Table 6.5 below the different factors which conditioned the pattern of electoral support enjoyed by the NSB are presented. The total set of 1,069 municipalities has been divided into five columns, each of which is divided into three categories according to the main influences mentioned above. Table 6.5 shows the average percentages of support for the NSB in all municipalities which have been categorised as indicated.

In broad terms, therefore, the NSB voters were not all that different from the membership of the party: in general they were well-off, from the urban areas of the country where socio-cultural and political segmentation was difficult to establish, and where special interest or social protest parties, often already authoritarian to some extent, had gained a foothold. Of course, this is only the profile relating to the average NSB supporter. Obviously one can find a lot of exceptions to the general picture, caused by such factors as the influence of individual personalities who attracted NSB votes where particular circumstances were favourable, or where associations, such as farmers' organisations, were either taken over or strongly

Table 6.5: NSB voters in different classes of municipalities (by %)

Wealth		Rural/ Urban		'Pillar' Parties		Liberals		Special Interest/ Protest Parties	
Poor	4.9	Rural	5.4	Strong	3.9	Weak	5.2	Weak	2.1
Av.[a]	5.5	Av.	6.5	Av.	6.9	Av.	5.9	Av.	4.7
Rich	8.7	Urban	8.0	Weak	10.3	Strong	7.5	Strong	8.9

Note: a. denotes average.
Source: Passchier and Van der Wusten, 'Het electoraal succes van de NSB in 1935; enige achtergronden van verschillen tussen de gemeenten', in P. W. Klein and G. J. Borger (eds.), *De jaren dertig. Aspecten van crisis en werkloosheid* (Amsterdam, 1979), tables 1, 2 and 3.

influenced by NSB members and used to generate support for Dutch fascism.

The bulk of *Verdinaso*'s following came from West Flanders and was probably recruited from the people who had voted for Van Severen while he was 'frontist' MP for a rural district in the province during 1921 and 1929. In its infancy, *Verdinaso* was essentially a fascist reinterpretation of Flemish nationalism, and it was only in its later stages of development that there was some change of course in the direction towards the radical right, but this seems to have only slightly affected its membership composition. There is no detailed information available indicating any sharp social bias among its membership, though there is a suggestion of working-class underrepresentation in the membership of the Bruges branch in 1940 analysed by Schepens, but this data is piecemeal and for a very late date.[29] Some support did come from Flemish students and from a few radicals who temporarily joined Van Severen's movement. Although Van Severen attempted to extend *Verdinaso* to the Netherlands, he appears to have secured only a minute response from young Catholic intellectuals and students. The total membership of *Verdinaso* never reached five thousand. It would appear that *Verdinaso* had two, perhaps even three, different sources of support, which had much to do with Van Severen's assets as a political leader. On the one hand he secured a personal following in his capacity as a local politician, partly based on his status as a local notable, and probably also facilitated by a West Flemish tradition of radicalism, which made his extreme views - after the war initially towards the left, and then increasingly towards the right - attractive. On the other hand he was the first politician to introduce fascism into Flemish nationalist circles. Its sheer novelty, international appeal and radicalism ensured him some access to a student body which was prone to radicalism due to the emotions whipped up by Flemish demands within the overall context of Belgian politics. In addition, Van Severen seems to some contemporaries to have been an electrifying personality. His fascism, in its expressive features very much Italian in style, was coloured by his cultural orientation towards France. The *Action Française* had influenced him. This aspect provided the link he was able to foster with a few Dutch Catholics.

In the literature on the VNV there is hardly any information to be found on the social composition of its rank and file. However, the milieu from which the VNV was able to recruit is fairly clear from the case histories of its most important leaders, and from the electoral results secured by specific politicians and by the VNV in general. One of the big issues of the Flemish nationalist movement had been the use of Flemish in university courses and the appointment of Flemish speakers to professorships at universities. As a consequence that section of a generation of Flemish youth which was university-educated was very consciously Flemish in outlook. Although a number of the Flemish graduates secured important posts at the national level, some were denied them, and many formed the nodes in the professional networks which covered the Flemish countryside in their capacity as solicitors, notaries, doctors, vets, teachers and lower clerics. These occupational groups, together with local branches of ex-servicemen's organisations, provided the backbone of the local VNV in the Flanders region.

Flemish nationalism, from the days of the 'Front' in the 1920s to the end of the inter-war period, when the VNV had become its main vehicle, gradually won electoral support, but the social basis of its support changed to some extent over time. Within Flanders it lost support in the urban, freethinking, anti-clerical milieu, but won support in the rural, Catholic parts of the region. Illustrative of this trend is the career of Herman

Vos, the parliamentary leader of the Flemish nationalists, who held a reasonably safe seat in Antwerp in the 1920s, which he lost in the 1932 election. By the time of the 1936 election the strongest support for nationalist candidates came from Limburg and West Flanders, the two most rural provinces of Flanders. In the more urbanised provinces of East Flanders, Antwerp and Brussels, seats were also won by nationalists in rural districts. This is not to suggest that Flemish nationalism was restricted solely to farming communities, since there is evidence that the nationalist gains in the province of Limburg in 1936 came not only from farming areas but also from the villages which had recently sprung up around the new coal mining industry.[30] The three traditionally large parties of Belgium all lost support in the 1936 election. The severest loss, about a quarter of its former support, was sustained by the Catholic Party in all parts of the country: Wallonia, Flanders and the Brussels regions. It is generally assumed that the majority of the former Catholic vote in Flanders went to the VNV, and that the VNV did not make any significant gains from the other two large parties. In assessing the nature of VNV support, one should also look at the politicians elected on its ticket. The two most radical MPs came from the province of West Flanders. It is probably no coincidence that R. de Tollenaere, the only Flemish nationalist MP to have had clear 'national socialist sympathies', won the West Flanders seat in 1936 which Van Severen had lost in 1929.[31] Born in 1909, De Tollenaere had only recently graduated from university, and was not only the propaganda leader of the VNV, but also a member of the hard core within the VNV which was responsible for steering it in a fascist direction. Other members of this core group were also university graduates from West Flanders, who had joined various radical groups while at university in the 1920s. Overall it would seem that the VNV attracted support from different layers of the Catholic population in the Flemish countryside, while its leadership corps came primarily from recent university graduates originating from West Flanders.

Less than a year after Degrelle had parted company with the Catholic Party, his *Rex* movement also participated in the national election of 1936. *Rex*, in the eyes of many at the time, had begun as a student affair, but soon developed a broader base, attracting diverse elements through the popular journalism of Degrelle's yellow press, in which the 'exposure of scandals' loomed large, as well as youth drawn to it by impressive, but also festive, mass meetings. It was Degrelle's hope and ambition to make *Rex* into an all-Belgian movement. But it was started, and was dominated, by French-speakers in Wallonia and Brussels, though Degrelle did learn some Dutch from Linguaphone records. The electoral results of 1936 show that the main support for *Rex* came from French-speakers, but the movement was by no means confined to the same extent to Wallonia and the French-speaking parts of the Brussels region as the VNV was to Flanders. Some of the *Rex* support in the Flanders region probably came from the French-speaking higher status groups, but it is generally held that *Rex* was able to extend its attraction beyond this circle. In Wallonia the movement generally polled higher, particularly in the very Catholic rural Ardennes region, and most of all in Luxemburg, Degrelle's province of origin. *Rex* was least successful in Wallonia in the socialist bulwarks around the mining areas in the province of Hainout. In Brussels, *Rex* candidates also scored very highly. When the support for *Rex* fell from 11.5 per cent in 1936 to 4.4 per cent in 1939, this pattern of support was maintained. Although *Rex* has been described as primarily an urban movement, this seems highly doubtful given the pattern of its electoral support described above, though this is not to suggest that it was merely a rural movement either.[32] *Rex* primarily attracted voters from the Catholic Party, the heavy loser in the 1936 election. But the movement seems to have drawn some support from the Socialist and Liberal Parties as well. If one assumes that in the 1936 election the VNV only attracted former Catholic Party voters, and the Communist Party drew all the socialist losses, and no significant change had occurred in terms of the differential joining and leaving of the body politic, then nearly 70 per cent of *Rex* voters would have come from the Catholic Party, with the remaining votes drawn almost equally from the Liberals and the Socialists. It is possible, however, given the *Rex* emphasis on youth, that it attracted relatively many new voters, which came from Catholic families, but there is no way of testing this hypothesis.

Rex was probably a refuge for the small businessman. Statistical evidence pointing in this direction is provided by the analysis of two partial lists of *Rex* candidates for the national election of

1936, and for the municipal elections of 1938.[33] There is also a membership list for one small commune within the Brussels region.[34] In all three lists the small businessmen, such as shopkeepers, merchants, publicans and hoteliers, are the largest category, accounting for a quarter to a third of the total. Although a useful indicator, the data is too limited to allow one confidently to generalise about the total *Rex* membership. What is clear is that Degrelle was capable of attracting not only sympathy but also support from well-connected circles. *Rexist* MPs included a famous mountaineer of noble stock, who was also a friend of the king, some important lawyers, and a mayor. Most of these individuals seem to have been asked to stand as *Rexist* candidates rather than joining the movement through their own initiative, and it is by no means clear as to how widespread the sympathy for, and approval of, *Rex* actually was among the national elite. But it is unlikely that support from the elite extended much beyond the spring of 1937, when Degrelle challenged the whole political elite in a by-election in Brussels, in which he was decisively defeated.

Though *Rex* support was circumscribed by the Catholic and by the French-speaking factors, Degrelle had some success in creating an all-Belgian movement, but he could only succeed in winning a significant following for a very short while. His extraordinary, though only temporary, success in Brussels was due in part to the concentration of his propagandistic efforts in the city. He had moved his party headquarters from Louvain to Brussels even before he made his final break with political Catholicism, at a time when he had already made clear his political ambitions at the national level.[35] It was in Brussels that he subsequently organised his most impressive mass meetings.

III

Neither the Dutch nor the Belgian polity experienced a major authoritarian nationalist threat, fascist or otherwise. The most important fascist movements peaked at moderate levels in the mid-1930s or even later. There were also a number of other efforts to create fascist organisations during the inter-war period which remained without any success at all. This was because the Netherlands and Belgium were thoroughly modern states situated in the capitalist core of Europe, where the chances for authoritarian nationalist victories after a breakdown of competitive mass politics, according to Hagtvet and Rokkan, were relatively small.[36] The conditions for such a breakdown that were present in the European semi-periphery were nearly totally absent in the Low Countries. Thus there was no widespread feeling of being part of the heritage of failed European empirebuilding, though both countries had, in some stage of their history, been part of former empires. Nor had the Low Countries become peripheral countries in an economic sense following the revolutions in world trade and industry during the sixteenth and nineteenth centuries, although the Netherlands had only been industrialised belatedly. No military-industrial alliances had, as a result, been formed to re-establish their international position. They had even been endowed with more colonial possessions than their European status warranted.

These factors largely explain why no massive fascist mobilisation occurred. In connection with the systemic shocks which happened around 1920 and 1930, they also account for the fact that fascism's most significant support was only mobilised at the later of these two occasions. Being only weakly predisposed to authoritarian nationalism, the relatively minor societal dislocations of the period around 1920 were insufficient to trigger a major fascist movement in the Low Countries. The period around 1930 was more disruptive and traumatic, and led some to question whether the institutions of democratic mass politics were working properly. An additional factor influencing developments in the 1930s was the example of alternative regimes and powerful fascist parties active in countries nearby, which produced a certain appeal for such movements, though rather late in the day. That these were ultimately more fascist, rather than of the radical or conservative right, is mainly due to the way in which the world was seen to be developing around the Low Countries. Italy and Germany were the relevant examples to follow or the relevant threats to oppose. Indigenous movements in the Low Countries, even if they started with different accents, could hardly avoid taking a fascist position.

While the Low Countries were similar in some of their significant macro-variables, and experienced fascist mobilisations which were only slightly different in their total size and timing, they did differ significantly in terms of their social profiles and in their degree of organisational cohesion. Support for Dutch fascism was particularly concentrated among high status groups in urban and suburban parts of the country, where politically organised religion was of minor significance and where social life was not strongly moulded by 'pillarisation'. Support for Belgian fascism came primarily from the Catholics, and was probably less confined to specific status groups, although the number of working-class people supporting fascism was relatively small. It would appear also that students, and youth in general, were more important in the Belgian movements than in the NSB. Finally, while in the Netherlands there was only one fascist organisation of some significance, in Belgium there were several. How can one account for these differences? Four factors appear to be relevant in explaining the various profiles: the differences discernible in the two countries as regards the influence of the Catholic Church, the historical role of the Liberal and of the Catholic parties, the experience of the First World War, and university involvement in major political issues. The first two factors provide explanations for differences in terms of the status groups involved in fascism, as well as in the former political allegiance, religion and place of residence of fascist supporters, while the latter two account for the different emphasis on the role of youth and of students in the fascisms of the Low Countries.

It is my impression that the Catholic Church in the Netherlands was more monolithic and controlled the behaviour of its members more effectively than its Belgian counterpart. This was the consequence of two reasons. The Dutch Catholics were perhaps more vigorous, because they had taken on some of the deadly seriousness of their Calvinist rivals. At the same time they were located at a religious frontier, which may have imbued them with a mentality designed to preserve and extend the community of true believers against all rival challenges. A Dutch study of the birthrates in neighbouring communities on both sides of the Dutch-Belgian and Dutch-German borders has in fact suggested such a difference between Catholics in the sphere of marriage and child-bearing.[37] In contrast to the unity of the Dutch Catholic Church, the Belgian Catholic Church was divided on the issue of the 'Belgian question'. While the leadership of the Catholic Church in Belgium was in favour of one nation encompassing all Belgians, the lower Catholic clergy in Flanders gave support to Flemish nationalism, some of the clerics supporting even its most extreme versions. The Catholic Church in Belgium was unable, despite efforts to do so, to effectively close its ranks in face of the fascist challenge.

The second significant factor relevant in determining the origins of fascist sympathies may have been the consequence of groups of individuals feeling that they were 'on the losing side' following the introduction of the new stage of competitive mass politics after 1918. In Belgium the Catholic Party had monopolised government cabinets from the 1880s up to the middle of the First World War. The dominance exercised by the Catholic Party was lost in the coalition governments of the post-war era. In the Netherlands the Liberals had slowly been removed from the centre-stage of Dutch politics since the 1880s. They finally lost their former pre-eminence, with seemingly no chance of staging a comeback, when the franchise was extended in 1918, and when united blocks of rival political support were organised all round them, in sharp contrast to their own fragmented and loosely organised parties. Disenchanted former Liberal voters in the Netherlands, and former Catholic voters in Belgium, affected by the feeling that their parties had lost influence politically after 1918, or holding the view that they could not win in the extended political arena of the post-war era, harboured feelings of resentment and frustration which could be exploited by fascist movements.

The relatively more important role of youth in general, and of students in particular, in the more important Belgian fascist movements has, I think, much to do with the First World War. It was war experience which accounts for youth, that is ex-servicemen, becoming a separate political category in Belgium, but not in the Netherlands. Many of the small radical youth groups of the 1920s are reflections of this development pattern, and 'fronters' such as Joris van Severen, and the *Légion Nationale*, provide the clearest example. The feature of youth organising itself separately was repeated in Degrelle's *Rex* movement. At first the by now older guard of ex-servicemen looked at *Rex* members as 'just kids', but in the end many of them joined the movement or expressed sympathy with it. In the Netherlands this outlook of youth was only weakly developed, and youth organisations were generally contained within the major political blocks. Finally, Belgian universities were the focus of the most salient issue of inter-war Belgian politics:

the language question. It is obvious that many students became involved in this issue, and that commitment to the language question, so central to nationalism, could easily lead towards involvement in fascism, even if such a progression was not inevitable. The road leading a university student towards becoming a fascist activist was a little wider in Belgium than it was in the Netherlands.

The fragmentation of the Belgian fascist movements has much to do with the linguistic divisions, and the ensuing alternative interpretations of nationalism. There were various efforts made to overcome the division, and Van Severen made some attempts to push the linguistic issue into the background. *Rex* and VNV tried to come to some agreement, but the efforts failed. Mussert, on the other hand, was able to defeat attempts by his opponents to form rival fascist movements due to his superior organisational ability and his cultivation of an image of respectability. Attempts to form alternative fascist organisations in the Netherlands, based to a large extent on the Catholic population, probably also failed on account of the tighter grip exerted by the Dutch Catholic Church on its following.[38] The linguistic divide in Belgium and the ensuing alternative nationalisms provided many opportunities for fascist mobilisation and therefore resulted in the fragmentation of Belgian fascism. These various movements did not, however, necessarily cancel each other out in terms of growth potential, as Schepens seems to conclude.[39] On the contrary, it could well be that Belgian fascism was, if anything, slightly more successful than its Dutch counterpart, since more than one nationalism was available in Belgium to serve as an appropriate and mutually reinforcing basis for different fascist organisations in various parts of the country.

Notes

1. G. Allardyce, 'What fascism is not: thoughts on the deflation of a concept', *American Historical Review*, vol. 84 (1979), pp. 367-88.
2. S. G. Payne, *Fascism. Comparison and Definition* (Madison, 1980), ch. 1.
3. M. H. Kater, *The Nazi Party. A Social Profile of Members and Leaders 1919-1945* (Oxford, 1983).
4. E. H. Kossmann, *The Low Countries 1780-1949* (Oxford, 1978), p. 630.

5. S. Rokkan, 'Towards a generalised concept of '*verzuiling*': a preliminary note', *Political Studies*, vol. 25 (1977), pp. 563-70; with respect to Belgium: L. Huyse, *Passiviteit, pacificatie en verzuiling in de Belgische politiek* (Antwerpen-Utrecht, 1970); on the Netherlands-Belgian comparison, see *Acta Politica*, vol. 19, January 1984, special issue.
6. Kossmann, *The Low Countries*, p. 574.
7. P. Merkl, 'Comparing fascist movements' in S. U. Larsen a. o. (eds.), *Who were the Fascists? Social roots of European fascism* (Bergen-Oslo-Tromsø, 1980), p. 778.
8. J. J. Linz, 'Political space and fascism as a latecomer' in Larsen, *Who were the Fascists?*, pp. 153-89.
9. A. W. Willemsen, *Het Vlaams nationalisme 1914-1940* (Groningen, 1958), p.332 and p. 381.
10. Payne, *Fascism*, p. 20.
11. Willemsen, *Vlaams nationalisme*, pp. 323-4.
12. Slightly different conclusions are reached by L. Schepens, 'Fascists and Nationalists in Belgium 1919-1940' in Larsen, *Who were the Fascists?*, pp. 511-4; Payne, *Fascism*, p. 20.
13. J. M. Etienne, *Le mouvement rexiste jusqu'en 1940* (Paris, 1968), pp. 79-80.
14. Schepens in Larsen, *Who were the Fascists?*, p. 512.
15. Willemsen, *Vlaams nationalisme*, p. 380, note.
16. A comparative overview of the NSB and of the VNV is provided by I. Schöffer, *Het nationaal-socialistische beeld van de geschiedenis der Nederlanden. Een historiografische en bibliografische studie* (Arnhem-Amsterdam, 1956), pp. 71-98.
17. J. F. Vos, 'Het ledenverloop van de Nationaal Socialistische Beweging in Nederland', unpublished thesis, University of Rotterdam, 1971, appendix 4. There are some problems with regard to small numbers of provisional members, secret members and members in foreign countries and the colonies.
18. Ibid., p. 31.
19. L. de Jong, *Het Koninkrijk der Nederlanden in de Tweede Wereldoorlog. Deel I. Voorspel*, ('s Gravenhage, 1969), p. 344; J. Zwaan (ed.), *De Zwarte Kameraden. Een geïllustreerde geschiedenis van de NSB* (Weesp, 1984), p. 76; Vos, 'Het ledenverloop van de Nationaal Socialistische Beweging', p. 52.

20. G. A. Kooy, *Het échec van een 'volkse' beweging. Nazificatie en denazificatie in Nederland 1931-1945* (Assen, 1964), pp. 146-53 and p. 160.
21. Vos, 'Het ledenverloop van de Nationaal Socialistische Beweging', p. 51.
22. Ibid., appendix 8.
23. Kooy, *Het échec van een 'volkse' beweging*, p. 139.
24. Vos, 'Het ledenverloop van de Nationaal Socialistische Beweging', appendix 8.
25. Kooy, *Het échec van een 'volkse' beweging*, pp. 136-8.
26. N. P. Passchier and H. H. van der Wusten, 'Het electoraal succes van de NSB in 1935; enige achtergronden van verschillen tussen de gemeenten' in P. W. Klein and G. J. Borger (eds.), *De jaren dertig. Aspecten van crisis en werkloosheid* (Amsterdam, 1979), pp. 262-73.
27. O. Schmidt, 'A quantitative analysis of support for the National-Socialist Movement (NSB) from 1935 to 1940 in the City of Amsterdam', *Acta Politica*, vol. 14 (1979), pp. 479-508.
28. Slightly different conclusions are reached by J. Th. Minderaa, 'Crisis en stembus. De NSB en de gevestigde orde' in H. W. von der Dunk (ed.), *In de Schaduw van de depressie. De NSB en de verkiezingen in de jaren dertig* (Alphen aan de Rijn, 1982), pp. 21-65.
29. Schepens in Larsen, *Who were the Fascists?*, p. 515.
30. Willemsen, *Vlaams nationalisme*, p. 363.
31. Ibid., p. 364.
32. Etienne, *Le mouvement rexiste*, p. 65.
33. Ibid., p. 64.
34. D. Wallef, 'The composition of *Christus Rex*' in Larsen, *Who were the Fascists?*, p. 519.
35. Etienne, *Le mouvement rexiste*, p. 27.
36. B. Hagtvet and S. Rokkan, 'The conditions of fascist victory' in Larsen, *Who were the Fascists?*, p. 147.
37. F. van Heek, *Het geboorte-niveau der Nederlandse Rooms-Katholieken. Een demografisch-sociologische studie van een geëmancipeerde minderheidsgroep* (Leiden, 1954).
38. Cf. L. M. H. Joosten, *Katholieken en fascisme in Nederland 1920-1940* (Hilversum, 1964) for an extensive description of the different efforts.
39. Schepens, in Larsen, *Who were the Fascists?*, pp. 513-4.

Chapter Seven

AUSTRIA

Gerhard Botz

Although historians dealing with the contemporary history of Austria have, since the mid-1960s, concentrated research on the First Republic (1918-1934), the Dollfuss-Schuschnigg dictatorships (1934-1938) and the *Anschluss* period (1938-1945), fascism in Austria is still one of the topics deserving further empirical research and attempts at general interpretation. This is surprising given that there are many specialised studies on historical events and aspects related to fascism in Austria[1] and given that we already have several useful summarising monographs, mostly from non-Austrian scholars.[2] There are also various contemporary attempts to develop a theory of fascism by Otto Bauer and other Austrian socialists,[3] which could have been used for shaping research on fascism in Austria.

Various reasons, such as the political failure of Austro-Marxism, the need to create an Austrian identity different from German nationalism after the Nazi period, the efforts to compromise about the historic past among the partners of the Great Coalition government after 1945,[4] can be blamed for this situation. Compared with the vast and sophisticated literature available especially on German National Socialism and Italian Fascism, studies on Austrian fascism display several systematic shortcomings.[5] First of all, they indicate a strong tendency to exclude Austrian pre-1945 history from its obvious international context, save simply blaming foreign powers - Mussolini's Italy and Hitler's Germany - for interfering in Austrian politics. Not surprisingly, many studies on Austrian fascism resist the use of explicit hypotheses and general theories on the nature and causes of fascism; they are often historicist in the traditional sense, and hence by virtue of this reliable when dealing with details, differentiations and in avoiding hasty conclusions.[6] The reverse side of the coin is that they have not contributed very much to the clarification of the guiding questions prevalent in international research on fascism. This is also partly true of the few attempts which have been made to apply Marxist theories of fascism to the Austrian case.[7] It is astonishing that political scientists, who have produced a good deal of research on German National Socialism, have not made any significant contribution to the understanding of our theme.[8]

As yet consensus has not been reached among scholars of Austrian fascism on questions such as 'Was there an Austrian fascism at all?', 'Was the *Heimwehr* movement, commonly held to be fascist outside of Austria, fascist in the proper use of the term?', 'What kind of regime was represented by the dictatorship of Dollfuss and Schuschnigg: was it mainly fascist, authoritarian or corporatist?', and 'Was Nazism simply imported from Germany into Austria or did it have its own base in the country?'. More specific questions and central issues of any analysis of fascism[9] are also still open to discussion, such as 'Where did the mass support of fascist movements come from in Austria?', 'Which economic, social and political reasons account for the support given by various social groups to fascism?', 'What was their collective motivation?', 'Did direct financial support from capitalists or from outside of Austria play a decisive role in giving rise to fascism in Austria?', 'What kind of relationship linked Austrian fascism with the bourgeois parties and pre-fascist political culture?', 'Why did the *Heimwehr* fail to become the dominant expression of fascism in Austria and not overthrow Austrian democracy as early as 1929 or 1931?', 'To what extent did Austrian Catholicism foster or inhibit the various kinds of fascism?', and finally 'Did these kinds of fascism compete with, and by doing so, thus block each other, or did one pave the way for the other?'.

Only a few of the many questions posed above will be examined in this chapter. First, the position of Austrian fascism within the general European context will be outlined, based primarily on theories of modernisation and models of explanation developed by modern social scientists and by the Austro-Marxist theoretician Otto Bauer. Secondly, a typology of strands of Austrian fascism, embedded in the politico-societal system of interwar Austria, will be developed. And thirdly, some generalisations concerning the social bases of the mass following of the main-stream of Austrian fascist movements will be made.

I

The concept of fascism used here is a generic one which is applicable to forms other than that of Italian Fascism. Emphasized also is the distinction which needs to be made between fascist *regimes* - or similar kinds of dictatorship - from fascist *movements* before the seizure of power.[10] Only the latter will be dealt with here, and I will not present an account of the changing patterns of the different forces and groups supporting regimes such as the Austrian 'Christian Corporate State' of Dollfuss and Schuschnigg.[11]

As an explanatory framework, fascism can be located, according to Stanley Payne, in an political continuum of various kinds of rightist nationalisms ranging from traditional right-wing conservatism to extreme fascism. Corporate or authoritarian nationalism and elitist right-wing extremism can be positioned somewhere in the middle of the range.[12] Among the common features which fascism shares with other right-wing political phenomena of nationalism are anti-Marxism, anti-liberalism and open aggressiveness towards ethnic or religious minorities. In contrast with the opposite end of this right-wing continuum, fascists tend to have a secularised, neo-idealistic *Weltanschauung*, display some anti-capitalist, pseudo-socialist tendencies and, even more so, tend to support mass mobilisation, which strongly affects their nationalism, the style of their organisation and propaganda, and the effectiveness of their violence in a typical way.

Fascism, despite being opposed to many aspects of modern society, is based on societies which are at least partially modernised or in the process of being modernised,[13] that is societies which have at least already left the quasi-static stage of pre-industrialism and which have been affected by the social consequences of the capitalist economy and the industrial revolution. There were, on the one hand, those countries in the west and north of Europe which were highly industrialised and already fully capitalist, where stable middle-class democratic societies with powerful labour movements had established themselves either through evolution or revolution; on the other hand there were the semi-feudal societies of small farmers in south-eastern Europe, where the traditional patriarchal structures still predominated.[14] In central and southern Europe there were mixed or strongly contrasting areas and areas of transition with significant gaps and discontinuities among the various elements involved in the modernisation process in comparison with the West European model. And it was precisely these partly and unevenly modernised societies which by and large proved to be ideal breeding grounds for fascism, primarily when special political and social preconditions, resulting from various crises after the First World War and during the World Economic Crisis, occurred.

The slow historical development of the trend towards fascism required, however, a new series of impulses before it could be finally established. Central Europe was to witness this in its starkest form. The most important developments which rocked this zone are common knowledge and relate on the whole to the First World War: there was an excited and frustrated nationalism; there was the complex of problems connected with the economic and political breakdown occasioned by the war, together with the re-formation of nations and states which took place in the areas where the races were mixed, in particular within the former Habsburg Empire;[15] there were the crises in the economic structure and, after the war, social problems aggravated by inflation and unemployment; and there were the strong social revolutionary movements and tendencies after the end of the First World War, though these were not wholly successful. These upheavals during and after the First World War sufficed for an initial wave of fascism to pass through parts of Europe in the early 1920s, starting from Italy and Bavaria. Austria, like almost all the other countries affected by the development of strong fascist movements during the 1920s, belonged exactly to this de-stabilised central zone of Europe.

To this was added a particularly critical development towards the end of the 1920s, namely the World Economic Crisis, which saw a drop in industrial productivity of between 33 per cent and 42 per cent. The social consequences thereof are well known. Once more Austria, together with Germany, belonged to the most severely affected countries. That is not to say that the economic crisis automatically led to the rise of fascist mass movements, but there is no doubt that it was a precondition for these movements and for the crisis which faced the democratic or the traditionalist government systems which had only recently (after the First World War) been established. Fascist movements now spread in almost all the other countries of southern, western and northern Europe, but nowhere to the same extent as in Germany, where it became possible for National Socialism to gain power. Towards the end of the nineteenth century the last relics of the feudal class system in Germany had come to terms with social reforms and no longer resisted national reunification from above. This led to a national development which is still discussed today under such slogans as 'The special German way'[16] or 'A delayed nation'[17], no solution to which has been arrived at to date. Similar socio-historic peculiarities applied also to the German-speaking areas of the old Austro-Hungarian Empire. There emanated from National Socialism a kind of after-effect which issued directly in the fascist satellite regimes of the Second World War.

One thing is clear: in this crises-shaken area of Europe the only states that were major powers also became the countries of 'classical' fascism[18] in Europe and the weaker fascist movements of the 1920s took their cue from there.[19] It was succeeded for the most part in its function as guide and gravitational centre of fascism by German National Socialism, which was even more powerful and radical. For a while, before Italy and Germany compromised on the basis of foreign policy, this led to a strong conflict among the competing strands of fascism, especially in the Alpine and Danubian regions, as well as in the Balkans.

Although it has as yet not been possible to put into clear categories all the multiplicity of social substrata, social structures, ideologies and forms of development of fascist movements in Europe, following the typology put forward by E. Weber and P. Merkl, I would like to propose the following divisions for the treatment of my theme:[20]

a kind of 'leftist' fascism in parts of southern and western Europe, with a strong *urban* bias, which would also include early Italian Fascism;

a *rural* conservative version of fascism which was responsible in Italy for the decisive increase in support for Mussolini and which was widespread in eastern and southern Europe;

> *German National Socialism*, which in its structure can also be taken as a model for a number of fascist movements in neighbouring countries and for those in northern Europe.

Austria had a special position in that it stood at the centre of the European constellation as described above from the point of view of its geographic situation, but also in terms of its economic and social structure and the intensity of the crisis. It also had an intermediate position with regard to the types of fascism which evolved, for at least two - if not elements of all three - types of fascist movements are found there. Furthermore, the Christian Corporatist regime of 1934 to 1938 is an interesting combination of features of corporate, authoritarian and fascist regimes comparable with Salazar's Portugal and Franco's Spain,[21] which makes 'Austro-fascist' dictatorship a kind of half-fascist authoritarian regime rather than a fully fledged fascist one.

II

There was in Austria, on the one hand, a secularised, German-nationalist, radical version of fascism, which in its social structure was more orientated towards the city and the town, namely National Socialism. On the other hand, there was a 'moderate' version tending towards Italian Fascism, which was essentially linked to the rural areas and undoubtedly had clear connections with the elitist radicalism and traditional conservatism of the right. This strand was represented by the so-called *Heimwehren*, which were only loosely unified.[22]

Thus fascism in Austria coincided to a great extent with the same cleavages which had defined to a large extent the middle-class sub-cultures - the so-called political 'camps' - of Austria for over one hundred years.[23] The 'pillarisation' of Austria[24] became more pronounced and decisive after 1918. This was due in part to the widening of the gap between the middle-class 'camps' and the Marxist 'camp', a result of the intensified and violent class struggle,[25] which developed out of the economic and social consequences of the First World War and the corresponding difficulties in starting again, as well as from Austria's permanent structural crisis and the market collapse of the world economy. It was also due in part to the national identity crisis and the problems connected with the *Anschluss* question,[26] which intensified the ideological antitheses within the middle-class 'camps', which in the final analysis go back back to the late nineteenth-century opposition between the anti-clerical German nationalists and the clerical pro-Habsburg Christian Socialists. This line of division among the middle-class groups was further exacerbated by the fact that after 1918 Austria found itself in a position where the spheres of influence of German and Italian imperialism overlapped. Particularly after 1918 Austria held a key position for the two major powers in the west and south in their efforts to establish themselves economically and extend their military and strategic influence, especially on south-eastern Europe.

The external influence of rival financial and propagandist expansionism on internal relations is also reflected in the development of fascism in Austria.[27] For these reasons a specific form of fascist movement may have developed both within the Catholic conservative 'camp' and among the German nationalist parties. This circumstance explains why the forces of fascism were split in Austria and why, in the end, fascism could only come to power with outside support, first with the backing of Italy, and then with the overt support of Germany, each in accordance with internal developments. Fascism in Austria was thus at first an *internal* phenomenon of both of the large middle-class 'camps'. It was only relatively late in the development of the fascist movements, that is shortly before or even just as these reached their high-point of mass attraction, that each of the two kinds of fascism moved towards the respective other camp and towards the margin areas of the socialist movement.

I am aware that this generalisation certainly leaves itself open to criticism on two points. First, the question arises as to whether in fact the *Heimwehren* of the late 1920s and early 1930s, which were decidedly regional and stamped with the social and political peculiarities specific to respective provinces, were sufficiently unified to warrant the kind of estimation made of them here.[28] This problem becomes even greater when we consider that the so-called Korneuburg Oath, which was taken in May 1930 by the leaders of the various *Heimwehr* organisations, was in fact only a kind of fascist minimum progamme[29] and was by no means capable of abolishing internal differences among the regional groups of the *Heimwehr* movement. On the one hand the Lower Austria wing of the *Heimwehr* movement, and to a certain extent the Tyrolean *Heimwehr* too, remained well within the boundaries of the traditional right when approaching the Christian Socialist Party,[30] while the tendency, on the other hand, of the Styrian *Heimwehr* to support the *Anschluss* became so strong that it was fascist in the full sense, belonging typologically to the National Socialist 'camp' even before it officially went over to the NSDAP.

The *Heimwehren* had developed in 1919 from the earlier 'Village Guards', 'Peasant Guards' and 'Civil Guards', as well as from the Carinthian Border Fighters and from offshoots of the German free corps. These self-defence formations were as yet as far from being fully fascist as were the *Einwohnerwehren* of Bavaria which influenced developments in western Austria.[31] But in 1926 they gave rise to an independent fascism - that of the *Heimwehr* movement described above - which came into being against a background of intensified structural and economic crisis in the agrarian sector. At the beginning the *Heimwehr* movement received strong support from the anti-Marxist parties - the Christian Socialist Party, the Greater German People's Party and the Peasants' League - and the organs of the state. As early as the mid-1920s they also got massive support from Mussolini's Italy. Influenced by this, and by the prestigious philosopher Othmar Spann,[32] the *Heimwehr* movement drew up, as mentioned previously, a corporate and fascist programme in 1930 and began to contest elections as opponents not only of Marxism but also of the middle-class parties. Hereupon the Christian Socialists and the other traditional middle-class parties began to distance themselves from the *Heimwehr* movement. The latter began to split up into regional wings at a time when its attraction for the masses had already passed its summit in 1931. An attempted coup by the Styrian faction in the same year[33] - as the movement was becoming more and more pro-Nazi - was more a sign of disintegration than of strength. Nevertheless, it is a curious fact that the Christian Socialist chancellor Engelbert Dollfuss, at the last moment as it were, took the *Heimwehr* representatives into his government. From here the *Heimwehr* movement, pushed by Mussolini, succeeded in leaving a strong fascist imprint on the authoritarian regime of Dollfus in 1934, the year of civil war. However, in 1936 the influence of the *Heimwehr* movement disappeared and the movement itself was silently submerged in the monopoly party of the authoritarian state, the so-called Fatherland Front, and in the army.[34] The incorporation of the *Heimwehr* movement into the government after 1932 was a consequence of the impact of the World Economic Crisis and of the critical political situation which arose as a result of the massive breakthrough of National Socialism in Austria, as elsewhere.[35]

At this point we can move on to consider the second kind of fascist movement active in Austria, namely National Socialism. Even more than is the case with the *Heimwehr* movement, the historical precursor of this kind of fascism cannot be subsumed under any clear, unified concept of fascism. For apart from Bohemia and the initial stages of National Socialism in Munich, it is only in Austria that we find a division of National Socialism into an older, as yet not fascist form, and a younger form or Nazism of the Hitler kind, which is radically fascist. The organisation which was the direct antecedent of National Socialism in Austria, the *Deutsche Arbeiterpartei* (DAP - the German Workers' Party), came into being as early as 1903 as a result of the superimposition of sharp national conflicts on class cleavages in northern Bohemia.[36] The DAP, which added 'National Socialist' to its name in 1918 to become the DNSAP, was for a long time nothing other than the political arm of the German or *völkisch* white-collar unions.[37] Thus it was, to say the least, just as democratic as the other German nationalist parties of the late Habsburg monarchy era and was certainly not more militaristically hierarchic or more given to violence than these - it was, for instance, less amenable to the leadership principle than the Pan-Germans of Georg von Schönerer.[38] As a national and social reform party, the character of the DAP places it slightly to the left of the centre rather than on the right of the political spectrum.

The stream of German-speaking transport officials and civil servants returning after the collapse of the Austro-Hungarian Empire in 1919 began to firmly implant the ideas and organisation of National Socialism in the area which today constitutes Austria,[39] but the DNSAP remained an unsuccessful splinter party. During the national elections of 1913 and 1920 it gained only 23,000 and 34,000 votes respectively throughout Austria. The inflation crisis and the political instability of the years 1922 and 1923 afforded it a temporary success (it had perhaps 30,000 members by mid-1923), but more important was its transformation into a real fascist party on the lines of Hitler's NSDAP in Munich. Hitler succeeded in maintaining his claim to leadership even in Austria up to 1926, even though this led to serious splits and setbacks among the Austrian National Socialists. The further development of the Austrian NSDAP ran more or less parallel to that of its counterpart in Germany up until 1933, though it was less spectacular quantitatively speaking. The reason for its slower growth in comparison with the Nazi Party in Germany may be the fact that the NSDAP in Austria had to contend not only with a unified Catholic conservative 'camp' and a strong leftist social-democratic labour movement (Austro-Marxism), but also with competing fascist opponents.[40]

By the time of the parliamentary elections in November 1930, in which the NSDAP gained a mere 110,000 votes in all of Austria, the party probably only had some 7,000 members. Its membership support increased by just over twofold during 1932 to reach 16,000 and again more than doubled in 1933 to the 40,000 mark. The membership remained a highly volatile mass, however, since more than 40 per cent left the party again shortly after entering it. It was not until 1932 that the NSDAP, helped immensely from abroad by the rise of Hitler in Germany, gained between 15 and 24 per cent of the votes - in total some 344,000 votes altogether - in four regional elections.[41] After brutal waves of terror the party was prohibited by Dollfuss in 1933, but in July 1934 the Austrian Nazis, with continued support from Germany, were able to attempt a *coup*.[42] Though the *coup* failed, Chancellor Dollfuss was murdered and under his successor Kurt von Schuschnigg, National Socialism succeeded in gradually undermining the Austrian dictatorship from within. After Mussolini, as a consequence of his turn towards Nazi Germany and of the formation of the Rome-Berlin 'Axis', withdrew his protecting arm from Austria in 1936, nothing stood in the way of German intervention.[43] Nevertheless, the *Anschluss* of March 1938 was a consequence not only of foreign military intervention, but also of a previous internal 'nazification' of Austria.[44]

In June 1933, when the NSDAP was outlawed in Austria, the party organisation had 68,000 members, but by the time of the *Anschluss* the membership had increased once more by more than double to reach 164,000, and at the end of 1941 there were (though now in the enlarged Austrian *Reichgaue*) more than 688,000 party members. This was roughly 8.2 per cent of the total population or 20 per cent of the working population. Overall, the quantitative development of the membership of the Austrian NSDAP can be seen as a double growth curve consisting of two S-shaped sections: from 1926 to about 1936, and from about 1934 to 1945. The flattening curve of the first section overlaps with the gradually ascending second curve in 1934. A third, independent process of growth must be assumed also for pre-Hitler Nazism, with its peak in 1923.[45]

Even this brief summary of a much more complex process which brought forth fascism in inter-war Austria should have made clear that there is more than one single, or only one typical, Austrian form of fascism. But it does not make much sense to argue about the question of whether there were two, three, four or five different fascist movements - such as National Socialism, the fascism represented by the pro-Austrian wing of the *Heimwehren* or that of the pro-German Styrian *Heimwehr*, a kind of 'officers' fascism' in the form of the Front Fighters Organisation,[46] and the Fatherland Front - in Austria. One could easily differentiate even further, but for the purpose of this analysis it should suffice to distinguish only between the two major forms of Austrian fascism. It is also obvious that the use of a rigid definition of fascism would mean forcing socio-political reality into a Procrustean bed. Therefore, a gradualistic concept of fascism, which might be able to embrace the horizontal and vertical variations of fascism, one which takes into account regional differences and changes over time, is being applied here. This should not exclude consciously built typologies, a pre-requisite for any systematic comparison.

III

This leads us to the consideration of the social groups recruited by fascism in Austria, which focusses on the membership rather than on the leaders, the militants, or the voters of the major fascist movements. Neither the Marxist class model nor that of the Western (American) type of social stratification will be used to determine the social categories for description and explanation of the social bases of Austrian fascism. Both models fit less well to those societies in the central

North-South belt of Europe which provided fertile breeding grounds for major fascist movements and which displayed a remarkable persistence of features of traditional society even in modernity. The use of occupational categories - or a perception of society according to labour legislative statuses which pre-served a good deal of estate (*ständisch*) structures[47] - seem more appropriate for a description of the social bases of fascist movements in Austria as well as in Germany.

The empirical grounding of the following generalisations is still weak, although it is no longer as weak as it was a decade earlier when virtually only raw statistical data from printed sources were available, some of which are certainly unique in Europe, such as the seperate count of male and female votes in parliamentary elections[48] and the separation of those entitled to vote for the Chambers of Labour according to their occupational status in different 'curias'.[49] Since the early 1970s, several studies dealing with the social structure of Austrian fascism have either been published[50] or are in progress.[51]

It is obvious that in an anti-feminist movement which fascism represents, with its concentration on male associations, women had only a minor role to play. As one would perhaps expect, they were not represented at all among the leaders of paramilitary formations, and there were practically no women in the *Heimwehren*. This reflects more or less the situation in the early Italian Fascist Party, in which only 1 to 2 per cent of members were women in 1921.[52] In contrast to the Italian situation, the number of women members in the DNSAP was higher, especially in its pre-fascist phase. Thus in 1919, 45 per cent of its votes came from women and one-seventh of its candidates were females. But as a result of the 'fascistisation' process in 1922 and 1923, the number of women among new party members dropped dramatically, to 6 per cent between 1926 and 1931 (see Table 7.1). Then a steady rise in female recruitment set in again, women accounting for 12 per cent of new members in 1933, and for 28 per cent during the 'illegality' period. The same seems to be true for the National Socialist electorate, 42 per cent of which were women in 1930. After the party acquired power in 1938, fewer women (some 22 per cent) joined the ranks of the NSDAP, but towards the end of the Third Reich there were more women joining the party again.[53] The situation outlined above is not surprising when we consider that in the

Table 7.1: The average age and percentage of women among the 'new party members' joining the Austrian NSDAP in the period 1926 to 1944

Period of party entry	Age (mean)	% of women members	Frequency (*N*)
1926-1931	29	6	72
1932	33	8	103
1933	33	12	128
May 1938	36	28	493
Nov. 1938-April 1939	37	15	109
1940-1941	39	22	542
1942-1944	23	36	168

Source: Sample from the Berlin Document Center.

years between the wars the female social pattern was - in simplified terms - determined by the three great C's: 'Church - cooking - children'. National Socialism as a movement of socially rather mobilised classes was hard pressed to spread among women who were more strongly attached to the family and to the traditional Catholic-conservative 'camp'. The reason why women were less attracted to National Socialism lies more in the importance of the Church as an immunising factor than in the pronounced fascist cult of masculinity which Nazism projected. Only during the last phase of National Socialism were the less mobilised groups, such as young women (and the rural population also) included organisationally, primarily due to orders from party headquarters. It would seem that after the marked decline in female participation in the period of 'fascistisation' between 1921 and 1923, the later increase of women members can be interpreted as a sign of the diminishing social and governmental distance of Nazism from the political culture and polity of Austria.

We cannot expect any surprising results as regards the age pattern of fascist membership. Fascist parties, and especially their paramilitary formations, were always explicitly youthful in comparison with the population as a whole and with most of the other political parties (with the exception of the Communists) in inter-war Europe. This is especially true for the National Socialists, whose paramilitary activists were on average four years younger (23 instead of 27) than those in the

Heimwehr movement.[54] From this perspective fascism presents itself as a kind of revolt of youth against the establishment in society, in politics and in the family. But in the age aspect, too, the pattern did not remain constant. The evidence shows that the average age of members of the NSDAP in Austria was 28 until 1939, but rose to 33 during the period of its greatest success in 1932 and 1933. Then, however, the only essential increase was that brought about by the aging of the existing membership. During the last three years of Nazi rule it sank again to 23 years as a result of the drive to take members of the Hitler Youth (HJ) and of the League of German Maidens (BdM) into the party. A similar development pattern also took place in Germany and in other fascist movements.

This means that National Socialism got its members by and large from the same age groups, in particular those born between 1894 and 1913 who formed the last generation socialised before the First World War - the so-called 'War generation' - and the generation which grew up immediately after the war (see Table 7.2).[55] It was not of much importance whether the fascist movement was in its infancy, was enjoying the support of the masses or was at the beginning of its regime phase. Certain conclusions can be drawn from this with regard to political socialisation processes specific to a given generation.[56] According to political socialisation theories a generation's politically formative period lies between the ages of fifteen and twenty. This age group was exposed to specific conditions of socialisation in the course of the historical events between 1909 and 1929: the nationalistic and youth-agitated atmosphere of fundamental change; the First World War; the revolutionary post-war crisis; border conflicts and nationalistic agitation; inflation and the subsequent stabilisation crisis; and structural rationalisation, unemployment and the world-wide economic depression. All these factors predestined almost exclusively those age groups to National Socialism, in Austria as in Germany. The younger age group (those born after 1914), people who became politically conscious at a later period, and also the older generation (those born before 1894) did not respond positively to the fascist appeal to the same extent. In simplified terms, the age classes between 1894 and 1913 were predestined for fascist ideas from their youth because of the ideology of national community, the cult of violence and the glorification of the experiences acquired in the

Table 7.2: The age structure of the membership of the Austrian NSDAP, 1926-38 (by %)

Year of birth:	New party members joining the NSDAP in the following periods: 1926-31	1932	1933	1934-38	The age distribution of the Austrian population (14 years and over), 1934
Before 1878	2.8	6.9	3.3	4.2	23.2
1879-1888	11.3	11.9	13.0	11.5	16.1
1889-1893	8.4	5.9	9.8	7.0	8.7
1894-1898	15.5	11.9	13.8	10.6	10.0
1899-1903	15.5	22.8	14.6	15.9	11.4
1904-1908	25.4	23.8	14.6	15.9	11.6
1909-1913	21.1	16.8	28.5	19.1	11.4
1914-1918	-	-	2.4	10.6	7.6
1919-1923	-	-	-	5.2	-
All age cohorts (%)	100	100	100	100	100
Frequency (*N*)	71	101	123	498	5,150,000

Sources: Sample from the Berlin Document Center; *Die Ergebnisse der österreichischen Volkszählung vom 22. März 1934* (Vienna, 1935), section 1.

front line. Consequently, the rise of National Socialism in Austria - as well as in Germany - was a phenomenon which was limited to specific generations and to a very few groups, in which the social unsettling of traditional values in the war and post-war years did not take effect until later.

This circumstance has been partly responsible for the fact that the earliest Marxist theories of fascism[57] often represent fascist movements simply as protest movements of persons uprooted by the First World War. This interpretation is in fact correct when applied to the early stages of most forms of fascism. There were armies of defeated and uprooted military men of the middle and upper rank drifting about, especially NCOs and young officers, for whom it was socially impossible to return smoothly to normal society or to put down roots again as white-collar workers, or as ordinary civil servants or even as labourers. These modern mercenaries could now make no headway against a public opinion which had been visibly shifted to the left by the revolutionary and anti-military movements of the period after 1918. They constituted a kind of dangerous social dynamite in Austria and in Germany and even more so in Italy and in Eastern and Central Europe.

Closely related thereto was the student problem at the time. For five years many of those who had finished secondary school were sent to the front as reserve officers instead of going on to university. After the war these young officers tried to commence, or continue, their university studies, or went to university for the want of something better to do. But the social problems of this group were by no means solved thereby. The number of student drop-outs was great and those who did finish were faced with a rapidly increasing unemployment rate among graduates. Both industrious students and loafers were very overrepresented in almost all fascist movements. We have no exact details about the number of students active in the *Heimwehr* movement, but university students formed 3.3 per cent of the NSDAP up to 1933, roughly five times greater than their number in Austrian society as a whole.

The youth problem which was channelled into the fascist movements again becomes obvious when we look at the occupational and social background of the fascist rank and file (see Table 7.3). Within the ranks of fascist party members who were under 30 years of age, irrespective of whether they were in the NSDAP or in the *Heimwehr* movement, two groups deserve attention: students and former soldiers, especially the demobbed officers, NCOs and special troops. The 'Association of Front Fighters', which represented a special form of 'officer fascism' in Austria, centred mainly on Vienna, recruited its members almost exclusively from war veterans who, paradoxically, were generally very young.

Another constant feature of all fascist movements in Europe was the overrepresentation of academics from many liberal (or 'free') professions, especially of lawyers and physicians, both in the rank-and-file membership and in the leadership. The degree of preponderence, however, does vary greatly. Members of the liberal professions accounted for 5.6 per cent of the membership of the Austrian NSDAP up to 1933, a representation that was five times higher than their number in Austrian society. We do not know if the proportions were similar in the *Heimwehr* movement. The social reasons for the increased

Table 7.3: The development of the social composition of the membership of the Austrian NSDAP, 1926-45 (by %)

Occupational subgroup	'New party members' joining the NSDAP in the following periods: 1926-31	1932	1933	1934-38	1939-41	1942-44	Total 'registered' NSDAP members 1945-46	Total working population of Austria, 1934
Farmers	3	14	12	10	13	2	12.8	10.8
Self-employed	11	6	5	10	7	3	22.3	12.3
Artisans[a]	8	12	23	-	-	-	-	-
Blue-collar workers	20	18	27	31	28	25	13.9	53.5
Private employees	22	15	11	11	12	9	10.8	11.0
Public employees	27	27	10	12	20	10	15.6	11.4
Free professions	6	4	8	1	2	2	4.2	1.0
Students	3	4	4	1	0	1	1.3	(0.6)
Others[b]	-	-	-	24	18	48	19.1	-
Total (%)	100	100	100	100	100	100	100	100
Frequency (*N*)	64	94	115	494	653	169	541,727	2,700,000

Notes:

a. Mostly self-employed craftsmen.
b. Mostly 'artisans' and housewives.

Source: Provisional analysis of sample (*N*: 1,617) drawn from the NSDAP membership files at the Berlin Document Center.

susceptibility of these professional groups to Nazism must lie partly in the previously noted unemployment rate among academics, as well as in the overcrowding of many of the liberal professions, which led to strong generational conflicts within them. They are to be sought even more in the collective feeling of these social groups that their social importance was not esteemed highly enough in post-war society, that they were cut off from further advancement, and that they were financially underpaid. This feeling of being relatively at a disadvantage also played a major role as a motivating factor in moving other more quantitatively important social groups towards fascism.[58] The extremely heterogeneous group of independent businessmen, from the entrepreneur down to the merchant and the small independent handicraftsman, forms an almost exact complement to the liberal professions. In Austria members of the independent middle class had the same representation in the NSDAP as in society at large, unlike the situation in Germany, where this social group was overrepresented in the Nazi movement. The immunisation effect of Catholic conservatism and the stronger attachment of the Christian Socials to their interest associations,[59] which continued unchanged - with the exception of the pro-Nazi small traders - into the corporate dictatorship period, seem to have been stronger in the Catholic areas than corresponding mechanisms within relative Protestant strongholds. On the other hand, the 'old middle classes' (*alter Mittelstand*), especially in rural surroundings, were - for a while - more heavily represented in the *Heimwehren*. The same applies to the farmers who, up to 1931, were hardly represented in the membership of the NSDAP in Austria, but whose recruitment increased rapidly in the early 1930s: they made up 14 per cent of new members in 1932 and 12 per cent in 1933. However, one must assume that rural social groups were extremely overrepresented in the *Heimwehr* movement, though the figure of 70 per cent for farmer representation reported in the *New York Times*[60] in 1928 is probably an exaggeration. In this respect the *Heimwehr* movement, although it was led by aristocratic landowners, was similar to the model of East European fascist movements, such as Codreanu's Iron Guard, the Slovakian Hlinka Party or the Lapua Movement in Finland, all of which had a strong rural base.[61] Estate owners, such as the aristocratic owners of forests, were represented only in the *Heimwehr* version of Austrian fascism. Together with the intelligentsia of small towns they occupied most of the top positions within the leadership, but they brought with them into the *Heimwehr* formations, as a kind of infantry, the masses of rural workers and day-labourers employed on their estates.

The 'new middle classes' (*neuer Mittelstand*) of salaried employees and civil servants were over-represented in almost all fascist movements in Europe. In the Austrian NSDAP, however, they enjoyed an unusually high representation. Up to 1932 civil servants constituted more than a quarter of the NSDAP's membership, but during the mass-movement phase and at the time of the prohibition and persecution of the NSDAP by the 'Christian Corporate regime' their numbers declined drastically, only to increase again to a quarter of the membership total after the NSDAP's assumption of power. Of the total number of the working population those in the public sector represented only about a little over ten per cent. Apart from those in the administrative branches of the civil service, a large number of the public servants in the party came from the middle and upper ranks of employees in the service of the state railway and in the postal service. These social groups, which are similar to the private employees to be discussed later, constitute from the point of view of their social structure a relic of the old pre-fascist Austrian National Socialism. For let us recall the designation of the DAP/DNSAP as the political wing of the *völkisch* white-collar unions. Up to the mid-1920s their main area of recruitment was the new middle class, and this to such an extent that early Austrian National Socialism can only be seen as specific to very few occupational groups. As the Hitler version of National Socialism developed[62] it too spread initially by and large among the white-collar unions in Austria. By doing this it also partly inherited the social structure of the old form of National Socialism. Thus until 1932 Austrian National Socialism was clearly distinct from the German NSDAP which, apart from its initial period in Munich, was never dominated by public (and private) employees to the same extent. For this reason it might have retained the original 'leftist' elements in its programme and ideology for longer than did its German counterpart. This was an exception by international standards as well. The public sector enjoyed the same degree of representation only in the fascist movements in eastern and southern Europe, in the National Socialism of the 'Sudeten-Germans' in Czechoslovakia and in the Swiss 'National Front'.[63] This is probably to be explained in part as a social consequence of the disintegration of the huge network of transport and administrative organisation of the Habsburg empire.

The situation was similar in the case of employees in the private sector. At the beginning these represented more than 20 per cent of the members of the Austrian NSDAP, but in 1932 and 1933 this number fell dramatically, though from the time of the 'illegality' period onwards, 15 per cent of all Nazi members were employees in the private sector. The reasons for this may be found in a disintegration process which, similar to that in the public transport sector, badly affected banking and trade in Austria. When the inflation period came to an end and even before bank after bank collapsed[64] and huge numbers of employees were laid off, there were many white-collar employees ready to align themselves with National Socialism.[65] Also because of a structural amenability which transcended national boundaries, private employees - especially those involved in commerce and holding or aspiring to higher positions - were driven into the arms of fascism in a way in which others were not. I have already referred to the feeling of being relatively underprivileged which academics in the liberal professions entertained. This applies also to those in the public services and to civil servants. All these groups were disappointed in that their hopes of further advancement were frustrated by the processes of industrialisation and the consequences of the First World War. In comparison with workers in industry - above whom the 'new middle classes' in Central Europe demonstratively, consciously and habitually placed themselves - the salaried employees and civil servants felt that their position had become relatively worse since 1918, even if their social situation, when objectively examined according to income level, employment and unemployment rates, had in no way grown worse than that of the workers.[66] The special features of the political and societal modernisation process in Central Europe - i.e. the corporatist (*ständisch*) views - had allowed such evaluations to harden into a deep-seated rightist bias within the 'new middle classes'. It now only required the climax of a crisis to direct the current of this potential into fascist channels.[67] It comes as no surprise therefore that private employees also constantly form an overrepresented group in all fascist movements, not only in Austria. The *Heimwehr* movement, however, akin to the type of agrarian fascism found in eastern and southern Europe, did not have such a strong overrepresentation of the 'new middle classes', and neither salaried employees nor civil servants were prominently represented in it.

It is well-known that fascist movements in general had few recruits from ordinary workers, especially from industrial workers. This was particularly true in Northern, Central and Eastern Europe and in the period when fascism acquired massive support.[68] Though workers and tradesmen always composed between a quarter and a third of the membership of the Austrian NSDAP, this was significantly less than their share in the total labour force (40 to 50 per cent, depending on the way the percentage is calculated). It was only when the World Economic Crisis was at its worst that workers and tradesmen accounted for almost half of the new members joining the NSDAP. We will leave the question open as to whether unemployment and political pressure from owners of businesses was more responsible for this than the collapse of the organisational network of the Austro-Marxist labour movement.[69] By contrast, *Heimwehr* fascism did not attract many workers from industry. Only in the federal state of Styria did the World Economic Crisis and the specific political aims of the employers force a large section of metal workers and those in heavy-industry to join the *Heimwehr* movement. But a large proportion of the participants in the *Heimwehr* units were, as has been mentioned already, agricultural workers, especially those employed in forestry. And they were even paid to participate. But we do not have as yet more precise details on record.

Before concluding, reference to two other aspects conditioning fascist recruitment needs to be made: religion and political provenance. Like other fascist movements outside of Eastern Europe, the Austrian NSDAP had greater success in recruiting from the more secularised parts of society, i.e. among Protestants rather than Catholics, among anti-clericals, the so-called 'believers in God' ('*Gottgläubige*') and the so-called 'Old Catholics'[70] rather than from groups attached to an established Church. In some mining communities in Alpine valleys and in some vine growing districts in eastern Austria we can establish a line of connection between the anti-democratic, anti-Austrian protest of the Nazis and the anti-Catholic, anti-Habsburg resistance to the oppression and the enforced conversion associated with the Counter-Reformation during the seventeenth century. The effects of proto-industrialisation and the early orientation towards a market economy also seem to have played an intermediary role in these areas. The regional and local political differentiations in the development of fascism in Austria might indeed relate to politico-religious attitudes which go back a long way in history.[71] In the case of *Heimwehr* fascism the situation was quite different. Apart from the Styrian wing, it entered more or less into a symbiosis with Catholicism. Here the connection with the majority religion is in line with the East-European fascist model.

A similar situation also presents itself as regards the political provenance of the adherents of fascist movements in Austria. As was the case with fascist forms in areas outside of Eastern Europe, the Austrian NSDAP gained the greatest part of its support from laicised and right-wing parties (from the German nationalists) rather than from parties with religious affiliations (such as the Christian Social Party). These were sectors of society which had up to then not been strongly politically activated or which had been organised in 'unpolitical' associations that represented their interests.[72] In contrast to this development pattern, the *Heimwehr* movement succeeded to a certain extent in attracting members from the Catholic, conservative 'camp' and the associations representing its interests. This means that it automatically attracted a wider range of social groups than just the peasantry. However, once these groups had broken out of the traditional Catholic milieu, they were more disposed to join the NSDAP when the *Heimwehr* movement broke up. One can but stress again the particular importance of politico-cultural 'camp' structures in defining the boundaries within which Austrian fascism was able to expand.

IV

To summarise the many findings evaluated here and presented in the various tables: the social basis of fascist movements in Austria (as well as in most other European countries) is very much like a chameleon. It takes on different colours which shift not only according to the various regional socio-economic contexts in which fascist movements operated, but also according to the stages of their development. It makes a great difference therefore if one looks at - say - the Austrian NSDAP when it was an obscure splinter party, or when it was at the point of breaking through to become a mass party, or when it was an outlawed, violent political opposition movement under a semi-dictatorship, or when it became the monopoly party of a totalitarian regime and acquired the role of dominating the political decision-making process and controlled the 'real wishes' of the people. The same applies to the *Heimwehr* movement when - say - it was little more than a weekly gathering of frightened farmers and male youth gangs in rural neighbourhoods, or when it became a strong protest movement combatting the 'weakness' of the 'bourgeois parties' towards Marxism, or when it was a competing force for domination inside a semi-pluralistic authoritarian regime. It is also quite obvious that a small political party which gains as little as three per cent of the national votes, as the Austrian NSDAP did in 1930, can still derive most of its support from a few specific social and age groups. But as soon as it gained as much as 16 per cent of the votes in various regional elections in 1932, it must to some extent have widened its social spectrum of mass support, otherwise it could not have reached that degree of (relative) electoral strength. This trend towards a people's party was strengthened even more when the party managed to control the public opinion of a nation, or at least a large segment of it. Therefore, a research question which tries to establish a fixed relationship between fascism and specific social groups might easily turn out to be misleading.[73] It would be equally wrong to apply a static general explanation to the rise and mass success of fascist movements.

Things become even more complex when considering the fact that fascists were involved in their 'movement' to different degrees, either as leaders, militants (in paramilitary or affiliated organisations), party members or simply as voters. And in fact there are different patterns in the social composition of each of these categories and, generally speaking, the social basis of a given fascist movement loses much of its specificity when stepping down from the leadership level towards the electorate. Nevertheless, bearing in mind these words of caution, the following relationships between social groups and Austrian fascist movements can be established. The National Socialist party elites, from their early democratic stage to their triumph in 1938, were always strongly based on public and private employees and on academically trained free professions (see Tables 7.4 and 7.5). This is true even in a comparison with the elites of other contemporary political parties.[74] Besides serious setbacks in the strength of public employees among Nazi elites during the Dollfuss-Schuschnigg dictatorship and a decline of the initially dominant role of railway or postal service workers, the National Socialist leadership always preserved important features of its founding periods in the years 1903 to 1904 and 1918 to 1919. The *Heimwehr* leadership of the early 1930s was clearly predominantly rural and indeed based strongly on aristocratic estate owners (of forests) and on farmers and on the so-called 'provincial intellectuals', but it comprised also a variety of other social groups, including workers and civil servants (see Table 7.5).

In contrast to these more or less established social groups among the fascist elites, the militants, often involved in street fighting and violent deeds, usually came from much less secure social positions. Being extremely young, solely male and professionally often marginal, they tended to be recruited from the unemployed and the lower classes, in contrast to the social make-up of the elites and of the membership of fascist movements. This is true for the Austrian NSDAP as well as the *Heimwehr* movement of the early 1930s.[75] Reliable information about fascist party membership is only available for supporters of the NSDAP, but it is clear that the *Heimwehr* organisation built up to compete in the parliamentary elections of 1930 must have included a greater variety of non-rural strata than the *Heimwehr* leadership and militants. On the level of simple party members, the Austrian National Socialist Party was for some years after its 'fascistisation' and takeover by Hitler, just the same as the DAP from Bohemia: mainly a party of the 'new middle classes', including the highly over-represented free professions and students. Only after 1932 were these groups partly overwhelmed by the influx of new party members who displayed a wider social spectrum, which caused a relative shift in the membership spectrum towards the farmers and blue-collar workers. Even after the *Anschluss* and the Nazi seizure of power in Austria the typical inclination of Austrian Nazism towards specific groups of dependent middle-class strata gained

Table 7.4: The social composition of National Socialist elites in Vienna and in Austria, 1919-38 (by %)

Occupational subgroup	DNSAP candidates for Parliament, 1919 for the whole of Austria	DNSAP candidates for Parliament, 1919 in Vienna	NSDAP Elected district councillors, 1932 in Vienna	NSDAP Members of four Provincial diets and 'Bundesrat', 1932	NSDAP Austrian members of 'Grossdeutscher Reichstag', 1938
Farmers	3	4	–	6	5
Self-employed	9	13	18	10	7
Free professions	9	12	4	13	11
Railway employees	14	13	)	13	3
Teachers	7	)	) 34	6	10
Military personnel	1	) 29	)	6	8
Other public employees	29	)	)	20	17
Higher private employees	–	)	8	10	19
Other private employees	13	) 29	22	6	6
Blue-collar workers	11	)	14	10	14
Others	4	–	–	–	–
TOTAL (%)	100	100	100	100	100
Frequency (*N*)	71	24	116	31	73

Sources: *Beiträge zur Statistik der Republik Österreich*, No. 2 (Vienna, 1920), pp. 12-20; *Land und Gemeinde*, vol. 1, No. 1 (Linz, 1932); *Ergebnisse der Wahl in den oberösterreichischen Landtag am 19. April 1931* (Linz, 1931), pp. 4-12; *Der Grossdeutsche Reichstag. IV. Wahlperiode* (Berlin, 1938); *Namensverzeichnis der Mitglieder des Landtages, des Stadtsenates, der Gemeindeausschüsse und der Bezirksvertretungen der Stadt Wien* (Vienna, 1932).

Table 7.5: The social composition of *Heimwehr* and Nazi candidates in Lower and Upper Austria, 1930-32 (by %)

Occupational subgroup	Candidates for parliamentary election (9.11.1930) in Lower Austria		Candidates for provincial diet election (24.4.1932) in Lower Austria	Candidates for parliamentary election (9.11.1930) in Upper Austria		Candidates for provincial diet election (19.4.1931) in Upper Austria	
	Heimatblock	NSDAP	NSDAP	*Heimatblock*	NSDAP	*Heimatblock*	NSDAP
Estate owners	12	2	5	3	0	0	0
Farmers	21	3	20	32	3	21	7
Self-employed (in trade and commerce)	16	6	9	21	8	21	11
Free professions	7	6	4	3	6	7	2
Public employees	19	47	43	14	49	24	44
Private employees	8	15	10	3	20	3	14
Blue-collar workers	13	13	8	21	14	21	20
Others	4	8	1	3	0	3	2
TOTAL (%)	100	100	100	100	100	100	100
Frequency (N)	68	53	98	29	35	29	55

Sources: *Ergebnisse der Nationalratswahl vom 9. November 1930 in Niederösterreich* (Vienna, 1930); *Ergebnisse der Wahl in den Nationalrat am 9. November 1930 in Oberösterreich* (Linz, 1930); *Ergebnisse der Wahl in den oberösterreichischen Landtag am 19. April 1931* (Linz, n.d.); *Ergebnisse der Landtagswahlen in Niederösterreich vom 24. April 1932* (Vienna, 1932).

strength again if one ignores the exceptionally strong membership recruitment from the very young and socially lower-class groups during the last years of the Third Reich. The groups of wage-earners who proved especially susceptible to Nazism were those with a kind of class consciousness and an ambition to get on, people who, for example, seem to have raised themselves within a firm above the level of the non-specialised manual worker by means of exercising certain supervisory functions. These people were primarily civil servants, white-collar workers, foremen, and master craftsmen, but also 'servants', chauffeurs, and engine drivers. Beyond these, Nazism was able to influence most easily only those workers who had not been actively involved in 'Marxist' or Christian unions or party organisations.

The social spectra of the electorate of the *Heimwehr* party and of the NSDAP are again markedly wider than those of their respective party memberships and elites. At least a provisional analysis of the ecological background of the electorate of these two fascist movements in November 1930, based on all Austrian communes (see Table 7.6), clearly shows that the NSDAP's as well as the *Heimwehr*'s voters were much less socially specific than those of the Social Democratic Party and of the Christian Social Party. The Social Democratic Party was clearly based on urban and industrial social ecological environments (which also explains the positive correlation of the socialist vote with professions in the tertiary sector of the economy), while the Christian Social Party was strongly non-urban, agrarian and Catholic. Compared to these class or religion based 'camp' parties, the NSDAP drew its electoral support from a large variety of social and political groupings, giving only slight preponderance to communes with urban, non-agrarian and economically tertiary environments. Surprisingly, the *Heimwehr* vote by and large shows the same features, which proves the hypothesis of its fascist character. Only the different relationship towards the traditional parties of German nationalism demonstrates the difference between the closeness of Nazism and the German national 'camp' and the close connection between *Heimwehr* fascism and the Catholic conservative 'camp'. The analysis of the 1930 parliamentary vote also proves those hypotheses which emphasise the role played in the success of fascism of the at least partly socially and politically mobilised strata not closely bound to the strong

Table 7.6: The electoral ecology of NSDAP and *Heimwehr* votes for the parliamentary election in November 1930 (Unweighted Pearson correlation coefficients, based on all Austrian communes)

	NSDAP	*Heimatblock*	Christian Social Party	Social Democratic Party
NSDAP	1	.06	-.25	.07
Heimatblock	.06	1	-.23	.02
Christian Social Party	-.25	-.23	1	-.65
Greater German People's Party and Peasants League	.08	-.34	-.50	.04
Social Democratic Party	.07	.02	-.65	1
Density of dwelling (urbanisation)	.15	.14	-.40	.60
Percentage of those employed in agriculture	-.20	-.15	.45	-.70
Percentage of those employed in the tertiary sector	.21	.15	-.31	.43
Percentage of Protestants	.04	.02	-.31	.17

Source: *Datenbasis Erste Republik*, L. Boltzmann Institut für Historische Sozialwissenschaft, University of Salzburg.

sub-cultural and ideological networks of either the Marxist or the Catholic-traditional type.

Summing up in an even more condensed form, it can be said that both kinds of Austrian fascist movements were very 'young', and strongly attracted those age cohorts born between 1894 and 1913. Even though the various professional groups in the fascist movements were represented very differently in relation to their size in society as a whole, the social spectrum of these movements was far too wide to simply accommodate the NSDAP in the middle-class hypothesis in its purest version, or the *Heimwehr* movement in the farmers-aristocracy hypothesis. We can also exclude from being true those hypotheses which emphasise the importance of only the petty-bourgeois or purely upper-class support for any kind of Austrian fascism. Generally it is only the absence of a proportionally strong representation of industrial workers and in addition to this, in the case of the NSDAP in Austria the weakness of support from farmers, and in the case of the *Heimwehr* movement the underrepresentation of private employees, which prevented each kind of fascism - due to different reasons - to be a 'people's party'[76] which mirrored all social groups and classes of society. Given their complementary relative strong-holds among the urban new middle classes on the one hand, and medium- and large-sized owners of land in agriculture and forestry on the other hand, the Austrian NSDAP and the *Heimwehr* can best be described as not equally successful 'catch-all-parties', or as '*asymmetrical people's parties*'.

Notes

1. For detailed bibliographies see P. Malina and G. Spann, *Bibliographie zur österreichischen Zeitgeschichte 1918-1985* (Vienna, 1985); P. Rees, *Fascism and Pre-Fascism in Europe, 1890-1945: A Bibliography of the Extreme Right* (Sussex, 1984), pp. 120-36; S. Mattl, *Bestandsaufnahme zeitgeschichtlicher Forschung in Österreich* (Vienna, 1983), pp. 36-42.
2. See primarily F. L. Carsten, *Fascist Movements in Austria: From Schönerer to Hitler* (London, 1977; C. E. Edmondson, *The Heimwehr and Austrian Politics, 1918-1936* (Athens, Ga., 1978); B. F. Pauley, *Hitler and the Forgotten Nazis: A History of Austrian National Socialism* (Chapel Hill, N.C., 1981); K. J. Siegfried,

Klerikalfaschismus: Zur Entstehung und sozialen Funktion des Dollfussregimes in Österreich (Frankfurt/M., 1979); U. Kluge, *Der österreichische Ständestaat 1934-1938* (Vienna, 1984); B. F. Pauley, *Hahnenschwanz und Hakenkreuz* (Vienna, 1972).

3. O. Bauer, *Zwischen zwei Weltkriegen* (Bratislava, 1936), pp. 139-59; G. Botz, 'Faschismustheorien Otto Bauers' in E. Fröschl and H. Zoitl (eds.), *Otto Bauer (1881-1938)* (Vienna, 1985), pp. 161-92; G. Botz, 'Austro-Marxist Interpretations of Fascism', *Journal of Contemporary History*, vol. 11 (1976), pp. 129-56.
4. W. Holzer, 'Erscheinungsformen des Faschismus in Österreich 1918-1938', *Austriaca*, special number 1 (1978), pp. 74-83. See G. Botz, 'Die Ausschaltung des Nationalrates und die Anfänge der Diktatur Dollfuss im Urteil der Geschichtsschreibung von 1933 bis 1973', in *Vierzig Jahre danach* (Vienna, 1973), pp. 31-59.
5. In general cf. G. Klingenstein, 'Bemerkungen zum Problem des Faschismus in Österreich', *Österreich in Geschichte und Literatur*, vol. 14 (1970), pp. 1-13; K. R. Stadler, 'Austria' in S. J. Woolf (ed.), *European Fascism*, 2nd edn. (London, 1981), pp. 93-115; G. Botz, 'Varieties of Fascism' in S. U. Larsen a. o. (eds.), *Who were the Fascists? Social Roots of European Fascism* (Bergen-Oslo-Tromsø, 1980), pp. 192-201; Holzer, 'Erscheinungsformen des Faschismus', pp. 69-155.
6. This is particularly true for L. Jedlicka, *Vom alten zum neuen Österreich: Fallstudien zur österreichischen Zeitgeschichte, 1900-1975* (St. Polten, 1975) and G. Jagschitz, *Der Putsch: Die Nationalsozialisten 1934 in Österreich* (Graz, 1976).
7. See Siegfried, *Klerikalfaschismus*, pp. 27-30, 72-9; M. Kitchen, *The Coming of Austrian Fascism* (London, 1980), pp. 265-81; E. Talós and W. Neugebauer (eds.), *'Austrofaschismus'* (Vienna, 1984); K. Gossweiler, 'Die faschistische Bewegung in Österreich' in E. Fröschl and H. Zoitl (eds.), *Der 12.Februar 1934* (Vienna, 1984), pp. 193-207.
8. As a positive example see A. Pelinka, *Stand oder Klasse? Die christliche Arbeiterbewegung Österreichs 1933 bis 1938* (Vienna, 1972); cf. E. Talós and W. Manosek, 'Politische Struktur des Austrofaschismus (1934-1938)' in Talós and Neugebauer, *'Austrofaschismus'*, pp. 75-119; W.

B. Simon, 'Democracy in the Shadow of Imposed Sovereignty: the First Republic in Austria' in J. Linz and A. Stepan (eds.), *The Breakdown of Democratic Regimes: Europe* (Baltimore, 1978).

9. F. L. Carsten, 'Interpretations of Fascism' in W. Laqueur (ed.), *Fascism: A Reader's Guide* (London, 1976), p. 415; for a comprehensive comparison see Larsen, *Who were the Fascists?*; W. Wippermann, *Europäischer Faschismus im Vergleich 1922-1982)* (Frankfurt/M., 1983).

10. Bauer, *Zwischen zwei Weltkriegen*, pp. 138-59.

11. See H. Mommsen, 'Theorie und Praxis des österreichischen Ständestaates 1934 bis 1938' in N. Leser (ed.), *Das geistige Leben Wiens in der Zwischenkriegszeit* (Vienna, 1981), pp. 174-92; Kluge, *Der österreichische Ständestaat*, pp. 67-135; G. Jagschitz, 'Theorie und Praxis des österreichischen Ständestaats 1934-1938' in L. Rettinger a. o. (eds.), *Zeitgeschichte* (Vienna, 1982), pp. 116-37; and K. D. Bracher, '"Austrofaschismus" und die Krise der Demokratien', *Politicum*, number 5 (1980), pp. 49-53 as opposed to E. Talós, 'Das Herrschaftssystem 1934-1938' in Talós and Neugebauer, *'Austrofaschismus'*, pp. 267-84; cf. also H. J. Krüger, 'Faschismus oder Ständestaat. Österreich 1934 bis 1938', unpublished university thesis, Kiel, 1970; for a balanced account see J. Rath and C. W. Schum, 'The Dollfuss-Schuschnigg Regime: Fascist or Authoritarian?' in Larsen, *Who were the Fascists?*, pp. 249-56, and J. Rath, 'The First Austrian Republic - Totalitarian, Fascist, Authoritarian or What?' in R. Neck and A. Wandruszka (eds.), *Beiträge zur Zeitgeschichte* (St. Pölten, 1976), pp. 163-88. My own account: G. Botz, 'Faschismus und "Ständestaat" vor und nach dem "12.Februar 1934"', in Fröschl and Zoitl, *12.Februar 1934*, pp. 311-32.

12. Cf. S. G. Payne, *Fascism: Comparison and Definition* (Madison, Wisc., 1980), pp. 4-21; J. J. Linz, 'Totalitarian and Authoritarian Regimes' in F. L. Greenstein and N. W. Polsby (eds.), *Handbook of Political Science* (3 vols., Reading, Mass., 1975), vol. 3, pp. 277-9; E. Holtmann, *Zwischen Unterdrückung and Befriedung* (Munich, 1978), pp. 11-20; P. C. Mayer-Tasch, *Korporativismus und Autoritarismus* (Frankfurt/M., 1971).

13. A. F. K. Organski, 'Fascism and Modernization' in S. J. Woolf (ed.), *The Nature of Fascism*, (New York, 1968), pp. 13-41; H. U. Wehler,

Modernisierungstheorie und Geschichte (Göttingen, 1975); A. J. Gregor, 'Fascism and Modernization. Some Addenda', *World Politics*, vol. 26 (1974), pp. 370-84; R. Dahrendorf, *Gesellschaft und Demokratie in Deutschland* (Munich, 1965), pp. 444-50; T. Parsons, 'Some Sociological Aspects of the Fascist Movements' in idem, *Essays in Sociological Theory* (Glencoe, 1954), pp. 124-41; cf. also: B. Moore, *Social Origins of Dictatorship and Democracy* (Boston, 1966); J. J. Linz, 'Some Notes Toward a Comparative Study of Fascism in Sociological Historical Perspective' in Laqueur (ed.), *Fascism*, pp. 3-121, esp. pp. 23-33.

14. Miklos Lackó, 'Ostmitteleuropäischer Faschismus', *Vierteljahrshefte fur Zeitgeschichte*, vol. 21 (1973), pp. 39-51; E. Weber, 'The Right. An Introduction' in H. Rogger and E. Weber (eds.), *The European Right. A Historical Profile* (London, 1965); S. J. Woolf, 'Introduction' in S. J. Woolf (ed.), *Fascism in Europe*, 2nd. edn. (London, 1981), pp. 4-10; F. L. Carsten, *The Rise of Fascism*, 2nd edn. (Berkeley, 1980), pp. 160-93; H. U. Thamer and W. Wippermann, *Faschistische und neofaschistische Bewegungen* (Darmstadt, 1977), pp. 84-91.
15. P. F. Sugar (ed.), *Native Fascism in the Successor States, 1918-1945* (Santa Barbara, 1971); B. Vago, 'Fascism in Eastern Europe' in Laqueur, *Fascism*, pp. 229-53; B. Vago, *The Shadow of the Swastika. The Rise of Fascism and Anti-semitism in the Danube Basin, 1936-1939*, (Farnborough, 1975).
16. J. Kocka, 'Der "deutsche Sonderweg" in der Diskussion', *German Studies Review*, vol. 5 (1982), pp. 365-379; F. Stern, 'National Socialism as Temptation' in idem, *Reflexionen Finsterer Zeit* (Tübingen, 1984); H. U. Wehler, *The German Empire, 1871-1918* (Leamington Spa, 1985). For a critical evaluation see D. Blackbourn and G. Eley, *The Peculiarities of German History: Bourgeois Society and Politics in Nineteenth-Century Germany* (Oxford, 1984).
17. H. Plessner, *Die verspätete Nation: Über die politische Verführbarkeit bürgerlichen Geistes*, 2nd edn. (Stuttgart, 1959); Bauer, *Zwischen den Weltkriegen*, pp. 139-59.
18. Thamer and Wippermann, *Faschistische und neofaschistische Bewegungen*, p. 250.
19. J. W. Borejsza, 'East European Perceptions of Italian Fascism' in Larsen, *Who were the*

Fascists?, pp. 354-66; J. Borejsza, 'Faschismus und Internationalismus', *Faschismus in Österreich und international: Jahrbuch für Zeitgeschichte*, vol. 2 (1980-1), pp. 121-36; M. A. Ledeen, *Universal Fascism* (New York, 1972), pp. 104-55.

20. Weber in Rogger and Weber, *The European Right*, pp. 1-28; P. Merkl, 'Comparing Fascist Movements' in Larsen, *Who were the Fascists?*, pp. 752-83; cf. Linz in Laqueur, *Fascism*, pp. 3-121.

21. Cf. S. G. Payne, *Franco's Spain* (London, 1968); J. J. Linz, 'From Falange to *Movimiento* Organisation: the Spanish Single Party and the Franco Regime, 1936-1968' in S. P. Huntington and C. H. Moore (eds.), *Authoritarian Politics in Modern Society* (New York, 1970), pp. 128-203; P. C. Schmitter, *Corporatism and Public Policy in Authoritarian Portugal* (London, 1975); H. J. Wiarda, *Corporatism and Development. The Portuguese Experience* (Amherst,1977).

22. O. Bauer, 'Um die Demokratie', *Der Kampf*, vol. 26 (1933), pp. 269-76; G. Botz, 'Faschismus und Lohnabhängige in der Ersten Republik', *Österreich in Geschichte und Literatur*, vol. 21 (1977), pp. 107-128; F. L. Carsten, 'Zwei oder drei faschistische Bewegungen in Österreich', in Fröschl and Zoitl, *Februar 1934*, pp. 181-92.

23. A. Wandruszka, 'Österreichs politische Struktur' in H. Benedikt (ed.), *Geschichte der Republik Österreich* (Vienna, 1954), p. 291; M. A. Sully, *Political Parties and Elections in Austria* (London, 1981), pp. 2-5.

24. R. Steininger, *Polarisierung und Integration* (Meisenheim am Glan, 1975).

25. G. Botz, *Gewalt in der Politik. Attentate, Zusammenstösse, Putschversuche, Unruhen in Österreich 1918 bis 1938*, 2nd edn. (Munich, 1983).

26. S. Suval, *The Anschluss Question in the Weimar Era* (Baltimore, 1974); R. Luža, *Austro-German Relations in the Anschluss-Era* (Princeton, 1975, pp. 3-17; N. Schausberger, *Griff nach Österreich* (Vienna, 1978); R. Neck and A. Wandruszka (eds.), *Anschluss 1938* (Vienna, 1981; J. Gehl, *Austria, Germany, and the Anschluss, 1931-38* (London, 1963).

27. L. Kerekes, *Abenddämmerung einer Demokratie* (Vienna, 1966); L. Jedlicka, 'Schicksalsjahre Österreichs (1932-1935)', part 1, *Die allgemeinbildende höhere Schule*, vol. 1 (1962); K.

Stuhlpfarrer and L. Steuer, 'Die Ossa in Österreich', in L. Jedlicka and R. Neck (eds.), *Vom Justizpalast zum Heldenplatz* (Vienna, 1975), pp. 35-64.

28. Carsten in Fröschl and Zoitl, *Februar 1934*, pp. 184-91.
29. See L. Jedlicka, 'The Austrian *Heimwehr*' in G. L. Mosse (ed.), *International Fascism*, (London, 1979).
30. See especially W. Wiltschegg, *Die Heimwehr* (Vienna, 1985).
31. L. Rape, *Die österreichischen Heimwehren und die bayerische Rechte 1920-1923* (Vienna, 1977); H. W. Nusser, *Konservative Wehrverbände in Bayern, Preussen und Österreich 1918-1933* (Munich, 1973); M. Kitchen, 'Militarism and the Development of Fascist Ideology', *Central European History*, vol. 8 (1976), pp. 199-220.
32. K. J. Siegfried, *Universalismus und Faschismus* (Vienna, 1974).
33. J. Hoffmann, *Der Pfrimer-Putsch* (Vienna, 1965); C. A Gulick, *Österreich von Habsburg zu Hitler* (3 vols., Vienna, 1950), vol. 3, pp. 233-40.
34. Edmondson, *The Heimwehr*, pp. 233-63; I. Baernthaler, *Die Vaterländische Front* (Vienna, 1971); E. Starhemberg, *Between Hitler and Mussolini. Memoirs* (London, 1962).
35. R. Matthes, *Das Ende der Ersten Republik Österreich* (Hamburg, 1979); G. Botz, 'Der "4.März 1933" als Konsequenz ständischer Strukturen, ökonomischer Krisen und autoritärer Tendenzen' in E. Fröschl and H. Zoitl (eds.), *Der 4.März 1933* (Vienna, 1984), pp. 13-36; E. März and F. Weber, 'Österreichische Wirtschaftspolitik in der Zeit der grossen Krise' in Fröschl and Zeitl, *Februar 1934*, pp. 15-34.
36. A. G. Whiteside, 'Nationaler Sozialismus in Österreich vor 1918', *Vierteljahrshefte für Zeitgeschichte*, vol. 9 (1961), pp. 333-59; idem, *Austrian National Socialism before 1914* (The Hague, 1962), p. 118; A. Ciller, *Deutscher Sozialismus in den Sudetenländern und der Ostmark* (Hamburg, 1939); idem, *Die Vorläufer des Nationalsozialismus* (Vienna, 1932); R. Jung, *Nationaler Sozialismus*, 3rd. edition (Munich, 1922).
37. L. Haubenberger, *Der Werdegang der nationalen Gewerkschaften* (Vienna, 1932); G. Botz, 'The Changing Patterns of Social Support for Austrian National Socialism (1918-1949)' in

Larsen, *Who were the Fascists?*, pp. 202-3; Carsten, *Fascist Movements*, ch. 4.

38. A. G. Whiteside, *The Socialism of Fools* (Berkeley, 1979); C. E. Schorske, 'Politics in a New Key: Schönerer', *Journal of Modern History*, vol. 39 (1967), pp. 343-86; R. Wistrich, 'Georg von Schönerer and the Genesis of Modern Austrian Antisemitism', *Wiener Library Bulletin*, no.39/40 (1967/7), pp. 20-29; E. Pichl, *Georg von Schönerer* (3 vols., Oldenburg, 1912-23).
39. E. B. Bukey, 'The Nazi Party in Linz, Austria, 1919-1938: A Sociological Perspective', *German Studies Review*, vol. 1 (1978), p. 303; E. Hanisch, 'Zur Frühgeschichte des Nationalsozialismus in Salzburg, 1913-1929', *Mitteilungen der Gesellschaft für Salzburger Landeskunde*, vol. 117 (1977), pp. 371-410.
40. B. F. Pauley, 'Nazis and *Heimwehr* Fascists' in Larsen, *Who were the Fascists?*, pp. 226-38; Pauley, *Hitler*, pp. 36-84; idem, 'Fascism and the *Führerprinzip*: The Austrian Example', *Central European History*, vol. 12 (1979), pp. 272-96; Carsten, *Fascist Movements*, chs. VII and IX.
41. W.B. Simon, 'The Political Parties of Austria', unpublished Ph.D. thesis, Columbia University, 1957, pp. 153-72; R. Danneberg, *Die Wiener Wahlen 1930 und 1932* (Vienna, 1932).
42. See especially Jagschitz, *Putsch*; idem, 'Zur Struktur der NSDAP vor dem Juliputsch 1939' in L. Jedlicka and R. Neck (eds.), *Das Jahr 1934: 25.Juli* (Vienna, 1975).
43. See L. Jedlicka and R. Neck (eds.), *Das Juliabkommen von 1936* (Vienna, 1977); K. V. Schuschnigg, *The Brutal Takeover* (London, 1969).
44. See W. Rosar, *Deutsche Gemeinschaft* (Vienna, 1971); J. Haag, 'Marginal Men and the Dream of the *Reich*' in Larsen, *Who were the Fascists?*, pp. 239-48; P. Eppel, *Zwischen Kreuz und Hakenkreuz* (Vienna, 1980).
45. G. Botz, 'Strukturwandlungen des österreichischen Nationalsozialismus (1904-1945)', in I. Ackerl a. o. (eds.), *Politik und Gesellschaft im alten und neuen Österreich* (2 vols., Vienna, 1981), vol. 2, pp. 174-8; G. Botz, 'Soziale "Basis" und Typologie der österreichischen Faschismen im innerösterreichischen und europäischen Vergleich', *Jahrbuch für Zeitgeschichte* (1980/81), pp. 15-78.

46. I have previously established this type of Austrian fascism - see Botz, 'Soziale "Basis"', pp. 27-8; idem, 'Faschismus', pp. 110-11; cf. I. Messerer, 'Die Frontkämpfervereinigung Deutschösterreichs', unpublished phil. diss., Vienna, 1965.
47. Cf. E. Bodzenta, 'Gesellschaft im Wandel' in O. Schulmeister (ed.), *Spectrum Austriae*, 2nd. edn. (Vienna, 1980), pp. 272-302; E. Bruckmüller, 'Sozialstruktur und Sozialpolitik' in E. Weinzierl and K. Skalnik (eds.), *Österreich 1918-1938: Geschichte der Ersten Republik*, vol. 1 (Vienna, 1983),pp. 357-454; E. Bruckmüller, 'Die verzögerte Modernisierung' in *Wirtschafts- und sozialhistorische Beiträge* (Vienna, 1979), pp. 289-307.
48. During parliamentary elections from February 1919 to November 1930, as well as in many regional elections, men and women cast their votes in different ballot boxes. One can, therefore, establish exactly the parties men and women voted for in the First Austrian Republik. See *Beiträge zur Statistik der Republik Österreich*, no. 2 (Vienna, 1920); *Statistische Nachrichten*, special no. '*Wahlstatistik: Nationalratswahlen vom 24.April 1927*' (Vienna, 1927); *Statistische Nachrichten*, special no. '*Die Nationalratswahlen vom 9. November 1930*' (Vienna, 1931).
49. Membership of the Chambers of Labour (*Arbeiterkammern*) was obligatory and the elections in which unions of each of the major parties ran their own candidates followed corporative lines. Therefore a complete political profile of the workers, private employees, workers in transportation and employees in transportation is provided by the printed statistics - see *Wirtschaftsstatistisches Jahrbuch 1926* (Vienna, 1927), p. 69.
50. Beyond my own books and articles cited here, see Pauley, *Hitler*, pp. 91-6; Bukey, 'Nazi Party in Linz', pp. 302-26; Hanisch, 'Frühgeschichte', pp. 371-410; idem, '1938 in Salzburg', *Mitteilungen der Gesellschaft für Salzburger Landeskunde*, vol. 118 (1978), pp. 257-309; G. Jagschitz, 'Die Anhaltelager in Österreich', in Jedlicka and Neck, *Vom Justizpalast*, pp. 128-51.
51. I am preparing a project at present, supported by the Humboldt Foundation, Bonn-Bad Godesberg, which researches the social structure of the

Austrian Nazi movement since 1918 on the basis of the membership cards housed in the Berlin Document Center. The L. Boltzmann Institute for Social Scientific History, University of Salzburg, recently published a computerised data basis of social, structural and electoral data for all Austrian communes, supported by the Austrian National Bank. J. Falter, Free University of Berlin, is conducting a quantitative analysis of German and Austrian Nazi votes in the late 1920s and early 1930s. At the University of Salzburg J. Dressel and F. Schneeberger are doing research on the social composition of the Austrian *Reichstag* Deputies of 1938 and on the social bases of *Heimwehr* fascism in Upper Austria respectively. H. Schafranek ('Verein für Geschichte der Arbeiterbewegung', Vienna) has completed a research project on the relationship of socialist workers to 'Austro-fascism' and Nazism.

52. R. de Felice, *Mussolini il fascista: La conquista del potere 1921-1925* (Turin, 1966), pp. 5-12.
53. M. Kater, *The Nazi Party. A Social Profile of Members and Leaders, 1919-1945* (Oxford, 1983).
54. Botz, *Gewalt*, pp. 325-7; also Jagschitz in Jedlicka and Neck, *Vom Justizpalast*, p. 150.
55. P. H. Merkl, *Political Violence Under the Swastika: 581 Early Nazis* (Princeton, 1975); idem, *The Making of a Stormtrooper* (Princeton, 1980).
56. N. D. Glenn, *Cohort Analysis* (Beverley Hills, 1976), pp. 21-4; E. H. Erikson, *Childhood and Society* (New York, 1950), pp. 261-3; A. Hainke, *Politische Sozialisation* (Hamburg, 1970), pp. 114-28.
57. J. Braunthal, 'Der Putsch der Faschisten', *Der Kampf*, vol. 15 (1922), pp. 320-3; G. Zibordi, 'Critica socialista del fascismo' in R. de Felice, *Il fascismo. Le interpretazioni dei contemporanei e degli storici* (Bari, 1970), pp. 39-53; cf. R. Sturm, 'Julius Braunthal und die Anfänge sozialdemokratischer Faschismusinterpretation', *Internationale Wissenschaftliche Korrespondenz zur Geschichte der deutschen Arbeiterbewegung*, vol. 17 (1981), pp. 1-4.
58. Haag in Larsen, *Who were the Fascists?*, pp. 239-48; cf. also M. Kater, *Studentenschaft und Rechtsradikalismus in Deutschland 1918-1933* (Hamburg, 1979).

59. P. G. Fischer and D. Stiefel, *Zur Geschichte der Handelskammerorganisation* (Vienna, 1978); K. Haas, 'Industrielle Interessenpolitik in Österreich zur Zeit der Weltwirtschaftskrise', *Jahrbuch für Zeitgeschichte*, (1978), pp. 97-126; Kluge, *Der österreichische Ständestaat*, pp. 34-51; G. Botz, 'Der Übergang der Mittelstände vom katholischen ins nationalsozialistische Lager', *Christliche Demokratie*, vol. 2 (1984), pp. 371-84.
60. C. Price, 'Austria's Hands Tied by Two Armed Parties', *New York Times*, 2 Dec. 1928, p. 4; cf. Pauley, *Hahnenschwanz*, p. 60.
61. P. H. Merkl, 'Comparing Fascist Movements' in Larsen, *Who were the Fascists?*, pp. 776-80.
62. G. Jagschitz, 'Faschismus und Nationalsozialismus in Österreich bis 1945' in *Fascism in Europe - Fasismus a Europa*, (2 vols, Prague, 1970), vol. 2, pp. 15-23; Carsten, *Fascist Movements*, ch. VII; Pauley, *Hitler*, pp. 36-68.
63. Merkl in Larsen, *Who were the Fascists?*, pp. 776-7; B. Glaus, 'The National Front in Switzerland' in Larsen, *Who were the Fascists?*, pp. 467-78; R. N. Smelser, 'Hitler and the DNSAP', *Bohemia*, vol. 20 (1979), pp. 137-50; J. W. Brugel, 'Nazis without Hitler?', *East Central Europe*, vol. 6.
64. K. Ausch, *Als die Banken fielen* (Vienna, 1968).
65. G. Botz, 'Angestellte zwischen Ständegesellschaft, Revolution und Faschismus' in J. Kocka (ed.), *Angestellte im europäischen Vergleich* (Göttingen, 1981), pp. 196-239.
66. R. W. Rothschild, 'Wurzeln und Triebkrafte der Entwicklung der österreichischen Wirtschaftsstruktur' in W. Weber (ed.), *Österreichs Wirtschaftsstruktur gestern - heute - morgen* (Berlin, 1961), vol. 1, pp. 55-6; W. T. Layton and C. Rist, *Die Wirtschaftslage Österreichs* (Vienna, 1925), pp. 5-141; D. Stiefel, *Arbeitslosigkeit* (Berlin, 1979), pp. 26-30.
67. Kocka, *Angestellte*; H. Speier, *Die Angestellten vor dem Nationalsozialismus* (Göttingen, 1977).
68. Merkl in Larsen, *Who were the Fascists?*, pp. 776-9; D. Mühlberger, 'The Sociology of the NSDAP: The Question of Working Class Membership', *Journal of Contemporary History*, vol. 15 (1980), pp. 493-511.
69. Cf. I. Kykal and K. R. Stadler, *Richard Bernaschek* (Vienna, 1976), pp. 101-170; J. Hannak, *Karl Renner und seine Zeit* (Vienna, 1965), pp. 612-35.

70. Cf. E. Weinzierl-Fischer, *Die österreichischen Konkordate von 1855 und 1933* (Vienna, 1960).
71. W. Daim, *Der Mann, der Hitler die Ideen gab* (Munich, 1954), pp. 233-4; Wandruszka in Benedikt, *Geschichte der Republik Österreich*, p. 373; M. Haydter and J. Mayer, 'Regionale Zusammenhänge zwischen Hauptwiderstandsgebieten zur Zeit der Gegenreformation und den Julikämpfen 1934 in Oberösterreich', *Zeitgeschichte*, vol. 9 (1982), pp. 392-407.
72. Simon, 'Political Parties of Austria', ch. VIII; idem, 'Motivation of a Totalitarian Mass Vote', *British Journal of Sociology*, vol. 10 (1959), pp. 338-95.
73. See conclusions reached in my article - Botz, 'Faschismus', pp. 123-5.
74. Ibid., p. 112.
75. Botz, *Gewalt*, pp. 325-34.
76. See H. Mommsen, 'National Socialism: Continuity and Change', in Laqueur, *Fascism*, pp. 189-95; H. Mommsen, 'Zur Verschränkung traditionaler und faschistischer Führungsgruppen in Deutschland beim Untergang von der Bewegung zur Systemphase' in W. Schieder (ed.), *Faschismus als soziale Bewegung* (Hamburg, 1976), p. 164.

Chapter Eight

EASTERN EUROPE

Raphael Vago

In analysing the social basis of fascism in Eastern Europe, focusing on the movements in those countries where they reached mass support and eventually came to power, one cannot help wondering if the vital question should be 'What drew people to fascism?' rather than 'Why were some people not drawn to fascism?'. If phrased in this way, the focus of research would shift away from the standard 'Who were the fascists?' to 'Why were others not attracted to fascism?'.

The student of fascism in Eastern Europe, as well as elsewhere, has now at his disposal an abundance of interdisciplinary works, which have certainly added much valuable insight to the understanding of the dynamics of fascism and the secrets of its appeal to various social classes and groups. The current trend in research is less oriented toward the political-diplomatic field, which was exhausted to a large extent in the post-war boom in diplomatic histories, and more toward the social, psychological aspects of fascism. One of the most evident conclusions of the latter analysis of the fascist phenomenon is not only the assertion that the movements were made up of elements drawn from an extremely mixed social background, but also that in some cases the mainspring which should be sought is not the social composition of fascism but the psychological factor behind it.

The Western researcher using such an approach, whether as social scientist, as historian or as researcher in any related discipline, needs a wealth of source materials. Here the limitations are indeed grave, amounting to a 'poverty of sources'. Today, the diplomatic and political history of Eastern Europe can be exhaustively written with sources available in the West, including those from

Nazi documentation. But for the social aspects of fascism, with very few exceptions, the Western researcher has to rely on material from Eastern Europe. As guardians of sources, the East European regimes, excepting Hungary to a limited extent, have been very consistent throughout. Not only is the Western researcher unable to reach directly the sources he is interested in, such as the background of known members of fascist organisations and parties on the national and local level, but even access to newspapers and periodicals from the inter-war period is restricted. Unfortunately, both the Western and some keen East European researchers are facing a stalemate: both sides have had to rely on almost the same meagre sources, turning and analysing them from diverse angles, hoping to secure some new insight from them. From time to time a small gush of fresh air breaks through, especially in the case of Hungary, where during the last few years researchers have not only tackled the social basis of fascism more and more objectively than their colleagues in other East European countries, but have also been able to present new, valuable data, which will certainly be the prey of Western researchers for years to come, until still more sources come to light.

It is very ironical that, in the current state of research relating to all aspects of fascism in Eastern Europe, the East Europeans are also victims of their own system in the emerging vicious circle of working and deducing from the same sets of data. Thus a well-known Hungarian historian, Ormos Mária, in a study of the Iron Guard, relies on and quotes Western studies, which seem to have helped her more than the ones made accessible or published by the Romanians.[1]

For years the issue of mass support for fascist movements, and their appeal to wide segments of society, frightened and put off the Marxist historians, as well as those faced with the historic task of building a new socialist society. Instead of concentrating on an in-depth study of what drew people to fascism, and who were drawn to it, they have emphasised the external aspects of the fascist influence, of the 'imperialist bourgeoisie' which furthered the spread of fascist ideology in conjunction with internal factors.[2]

The very definition of Eastern Europe and its subdivision is disputable. Fascist movements flourished in the area east of Germany and Austria, which will be treated in the present study as

Eastern Europe. Four fascist movements seized power close to the end of the Second World War, and only for a short period, in Romania, Hungary, Slovakia and Croatia.[3] The search for the social bases of the movements must necessarily also include the various fascist parties and groups in the other states of the area.

I

Independent Eastern Europe emerged out of the ruins of the Ottoman, Habsburg, German and Russian empires. No state in the area, including the nation states born before the end of the First World War, came out unchanged from the turmoil of the Great War. The new states had one common feature, an almost in-born instability which turned them from the nominal democracy following the First World War towards various forms of authoritarian rule. Victors and losers alike shared a feeling of insecurity, dissatisfaction and of growing uprootedness, factors which proved to be crucial in the process of radicalisation and in the shift to the right.

Generally speaking, Eastern Europe was made up of backward agricultural societies, which rushed into the race towards modernisation without being adequately equipped for it, as well as lacking a liberal-democratic tradition. Nation states were born, yet they faced the serious problems of national integration - Poland and Romania had to cope with the unification of different regions which had various levels of economic and social development, and with populations of diverse mentalities. The issue of Czech and Serbian domination over their respective partners, the Slovaks and the Croats, defined from the very beginning the nature of the Czechoslovak and Yugoslav states, just as this issue had been predominant in their emerging national movements in the nineteenth century. And there were the truncated states, Hungary and Bulgaria, which fuelled the revisionist-irredentist ethnic and territorial disputes. The loss of national and economic resources, especially in the case of Hungary, brought about an almost unified national response to the peace treaties - vehement opposition to the settlement and ardent nationalism.

Ethnic tensions were a constant concomitant of the history of the area, constituting one of the main sources of conflict. The new states contained in this respect, as well as in others, the characteristics of the former empires from whose ruins they had sprung. Thus, the Jewish question was not a new one and not an invention of the peace treaties in Romania, Poland or Hungary, but a legacy of the pre-war era, which assumed a new dimension against the background of the never-ending crisis that accompanied the East European societies between the two World Wars. The ethnic tensions fuelled all the various extremist movements, which were dedicated to the redeeming of the 'nation' from its internal enemies. And there were the Germans, manipulated after 1933 by Nazi Germany, destabilising the regimes of at least two nation-states, Czechoslovakia and Poland, many of them serving as a fifth column to the upstart and menacing Third Reich.

In Eastern Europe there were too many negative factors at work. There was no strong middle class, no strong working class, with the exception perhaps of Czechoslovakia, and there was no tradition which could have prevented the spread of extremist ideas during the crucial years of nation and state building. Joseph Rothschild emphasises[4] the emergence of the bureaucracy, allied with and recruited from the intelligentsia, which served as the ruling political class. This class descended from the gentry, the middle class or the peasantry. Its nature, its interests and the ways in which it influenced the political life of the states involved, had an important effect on the developing competition between what later could be identified as 'fascism from above' and that from below. The 'ruling political class' may serve as a convenient working tool, as East European societies were of a much more complex nature than to allow the modern researcher to define them merely by means of simple class definitions. In analysing Hungarian society, Berend and Ránki justly point out that the picture of class structure ignores fundamental aspects of social structure since 'social hierarchy, historical traditions, religious and national differences and prejudices, share in national product, social prestige and status'.[5] Such an approach would make it more easy to understand the almost caste-like differences that are outside the known factors that determine class. A similar approach characterises Romanian society as a 'status' one, rather than as a 'class' society.[6] As a matter of fact, all the societies in Eastern Europe can be better understood by such methods of research.

All over the area the gap between the haves and have-nots remained a critical issue even if, as in the example of Czechoslovakia, it caused less tension than elsewhere. The existing economic conditions, and of course the effects of the fluctuations and crises of the world economy, only deepened the frustrations of those groups that remained outside the political system - the peasants and the urban proletariat. Peasants did reach power nominally through their movements and parties in Bulgaria and in Romania, but the politicians used the name and ideas of peasantism as an alternative to modern materialistic society, as a disguise for their greed and ambition.

The emergence of the various types of dictatorship - be it royal or military - was due to internal and external factors, and signalled the 'beginning of the end' for inter-war Eastern Europe. The growing political polarisation, the imminent struggle between the 'old' and the 'new' right opened up a chapter which was soon to end with the approach of the Second World War. Post-First World War Eastern Europe was born into a vacuum left by the dying empires, and a mere twenty years later the area succumbed once again to turmoil. Among the internal forces which contributed to the disintegration on the eve of the Second World War and during it, fascism assumed a main, leading role. The movement which promised *élan*, and according to some researchers a 'revolutionary *élan*', hurled the area into the outstretched hands of Nazi Germany.

II

Fascism has often been characterised by the leaders of the movements, as well as by researchers, as a revolt of the young generation following the Great War. It was a revolt of those who were disappointed with the existing social and political order and resented from the beginning the character of the new nation states - be it truncated Hungary, or Greater Romania with its nationality problems. These youngsters were drawn by the magnetism of an idea that was taking shape at that time, which promised a radical change in every aspect of their lives. It was they who turned the idea into a movement and fused the vigour of youth into political deed.

Many of the first generation students at the universities were battle-tested in the War, and thus there was a strong overlap between those who formed the first shock troops of the fascist movements at the universities and young army veterans. Carsten refers to this overlapping between these two groups, but in many cases we can actually speak of one integrated group - the veterans who became students.[7]

There was no correlation between the input into higher education and society's capacity to absorb the young job-hungry graduates. The predominantly agrarian societies of Eastern Europe did not need all those graduates in the humanities and law who flooded the limited job market. It was an era when the prestige of being a 'student' and studying at a university was sought after, while the chances of finding employment were rather scant. The intellectual proletariat that was formed at the universities in the first post-war years was politically inexperienced, with only a dim image of the future in store for them, yet well equipped to absorb radical ideas and to find scapegoats for their nation's plight, usually in the shape of the ethnic minorities in their societies.

Who were the students who manifested the feeling of lost illusions and unrealised expectations in their political activity? Data on the student generation of the early 1920s is very scant and to a large extent unreliable. The Romanian case is the only one from which more solid conclusions can be drawn. The nucleus of the Romanian fascist movement, which was to become the Legion of Archangel Michael (founded in 1927) and later the Iron Guard, was made up of young university students. Eugen Weber defined their social origin as provincial, only recently urbanised intelligentsia, a large segment of whom were the sons and grandsons of peasants, teachers and priests.[8] Weber's findings, mostly based on the 'Papanace list', refer to the Legionaries interned in Germany following the failure of the Iron Guard 'rebellion' in January, 1941. Their age averaged 27.4 years in 1940, and 60 out of the 251 were students. His data bears out the continuity of the strong student basis of the Iron Guard over a period of almost 20 years. Zeev Barbu added another dimension to Weber's findings and analysis. As a social group the Legionaries were climbing the social ladder in the direction of the middle class, without, however, breaking away from their traditional background. Elaborating on this thesis, Barbu's conclusion was that 'we are dealing here with a psychological rather than a social group'.[9]

An analysis of the continuity and change in the students' role in the Romanian fascist movement will necessitate a short survey of their place in the formation and establishment of the movement, against the background of the intellectual ferment of inter-war Romania.

Corneliu Zelea Codreanu was the son of Ion Zelenski, a school teacher from Austrian Bukovina, and a German-Protestant mother. Codreanu missed the opportunity to qualify as a 'war veteran cum student' - he was not drafted due to his youth. From a similar social, if not ethnic, background came Ion Moţa, the 'martyr of Majadahonda', who was killed in the Spanish Civil War and was the son of a country priest and the grandson of a peasant.

Codreanu, Moţa and their colleagues were typical representatives of the students enrolled at the centres of higher learning, some of them situated outside the 'Old Kingdom', in the territories recently integrated into Greater Romania. In Transylvania, for example, Romanian students of peasant stock had for the first time the opportunity to enrol in universities, which had been practically out of their reach under the Austro-Hungarian monarchy.

Xenophobic manifestations among the Romanian students were aimed first of all against the Jews, especially their colleagues at the universities. Various figures, inflated by contemporary authors, point to a disproportionately high number of Jews in the universities. A. C. Cuza, Professor of Law at the University of Iasi, who in 1923 merged several anti-Semitic organisations into LANC (League of National Christian Defence), claimed that in the academic year 1919 to 1920 there were 546 Jewish students as against 392 Romanians in the Faculty of Law in Cernauti, and in the Faculty of Pharmacology in Iasi, in 1922 to 1923, there were 299 Jews as against 97 Romanians.[10] At the Medical School of Cluj University in 1921 to 1923, Jewish students accounted for 38 per cent, drastically reduced in the following years due to anti-Semitic violence and official restrictions. In the early 1920s about 20 per cent of the student body in Romania was Jewish, so their presence in higher education was indeed sizeable and conspicuous in a country where they represented four per cent of the population. Many Romanian students, among them Codreanu's Legionaries, did not manage to complete their studies, and in fact only eight per cent of the enrolled students between 1921 and 1932 ever graduated. This should be attributed to several factors, among which the attraction of still available jobs in the rapidly expanding bureaucracy was not a negligible one.

The Romanian intelligentsia, and the staff of the universities, encouraged Romanian youth not only to join the universities but to take them over and transform them into bastions of 'true Romanian learning'. The groundwork was prepared for the activities of Codreanu and his friends in the various academic centres, where they created a battlefield of national salvation, declaring an all-out war against the Jews, whom they viewed as alien to Romanian culture and civilisation. The radical student elements led by Codreanu, Marin and Mota gathered strength during 1921 to 1922, and provoked anti-Jewish incidents, mainly in the urban areas and in the market towns of Moldavia, Bessarabia and Bukovina. Their anti-Semitic, anti-communist slogans were favourably received among wide segments of the population in these areas.

Codreanu's ACS (Association of Christian Students), which aspired to become a student-led national youth movement, organised the student riots of 1922 to 1923, demanding a *numerus clausus*. The ACS platform emphasised the role of the students in the forthcoming national struggle against the 'Jewish spirit and way of thinking', and against Jewish poisoning of the intellectual and artistic life.[11] The fact that thousands of students joined the student strike proclaimed by the ACS on 10 December 1922 is indicative of the successful penetration of radical ideas into wide segments of the student body. That day, labelled 'student day', was to be officially celebrated by the Legionnaire movement.

The spiritual supporters of the fanatic student movement, like the great national poet Octavian Goga, enthusiastically acclaimed the 'patriotic' activities of the youth in those troublesome years of violence at the universities. For Goga the student movement represented the 'honest manifestation of collective conscience', a process of national rebirth. By 1925 support for LANC was spreading far beyond the small circle of activists rallied around Cuza and Codreanu in the early years. Following the acquittal of Codreanu on murder charges in May 1925, he was cheered at the Bucharest railway station by some 50,000 people - grim statistics on the popularity of the 'Captain', glossed over in modern Romanian historiography. This was the first indication of the growing mass basis of the movement, which at the 1926 elections polled 4.76 per cent of the votes, receiving 10 out of the 387 seats in the Chamber of Deputies.

The 'generation of 22', as the wreckers of Romanian universities were called, took great care from the very beginning to prepare 'ideologically' the next generation that was to come to maturity in the late 1920s and early 1930s. Student activists were a force in the high schools of the large cities and in smaller towns, where combined gangs of high school pupils, led by their teachers and by students, were not unusual participants in assaults against Jews and Jewish property. Ion Moţa's elitist 'Brotherhood of the Cross' was instrumental in indoctrinating the next generation of pupils and village youth. From the age of ten, thousands of Romanian youngsters were drawn into the circle of the Legion, supplying to a large extent the backbone of the Legion, whose 'nests' numbered some 12,000 by 1937.

The split between Codreanu and Cuza in 1927 was due to a certain extent to the generation gap between the followers of Codreanu, whose average age was 28 in 1927, and the older followers of the conservative Cuza. The latter, who shared Codreanu's violent approach to the Jewish problem, did not advocate the destruction of the Romanian political order, and was much more conservative in his social views than Codreanu. At the 1927 elections the Legion of Archangel Michael, founded by Codreanu, received only 0.39 per cent of the votes, a drastic fall compared to the previous elections, when it was still part of the LANC. The failure in the 1927 elections was not indicative of the movement's continuing support among the students.

The Iron Guard, formed in 1930, was to become the mass movement of the elitist Legion, but actually the two names were used alternately to designate the movement. From then on Codreanu acted successfully to enlarge the movement's mass base, appealing to wider segments of the population. The Iron Guard literally embarked on a new road - the marches through the villages and the summer work camps - with a view to exerting a mystical attraction on the peasants. The widening base of the Iron Guard was borne out by the participation of nationalist intellectuals and local Orthodox clergymen at the anti-Jewish excesses organised by students. For many of the students the political agitation in the poor, underdeveloped rural areas meant a return to their roots, a populism that was to characterise the later activities of the Guard.

Following the assassination of Prime Minister Duca by a death squad of the Iron Guard in December

1933, the Liberals unsuccessfully tried once again to dissolve the Guard. When, in 1934, several Legionnaires were killed by the police, Codreanu and Moţa warned Romanian youth that a 'wide coalition of Jews, Cuzists, Peasantists and the Senates of the Universities' were bent upon destroying them.

By the mid-1930s a new generation of students that had recently graduated from the high schools continued to form the hard core of the movement. The annual student congress became a peculiar, overt decision-making forum where the movement outlined its operational plans to the smallest details. At the 1936 student congress it was decided to form death squads assigned to execute the growing number of enemies, including former comrades. In July 1936 one such hit squad, among whom five were theology students, executed Mihail Stelescu at a Bucharest hospital. He had been a former student activist and the youngest representative of the Iron Guard in Parliament, who had formed a rival fascist organisation following his break with Codreanu. The execution, which was carried out in the form of a bizarre ritual, with the members of the team chopping up the body with an axe, kissing each other, and dancing around the body, was hailed by the National Union of Romanian Christian Students. Such acts once again highlight the need for psychological profiles of the fascists, no less than their social background.

'Student police' units were formed at the main universities, which served as shock troops for the students in enforcing Legionnaire concepts of 'law and order'. Members of such a student police unit punished a student, who belittled the activities of Moţa and Marin, with beatings and torture. The latter were two prominent student leaders of the 'first generation', who had been killed during the Spanish Civil War in 1937. The trial of the seven students involved in the assault was reported by the Legionnaire press, and is a testimony to the leading roles of the students in the period of the radicalisation in Romanian political life.[12]

Viorel Trifa (expelled from the United States in 1984!) was in charge of the student police at the time and was a representative of the new generation of student activists in the movement. He was the son of a small livestock farmer in Transylvania, matriculated in 1931 as a theology student at the Chisinau branch of Iaşi University, and enrolled as a philosophy student at the Bucharest University in 1936.

In the elections of December 1937, the political party founded by Codreanu in 1934, the TPT (All for the Fatherland) became the third largest faction in the Parliament, having received 15.58 per cent of the votes. This was an electorate with a large mass base, capitalising largely on what Eugen Weber has characterised as retarded areas, and among social strata neglected by other parties. Yet a closer scrutiny of the activities of the party, now with 66 members in Parliament, reveals that the nerve centre of this party-movement was still based among the student body of the universities, especially in Iași and Bucharest. It may look anecdotal, but at the time when the party grew into a mass movement, and Nazi diplomats were in touch with Berlin on how to assess the electoral success of the Iron Guard, highest-level decisions were taken at nightly meetings at places like the student dormitory of the Medical Faculty in Bucharest.

Following the short-lived Goga-Cuza government, King Carol's coup of February 1938 brought about the dissolution of the TPT and the intensification of the rivalry between the King and the extreme right. Carol's royal dictatorship was rightly characterised as intending to 'stymie the Iron Guard and steal its ideological appeal', including the formation of a youth movement patterned on the Legionnaire system of youth mobilisation.[13]

The execution of Codreanu and his group of followers in November 1938, and the persecution of thousands of Legionnaires eliminated the original leadership. Thus, as Eugen Weber notes, the 'Legion always remained a young movement'. The continuity in the predominant role of the students was borne out in 1940, when Viorel Trifa, at that time the president of the Union of Romanian Christian Students, said that 'one can proudly declare that very often the Movement meant the students, and the students were the Movement'.[14]

Available data confirms the high percentage of students among the activists of the movement, as described by Trifa. The list of 32 Legionnaires executed in September 1939 at Vaslui included 14 students and one high school student.[15] The students continued to play a central role during the National Legionary State between September 1940 and January 1941, as well as during the unsuccessful 'rebellion', which was followed by the brutal repression of the Iron Guard by Antonescu's regime. During the Legionary regime, activities organised by and for students played a prominent role, and the universities became for the first time official bastions of the movement, albeit for a short time.

Communist historiography belittles the role of student elements in the history of the Legionary movement. An 11-page analysis of the social-economic base of fascism in Romania, published in 1971, devotes a mere three lines to the student element: '... the fascist movement, using the spirit of adventure, and capitalizing on the fear of intellectual unemployment, wished to recruit more and more students'.[16] The issue was treated likewise in another Romanian study, which mentioned 'young frustrated intellectuals' in a list of groups and strata which supported the fascist movement.[17]

In his frequently-quoted 'Under Three Dictatorships', Lucreţiu Pătrăşcanu, the Romanian national Communist, posthumously rehabilitated by Ceausescu, did not minimise the decisive role of students and young intellectuals.[18] Yet recent Romanian sources usually refrain from elaborating on this aspect of Pătrăşcanu's work.

The late Romanian historian, Constantin C. Giurescu, writing about his experience at the Faculty of Humanities at the University of Bucharest during the Legionary regime, presents a mild picture of fascist influence among the academic staff and students.[19] He mentions one professor among the faculty's 24 professors who adhered to the Iron Guard, and among the students he mentions that only a minority, albeit a noisy one, belonged to the Iron Guard. These students are presented as ineffective *vis-à-vis* the democratic student elements. This rosy survey of one faculty at the University of Bucharest is refuted by the picture emerging from the press during the National Legionary State. The newspaper reports and pictures testify to the participation of thousands of students and their lecturers at the first 'Legionary Student Day' in 1940.[20]

The role of the students in the history of the Romanian fascist movement is much more emphasised in recent Hungarian historiography. Ormos Mária refers to the role of the student organisation emerging from Iaşi, and quotes sources, as already mentioned, which are Western ones.[21] Due to the lack of new sources, Hungarian historians of the fascist movements, the most productive ones among the East Europeans, are unable to elaborate on the social background of the members of the fascist movements.

In Hungary the students also played an important role in the Arrow Cross and other fascist organisations, although to a lesser extent than in Romania. Students and young intellectuals from the lower strata of the gentry class flocked to the various right-wing extremist movements. The rapid expansion of the Hungarian educational system turned out more and more young graduates, who responded to the nationalist, irredentist appeal of the secret and open 'patriotic' societies. Many of them, and unfortunately there is not enough statistical evidence, originated from the half a million refugees from the territories that Hungary lost in the Treaty of Trianon.[22] A new generation of young intellectuals turned to the right, including the extreme right, where they found a haven for their populist views. It was a strange odyssey of the 'village explorers' who were searching after a solution for the plight of the Hungarian peasant. Their appeal to the generations of students was very evident through the 1930s.

As in all East European states where fascist movements were active, in Hungary, too, groups competed in recruiting youth and students. The 'Levente Egyesület', formed in the early years of the Horthy regime, had a paramilitary, fascist character aimed at educating the youth in the spirit of revisionism. The 'Levente', and other similar organisations, were manipulated from above, or by persons on the road to political power, like Gömbös. In Hungary, unlike Romania, there was no grass-roots student movement which later formed the backbone of a mass movement.

The Turul association, under the patronage of Gömbös, acted to combine the demands of university students on daily 'bread and butter' issues with higher national goals. This was especially evident in the 1930s with the second generation of students, characterised by the well-known Hungarian historian Szekfü Gyula, as a generation which was born in the old middle class, became more and more *déclassé*, striving for contacts with the social strata below the middle class.[23] The students and youth organisations, like Turul, resorted in due time to social demagoguery in order to also attract young industrial and agricultural workers. In the 1930s, disturbances in the Hungarian universities echoed the events of the 1920s in the Romanian universities. Debrecen played to a certain extent the role of Iaşi in the vanguard of anti-Semitic outbursts by students, which were sanctioned in 1933 by Gömbös himself, who was interested in anti-Semitic measures directed and controlled from above, rather than in the spontaneous excesses of the students.

The land problems in Hungary and the situation of the farmers became a favourite issue of Turul, which kept in tune with the populist trend of many right-wing, as well as left-wing, groups during the era of the 'village explorers'. Turul's press organ noted in 1934 that 'we are waiting for miracles with our heads in the sand, instead of strengthening the only solid base of our national life - the peasants'.[24] But the pilgrimage of the Hungarian students to the village was not a return to the roots, as was the case among the Romanian students, since Hungary's rigid social system did not allow the mass flocking of rural youth to the universities, as was the case in Romania.

Following the Bethlen era, his successors applied the *numerus clausus* against Jewish students, and thus took, to a certain degree, the wind from the sails of the Magyar students. During the successful and rapid transformation of the Arrow Cross into a mass movement after 1937 to 1938, the students did not play a leading role, which was assumed by people with a more distinct background, especially army officers.

Fascism in Yugoslavia did not have a strong mass support, except for the Ustasha separatists who recruited mostly among the urban population, but it did have a strong base among students, both lay and religious. The Zbor movement of Dimitrije Ljotić and the Croat Ustasha are considered the most explicitly fascist movements in Yugoslavia. Ljotić's movement, based primarily on students and young intellectuals, did not seek to destroy Yugoslavia, as did the Ustasha, but to transform it into a centralised, corporative state. It received only 0.86 per cent of the votes in 1935, and 1.01 per cent in 1938. The students and young intellectuals were mainly of urban middle-class origin, some of them from well known families. Milan Stojadinovic's regime, just as the royal dictatorship which preceded it, succeeded in tapping the young generation, not unlike the situation in Hungary or that during King Carol's royal dictatorship in Romania. The Yugoslav universities, especially that of Belgrade, were strongholds of Zbor, which projected an anti-Semitic, anti-communist platform. Violent clashes at Belgrade University in 1940 were among the highlights of Yugoslav fascist activism.[25]

The Ustasha were much more successful in recruiting students to their separatist idea than the Ljotić movement in Serbia. In Croatia, too, the fascist students were mostly of urban origin. By

1940 they were the largest student group at Zagreb University, having received 15 per cent of the votes in the student elections of 1939 and 1940, still a poor showing compared to the trend in Romania. Their strength lay especially in the faculties of law, agriculture and veterinary medicine.[26]

In Croatia and Slovakia students in the theology seminaries played an important role in the fascist presence among the students. Here the pattern was similar to that in Romania, including the social composition of the students who were of rural origin and tended to be poorer than their colleagues in the faculties of law and humanities. The strong clerical element in Croatian and Slovak fascism, as well as the seminarists' role in the Iron Guard, assured the continuity of their activities through the years until the Second World War. Thus many of the clergymen active in the Ustasha were the ones who had supported the movement since its early days. Various educational establishments and schools run by the Church became strongholds of the Ustasha, and carried on the ideas of the movement to the new generations of students.[27]

In Slovakia, Hlinka's Slovak People's Party was led by the clergy, and as most researchers agree, was made up of the rural petty bourgeoisie and peasants, with a strong following among theology students, who supplied the young clerical element in the movement. The young Slovaks, both religious and lay, detested the Czech tutelage of Slovakia, while the danger of unemployment loomed high among the young intellectuals. For many of them Slovak separatism meant jobs, power and advancement up the social ladder.

Czech fascism had a short history, as the rise and the menace of German fascism hung over the fate of Czechoslovakia. Several fascist groups, which never attained a mass base, attempted to attract the students. Unlike the situation in Romania, the Czech fascist appeal to the students was similar to that in Hungary, in that it was not the students who built up the movements, but rather the movements which strove to woo them. While nationalist demands by students in Prague in 1934 were supported by the small fascist groups, the movements could never gain a strong foothold at the universities. Fascism among the Czechs was of a clear urban character, or to be more precise, it was a Prague phenomenon. Unlike their Romanian counterparts, the relatively well-to-do Czech students, and even those of a lower origin, did not have an *a priori* feeling of failure, frustration and rejection by the existing order. Czech society did promise jobs and advancement to its young graduates. In other words, for the Czech student there was no need to conquer the universities and transform them into bastions of nationalism. On the contrary, the more serene the atmosphere was, the more rapid their prospects of advancement. With a diploma in his hands the Czech student had every chance of getting a teaching or administrative job in Slovakia. Thus it was the Czech student who in many respects fuelled the fascism of his Slovak counterpart of a lower social origin.

Without attempting to answer the ever-present question on Poland, if there was a fascist movement at all, and, if so, who were the fascists, it should be noted that among the right-wing extremist groups, youths and students constituted an important element. The danger of unemployment and economic competition especially faced the Polish students from an urban background. Anti-Semitism flourished at the Polish universities, and the existing discontent was translated into right-wing anti-Semitic activism. Numerous students were attracted by the Great Poland Camp set up in 1926 by Dmowski. The nationalist, xenophobic platform appealed to the young generation, and the various youth and student movements, which sprung up in the early 1920s, played a major role in the student politics of the late 1930s. The OZB (Camp of National Unity) formed in 1937, and its paramilitary organisation attempted to organise the youth, and skirmishes at the universities between the various groups became a constant feature of academic life. Overall, the fascist movements, which did not have a mass basis in Poland, also lacked it among the students.

III

War veterans, and the military of all ranks, represented an important base of the fascist movements, especially in Hungary. Following the First World War, young officers found their careers interrupted, their future uncertain, and their integration into the new states difficult. The defeated countries, Germany, Austria and Hungary, all represented classic cases of the veterans' inability to cope with changing reality. Former career officers, especially junior ones, played a major role in the mushrooming nationalist organisations, and in the formation of right-wing and fascist movements.

The case of Hungary is the best documented in Eastern Europe as far as the role of the veterans and the military is concerned. According to Lackó, whose studies are well received by Western researchers, one of the main bases of the extreme right wing, and socio-politically the important one, was the officer and civil servant stratum of the 'Christian Hungarian middle class'.[28] This layer was to be found in the lower strata of the gentry class, and later on it provided most of the top leaders of the Arrow Cross. This rather 'peculiar agglomeration' represented the lower stratum of the Hungarian ruling class, and reflected the deep crisis of inter-war Hungarian society.[29] During the period of the 'white terror' following the downfall of the Kun regime, the various official and unofficial detachments were manned by such elements. These *déclassés* of the lower gentry made up the dozens, if not hundreds, of 'patriotic' organisations responsible for the murder of 5,000 to 6,000 persons. The restrictions of the Trianon Treaty - an army of 35,000 and a gendarmerie and police of 12,000 each - left unsolved the problem of the demobilised masses, especially those with higher training, starting from junior officers upwards. The army itself became a hotbed for nationalist, anti-democratic and anti-Semitic ideas, and parallel to the army's strong role in Hungarian society, the former veterans outside the military establishment continued to fuel and staff the dozens of extremist organisations. It should be emphasised that many of the officers' detachments were formed from officers from the territories which Hungary had lost. The radicalisation among these elements contributed to the general trend that started with the 'Szeged idea' of Horthy and his followers.

Gyula Gömbös, of Swabian origin, the son of a village schoolteacher, was a professional officer who organised and led such official and unofficial groups. He had been close to the military before his appointment as Minister of Defence in 1929. By 1930 there were some 40,000 commissioned and non-commissioned officers in the various branches of the military and security forces. Many of these were living in modest circumstances, did not climb up the social ladder, and later on embraced the more extremist nationalist solutions.

Gömbös' fascist experiment failed, and to a certain extent it may even be debated what kind of fascism he represented, but the fact remains that the extreme right wing of the gentry, wide segments of the officer corps, landowners and the new post-war bourgeoisie deserted him and his ideas even before his death in 1936. However, his legacy was there in the form of the growing participation of the Army in civilian administrative affairs, and its political involvement received a new impetus during his period of activity, even before he became Premier.

Ferenc Szálasi, a retired General Staff major, launched his movement, the Party of National Will, in 1935, and appealed to Hungarians in the name of 'God, peasant, citizen and soldier'. He believed that the Army was the 'Messiah which could force the country on the true road'. Szálasi had followers among the junior as well as the senior officers, who were generally of a higher social origin than the lower ranks. Disillusioned by the conservative character of the previous regimes, the officer corps wanted change. The example, and not only the influence, of Germany was evident, and the pattern of military involvement in the most extremist right-wing movements was repeated in Hungary. Some of the high-ranking officers supported the extremists from the period of Bethlen's 'era of consolidation'. As an example one can cite General Beregffy, member of the Arrow Cross cabinet in 1944, who had for many years been the commander of the Ludovika Military Academy.

It would be inappropriate to characterise the Horthy army officers, in the words of Lackó, as an 'anti-popular, anti-progressive, uneducated, low-minded stratum indulging in chauvinistic wish-dreams'.[30] Unfortunately, there are too few detailed studies which could shed more light on the social, and perhaps psychological, profile of the Hungarian officer corps to draw general conclusions. But the undisputed fact is that Szálasi had enjoyed the support of the higher military echelons from 1938 onwards, and the Arrow Cross leadership in 1938 and 1939 was drawn mainly from the officer corps. The 'Hungarist' military formations were led by officers, some of whom had demobilised themselves in order to take up tasks in the Szálasi movement. Their social origin was far from humble. László Baky, the son of a county chief auditor, as presented by Lackó was the 'prototype of the morally altogether depraved adventurer of sadistic disposition, ready to undertake anything for money and career'. During the German occupation of Hungary he was named Under-Secretary of State in the Ministry of the Interior.

Former officers, *déclassé* members of the aristocracy, were also active in the Arrow Cross. Count Pálffy, for example, demobilised in 1920, was active in various extremist organisations, having lost all of his estates, and in 1940 he joined the Arrow Cross. Before that he had been a member of the more 'moderate' Hungarian National Socialist Party.

By 1937 some 17 per cent of the Arrow Cross members were officers, the highest percentage of military personnel in any East European fascist movement. In 1938, in Szálasi's words the 'year of the movement', when the Arrow Cross was transformed into a mass party, more persons in active or reserve service joined the party. However, due to the rapid influx of other social groups, especially workers, the percentage of officers in the membership, but not in the higher echelons of the party, must have been lower at the outbreak of the Second World War than it had been in 1938 to 1939.

In Romania the military did not provide the Iron Guard with a solid base. Modern Romanian historiography emphasises that the Romanian army, composed of 'peasants and workers' who had fought against the Central Powers in the First World War, were not attracted by the pro-Nazi trend of the Iron Guard and of the other extreme right-wing organisations. As to the officer corps, by the beginning of the Second World War it supported Antonescu's brand of authoritarian regime, having sympathised for a long time with the right, but it was also anxious to restrain the advancement of the Codreanu type of hoodlums.

Some high-ranking officers did support Codreanu's movement, and one of these was General Gheorghe Cantacuzino, who was appointed the nominal head of the 'All for the Fatherland' organisation, set up by Codreanu in 1935. He was characterised by Nichifor Crainic, one of the leading young fascist intellectuals, as a 'degenerate aristocrat', a label that indeed fits into the pyscho-social profile of the General and of other high-ranking retired or active officers among Codreanu's adherents.[31] The 'legionary Senate', one of the bodies set up by 'All for the Fatherland' to serve as a respectable façade, was made up of leading intellectuals and some high-ranking officers, like Generals Macrodescu, Tarnoschi and Bucharest's Chief of Police. The movement strove to bring about a rapprochement between the active and retired military personnel, yet without immediate success. There was no doubt at the time that the security offered by the establishment was more attractive to the officer corps than the promises made by Codreanu. In the 1937 elections, when 'All for the Fatherland' received 15.56 per cent of the votes, there were only 11 retired Army officers among the movement's 388 parliamentary candidates, bearing out Codreanu's failure among the military establishment. The data available in the 'Papanace list' includes 3 officers out of the 251, and there was only 1 officer among the 39 legionnaires executed in September 1939.

Neither did the military in the other East European states provide the fascist movements with a solid base. Prominent personalities linked with the military did play major roles in the leadership of extremist movements, but not in the membership. The group gathered around General Radola Gajda in Czechoslovakia lacked any mass following. Gajda established the 'Národní Obce Fašistická' (National Fascist Community) in 1925 while he was in service as Acting Chief of Staff. He was removed from office in 1926 in what is still considered the enigmatic 'Gajda affair', and soon lost his power base among his fellow officers.[32]

The same picture emerges in Bulgaria between the two World Wars. Bulgarian Communist historiography regards the 1923 *coup* which removed the Stamboliski regime as a fascist one.[33] This characterisation should be treated carefully since Bulgarian fascism did not have any mass basis. The Military League was a small organisation composed of active and reserve officers. The Union of Reserve Officers drew its membership from officers who had lost their positions due to the restrictions imposed on the Bulgarian army in the peace treaties. However, these organisations did not reach the extremism manifested by the frustrated members of the Hungarian officer corps. Although the role of the military remained prominent in Bulgaria's inter-war history, the organisations and movements manipulated by the army had no mass basis nor did they have mass support.

IV

Fascism practically everywhere in Eastern Europe started in the towns, and was carried from the towns into the villages. Today there is no doubt about the validity of this assertion, but the question remains, as it was during the debates of the Comintern: to what extent does fascism represent a certain stage in the development of the bourgeoisie? The arguments on the role of the middle classes in fascist movements were, and still are, highly emotional: the more fascists you find among the middle classes, the less you have to disprove the participation of the working class in the fascist movements. The Comintern made its 'blunders', which are frankly discussed by Marxist researchers such as Nicos Poulantzas, in his *Fascism and Dictatorship*. In the 1930s the leading figures of the Communist movement approached the study of fascism in a very clear way: they seemed to know the answers before the questions, and were eager to prove their theories, not bothering with the facts. The result was a gross generalisation of the nature of the fascist movements and the avoidance of any in-depth understanding of the growing mass basis of the movements in the respective East European countries. Whenever the facts somehow did not fit into the theory, one could always resort to the *Lumpen* elements, the favourite targets of Marx, who could be quoted at length.

Contemporary Marxist historians in Eastern Europe have not given up the emphasis on the various segments of the middle classes as recipients and carriers of fascism, but have broadened our horizon on the social basis of the movements. Once again, the Hungarian historians have taken the lead in rather frank exposures of the issues involved. In his discussion of Hungarian fascism, Ránki correctly summed up that 'considering fascism simply as a regressive mass movement or as the reactionary manifestation of big capital is a dangerous oversimplification'.[34] This is certainly a more realistic approach than that of the classic Dimitrovian thesis.

In analysing the participation of certain segments of the middle classes in the fascist movements, one is immediately struck by a common denominator that runs through them, namely their uprootedness, their vulnerability to be threatened, be it by Jews, other ethnic elements, by Communists and, in particular, by every upward-aspiring element in society.

Hungarian society, which - along with that of Romania - bred the most important fascist mass movement in Eastern Europe, was a strange combination of the forces of the past and of the future, a society in which the old gentry and the new bourgeois society coexisted, but, as Hungarian historians emphasise, remained segregated. The forces of the old order and their conflict with new forces were manifested in the pressures which pushed, or rather pulled apart, Hungarian society in the inter-war period. Theoretically the ruling classes in Hungary, from the large landowners downwards, did not need to adopt fascist ideas. Yet in Hungary *déclassé* elements of the upper and middle classes did play a major role in the fascist movements. Imrédy Béla's movement, the Party of Hungarian Revival, attracted in the late 1930s the new elements of the middle class and some intellectuals, along with persons from the upper classes. Hungarian historiography treats Imrédy's movement before he became Prime Minister in 1938 as a classic example of conservative fascism of the 'haves', which had nothing to do with the social demagoguery of Szálasi's Arrow Cross.[35]

In Hungary there were numerous fascist and extreme right-wing groups that did not reach, and perhaps did not endeavour to reach, a mass basis. Organisations such as the Association of Awakening Magyars, or the Hungarian Association for National Defence (MÖVE) were practically the personal properties of their leaders.

Szálasi's was the only movement to reach a mass basis. From data collected and analysed by such Hungarian researchers as Ránki and Lackó, it is possible to draw quite solid conclusions concerning the social basis of the movement, especially after 1938. According to the Hungarian researchers, several layers formed the social basis of the Arrow Cross: the layer of army officers, of the gentry, civil servants and intellectuals from the lower strata of the gentry class, *Lumpen* elements of the various strata of society, petty-bourgeois elements of towns and villages, and the backward stratum of urban and village semi-proletarians and proletarians. The Arrow Cross grew into a mass party in a relatively short time, following the *Anschluss*. The influx of the lower strata of the middle class, and of various elements of the working classes, took place within a year to a year and a half.

According to Lackó those who flocked *en masse* to the Arrow Cross, and supplied the top and medium leadership of the movement, were the 'most reactionary, most corrupt, most fanatic, chauvinistic' elements of the lower middle class. Just as the study of the Iron Guard membership in Romania led researchers to concentrate on psycho-sociological criteria rather than purely social origin, so did similar research in Hungary yield some interesting results. Once again, Western researchers until now have had to rely mostly on data made available by Hungarian researchers. It emerges from Lackó's work that one fourth of the 'activists' in the movement whose background was analysed were criminals, or of a criminal disposition.[36]

The emphasis on the criminal past or disposition of the Arrow Cross activists, and of its rank-and-file members, and of the *Lumpen* elements which are the 'inevitable product of any social system', is understandable, but such conclusions should not conceal the fact that tens of thousands of individuals from the middle class, as well as from the working class, supported the movement. And not all the 900,000 who gave their votes to the Arrow Cross and other similar fascist groups in 1939 were *Lumpen*, *déclassés* or elements with a criminal record. It was a tragic shift of a nation to the extreme right, encompassing all segments and layers of society.

Various levels of civil servants supported the Arrow Cross and represented the trend to the extreme right among Hungary's bureaucracy. They were the products of the overstaffed state apparatus, an inheritance from the pre-war period of the Monarchy. In 1930 there were some 250,000 civil and public servants, many of them with diplomas, constituting one third of all white-collar workers. In their discontent they became the most reliable supporters of the extremist-rightist movements.

One of the largest groups to support the Arrow Cross were the petty-bourgeois elements made up of innkeepers, urban and rural shopkeepers, clerks and pensioners. These groups opposed the labour movement and big business, and felt threatened by both. They saw the labour movement in action - the drastic steps taken by the short-lived Kun regime - and they did not entirely trust the oscillations of the Horthy regime. Before 1938 this layer concentrated more around the Centre, and was radicalised during and after 1938, not only by internal developments in Hungary, but by the influence of the advancement of Nazism, especially after the *Anschluss*. Lackó referred to this layer as those who were 'dragged' into the Arrow Cross. It seems more realistic to presume that they had no difficulty in integrating into the Arrow Cross, which offered, just as the fascist movements in other states did, an answer to their problems *vis-à-vis* the society in which they lived.

The success of the Arrow Cross among the discontented elements of the middle class, artisans and small businessmen, is reflected in the study of the 1939 election results in Budapest.[37] The Arrow Cross received very strong backing in some working-class districts, but its success in middle-class areas, albeit not in all, was also demonstrated. Overall, István Deák's assessment that in 1937 some 19 per cent of the Arrow Cross members belonged to the middle classes seems correct.

While the participation of sections of the middle classes in Hungary is easy to trace and understand, the situation in the Romanian extremist movements, especially in the Iron Guard, is more difficult to define. Romanian fascism had a distinct populist character, relying on the 'masses', which Codreanu never actually clearly defined. Romanian society was typically agrarian, with a rather small middle class, in which foreign elements, especially Jews, played a major role. The process of urbanisation and industrialisation was received with suspicion by the masses, especially the peasants. Anti-Semitic, anti-industrial and agrarian populism had its roots in the late nineteenth-century Romanian intellectual history, and its doctrines burgeoned in various forms following the First World War. The anti-capitalistic appeal of the Iron Guard remained one of the constant features of the movement, although in later years the emphasis shifted to the need for industrialisation, and it turned more to the urban segments of the population. As in Romania, there was no bourgeoisie comparable in size to that of Western or Central Europe, and it is almost futile to search for a strong middle-class basis in the Romanian fascist movements. Marxist analysts, especially Pătrăşcanu, admitted the strong appeal of fascism to wide segments of the Romanian masses, peasants, workers and especially *Lumpen* elements, but at the same time also stressed the role of the middle and lower middle class.[38]

If Codreanu and others of his ilk posed for long as defenders of the 'masses' against corrupt bourgeois values, then which segments of the middle class could react to his ideas? The petty bourgeoisie, made up of artisans, craftsmen and small traders, was menaced by the process of industrialisation and the advance of 'big capital' with its dire consequences for their economic stability. Such strata willingly absorbed the racist slogans of the Iron Guard. Codreanu's young Legionnaires exploited the frustrations of the petty bourgeoisie, and presented the Legion as the defender of the 'middle class of traders and industrialists' which, according to the Legion's doctrine, were about to flourish through the 'legal aid of the state aimed at encouraging the capable Romanian national energy'.[39]

In the small towns where, following their break in 1927, both Cuza's LANC and Codreanu's 'All for the Fatherland' competed with each other, the two movements could tap the frustrated small urban bourgeoisie 'threatened' by the Jewish presence. Along with the Orthodox mysticism and nationalism in Codreanu's philosophy there were also some very pragmatic aspects in the fascist doctrine, namely the removal of the foreign element, be it Jewish or Hungarian, which blocked the way to Romanians securing higher positions in an era of economic crises.

E. Weber's analysis of the regional strength of LANC and Codreanu's movement is perhaps the most comprehensive study available to Western researchers, on which even East European scholars rely. However, what is still lacking today - and it does not seem probable that Romanian historians will shed more light on it in the future - is analysis at the local level such as, for example, the appeal of the Iron Guard to the population in certain precincts of Bucharest. Such data, elaborated by Ránki in the case of Budapest, would illuminate the changing social basis of the Iron Guard (in its various forms) and its penetration into certain strata of society.

It should not be ignored that parallel to the Legion's march into the countryside, to the poor, isolated areas, and into the small market towns, the Legion was gaining growing support in the urban centres, including Bucharest. The financing of the Legion by the capitalists is not merely a favourite theme of recent Romanian historiography, but treated as an undisputed fact. Besides emphasising the support of increasing numbers from the ruling classes, the adherence of thousands of individuals from the middle and lower middle class should also be noted. In spite of this trend, in overall terms the Legion remained a populist movement. It seems that during the short-lived National Legionary State, Codreanu's heirs, such as Horia Sima , tried to enlist broader segments of the urban middle class, especially those in Bucharest.

The small fascist movements in Poland could never reach the middle and lower middle classes, although under the conditions of economic competition anti-Semitic slogans were effective among these classes. Yet overall Polish fascism remained an 'artificial and imported product'.[40] The attempts of Communist historiography to prove the adherence of the middle and lower middle classes to fascist movements are not successful and, except in a few cases, there is not enough empirical evidence on the social basis of the fascist groups in Poland.[41]

Although the Nazi movement among the Germans in Czechoslovakia is usually excluded from studies on East European fascist movements, it should be emphasized that Henlein's movement, not unlike Szálasi's in Hungary, captured the middle class and the working class. The growth of Henlein's movement was very rapid between 1933 and 1935 and, of course, it should be attributed not only to the objective situation of the German minority in Czechoslovakia, especially the impetus given by the Nazi rise to power in Germany, but also to the impact of the economic crisis. In the Czech areas - as has been noted - fascism was and remained a small urban phenomenon. The Czech middle classes were not attracted by demagogic slogans of the small fascist groups, and the Nazi menace looming over Czechoslovakia concentrated the great majority of them around the established centre and moderate-centre parties. Even the gains by the fascists in Prague in the 1929 and 1931 elections, five and eleven per cent respectively, did not indicate a fascist thrust among the middle classes.[42]

V

By the start of the Second World War the fascists had penetrated into all strata of those East European societies in which fascist movements were active. The understanding of the participation of all the social groups included under the general heading 'below the middle classes' is crucial to the study of the social basis of the fascist movements. It would be difficult to answer briefly why members of the working class, unskilled workers and agrarian proletarians joined the fascist movement. Certainly it was to a large extent an outlet for their frustration over their humiliating place in society, and as one of the leading newspapers of the National Legionary State in Romania remarked in 1940, the 'worker is the most loyal soldier of the Captain

(Codreanu) because he has given him the honour that before only the intellectual and the capitalist had'.[43]

Codreanu's movement, as well as Szálasi's to a certain extent, presented itself as the champion of radical social change. In academic circles there are still debates on the revolutionary character of the fascist movements due to the fact that, from the point of view of the lower classes, the fascists did promise a radical change in their place in society. In this sense, the 'Captain' in Romania did indeed give the worker the 'honour' due only to the capitalist and the intellectual, but at the same time the movement was courting both these groups through other means of appeal.

Among the fascist movements in Eastern Europe the Arrow Cross captivated the largest segments composing the lower classes. Following the failure of the working-class movement and the persecution of the left by the Horthy regime, the fascists constituted by the late 1930s the only radical force that could promise political participation to the workers, as well as a brighter future for the mass of unskilled urban and rural proletarians.

The Arrow Cross did not have much success outside of Budapest and the main urban centres until the breakthrough of 1937 to 1938, when significant categories aligned themselves with the movement: firstly, the new generation of industrial workers, workers in smaller industries, as well as miners; and secondly, the most backward elements of the proletariat, both rural and urban, living in poverty. The large section of workers in public transport and urban services, who in 1930 accounted for some 12 per cent of the urban proletariat, lived under better conditions than other workers, coming close to the petty bourgeoisie in some features of their life-style, such as enjoying fixed salaries and pension rights. It is only natural that they should have endeavoured to preserve their position fostered by the regime. From this segment of railwaymen, postmen and other workers in the utility companies, the Arrow Cross could draw a considerable number of voters, members and supporters.[44]

Among the proletariat working outside of industry a great number were of rural origin. According to the 1930 census 63 per cent of the domestic servants, 54 per cent of the auxiliary personnel in public service, 15 per cent of transport workers, and 45 per cent of day labourers were from such a background.[45] They were not integrated into the petty bourgeoisie, although in general their standard of living was quite reasonable. They too were drawn to the dynamic solutions offered by the Arrow Cross. The reservoir of semi-skilled or unskilled workers was also tapped by the fascists, and in the 1939 elections they showed their true colours.

There is no doubt, and Hungarian historians acknowledge the fact, that the working class contributed heavily to the 900,000 votes received in 1939 by the 'National Socialists', the loose alliance of fascist parties led by the Arrow Cross. In the proletarian suburbs of Budapest, the Arrow Cross received more votes than the Social Democrats, and the general picture in the suburbs of Budapest was as follows:

Table 8.1: Election results in the suburbs of Budapest (by %)

	1935	1939
Government Party	35.7	27.5
Christian Party	13.5	6.9
National Socialists	-	41.7
Social Democratic Party	33.3	17.1

Source: M. Lackó, 'The Social Roots of Hungarian Fascism: The Arrow Cross' in S. U. Larsen a. o. (eds.), *Who were the Fascists? Social Roots of European Fascist Movements* (Bergen-Oslo-Tromsø, 1980), p. 399.

The overall results in Budapest are also indicative of the dramatic breakthrough of the Arrow Cross (see Table 8.2). In the provinces the working class voted for the Arrow Cross in the main mining and industrial centres of Pecs, Veszprèm and Nogràd. Szálasi, the 'defender of the worker', succeeded in captivating the Hungarian working class by social demagoguery. If indeed some 41 per cent of the Arrow Cross members in 1937 were workers, this would certainly represent a great victory for a movement long seen as a bastion of the *Lumpen* and criminal elements of society.

In the case of Romania, E. Weber attributes the success of Codreanu among the working class to the absence of an effective labour movement, which turned the workers to the one movement that offered more extreme and radical solutions than those of the

Table 8.2: Election results in Budapest as a whole (by %)

	1935	1939
Government Party	26.0	33.1
Christian Party	25.8	5.5
National Socialists	-	29.9
Liberals	19.0	16.4
Social Democratic Party	22.3	12.7

Source: Lackó in Larsen, *Who were the Fascists?*, p. 399.

established parties.[46] In a sense this was true since, except in the case of Czechoslovakia, there were no effective labour movements in Eastern Europe. Romanian historiography is very vague about the participation of the working class in the fascist movements. Although Pătrăşcanu does admit that working-class elements did support Codreanu, the phrasing of the Romanian studies is very cautious and they do not contain precise data. The volume *Against Fascism* categorically states that among the 'great masses of workers, fascism had no success'. According to this source, its influence was 'sporadic and local' mainly among non-skilled workers who were not yet part of the 'real working class' and thus lacked working-class consciousness, such as transport workers in Bucharest. Fascist strongholds, such as the Malaxa works in Bucharest, are accounted for by the pressures of the pro-fascist management. It is much easier, of course, for Romanian historiography to mention that N. Malaxa, one of the leading Romanian industrialists, paid the sum of 2,000,000 lei in 1934 for the subsidising of the Iron Guard, than to publish data about the number of workers who supported Codreanu.

In October 1936 Codreanu set up the 'Legionary Workers Corps', his first direct appeal to the workers' anti-capitalism fuelled by anti-Semitism. No exact figures are available on the strength of the 'Corps' but it was reported to have had some 8,000 members in Bucharest before its dissolution between 1938 and 1940, when Carol's royal dictatorship toyed with social demagoguery. Contemporary Romanian historiography emphasises the successful activities of the Communist Party in preventing the Iron Guard from getting a foothold among the working class. Yet while there is no doubt that the small illegal Communist Party did act firmly in this direction, the fact remains that the fascist plague attacked some segments of the Romanian working class. The radical reforms advocated by Codreanu were welcomed by the young workers, many of them of rural origin, who saw no contradiction between their struggle for work and Codreanu's vision of an Orthodox, anti-industrial society. It is true that the electoral success of the Iron Guard in the 1937 elections was greater in isolated and neglected areas, and in counties affected by industrialisation, but at the same time, unfortunately, many Romanian workers did attest through the ballot that they were the 'most loyal soldiers of the Captain'.

The success of fascist movements among the working class in Romania and Hungary had no other parallel in Eastern Europe. Gajda's movement failed in the 1935 elections in the industrial areas of Czechoslovakia. Czechoslovak conditions were exactly the opposite of those prevalent in Romania or Hungary - a sound balance among the social classes, a strong middle class, a class-conscious working class, and a tradition of political activity and participation.

The weakness of fascism in Yugoslavia was also reflected in the lack of working class support for the two main fascist movements, that of Ljotić and Pavelić. Leftist organisations, including the Communists, whether they acted legally or illegally, captured a large section of the Yugoslav working class, and the rest were easy prey to the social demagoguery of Stojadinovic's regime. Those of the working class who supported the fascist movements were usually young workers and apprentices, but the great majority of workers, including those in Croatia, were not attracted by fascist ideas.

VI

The interaction between the peasantry and fascism in Romania can best be described by Codreanu himself. At the beginning of 1930 at a rally in Cahul, Bessarabia, at which Codreanu addressed 20,000 peasants, he promised that

> we would not abandon them to Jewish slavery, that they would be free, masters of the fruits of their labour, masters over the land and the country, that the

> dawn of a new day for the people was approaching, that in the fight we have begun, all we expect the peasants to give would be faith - faith to the death - and in exchange they would receive justice and glory.[47]

According to Codreanu, the Romanian countryside was made up of

> a crowd of several million peasants lacking humane means of existence, drained and impoverished, cultureless, poisoned by drink, led by enriched Jews who now have become the masters of Romanian towns, or by the Romanians... who are administrators in name only, because they are nothing but the supine executors of Jewish plans.[48]

The populism of Romanian fascism captured the masses of peasants. Codreanu preached not only a return to the true religion, to Orthodoxy, not only the dawn of a better tomorrow, but the peasants' integration into a society which rejected their values, but also exploited their misery for political needs. The impotence of the peasant parties was clearly borne out by the appeal of fascism in the Romanian countryside. The National Peasant Party of Iuliu Maniu, which received 77.76 per cent of the votes in the 1928 elections, failed to introduce reforms which would have satisfied the masses of peasants. It seems that they were waiting more for psychological reinforcements, for somebody who could give them dignity and a place in society, than for practical measures to cope with their situation. The Romanian peasantry was easy prey for the rising right-wing extremists since the early 1920s, such as Petrache Lupe's movement, and the various factions that appeared in the 1933 elections in Cuza's LANC. The Romanian National Socialist Party, for example, claimed that it had received some 50,000 of the 159,000 votes of the LANC list, and that they gained a part of their share from peasants who were fed up with the 'economic anarchy prepared by the old parties'.[49]

Among the largest extremist groups the contest for the peasants was strongest between the LANC and Codreanu's movement. The main difference between the two, according to E. Weber's analysis, was that the LANC stronghold was poor and decaying, while the Legion's support came from isolated and less densely populated areas.[50] Actually the two movements supplemented each other in their breakthrough into the Romanian village communities. Cuza did not exactly abandon the peasants in the 1920s, but the *élan* was provided by Codreanu.[51] Later on, Cuza did refrain from flirting with the agrarian problem, and the platform of the National Christian Party (NCP) formed by Cuza and Octavian Goga included no references to the agrarian issue.[52]

In spite of Codreanu's deep penetration into the countryside, the NCP still enjoyed peasant support, as evidenced by the mass participation of peasants from the provinces among some 100,000 who greeted Goga and Cuza, with the Nazi salute and armbands with swastikas, at the NCP rally in Bucharest in November 1936.

Romanian communist historiography makes it rather difficult to glean any substantial factual data on the degree of success enjoyed by the Iron Guard in the rural areas. In analysing the situation of the peasants, Romanian historiography emphasises the rapid trend of the concentration of landed property in the hands of capitalist landowners, a process in which the peasantry was transformed into an agricultural proletariat.[53] This school of thought presents the Iron Guard as the defender of the rights of the landowners, while capitalising on the peasants' religious feelings and their traditional anti-Semitic attitudes.

Ironically, the very issue that Romanian historians try to shun and pass over, namely the working-class support for the Iron Guard, becomes by inference an admission of the Guard's success among the rural classes. Romanian historiography correctly underlines the influence of the lower clergy and village teachers upon the peasants and over the rural population in general. But once again, there is practically no reliable data on the forces that shaped the villagers' outlook and political allegiance in the various areas of the country.

Romanian fascism filled a vacuum in the life of the Romanian peasants that no other political movement of the centre or left succeeded in achieving. In Hungary this was also the key to the successful penetration of extremist movements into the villages. In Hungary's rigid social hierarchy, the various layers of peasantry virtually represented a society in itself, alongside the gentry and the bourgeois classes. This rural society was likewise subdivided into several layers, hostile to each other, with each of them, except the top section, attempting, mostly unsuccessfully, to break away and climb the social ladder. The mass of Hungarian peasantry stood midway between the smallholders and the village proletariat. It consisted of about 200,000 families after the First World War, and doubled during the inter-war period, especially after the land reform of 1921, which swelled its numbers. According to the 1930 census, among the agrarian proletariat the servants of the big estates numbered 220,000 families, and there were as many as 560,000 families of landless agricultural labourers. The Hungarian historians are much more honest than their Romanian or other East European counterparts in recognising the success of the rightist movements among the peasantry. Berend and Ránki acknowledge that 'most of the rural masses looked to religion for consolation, or became supporters of the social programs of the rightist radical movements'.[54] Carsten, on the other hand, claims that the 'majority of the peasants were and remained loyal to the Regent and disinclined to support political radicalism'.[55] While it is true that peasants were underrepresented in the Arrow Cross, and that they were loyal to the regime, no matter who was at the helm, peasant participation in the extremist movements was still very evident.

The most radical fascist peasant movement was the 'Brotherhood of the Scythe Cross' led by Böszörmèny Zoltan, a journalist who called himself the 'prophet of the poor'. He successfully appealed to the 'three million paupers', preaching land reform and a better life in a society which until then had rejected them. The Scythe Cross was violently anti-Semitic, used religious chiliastic terminology, but lacked the mystical aura that accompanied Codreanu's sway over the backward rural areas of Romania. Böszörmèny's 'Ten Commandments' were a mixture of social demagoguery under a religious guise. The movement flourished between 1931 and 1936, when its membership grew from 20,000 to 250,000. The authorities obstructed the movement's participation in the 1935 elections, and thus Böszörmèny could not translate his success among the mass of the rural poor into political power.

In 1936 Böszörmèny organised a peasant army that was supposed to march from the countryside to Budapest, where the peasants were expected to raze the sinning city of 'lords and communists'. The police stopped the march, tried several hundred of the peasants, after which the movement dispersed, and the leader fled to Germany. Hungarian historiography recognises the movement's success in building a strong mass base of impoverished peasants, especially in eastern Hungary.[56] The consequences of the depression were used by several small extremist groups, which in their greed for power resorted to empty slogans, promising the peasants a solution to the land problem. Gömbös, who became Prime Minister in 1932, postponed the tackling of the agrarian problem, but at the same time promoted the idea that Hungary was to become a country of small and medium sized estates. It seems that Gömbös' and his colleagues' anti-feudalism appealed at least to a part of the Hungarian peasantry. In the Arrow Cross, according to an estimate of the membership in 1940, some 13 per cent were peasants, certainly less than in the Romanian Iron Guard. In the 1939 elections the Arrow Cross had received good results in the most underdeveloped areas, an indication that Szálasi had succeeded in capturing tens of thousands of peasants, especially the agrarian proletariat. Rothschild attributes Szálasi's success among the peasants in 1939 to his 'authentic commitment to land reform'.[57] In fact, Szálasi's record did not contain many authentic commitments, and it seems that his attitude to the land problem was part of his demagoguery, rather than a reflection of a genuine interest in solving the real problems of the Hungarian countryside.

The structure of Slovak society made it almost natural that Hlinka's Slovak People's Party received the strongest support among the peasants. Agrarian Slovakia suffered from the structure of the Czechoslovak state, and from what seemed like Czech tutelage to wide segments of Slovak society. In the poor rural areas where Hlinka's party always received more than 50 per cent of the votes, the social groups and classes that supported him were similar to a large extent to those in Romania: the local lower clergy, many of them sharing the same living conditions as the peasants, and the peasantry. There is no doubt that the driving power behind Slovak fascism was nationalism and separatism, but we should not ignore the economic plight of the peasantry, which felt that it was not elevated on the social scale after hundreds of years under the Magyar yoke. The support of the peasantry in Croatia for the fascist movements can be explained in similar terms: dissatisfaction with the framework of the Yugoslav state, and a feeling of frustration *vis-à-vis* what seemed to them Serb economic advancement. However, compared to Slovakia, the Ustasha had less success among the peasants than Hlinka's movement. Pavelić's brand of agrarian socialism did not appeal to the Croat peasant.[58]

VII

Hungarian aristocrats, generals and miners, Romanian professors and backward peasants, Czech officers, Slovak and Croat clergymen are just a sample of the social and occupational backgrounds of the people who adhered to the various fascist movements in Eastern Europe. Societies in crisis in an era of upheaval, of economic fluctuations, and of rapid modernisation turned to radical solutions offered by fascism in all of its forms. Mostly led by young intellectuals (as in Romania), army officers (as in Hungary) or clergymen (as in Slovakia and Croatia), the fascist movements reached wide segments of the population, often encompassing antagonistic groups. Thus the Iron Guard could attract, through its populism and mysticism, the Romanian peasant and the Bucharest merchant, while in Hungary the Arrow Cross reached its electoral peak through the support of high-ranking officers, rural proletarians and young intellectuals.

The East European case indicates that except for those groups which were the targets and victims of fascism, especially the Jews, all others were potential reservoirs of the fascist movements. Thus fascism was an ideology for the bad seasons of inter-war Eastern Europe, an ideological cocktail that combined conservatism with revolutionary *élan*, religious fanaticism and mysticism with a secular *Weltanschauung*. Szálasi's and Codreanu's writings are an amalgam of solutions for all their discontented countrymen in desperate need of change or security in the face of real or imaginary enemies. Tragically, fascism was for many East Europeans the ultimate insurance policy against all evils. Nothing would be more erroneous than to treat all East European fascists as young disturbed hoodlums, thugs and people on the fringe of society. Electoral results in Hungary and Romania bear witness to the dissemination of fascism among all segments of society, embracing people from the most backward to the most advanced areas of the country.

It is very difficult to assess the impact of the rise of German Nazism in quantitative terms on the growth of the fascist movements in the countries of the area. There is no doubt that it did influence the spread of the movements, while it also affected them in peculiar ways, eliciting self-defensive responses in the East European countries: thus small groups in Czechoslovakia, Poland and Romania adopted local forms of fascist ideologies with a view to safeguarding their societies from the German menace. Paradoxically, the German challenge also promoted the emergence of local, or 'native', fascism in the area. The fact that fascist movements reached power very late, on the eve of or during the Second World War, should not underrate their previous achievements. In some cases, especially in Romania and Hungary, the fascists were ready to seize power in their respective states, having built a mass basis and a leadership, but only the machinations of the existing regimes prevented them from doing so.

One of the most problematic aspects of fascism in Eastern Europe is its success, mainly in Hungary and Romania, in also attracting the working class. It was tragic that the Communists at the time were more busy fighting their factional wars than fighting fascism. While their leaders, on orders from Moscow, were analysing the trends in the middle class in order to demonstrate its affinity with fascism, workers - and not only the unskilled urban proletariat - joined the fascist movements and voted for them in the elections. This is a painful legacy, with which East European research, with very few exceptions, has not been able to cope as yet. It is just possible that we in the West are lacking empirical data from East European sources which might show that for wide segments of the population in need of radical change, fascism was the inevitable logical solution. If this is the case, then fascism should not be seen as a manifestation of social marginality and psychological deviation but as evidence of society's weaknesses.

The unravelling of fascism's past in Eastern Europe lies ahead of us still, and one can but hope that honest scientific research will lead to a better understanding of the conditions and the dynamics under which some societies were liable to succumb to the various forms of totalitarianism.

Notes

1. Ormos Mária, 'A Vasgárda', *Történelmi Szemle*, vol. 25 (1982), pp. 426-42.
2. G. Zaharia and M. Fătu, '1940 - România', *Anale de Istorie*, vol. 25, no. 6 (1979), p. 165.

3. B. Vago, 'Fascism in Eastern Europe' in W. Laqueur (ed.), *Fascism. A Reader's Guide* (London, 1979), p. 216.
4. J. Rothschild, *East Central Europe between the Two World Wars* (Seattle, 1974), p. 19.
5. I. T. Berend and G. Ránki, *Underdevelopment and Economic Growth* (Budapest, 1979), p. 194.
6. For an analysis of current research into inter-war Romanian society, see Michael Shafir, *Romania* (London, 1985), pp. 4-8.
7. F. L. Carsten, 'Interpretations of Fascism' in Laqueur, *Fascism*, p. 460.
8. E. Weber, 'The Men of the Archangel', *Journal of Contemporary History*, vol. 1 (1966), p. 107.
9. See Z. Barbu, 'Psycho-Historical and Sociological Perspectives on the Iron Guard, the Fascist Movement in Romania' in S. U. Larsen a. o. (eds.), *Who Were the Fascists? Social Roots of European Fascism* (Bergen-Oslo-Tromsø, 1980), p. 391.
10. A. C. Cuza, *Despre poporatie, statistica, teoria, politica ei* (Bucharest, 1929), p. 659.
11. I. Z. Codreanu, *For My Legionaries* (Madrid, 1976), p.34.
12. *Buna Vestire*, 2 April 1937.
13 Rothschild, *East Central Europe*, p. 311.
14. *Cuvîntul Studentesc*, 1940.
15. *Buletinul Informativ*, 25 August 1940; see also Weber, 'The Men of Archangel', p. 109.
16. Ç. Bogdan, 'Baza Social-Economicӑ A Fascismului În România', *Împotriva Fascismului* (Bucharest, 1971), p. 40.
17. Zaharia and Fӑtu, 'România', p. 168.
18. See L. Pӑtrӑşcanu, *Sub Trei Dictaturi* (Bucharest, 1970).
19. C. C. Giurescu, 'Amintiri de la Facultatea de litere din Bucuresti privind perioada regimului legionar', *Împotriva Fascismului*, pp. 206-11.
20. See, for example, *Universul*, 12 December 1940.
21. See Ormos Mária, 'A Vasgárda', p. 429.
22. For a recent study of the role of the Hungarian refugees on the radicalisation of Hungarian political life, see I. I. Mocsy, *The Effects of World War I, The Uprooted: Hungarian Refugees and Their Impact on Hungary's Domestic Politics, 1918-1921* (New York, 1983).
23. Toth Pàl Pèter, 'Az Egyetemi Hallgatok Mozgalmai Debrecenben 1933-1936', *Szàzadok*, vol. 115 (1981), p. 1192.
24. Ibid., p. 1207.

25. D. Djordević, 'Fascism in Yugoslavia: 1918-1941' in P. F. Sugar (ed.), *Native Fascism in the Successor States* (Santa Barbara, 1971), p. 131.
26. I. Avakumovic, 'Yugoslavia's Fascist Movements' in Sugar, *Native Fascism*, p. 141.
27. Y. Jelinek, 'Clergy and Fascism: The Hlinka Party in Slovakia and the Croatian Ustasha Movement' in Larsen, *Who were the Fascists?*, p.371.
28. M. Lackó, *Arrow Cross Men - National Socialists 1935-1944* (Budapest, 1969).
29. G. Ránki, 'The Problem of Fascism in Hungary' in Sugar, *Native Fascism*, p.65.
30. Lackó, *Arrow Cross Men*, p. 7.
31. M. Fătu and I. Spălăţelu, *Gărda de Fier* (Bucharest, 1971), p. 129.
32. See J. Zarach, 'The Enigma of the Gajda Affair in Czechoslovak Politics in 1926', *Slavic Review*, no. 4 (1976).
33. See, for example, L. B. Valev, *Bolgarskoj narod v borbe protiv fasizma* (Moscow, 1964).
34. Ránki in Sugar, *Native Fascism*, p.72.
35. See, for example, P. Sipos, *Imrèdy Bèla es a Magyar Megujulás Pàrtja* (Budapest, 1970).
36. M. Lackó, 'The Social Roots of Hungarian Fascism: The Arrow Cross' in Larsen, *Who were the Fascists?*, p. 397.
37. G. Ránki, 'The Fascist Vote in Budapest in 1939' in Larsen, *Who were the Fascists?*, p. 416.
38. See Pătrăşcanu, *Sub Trei Dictaturi*.
39. Bogdan, 'Baza Social-Economică A Fascismului În România', p. 39.
40. P. S. Wandycz, 'Fascism in Poland' in Sugar, *Native Fascism*, p. 97.
41. On some further aspects of the social basis of Poland's fascist movements, see S. Anderski, 'Poland' in S. J. Woolf (ed.), *Fascism in Europe* (London, 1968), pp. 187-9.
42. See J. F. Zacek, 'Czechoslovak Fascisms' in Sugar, *Native Fascism*, pp. 56-62.
43. *Libertatea*, 10 November 1940.
44. Berend and Ránki, *Underdevelopment*, p. 210.
45. Ibid., p. 211; see also A. C. Janos, *The Politics of Backwardness in Hungary* (Princeton, 1982), ch. VI.
46. Weber, 'The Men of Archangel', p. 118.
47. Codreanu, *For My Legionaries*, p. 275.
48. Ibid., p. 67.
49. *Buletinul National Socialist*, 1933.

50. Weber, 'The Men of Archangel', pp. 116-7.
51. S. Fischer-Galati, 'Fascism in Romania' in Sugar, *Native Fascism*, p. 114.
52. P. A. Shapiro, 'Prelude to Dictatorship in Romania: The National Christian Party in Power, December 1937 - February 1938', *Canadian-American Slavic Studies*, vol. 8, 1 (Spring 1974), p. 51.
53. Bogdan, 'Baza Social-Economică A Fascismului În România', p. 39.
54. Berend and Ránki, *Underdevelopment*, p. 210.
55. F. L. Carsten, *The Rise of Fascism* (London, 1967), p. 174.
56. For the most important Hungarian study of the movement, see S. Kálmán, *Kaszakeresztesek* (Budapest, 1963); see also Ormos Mária and Incze Miklós, *Europai fasizmusok* (Budapest, 1976), p. 89.
57. Rothschild, *East Central Europe*, p. 181.
58. On Pavelić's ideology, see B. Krizman, *Pavelić I Ustase* (Zagreb, 1978).

Chapter Nine

THE IBERIAN STATES

Martin Blinkhorn

To attempt to discuss the social basis of Iberian fascist movements is to be faced, first of all, with the question of what precisely to examine. Unlike the writer on Italian, German or even British fascism, for whom the identification and isolation of 'fascism' presents few problems, the student of Spanish and Portuguese fascism must come to terms with the absence of any scholarly consensus as to how the term may best be applied to the various right-wing, authoritarian movements and regimes which have existed in the Iberian countries since the First World War. Recent writers on the subject have divided broadly between those who see fascism as an essentially self-defining phenomenon identifiable by its 'radical' programme and distinctive style, and those for whom, on the contrary, it constitutes an objective reality definable not in artificially rigorous ideological, programmatic or cultural terms but in those of its historical 'role'. For followers of the former tendency, Iberian fascism is effectively confined to the *Juntas de Ofensiva Nacional Sindicalista* (JONS - Committees of National Syndicalist Offensive) and the Falange in Spain and the National Syndicalists in Portugal; for those of the latter, the label may also be applied to other movements of a generally rightist but ostensibly 'non-fascist' character, as well as to the Franco and Salazar regimes.[1]

In the context of this volume, it is necessary to focus in the first instance upon those movements, identified above, which openly declared themselves fascist - or, to use more conventional Iberian terminology, national syndicalist. Since, however, the radical right in Spain before 1936 and in the Portugal of the early 1930s enjoyed only limited mass support, some consideration of the social basis of the right in general is also desirable in order that light may be shed upon the meaningfulness or otherwise of distinctions between the 'fascist' and 'non-fascist' right.

To problems of definition must be added problems concerning sources. The manner of the rise of Italian Fascism and German National Socialism, the sustained electoral activity of the NSDAP, and the availability of party records seized by the Allies in 1945 have presented historians of Italy and Germany with abundant data relating to the membership and, in the NSDAP's case, electoral support of those movements. In Spain, on the other hand, the holocaust of documentation which occurred not only during the Civil War but also throughout the Franco regime has made excruciatingly difficult any systematic sociological analysis of the very political forces out of which the regime itself was forged. Most records of the early Falange were destroyed in 1936, with the result that the membership details of the Madrid Falange in 1936, published by Stanley Payne a quarter of a century ago, remain the only serious source on Falangist membership before the movement's explosive expansion in 1936 and 1937.[2] Evidence on the wartime Falange and its militia is uneven, and in any case says little of interest about the Falange *as a movement*;[3] something may nevertheless be gleaned from Miguel Jerez's study of office-holders within the Franco regime between 1938 and 1957.[4]

Information of the desired kind on other movements of the Spanish right is no easier to come by. The membership file of the Carlist *Comunión Tradicionalista*, held in the party headquarters in central Madrid, was lost, destroyed or all too successfully hidden on the outbreak of war, and evidence is similarly lacking - perhaps for similar reasons - on the Catholic-conservative *Confederación Española de Derechas Autonómas* (CEDA - Spanish Confederation of Autonomous Right-Wing Groups) and the monarchist *Renovación Española*. Studies dealing with Carlism, the CEDA and *Renovación* have therefore been limited, in discussing these movements' social base, to reasonably confident and well-grounded assertions concerning leadership cadres and cautious generalisations about the rank and file.[5] The position is little better where electoral data are concerned, since the idiosyncracies of the Spanish Republic's electoral system and the actual methods of recording votes make impossible anything but the crudest excursions into electoral sociology.

In one respect, at least, the Portuguese situation is less bleak. It is true that the precise social foundations of the Salazar dictatorship remain unverified, thanks to the reluctance of the post-1974 authorities in Portugal to grant access to the membership lists of, for example, Salazar's single party, the paramilitary and youth organisations of the regime, and the police forces; publication of this material, for which historians are still pressing, would, it is presumably feared, be political dynamite.[6] Fortunately, from the point of view of this essay, however, valuable evidence has come to light regarding the social composition of the National Syndicalist rank and file.[7] Apart from this welcome exception, the present chapter, compared with some in this volume, will be regrettably deficient in hard statistical evidence.

I

During the period of fascism's rise in Italy, Spain too was affected by post-war socio-economic convulsions, left-wing militancy, and the writhings of an oligarchic liberal-parliamentary political system which appeared incapable of evolving successfully towards genuine democracy. Spain did not, however, witness significant fascist or even pre-fascist stirrings in the years before the military *pronunciamiento* of General Primo de Rivera in 1923. The 'Young Maurists' who took to the streets during the 1910s in support of the Conservative leader, Antonio Maura, lacked both ideological thrust and 'revolutionary' direction.[8] The military '*junteros*' who participated in the near-revolutionary crisis of 1917 proved in the event too preoccupied with professional concerns to be able to develop into anything more far-reaching.[9] Ironically, the most vigorous popular force of the right before 1923 remained, despite its chronic decline since the 1870s, the century-old Carlist movement. The historic vehicle for Spanish anti-liberalism, Carlism still possessed a degree of populist *élan*; it boasted a paramilitary wing, the *Requeté*; and in industrial Catalonia it was beginning, by the early 1920s, to display signs of a social radicalism which hinted at possible 'fascist' tendencies.[10] Although Carlism nevertheless remained, in the minds both of the general public and of its own leaders, too associated with all forms of traditionalism to have a serious chance of evolving into a movement of the modern, radical-authoritarian right, it may by its mere existence have inhibited the growth of radical-rightist alternatives.[11]

The reasons for the absence, to all intents and purposes, of anything seriously resembling Italian-style fascism in Spain before 1923 are not especially difficult to discern, especially when the always useful Italian comparison is borne in mind. Despite superficial similarities between the two countries, the general climate in Spain was simply less conducive to the emergence of movements remotely describable as fascist. Post-war economic and social dislocation, while considerable, was far less acute in Spain, a former neutral, than in Italy, an ex-belligerent forced to grapple with such problems as mass demobilisation and wounded national susceptibilities. Mass politics, suddenly thrust upon Italy thanks to suffrage and electoral reform and the appearance of large, modern socialist and Catholic parties, still lay in the future in Spain: to be precise, in the 1930s. Furthermore, whilst the threat of left-wing revolution, or even merely of left-inspired social reformism, was a real one for Spain's agricultural-financial-industrial oligarchy, there was as yet no reason for its members to seek salvation outside the familiar and reliable police and military resources of the established state.

All this could, and much of it would, alter. Other, more chronic factors were also present, however, which made it unlikely that fascism of a type closely resembling Italy's would prosper in Spain, either in the 1920s or later. Assuming that the likeliest sources of fascist activism and support include the urban lower middle class and the middling peasantry, Spain was infertile soil for actual or future radical fascists. Where the urban petty bourgeoisie was concerned, the problem lay not so much in lack of numbers as in its peculiar characteristics and distribution. A 'progressive' urban lower middle class produced by industrialisation and modernisation, as well as more vulnerable, 'traditional' sectors imperilled by the same processes, did exist in Spain's larger cities and industrial conurbations. Dominated by a wealthy bourgeoisie which had largely failed by 1920 to play a politically reforming role *vis-à-vis* the 'liberal' monarchy of Alfonso XIII, the urban lower middle class and intelligentsia were emerging by this time - in a manner not replicated in Italy - as a major element within the popular support for democratisation and even republicanism.

An overlapping complication, absent in Italy and insufficiently remarked by commentators in Spanish fascism, is the role of regionalism and 'regional nationalism'. With the major exception of Madrid, those regions where there can be said to have existed a numerous urban lower middle class - part 'modern' and upwardly-striving, part 'traditional' and insecure - were principally those - Catalonia, the Basque country, Valencia - where petty-bourgeois frustration with 'oligarchy and *caciquismo*'[12] was least likely to find an outlet in extreme Spanish, i.e. Castilian, nationalism. The gradual emergence of left-wing, petty-bourgeois Catalanism, the growth of the Basque Nationalist Party, and the local dominance of the Autonomous Republican Party in Valencia, all tended to channel petty-bourgeois political life in directions that were broadly democratic *and* decidedly anti-centralist. Whilst, in the 1930s, this was to prove a less than ideal base for Spanish democracy, it also deprived 'Spanish fascism' of a putative source of support.[13]

By no means all of the Spanish lower middle class was of this kind, however. Ronald Fraser has provided us with an illuminating portrait of a deeply conservative petty bourgeoisie whose members had been less obviously or immediately affected by economic change than their counterparts in Barcelona, Bilbao or Madrid.[14] Present throughout provincial Spain, *this* sub-class, individual members of which were often landowners on a relatively modest scale, was proportionately strongest in central Spain, and especially in small-town Castile, Leon and Aragon. It was this constituency, together with the peasantry with which it was intimately linked by economic and family ties, that both the Falange and the Catholic right were to idealise and woo after 1931. Before 1923, however, it was still for the most part either politically unmobilised, trapped in the web of *caciquismo*, or else caught up in the rather different network of social-Catholicism. Overwhelmingly and devoutly Catholic, the provincial petty bourgeoisie and peasantry formed, by the early 1920s, the rank-and-file personnel of such powerful social-Catholic bodies as the National Catholic-Agrarian Confederation (CNCA), a vast organisation composed mainly of smallholding peasants but dominated by landholding and clerical interests. The ideological and social conservatism of the Spanish Church, and its intimate relationship with the monarchical state, precluded any leftward radicalisation of social-Catholicism such as had occurred in the very different Church-state climate of Italy, and ensured that in Spain organised Catholicism could be depended upon to defend existing property relationships.[15]

The effective conquest of Spanish society's middling layers by, variously, demo-republicanism, regional nationalism and social Catholicism made unlikely the appearance of an autonomous fascist movement during the early 1920s, and was to create serious problems for those that did eventually emerge in the 1930s. Looked at in another way, however, the extensive and potentially still larger mass base of a social-Catholicism with distinctly reactionary tendencies might be said to have constituted the basis for a different, distinctively Spanish, version of fascism.

Political instability, social unrest and parliamentary assertiveness during the early 1920s came to an abrupt end in September 1923 with the *coup d'état* of Primo de Rivera, a wholly military affair which possessed widespread passive civilian support but, for the reasons discussed above, was based upon no prior mobilisation of popular forces, fascist or otherwise. During his six-year dictatorship, which eventually collapsed in January 1930, Primo stumbled towards the establishment of a broadly Italian-style corporate state. An important element in his political design was an artificially created single party, *Unión Patriótica*. Intended principally to give his regime legitimacy and permanence, *Unión Patriótica* is usually dismissed as an essentially passive, manipulative device with little active role save that of, in the words of one of Primo's own henchmen, saying 'Yes' to the dictator. Since a true 'movement' must surely arise independently of such official sponsorship, *Unión Patriótica* can scarcely be considered a 'movement' in any serious sense, still less a fascist one; Shlomo Ben-Ami has nevertheless suggested that it played an important transitional role in the creation of what he terms the 'agrarian fascism' of the 1930s, by schooling new right-wing political leaders and activists and by speeding up the political mobilisation of extensive sectors of the petty bourgeoisie and peasantry, especially in central Spain. And whilst Primo himself may have been reluctant to don the fascist label that others, both friends and enemies, attempted to pin on him, many of those surrounding him nursed no such reservations and actually strove to maximise the regime's resemblances to that of Mussolini. Following their master's fall, many of these elements regrouped in the *Unión Monárquica Española*: a vital ideological and human bridge, as Ben-Ami has demonstrated, between *Unión Patriótica* and the right of the 1930s.[16]

In the short term, the failings of the Primo de Rivera dictatorship discredited authoritarianism in Spain at a time when it was on the advance throughout much of Europe - not least in Portugal. More particularly it refuelled democratising zeal among the 'progressive' lower middle class of Spain's cities and larger towns. In the longer term, and given the nostalgia with which wealthy Spaniards were soon to regard the dictatorship, it may have restricted the prospects of radical fascism in another way: by reminding the rich, and the more traditional sectors of the lower middle class and peasantry, that the army - after half a century of relative non-involvement in politics - could in a crisis be expected to act as the 'spinal column of the fatherland' and a shield against 'bolshevism'. This comforting thought was one of which Italians, with their different civil-military tradition, were largely deprived.

The collapse of the dictatorship, followed in April 1931 by that of the monarchy and the installation of the Second Republic, created in Spain a new socio-political climate which proved far more conducive than that of the early 1920s to activist forms of right-wing authoritarianism. Like Italy after 1919, Spain was suddenly thrust into the arena of mass politics. Although *caciquismo* at the local level was still far from dead, the days of manufactured electoral and parliamentary majorities were effectively past as large, modern parties began to compete for popular allegiance within what, by 1933, was a system of universal adult suffrage. As Italy and other countries had already discovered, adjustment to such a sudden political change, certain to be difficult in itself, was all the more so when economic and social problems were especially pressing; in Spain, where many such problems had been artificially muffled by the dictatorship, by far the most acute and urgent was that of the land.

The republican-socialist governments of 1931 to 1933, for all their shortcomings in the sphere of social and especially agrarian reform, nevertheless significantly altered short-term conditions in favour of urban workers, rural labourers and tenant farmers. Against the background of agricultural depression, capitalist farmers and traditionalist landlords found profits squeezed and rents controlled as rural trade unionism embraced increasing numbers of day labourers and poor peasants. The anarcho-syndicalist *Confederación Nacional del Trabajo* (CNT - National Confederation of Labour), driven underground during the dictatorship, resurfaced in 1930 to 1931 and began to undergo both expansion and radicalisation; the socialist *Unión General de Trabajadores* (UGT - General Workers' Union), which under Primo had enjoyed and exploited a favoured position, now built upon this to increase both its membership and - as an unforeseen consequence - its militancy. Spain's wealthy classes accordingly found themselves faced not only with the reality of lower-class advancement but also with what they believed - or claimed to believe - was the prospect of a Russian-style slide from 'provisional' democracy into 'bolshevism'. Until early 1933 the left-wing republicans and socialists held the initiative and their right-wing opponents remained, relatively speaking, on the defensive. Thereafter, however, with the republican-socialist alliance in tatters, popular disillusionment widespread, and the examples of Germany and later Austria available to inspire those already fascinated by that of Italy, the climate for some sort of 'fascism' was more propitious than ever before. Given the agrarian predominance within the economy and society of Spain, and the role of militant Catholicism within Spanish culture, it was more than likely that these features would strongly influence whatever forms of organised response the right produced.

The right during the Second Republic developed along four main channels: one overtly fascist or at any rate 'national syndicalist', one monarchist with distinct and unashamed fascist tendencies, and two - Carlism and Catholic 'accidentalism' - officially non-fascist. Of these the oldest by far was Carlism, which, divided and seemingly moribund in the 1920s, revived strongly in the anticlerical and socially charged atmosphere of the Republic. Most securely established in Navarre, where it held a virtual political monopoly, Carlism nevertheless spread into most regions of Spain between 1931 and 1936, grafting onto its traditional rural populism and crusading Catholicism a new element of militant and increasingly violent anti-socialism. Although its ideology and programme may have been far from fascist in any strict sense, its role and behaviour wherever its numbers permitted persuaded left-wing opponents and victims of its 'objectively fascist' nature.[17]

The most numerically powerful strand of the Spanish right from 1931 down to the spring of 1936 was that of Catholic 'accidentalism'. Beginning in 1931 as an umbrella organisation of the right, *Acción Nacional*, and relabelled *Acción Popular* in 1932, this strand assumed its definitive form in early 1933 with the creation of the CEDA, the largest political party in Spain. Under the sinuous leadership of José María Gil Robles, the CEDA from 1933 to 1936 was officially committed to obtaining power peacefully within the Republic and then 'revising' its constitution and institutions along what seemed likely to be more authoritarian and corporativist lines. Between November 1933 and December 1935 the CEDA exercised considerable influence over and within a succession of centre-right governments without ever achieving complete cabinet or electoral dominance. Although it contained a sincere social-Catholic element which has inspired some commentators to see it as a potentially Christian Democratic party forced by republican and socialist intolerance to retreat into rightist positions, the CEDA - especially at grassroots level - was at heart antagonistic to republican democracy; from the outset, many of its activists and in particular its youth sections displayed a fascination with foreign authoritarianism and even outright fascism.[18]

Unlike Carlism and the CEDA, devotees of 'Alfonsine' monarchism made little attempt to conceal their *fascisant* tendencies. Under the influence, first of the post-*primoderriverista Unión Monárquica Española* and then of the intellectual coterie *Acción Española*, Alfonsine monarchism quickly abandoned its liberal heritage in favour of what its own protagonists were happy to acknowledge was a species of monarcho-fascism. In the form of the political party *Renovación Española*, and later in 1934 to 1935 in that of the more ambitious *Bloque Nacional*, this radical-monarchism possessed an important base within the Spanish socio-economic elite and the Catholic intelligentsia but attracted little popular support. Rather than an attempt to recruit or mobilise masses, it served throughout as a front for the ideological subversion of the Catholic middle class and for anti-republican conspiracy.[19]

Overt fascism, in the guise of national syndicalism, was represented in pre-civil war Spain by the JONS and the Falange. The former were formed in October 1931 out of two smaller 'groupuscules', the Madrid-based *'La Conquista del Estado'* group led by Ramiro Ledesma and the *Juntas Castellanas de Actuación Hispánica*, led by Onésimo Redondo and based in the Castilian city of Valladolid. The JONS languished, however, and in November 1933 a rival on the self-consciously 'radical' right appeared in the shape of the Falange and its principal figure José Antonio Primo de Rivera, son of the late dictator. In February 1934 the two movements merged to form a single national syndicalist party, *Falange Española de las JONS*. Although from time to time both José Antonio and Ledesma were to deny the Falange's fascism, the inescapably radical-fascist character of its 'Twenty-Seven Points' indicated that this was no more than a matter of nomenclature.[20]

Portugal's experience during the years just covered in discussing Spain was in some respects very similar to her neighbour's and in others very different. Like Spain, Portugal witnessed a military *coup d'état* during the 1920s which put an end to a parliamentary regime; the Portuguese *coup* of 28 May 1926, however, instead of merely producing a shortlived dictatorship, proved to be the first step along a road which led ultimately to the erection of António de Oliveira Salazar's long-lasting *Estado Novo*. Most importantly, at no time in this period can Portugal be said to have known anything remotely approaching mass politics. As a result, although *fascisant* tendencies were at work during the 1920s, when a significant fascist movement *did* appear it was against the background not, as in most cases, of a troubled democracy, but of an authoritarian regime of essentially conservative character.

The Portuguese republic that was born in 1910 was never the affair of much more than an urban, mainly middle-class minority of the population. Plagued by governmental instability, political irresponsibility and financial chaos, the republican regime had certainly aroused by the early 1920s widespread hostility extending well beyond its inveterate monarchist enemies. The 1926 *coup* therefore met with even broader public acceptance than had greeted its Spanish precursor three years before.[21]

As in Spain during the early 1920s, Portuguese politics as yet showed no sign of producing any fascist or fascist-style mass movement. Four main reasons may be adduced for this not very surprising fact: the traditional, undeveloped character of the country's economy and society; the very low level of political involvement throughout the 1910 to 1926 period; the weakness of the Portuguese left; and the strength of other, broadly rightist alternatives to the 'democratic' *status quo*. In a country which had undergone considerably less economic and social transformation during the previous fifty years than Spain, only in the two big cities, Lisbon and Oporto, did anything remotely approaching a 'modern' society exist by 1926. The limited numbers and assertiveness of the Portuguese middle class meant not only that republicanism was unable to widen its base and thereby increase its viability, but also that in the 1920s the popular basis for a right-wing radicalism was equally lacking. Although a traditionalist, provincial lower middle class and peasantry, roughly comparable with those in parts of Spain, did exist, their members were even less politically active than their Spanish counterparts. This was especially true north of Lisbon, thanks to the influence of a profoundly conservative upper and lower clergy. Not even the impact of military demobilisation after 1919, affecting in the main the peasantry, was able seriously to destabilise this social order.

An important consequence of Portugal's low level of industrial development was the smallness of the urban working class. The related absence of a serious left-wing challenge to the Republic made irrelevant any experiments with radical-rightist demagogy which would, for the same reason, have held little appeal for conservative interests. Instead, the effect of growing disillusionment with liberal-parliamentarism was not the appearance of right-wing activism so much as a growing reliance on military intervention - two shortlived military dictatorships were set up during the 1914-18 war - and a perceptible middle-class retreat into Catholic traditionalist postures during the early 1920s.

The closest approach to a fascist movement in pre-Salazar Portugal was *Integralismo Lusitano*, an organisation founded in 1913 in conscious imitation of *Action Française* and advocating for Portugal a political system - monarchical, non-parliamentary yet decentralising - roughly similar to that proposed in Spain by some, more modern-minded, Carlists. Unlike Carlism, with its populist tradition, but like *Action Française*, the Italian Nationalist Association and, in Spain later, the *Renovación*

Española, Integralism sought not to create a mass movement but to conquer the social elite from which most of its own members came. The Integralists' strongest base was among university students. In a country which in 1926 still had fewer than 7,000 students in higher education, this was a predominantly upper- and upper middle-class preserve; indeed, the founders of Integralism included the sons of some of southern Portugal's richest landowning families. By 1926, although Integralism as a cohesive movement had passed its peak, it had successfully radicalised, in an authoritarian direction, much of this sector of Portuguese elite society. Also susceptible to the Integralist message was the army officer corps, within which authoritarian leanings were visible and increasing throughout the Republican period; in 1917 to 1918 the Integralists, indeed, provided enthusiastic support for the brief 'New Republic' of the army officer Sidónio Pais, the first of the twentieth century's corporativist dictatorships. Many officers before and after the 1926 *coup* were also Integralists or fellow-travellers, though it cannot honestly be said that this fact materially affected the general course of events by which Salazar emerged, by 1932, as prime minister and dictator of Portugal. The importance of Integralism to any attempt at explaining the delayed appearance of radical fascism in Portugal is nevertheless great. Through capturing the minds of educated, middle-class youth before 'fascism' had even appeared on the European scene, it helped to deflect what slight chance there might have been of a serious, mass-mobilising movement emerging, either during the years before the 1926 *coup* or in the highly fluid, transitional period between the *coup* and the establishment of the *Estado Novo*.[22]

Salazar himself, and the regime which after 1932 he directed, nevertheless owed less to Integralism than to those powerful conservative currents within Portuguese Catholicism to which the prime minister himself had belonged. As a university professor and as a political activist, Salazar and his associates - comprising another academic and student coterie - had, especially in the Academic Centre of Christian Democracy (CADC), espoused broadly similar socio-political ideas and accidentalist tactics to those later embraced in Spain by the CEDA. Even more than the Integralists, Catholic political activists distrusted the masses and had no wish to see truly popular movements develop, either within the republican system in which they found themselves obliged to militate or within the authoritarian system with which they dreamed of replacing it.[23] The *Estado Novo* thus gave birth to officially sponsored organisations which were nevertheless designed not to mobilise the masses so much as to discipline them. The single party, *União Nacional*; the paramilitary *Legião Portuguesa*, set up in 1936; and the youth movement or *Mocidade*: these and other official organisations would certainly repay sociological analysis were the necessary data available. Like *Unión Patriótica* in Spain, however, bodies such as these, artificially created by a regime never more than superficially 'fascist', can scarcely be said to demand close study in an essay of this kind.

One movement which does, and which will be discussed later, is the National Syndicalist Organisation (ONC), formed autonomously of the *Estado Novo* yet under its protection in 1932, suppressed and driven underground in 1934, involved in an unsuccessful rising against the *Estado Novo* in 1935, and effectively extinct by 1936. Despite the oddity of its genesis and the particular context within which its life was lived out, National Syndicalism represents the only indisputable fascist *movement* in the history of Portugal between 1919 and 1945.

II

Like other radical-fascist and national socialist movements, the JONS and the Falange sought to become 'national' movements transcending class differences. By February 1936 it was clear that they had so far failed utterly, both in crude quantitative terms and in their attempts to woo particular social constituencies. The national membership of *Falange Española de las JONS* in early 1936 was at most 25,000, including around 10,000 'front-line' activists and at least as many 'illegal' student adherents.[24] In the February 1936 election, Falangist candidates polled a mere 40,000 votes nationwide; though only seventeen out of sixty constituencies were contested, this result, with the Falange obtaining only 4 per cent of the votes cast in Valladolid, just over 1 per cent in Madrid, and 4.6 per cent in José Antonio's home district of Cadiz, hardly suggested a large reservoir of passive support beyond the movement's actual membership. The chief task of the historian in the face of these facts is therefore to examine, and try to explain, 'radical' fascism's failure to recruit in the various social layers to which it had attempted to appeal.

If there is one feature which distinguishes the self-image of radical fascism and national socialism from that of more frankly conservative forms of authoritarian rightism, it is its attempt to poach working-class support away from the left. The Spanish radical right was no exception. From the start, Ledesma had hoped to attract Spanish workers through a raucous anti-capitalism and the notion - used by Italian revolutionary syndicalists a decade and more earlier - of 'national syndicalism'. Ledesma's particular target was the rank and file of the CNT, supposedly more 'Spanish' and more susceptible to ideological subversion than that of the socialist UGT.[25] José Antonio's own dabbling with 'syndicalism' in an ephemeral organisation, the *Movimiento Sindicalista Nacional*, early in 1933 indicated a similar, albeit more paternalistic, acceptance of fascism's need to win over the workers.[26] After the JONS and the Falange merged in 1934 a new labour organisation, the *Confederación de Obreros Nacional-Sindicalistas* (CONS - Confederation of National Syndicalist Workers), was created to execute the task.

Hopes for the CONS's success were inspired in large part by that during the 1920s of the *Sindicatos Libres*. These right-wing unions, founded by radical Carlists and strongest in urban Catalonia, had under Primo de Rivera built up considerable support, especially among workers in the service sector and in small industrial concerns. This achievement was despite rather than because of the fascist proclivities of the *Libres'* leadership, however, and in 1930 to 1931 the tide turned decisively. With the governmental patronage enjoyed under the dictatorship replaced by an official ban and CNT/UGT antagonism, the *Libres* withered rapidly in a manner that actually boded ill, first for the JONS and then for the CONS.[27] And so it proved. JONSista appeals to the workers fell on deaf ears in the left-wing heyday of 1931 to 1933, and although the climate thereafter became more favourable, the CONS in its turn made a negligible impact upon the Spanish working class; only among such service-sector groups as waiters and taxi-drivers were a significant number of converts won. Although the membership of the Madrid Falange in early 1936, studied by Stanley Payne, at first sight seems to indicate a predominantly lower-class, even working-class composition, the fact that labourers, service employees and skilled workers comprise 545 out of a total membership of 1,103 is, as Payne points out, evidence not of strength in that quarter but of weakness, given Madrid's workforce of several hundred thousands. Even in percentage terms, the working-class proportion of over 49 per cent is highly deceptive in view of the non-inclusion of the strictly 'illegal' student element which overwhelmingly dominated the movement in the Spanish capital.

One factor contributing to the CONS's failure to recruit workers was the response of the left. As the experience of the 1920s had suggested, and as the early months of the Civil War were to confirm, fascist syndicalism could flourish only against the background of a rightist regime which restricted or repressed alternative forms of labour organisation. Elsewhere in Europe, moreover, radical-rightist appeals to the working class rarely prospered when the left and its union organisations were undergoing a phase of expansion and confidence. In Spain, despite the loss of initiative after 1933, the right's grass-roots counter-offensive of 1934 to 1935, and the official repression during and after the Asturias rising of October 1934, the left stubbornly refused to show those signs of deep demoralisation that might have presaged a major leakage of support to the CONS. During 1934 to 1936, CONS recruitment drives among such potentially vulnerable sectors as construction workers were successfully countered by resolute UGT and CNT action. One final point needs to be made concerning the CONS's failure. Thousands of non-leftist workers did exist in Spain, yet these too remained mostly immune from the allure of the CONS; instead it was the workers' sections of the CEDA and the Carlists, with their emphasis upon Catholicism, which showed signs of growth as the 1930s wore on.

'*Obrerismo*' ('workerism') represented one of two main elements in JONSista and Falangist efforts to attract the Spanish masses. The second was the stress upon the middling strata of Spanish society, the lower middle class and the peasantry, evident - albeit with different shades of emphasis - in both Redondo's and José Antonio's ideas and propaganda. In their idealisation of the supposed honesty, industriousness, austerity and all-round '*hispanidad*' ('Spanishness') of the 'neutral masses' in general, the peasantry in particular, and that of Castile above all, JONSism and Falangism differed only in matters of nuance from other factions of the right.[28] Unlike their rivals, however, the fascist movements met with little success in actually enlisting them. For all Redondo's much cited base among the sugar-beet producing small farmers of Valladolid in Old Castile, no more than 600 of the province's 1,600 Falangists - this being the movement's strongest provincial outpost - came from *pueblos* where this activity was concentrated, most of the majority being drawn from the urban middle class of the provincial capital and other, smaller towns. In the February 1936 general election, Redondo's personal standing won him 5,435 votes in the province, indicating that a mere four out of every 100 *vallisoletanos* had cast one of their four votes for him; even more significantly, perhaps, only 2,793, 2.2 per cent of those voting, had opted to use a second vote to support the party leader, José Antonio.[29]

The broad pattern of support evidenced in Valladolid was repeated, with still lower numbers, elsewhere. Although between 1933 and 1936 the Falange established organisations in most provincial capitals and larger towns, some - in, for example, Seville, Santander, Badajoz and Cáceres - with several hundred members, peasant support proved largely unforthcoming. Falangism's appeal to the 'neutral masses' remained mostly confined to a minority within the provincial lower middle class. Lack of detailed data makes it impossible to establish with certainty any clear distinction between this 'fascist' minority and the rest of the non-republican provincial petty bourgeoisie. The modernising, 'productivist' strand in Falangist propaganda was undoubtedly aimed at better educated, professional and 'technocratic' elements within the 'neutral masses', but evidence as to the degree of its success is limited. Miguel Jerez's study of the Francoist elite is at least suggestive in this regard. Over two-thirds of those of Falangist descent who held office between 1938 and 1957 were, he concludes, of urban provenance, and of these over 90 per cent possessed degrees or other qualifications obtained, for example, in the armed forces. Whilst Jerez's is anything but a representative sample of Falangist members, it does offer some indication of the party's relative success in wooing better-educated members of the middle class. The evident eagerness of many office-holders to exploit their position in order to enrich themselves by joining boards of directors of banks, etc. may also be evidence of their origins in the 'ambitious', progressive sector of the provincial bourgeoisie, rather than in the numerically dominant traditional sector.[30] Although Madrid represented a very different environment from that of provincial capitals, the presence of 106 professional men (9.6 per cent of the total) in the Falangist membership list for the city also suggests that some inroads were made into this group.

It was among the educated young, however, that the Falange's only real success was recorded. Recent graduates, university students and high-school students, in Madrid and other Spanish cities, probably constituted over half the Falange's membership in early 1936. The fact that students below voting age were banned by Republican law from joining political organisations means that most of these enthusiasts are missing from such figures as exist; in the Madrid lists, students officially number a mere 38 out of 1,103 (3.4 per cent), even though the true figure was between 1,000 and 2,000. Students, especially in the law and medicine faculties where the Falangist *Sindicato Español Universitario* (SEU) was strongest, were likely to represent the upper layers of the middle class, not to say the upper class.[31] Their importance to the Falange reinforces a more general but nevertheless vital point: that the radical, alienated intelligentsia to which Ledesma, Redondo and even José Antonio belonged, which possessed representatives in most cities and larger towns, and of which the educated, middle- and upper-class young constituted the audience, was central to the very existence of Spanish radical fascism in the 1930s.

Apart from students and a handful of the intellectually alienated such as José Antonio himself, few members of the very highest layers of Spanish society showed any interest in actively involving themselves in the Falange - and fewer still, earlier, in the more determinedly plebeian JONS. In the main, elite interest in the Falange took the more calculating and manipulative form of financial assistance from some Andalusian latifundists and Bilbao bankers who viewed it as a possible future vehicle for violent anti-leftism and/or a strong-arm extension of militant monarchism.[32]

By February 1936, then, the Falange possessed, in numerical terms, little more significance in Spanish politics than that of the BUF in the affairs of Britain. However, whilst the growth of fascism in Great Britain was restrained by a socio-economic climate less helpful to extremism than superficial appearances suggested, and by the existence of a powerful Conservative Party fully committed to democratic politics, the Spanish situation could hardly have been more different. Radical fascism, in the form of the JONS and the Falange, failed before 1936 to attract mass support because, in an otherwise by no means unpropitious social and political atmosphere, all sources of possible support were more successfully tapped by other organisations: the working class mainly by the left, and the rest by rival rightist parties whose hostility towards republican democracy differed from that of the Falange on points of style and tactics rather than of principle.

Alfonsine monarchist organisations such as *Acción Española* and *Renovación Española* played their part in rendering Falangist expansion difficult by providing a rallying point for the neo-monarchist intelligentsia and those sectors of the old social elite who rejected CEDA accidentalism. Given the markedly *fascisant* trajectory of these organisations, however, this clearly does not mean that their members were immune from the attractions of fascism as such, or at any rate of a species of fascism consistent with their material interests and general outlook. Where popular support was concerned, it was nevertheless not the elitist *alfonsinos* who were responsible for frustrating Falangist ambitions but the Carlists and the CEDA.

Carlism, despite its long-term decline since the 1870s, still possessed in 1931 a residual organisation and, here and there, a vigorous local and family tradition upon which a dramatic revival was quickly based. Whilst remaining strongest in Navarre and Alava, the Carlist *Comunión Tradicionalista* established itself as a presence in most parts of Spain during the years of the Republic; by 1934 it claimed 700,000 members, this being perhaps twice its true strength.[33] Carlism's popular appeal, where it existed, was due to a potent combination of militant Catholicism and, increasingly, defence of private property against the threat of 'bolshevism'. Although it cannot be said to have possessed much to attract the genuinely modern-minded, the movement, especially its youth and student sections, did now begin to display signs of a renewal of that social radicalism which over a decade earlier had spawned the *Sindicatos Libres*.[34] This demagogy - for in practice it was little more - was combined in the paramilitary *Requeté* with a taste for anti-leftist violence which its victims not unnaturally considered bore comparison with Italian *squadrismo*. The *Comunión Tradicionalista* acquired a mass base among peasant farmers, mainly in northern and north-eastern Spain, and a section of the provincial, Catholic middle class. In western Andalusia, where it emerged as a significant force for the first time, it attracted some support from large landowning interests; in Navarre, still its principal bastion, its prosperous middle-class leadership was firmly established within the organisations of local social-Catholicism and within landowners' and businessmen's pressure groups.[35]

In this last respect, as in several others, Carlism differed little from its fellow-Catholic competitors, *Acción Popular* and the CEDA. Unlike Carlism these were new organisations, which none the less represented fusions of, in the main, pre-existing provincial parties, interest groups and, above all, such social-Catholic agrarian entities as the CNCA. Overall the CEDA was a truly mass party, essentially controlled - as studies of its leadership indicate - by members of a landholding oligarchy based chiefly in Castile and Andalusia, with considerable strength also among the Catholic professional classes but rather less in those industrial and banking sectors whose members tended to incline, depending upon conviction or tactical calculation, towards either Alfonsine monarchism or conservative republicanism; as with the *Comunión Tradicionalista*, but on a much larger scale, the CEDA's mass base was to be found among the Catholic peasantry, especially in Castile, Leon, Aragon and Valencia, and the provincial petty bourgeoisie.[36]

Of particular significance for the prospects of radical fascism in Spain were the size of the CEDA Youth, the *Juventud de Acción Popular* (JAP) and, eventually, of CEDA-linked workers' organisations. The JAP may never have commanded the numbers, discipline or fanaticism of the Hitler Youth so admired by Gil Robles during his 1933 visit to Germany, but it was able to muster 50,000 members for its first mass rally in 1934 and improved on this turnout on subsequent occasions. The JAP, and the Carlist Youth and *Requeté*, whilst lacking the supposed ideological radicalism of fascism, provided sufficient opportunity for radical and militant behaviour to satisfy bitterly anti-socialist, Catholic, mainly middle-class young Spaniards. On the working-class front, the CEDA struggled to achieve success, but by late 1935 had accomplished the unification of various Catholic workers' organisations within the *Confederación Española de Sindicatos Obreros* (CESO - Spanish Confederation of Workers' Syndicates), which claimed over 240,000 members. If this remained well behind the CNT and UGT, it nevertheless demonstrated the existence of a Catholic working-class sector which the Falange and the CONS had utterly failed to penetrate.[37]

The general election of February 1936, won by the Popular Front, clearly indicated the strength of the Spanish accidentalist, Carlist and Alfonsine right, which even in defeat accumulated (different interpretations of the results vary widely) over 40 per cent of the popular vote. The right's defeat had a convulsive effect, however, on the allegiance of CEDA supporters. The clear failure of the CEDA's gradualist tactic and a growing fear of 'bolshevism' caused the CEDA itself to disintegrate as tens of thousands of its members and supporters departed to throw in their lot with the tactically more radical Carlists or, in far greater numbers, the Falange. The flight towards unambiguous fascism was most pronounced in the JAP, many of whose local organisations transferred to the Falange *en bloc* or, as in Valencia, simply took up violent and conspiratorial activity on their own account. The Falange's phenomenal growth was not appreciably stayed even by the government's attempts at repressing the party; after the outbreak of the civil war in July 1936 the process, in the Nationalist zone, accelerated still further as both opportunistic conservatives and prudent leftists joined a party that seemed willing to admit anyone. Between March 1936 and April 1937, when it was arbitrarily merged by Franco with the *Comunión Tradicionalista* and other, much smaller rightist organisations to form the single party of his emerging new regime, the Falange became a truly mass movement.[38] During this period, and despite the deaths of José Antonio, Ledesma, Redondo and other front-rank leaders, the party retained its 'radical' image. For its true militants, its ex-leftist 'converts' and its conservative and Carlist rivals this was a matter of great significance. For tens, perhaps hundreds of thousands of new members, however, it must be doubted whether this was so. Much of the new Falange's mass base was indistinguishable from that of the 'old' right, 'radicalised' in its acceptance of Falangism's combative style and tactics rather than its fascist ideology and programme.

A socio-political order such as that of Spain in the 1930s (or Italy in the early 1920s) constitutes one environment favourable to the emergence of some kind or kinds of fascist movement. Portugal offers an alternative example, that of an authoritarian regime of essentially conservative character in relation to which fascism arose as an attempt to achieve the pursuit of more dynamic, mass-mobilising policies than were acceptable to those in power.

The blueshirted National Syndicalist Organisation (ONS) was founded in 1932, its chief protagonists being, like its two leading figures, Francisco Rolão Preto and the Count of Monsaraz, founder members of *Integralismo Lusitano* and later spokesman for that movement's more radical and socially concerned wing. Presenting themselves initially as a kind of elite militia for Salazar's use in a 'National Revolution' he was never likely to desire, they quickly developed into a force for radical-rightist opposition to Salazar's conservatism. The rhetoric of Rolão Preto and other leading Blueshirts was characteristically fascist in its reiterative but vague anti-capitalism, its stress upon youth and the youthful 'spirit', and even its expansionist appetite for Spanish Galicia. Its message was transmitted through a national newspaper, *Revolucão Nacional*, a provincial press consisting of thirteen weeklies, and a campaign of banquets, public meetings and rallies.[39]

By 1933 the ONS claimed a membership of 50,000, a figure accepted by most later commentators. However, António Costa Pinto has calculated, on the basis of the ONS's own membership files, that the highest figure actually reached was 25,000 - still in no sense a meagre achievement against the background of a right-wing regime and the country's low level of political mobilisation. Costa Pinto's examination of available figures - not a strict 'sample' - representing some 14 per cent of the ONS's national membership makes it possible to offer some conclusions as to the movement's appeal. Of 3,466 members studied, no fewer than 830 (24 per cent) were urban or rural workers, 260 (7.5 per cent) 'independent workers' or artisans, and a further 529 (15.2 per cent) 'private-sector employees'. Whilst this indicates proportionately considerable support among blue- and white-collar workers, these were apparently recruited mainly outside the principal industrial areas and were not converts from anarcho-syndicalism and communism. Other significant elements were the 399 (11.5 per cent) owners of small businesses, the 222 (6.4 per cent) civil servants, the 209 (6 per cent) 'intellectuals, teachers and members of liberal professions', and above all the 456 students (13.1 per cent), together adding up to an appreciable middle-class presence; all in all, the picture is not very different from that presented by the Falange at the start of 1936. What the ONS figures do not show is the considerable support of army officers, strictly forbidden to join political organisations and perhaps restless at their reduced role in Salazar's emergent new order.

The overall impression of National Syndicalism at its peak in 1932 to 1933 is thus of a movement with some appeal to previously unorganised workers, but whose solid core was to be found in the educated and economically active lower middle class of Lisbon and other larger population centres; considerable support was forthcoming from army officers and from the liberal professions, intelligentsia and student population, and some sympathy aroused among landowners and large-scale commercial and industrial proprietors (there were 277 of these: 7.9 per cent). In so far as it is possible to draw a more ambitious conclusion from these figures, it is perhaps that for a brief period National Syndicalism offered an outlet for groups within Portuguese, mainly urban, society who yearned for greater dynamism and mobility than was envisaged by Salazar or possible within the structures and policies of the *Estado Novo*.

These elements were a minority, however, and the limits to the ONS's potential were clear. Like Spain, Portugal lacked the displaced, *déclassé* groups whose members nurtured fascist activism in Italy and Germany; at the same time conservatives, of the kind who in Spain in 1936 embraced radical fascism, were by definition likely to be content with the very regime that National Syndicalism sought either to radicalise or replace. Short of a major internal crisis of the regime or an unlikely challenge from the left, it is hard to see how National Syndicalism could have attracted much more popular support than it did. To Salazar it was nevertheless an increasing nuisance. As early as July 1933 the authorities began to harass the National Syndicalist press; its leaders were pointedly urged to be more restrained in their language and conduct; and in July 1934 the movement was suppressed altogether. A shadowy organisation remained in existence and in September 1935, together with elements from the democratic and anarcho-syndicalist left and the army officer corps, engaged in an unsuccessful *coup* attempt in Lisbon. By 1936, when it finally disappeared, the underground movement's membership had fallen to a mere 1,200. Many of the less determinedly radical National Syndicalists had by then retreated into the cosier world of the *Estado Novo*'s official organisations; the rest, including Rolão Preto, persisted in increasingly futile opposition to Salazar's conservative and authoritarian regime.

III

In so far as a 'fascist movement' may be defined as one of ostensibly radical, rightist, mass-mobilising type, arising autonomously within either a pluralistic or a conservative-authoritarian system, then such movements enjoyed very limited success in attracting popular support in Spain before 1936; in Portugal, fascism thus defined was all but non-existent in the years before the establishment of the *Estado Novo*, and thereafter took the form of a shortlived, minority movement of radical protest. In both countries, radical fascism during these periods failed to attract more than a minority within the lower middle class, most of whose members were either Catholic and traditionalist in culture and political allegiance or, in Spain's case, caught up in the often linked causes of democracy and regional autonomy. In both countries, too, fascist movements failed to recruit an overwhelmingly Catholic peasantry and an urban and rural working class which remained stubbornly loyal either to the left or, in lesser numbers, to social Catholicism.

The Iberian countries' social fabric, their lack (notwithstanding Portugal's participation in the First World War) of 'uprooted masses' like those whose members swelled the ranks of Italian and German fascism, and the absence of the kind of 'pre-fascist culture' to which Italian fascism owed many of its external features,[40] all no doubt help to explain the non-appearance, on any scale, of fascist movements more or less resembling the Italian paradigm. None of this is exactly surprising, however, and it is surely more useful to try to account for the slow development of movements combining indisputably 'fascist' with authentically 'Iberian' attributes, and then to assess their significance once they did appear.

In Spain, the Primo de Rivera dictatorship preempted the possible appeal of radical rightism by resolving in an essentially conventional manner the convulsions of the early 1920s; in the longer term, none the less, it nurtured fascism by providing an atmosphere favourable to *fascisant* ideas and schooling future right-wing activists. At the same time, the social and political organisations of Spanish Catholicism created foundations upon which later counter-revolutionary, whether or not openly fascist, movements could be built. After 1930 the transformation of Spanish politics and the releasing of social pressures appeared likely to give 'fascism' a relevance it had not previously possessed, and to offer at least the possibility of mass support. That this support did not materialise before 1936 was due not to the lack of potential social constituencies but to the simple fact that their members' political loyalties lay for the time being elsewhere: with the Republic itself, with regional nationalism and, more importantly, with various forms of authoritarian, corporatist Catholicism.

In the light of this last point, and of developments after February 1936, it would be unwise to conclude that the slowness of the JONS and the Falange to attract mass support was the consequence of those features which made them distinctively 'fascist', or to the absence of a base for what Ben-Ami calls 'agrarian fascism'. For the leaders, ideologues and front-line activists of rightist movements in the Spain of the 1930s, ideological and programmatic nuances were doubtless of burning importance, but it is anything but clear that such concern extended much further. When the Falange, and to a lesser extent the Carlist *Comunión Tradicionalista*, suddenly expanded during the spring of 1936, it was in no real sense the result of mass conversions to the ideas and programmes either of fascism or of Carlist traditionalism; rather than abandoning the precepts of the papal encyclicals in favour of the Falange's Twenty-Seven Points, the latter's new members, like the 'new' Carlists, were simply repudiating right-wing gradualism in favour of impatience and violence. As the Falange became a truly mass movement during the months before and after the outbreak of hostilities in July 1936, it retained its outward radicalism despite the death of most of its early leaders. Its mass base, nevertheless, was becoming increasingly similar to that once possessed by the 'non-fascist' right and in particular by the CEDA. Whilst the 'new' Falange's official commitment to radical policies made it, in and after April 1937, a convenient tool for Franco, the essential conservatism of its mass base, reinforced still further after the fusion with Carlism, rendered it ultimately toothless.

Spain's case may or may not have implications for a wider understanding of fascism and its social base. What, certainly, it does demonstrate is that while self-conscious radicalism, taken seriously by genuine activists, did perhaps distinguish the 'fascist' from the ostensibly 'non-fascist' right, and may even have inhibited the former's growth, in the end it was the Falange's ability to absorb conservatives, rich and poor alike, which brought it success and a share of power. Whilst, therefore, it is only proper to recognise the existence of contending strands within the right as a whole, it equally cannot be denied that those on the Spanish left in the 1930s who viewed Carlism, Alfonsism, CEDA accidentalism and Falangism as the four horsemen of a single 'fascist' apocalypse grasped an essential truth.

The Portuguese experience serves, in its own very different way, to confirm these conclusions concerning the importance or otherwise of the distinctiveness of 'fascism'. In attempting to break away from the stifling structures and attitudes of the *Estado Novo*, National Syndicalism represented an unusually 'pure' version of radical fascism; as such it managed to mobilise what appear to have been relatively dynamic social groups within a traditionalist society governed by an authoritarian, conservative regime. The mere existence, and modest success, of National Syndicalism proves that fascist radicalism, in Portugal as in the very different political context of contemporary Spain, possessed for a small minority very real meaning. On the other hand, and without question more importantly, National Syndicalism's failure to recruit more successfully than it was able to do provides graphic illustration of radical fascism's limitations against the background of a regime which clearly satisfied the kind of conservatives who, a couple of years later in Spain, flooded into the Falange. Self-conscious radicalism may thus give fascism its initial impetus and identity, but in Iberia at least it was the ability to appeal to conservative interests that was the key to real success.

Notes

1. The first of these two broad approaches is represented, par excellence, by Stanley Payne: see his 'Spanish Fascism in Comparative Perspective' in Henry A. Turner Jr. (ed.), *Reappraisals of Fascism* (New York, 1975) pp. 142-69, and 'Salazarism: "Fascism" or "Bureaucratic Authoritarianism"?', *Estudos de História de Portugal, vol. II, secs. XVI-XX. Homenagem a A. H. de Oliveira Marques* (Lisbon, 1983), pp. 525-31. For opposing views see, on Spain, Paul Preston, 'Spain' in S. J. Woolf (ed.), *Fascism in Europe* (London, 1981), pp. 329-51 and, on Portugal, Tom Gallagher, *Portugal. A Twentieth-Century Interpretation* (Manchester, 1983), passim.
2. Stanley G. Payne, *Falange. A History of Spanish Fascism* (London, 1962), pp. 81-2. See also the contribution by the same author to S. U. Larsen a.o. (eds.), *Who Were the Fascists? Social Roots of European Fascism* (Bergen-Oslo-Tromsø, 1980), pp. 425-6.
3. The Falangist militia is examined in R. Casas de la Vega, *Las Milicias Nacionales* (2 vols., Madrid, 1977) and *Las Milicias Nacionales en la Guerra de España* (Madrid, 1974).
4. Miguel Jerez Mir, *Elites políticas y centros de extracción en España 1938-1957* (Madrid, 1982), pp. 49-175.
5. On Carlism see Martin Blinkhorn, *Carlism and Crisis in Spain 1931-1939* (Cambridge, 1975). The most complete study of the CEDA is José R. Montero, *La CEDA. El Catolicismo social y político en la II República* (2 vols., Madrid, 1977). *Renovación Española* awaits a detailed study, but see Paul Preston, 'Alfonsine Monarchism and the Coming of the Spanish Civil War' in Martin Blinkhorn (ed.), *Spain in Conflict 1931-1939* (London, 1986).
6. *Diário de Noticias* (Lisbon), 24 November 1985. See also the comments by Philippe C. Schmitter in Larsen, *Who Were the Fascists?*, p. 435.
7. I am immensely grateful to António Costa Pinto for these details and for permission to use them. His book, *O Nacional Sindicalismo. Anatomia de um Movimento de tipo Fascista no anos Trinta*, will be published during 1986.
8. In the absence of a scholarly study of Maurismo, see José Gutiérrez-Ravé, *Yo fuí un joven maurista* (Madrid, 1946).

9. Carolyn Boyd, *Praetorian Politics in Liberal Spain* (North Carolina, 1979) provides the most up-to-date account of military politics in Spain during the period 1917 to 1923; see also Juan Antonio Lacomba, *La crisis española de 1917* (Madrid, 1970).
10. Colin M. Winston, *Workers and the Right in Spain, 1900-1936* (Princeton, 1985) provides a fascinating account of what he terms Carlist 'proletarian fascism'; see particularly pp. 65-170.
11. Blinkhorn, *Carlism and Crisis*, pp. 1-40.
12. *Caciquismo*: the system of local power networks, bossism and clientelism characteristic of Spain in the late nineteenth and early twentieth centuries.
13. On this subject, see Enric Ucelay Da Cal, *La Catalunya Populista. Imatge, cultura i política en l'etapa republicana (1931-1939)* (Barcelona, 1982), pp. 21-120, and Alfonso Cucó, *El valencianismo político 1874-1939* (Barcelona, 1977), passim.
14. Ronald Fraser, *Blood of Spain. The Experience of Civil War 1936-1939* (London, 1979), especially pp. 522-30.
15. Juan José Castillo, *Propietarios muy pobres. Sobre la subordinación política del pequeño campesino. La Confederación Nacional Católico-Agraria, 1917-1942* (Madrid, 1979); see also Josefina Cuesta Bustillo, *Sindicalismo católico agrario en España (1917-1919)* (Madrid, 1978) and José Andrés-Gallego, *Pensamiento y acción social de la Iglesia en España* (Madrid, 1984).
16. Shlomo Ben-Ami, 'The forerunners of Spanish Fascism: Unión Patriótica and Unión Monárquica' in Blinkhorn, *Spain in Conflict*. For a complete analysis of the Primo de Rivera dictatorship, see Ben-Ami's *Fascism from Above. The Dictatorship of Primo de Rivera in Spain 1923-1930* (Oxford, 1983).
17. Blinkhorn, *Carlism and Crisis*, passim; Carlist anti-leftist activity in Navarre is discussed in Martin Blinkhorn, 'War on two fronts: politics and society in Navarre, 1931-6' in Paul Preston (ed.), *Revolution and War in Spain 1931-1939* (London, 1984), pp. 59-84.
18. The 'Christian Democratic' interpretation of Gil Robles and the CEDA receives its classic presentation in Richard A. H. Robinson, *The Origins of Franco's Spain. The Right, the Republic and Revolution, 1931-1936* (Newton

Abbot, 1970), and is countered by Paul Preston in *The Coming of the Spanish Civil War. Reform, Reaction and Revolution in the Second Republic 1931-1936* (London, 1978). Also on the CEDA see Montero, *La CEDA* and Javier Tusell, *Historia de la Democracia Cristiana en España*, I (Madrid, 1974).

19. Preston in Blinkhorn, *Spain in Conflict*; Raul Morodo, *Los orígenes ideológicos del franquismo: Acción Española* (Madrid, 1985).
20. The most up-to-date study of the Falange is that by Sheelagh Ellwood, *Prietas la filas. Historia de Falange Española. 1933-1983* (Barcelona, 1984); see also Stanley G. Payne, *Falange*.
21. Douglas L. Wheeler, *Republican Portugal. A Political History 1910-1926* (Madison, 1978), pp. 214-45.
22. The most satisfactory description and analysis of *Integralismo Lusitano* remains that by H. Martins in his chapter on Portugal in Woolf, *European Fascism*: see, in particular, pp. 302-12. Other useful accounts are those by Gallagher, *Portugal*, pp. 26-47 passim; Richard Robinson, *Contemporary Portugal* (London, 1979), p. 40 and p. 51; and Manuel Braga da Cruz, 'O Integralismo Lusitano e o Estado Novo' in the collection *O Fascismo em Portugal. Actas do Colóquio realizado na Faculdade de Letras de Lisboa em Março de 1980* (Lisbon, 1982), pp. 105-39.
23. Manuel Braga da Cruz, *As orígens da democracia cristã e o Salazarismo* (Lisbon, 1980), provides a meticulous analysis of the Catholic origins of the *Estado Novo*.
24. These and later references to the Madrid membership lists of the Falange are drawn from Payne, *Falange*, pp. 81-2 and Payne, 'Social Composition and Regional Strength of the Spanish Falange' in Larsen, *Who Were the Fascists?*, p. 425.
25. Ramiro Ledesma Ramos, *¿Fascismo en España? Discurso a las Juventudes de España* (Barcelona, 1968), pp. 64-8.
26. Ellwood, *Historia de Falange Espanola*, pp. 36-7.
27. Winston, *Workers and the Right in Spain*, pp. 108-292 passim. On the CONS, and in particular their relationship with the remnants of the *Libres*, see ibid., p. 306 and p. 313.

28. Javier Jiménez Campo, *El fascismo en la crisis de la II República* (Madrid, 1979), pp. 224-41.
29. Javier Tusell, *Las elecciones del Frente Popular en España* (2 vols., Madrid, 1971), 2, pp. 268-97.
30. Jerez, *Elites políticas*, pp. 49-175 passim.
31. The most useful source on the SEU remains David Jato Miranda, *La rebelión de los estudiantes* (Madrid, 1953).
32. Juan Antonio Ansaldo, *¿Para que...? De Alfonso XIII a Juan III* (Buenos Aires, 1951) provides valuable information concerning links between the monarchist elite and the Falange; so, too, do Pedro Sainz Rodríguez, *Testimonio y recuerdos* (Barcelona, 1978), pp. 220-24 and Winston, *Workers and the Right in Spain*, pp. 293-322.
33. Blinkhorn, *Carlism and Crisis*, p. 133.
34. Ibid., pp. 171-5; Blinkhorn in Preston, *Revolution and War in Spain*, pp. 78-80.
35. Blinkhorn in Preston, *Revolution and War in Spain*, pp. 64-5, 74-7.
36. Montero, *La CEDA*, I, pp. 307-779 passim.
37. Ibid., pp. 747-79; Antonio Elorza, 'El Sindicalismo católico en la Segunda República: la C.E.S.O. (1935-1938)' in his collection *La utopia anarquista bajo la segunda república española* (Madrid, 1973), pp. 295-350. During the Civil War the greater part of the CESO joined the Carlist-dominated *Obra Nacional Corporativa* before being absorbed within the wider *franquista* apparatus in 1937: see Blinkhorn, *Carlism and Crisis*, p. 275.
38. Payne, *Falange*, pp. 116-31, 142-7; Ellwood, *Historia de Falange Espanola*, pp. 72-110.
39. Pending the appearance of António Costa Pinto's study, the most revealing work on National Syndicalism, containing an interview with Rolao Preto, is Joao Medina, *Salazar e os fascistas. Salazarismo e Nacional-Sindicalismo. A história dum conflito 1932/1935* (Lisbon, 1978). See also H. Martins, 'Portugal' in Woolf, *European Fascism*, pp. 319-22 and Tom Gallagher, 'Portugal' in Martin Blinkhorn (ed.), *Fascists and Conservatives in Europe* (forthcoming, 1987).
40. See Payne in Turner, *Reappraisals of Fascism*, for a discussion of the 'pre-fascist culture' issue.

INDEX